MADAME CATHERINE

MADAME
Catherine

Irene Mahoney

LONDON
VICTOR GOLLANCZ LTD
1976

ISBN 0 575 02037 7

All the photographs reproduced in this book, with
the exception of those listed below, are from
Photographie Giraudon, Paris.

François II and Mary Stuart from
Rare Books Division
The New York Public Library
Astor, Lenox and Tilden Foundations

Marguerite de Valois from
General Research and Humanities Division
The New York Public Library
Astor, Lenox and Tilden Foundations

Elizabeth of England from
Pinocoteca de Siena, Italy

Philip II of Spain from
Prado Museum, Spain

Printed in Great Britain by
Lowe & Brydone (Printers) Ltd, Thetford, Norfolk

Contents

Illustrations may be found following pages 128 and 256.

To my sister
Margaret Mahoney Loughlin .

Preface

Everyone, of course, knows Catherine de Medici: a dark, sinister figure, nourished on the subtle, political philosophy of Machiavelli, surrounded by her scheming Italian courtiers, her magicians and seers; her secret cabinets filled with poisoned daggers, poisoned rings, poisoned goblets; her castles replete with hidden staircases and terrible dungeons—and everywhere, the heavy smell of evil.

The legend is complete. Too complete for credibility.

The fact is, as I have discovered through five exciting and arduous years of research, there are few who know her beyond linking her name with something vaguely cruel and sinister. Even then, she is inevitably confused with the earlier Medici or with the Borgias, and even those who know that most of her life was spent in France, not Italy, confuse her with her distant cousin Marie de Medici, who ruled France several decades later.

It was precisely the legend of the Sinister Queen—a legend I could neither believe nor dismiss—that led me to seek the woman who had given rise to such a distorted image. Where would I find her, this child orphaned before she was a month old, this young Florentine sent at the age of fourteen to marry into the royal family of France, this widowed mother set over an imperilled kingdom?

I found her first of all in her astonishing collection of letters and then in the hundreds of diaries, letters, memoirs of her contemporaries. I found her in the detailed and gossip-laden reports of ambassadors and secret agents and in the monumental research of later historians.

" 'How did you contrive to grasp / The thread which led you through this labyrinth?' " asks a character in Robert Browning's "Mr. Sludge the Medium." Looking back, I am amazed at my own tenacity, for often it was a labyrinth, a labyrinth in which I stumbled, lost my path, retraced my steps, started again. But bit by bit I found my way. The pieces of the legend began to slip aside, like one of Catherine's own concealing panels, and behind it, in a dim light, I began to see a portrait: dark, obscure, far from beautiful, but very human.

My initial encounter with Catherine de Medici had occurred during my research for a biography of her Huguenot son-in-law, Henri de Navarre. Although doomed to be antagonists, they were in many ways closely akin. Henri's keen political sense, his realism, his pragmatic attitude towards religion were qualities he shared with his mother-in-law. It is ironic that religion was the issue that set them in conflict, for unlike many of their fellow sovereigns, neither of them considered creed or cult a valid subject for war.

It was their misfortune to come to power at a time when the myth of a united Christendom was failing. It was a terrifying prospect for both churchmen and statesmen, for it opened up waters more vast and uncharted than any Columbus had described. For many, it was the end of the world as they had known it, and in their desperation they determined to keep the myth alive. Their efforts were countered by those of the New Religion, equally determined that a new order should prevail. Both sides maintained that they were "true Christians," and both sides fought like beasts to prove it.

Those heretical opinions, which had been matter for academic discussion a few years earlier, became during Catherine's reign the stuff of civil war. "Heresy" had grown strong enough to fight for its freedom.

At first, Catherine saw no problem in granting certain liberties. She saw no reason why theology should make a man less a Frenchman. In this she was far more tolerant than her fellow sovereign, Elizabeth of England, who knew that while a man's religion might not make him less an Englishman, it could certainly make her less a queen: how a man's head was turned towards Rome determined whether she was England's legitimate sovereign or merely her father's bastard. But for Catherine, religion posed no personal threat. A Huguenot, she felt, could be as loyal to the fleur-de-lys as a Catholic.

Theoretically, she was, of course, dead right. Had she to deal solely with sincere religionists her policies would have kept France strong and peaceful. But she had not reckoned with those on both sides who would use religion as a political weapon, those who—as her son-in-law so aptly put it—"hide their ambition beneath the cloak of religion."

Religion had long been a weapon in the political power struggle, but during the Wars of Religion (surely one of history's most ironic epithets) it became the standard that hid the greed, the vindictiveness, the ambition of men and nations. During Catherine's lifetime the issues became so complex and the struggle so deadly that her every effort towards conciliation only increased the hostility towards herself. From both sides came those contradictory accusations which shaped the legend of the Sinister Queen: She is an atheist; she is a murderer of Huguenots; she employs magicians and sorcerers; she defies the Pope; she sells France to her Italian hangers-on.

Small wonder the portrait was lost behind the lurid colours of the legend. To the extent I have rediscovered it, I have succeeded by standing on the shoulders of those who have been there before me. "They are what we know," T. S. Eliot has commented. I had hoped at one time to acknowledge them all in my bibliography, but as my research progressed, I realised that such an exhaustive bibliography was neither possible nor feasible. I have consequently limited myself to listing those items which were directly helpful in preparing the manuscript. Throughout the work, the translations are my own.

In an age when authors and editors often seem engaged in a cold war, I have been extremely fortunate in having as editor Patricia Brebant Soliman, whose enthusiasm and personal involvement in every aspect of my book have been extraordinary. To my agent, Claire Smith, I wish to express my thanks for her constant interest and her uncanny ability to restore my flagging confidence.

In addition, I wish to acknowledge my debt to the Musée de Condé and the Bibliothèque Nationale, to the staffs of the Widener and Houghton libraries, at Harvard University, and of the New York Public Library. I am particularly grateful to the latter for according me the privilege of working for many months in the Frederick Lewis Allen Room, a haven from the distractions which imperil every writer and where I had at my service all the necessary tools for my research.

Far more than this, however, the Allen Room provided me with a community of writers whose generous understanding and encouragement sustained me in the bad days and renewed my hope in the good. I learned from them, and in their company found the courage to pursue my goal. For that, above all, my gratitude to Richard Petrow, Susan Brownmiller, Ruth Gross, Nancy Milford, Robert Caro, Ferdinand Lundberg, Peter Burchard.

For other friends I am also grateful—friends who, though bewildered by months of silence, by elations and depressions, never gave me up. A very special part of this book—and of myself—belongs to them.

New Rochelle, New York   I. M.
February 2, 1975

"The Solitary Branch"

She is not beautiful, but she is gifted with extraordinary wisdom and prudence.
—LORENZO CONTARINI

Chapter I

On October 9, 1533, a fleet of sixty ships sailed from the harbour of Villafranca, close to the French border. Clement VII had at last set out for his long-anticipated meeting with the King of France. It was a scene of great splendour and of high public interest, for Italy, long a prey to the conflict between French and imperial interests, hoped that this meeting would bring it a measure of security.

It was just a month since the Medici Pontiff had left Rome, making his slow, careful way northward, avoiding—by design, it would seem—his native Florence, and crossing the narrow stretch of the Ligurian Sea that would lead him to the French border. Although Clement was far from the most luxurious of Renaissance Popes, he surrounded himself with what he considered to be the pomp befitting his position. The papal galley was covered with gold brocade, marked with the insignia that indicated that it housed the Corpus Domini—the Body of the Lord—part of that special ritual of a travelling Pontiff. Another galley, almost as ostentatious as his own, but marked with the coat of arms of France, carried the Pontiff's niece: Caterina Maria Romola, Duchess of Urbino and only living shoot of the once-great house of Medici. In fact, she, rather than her uncle, was the central figure in this elaborate and complex tapestry, for the fleet that gathered was her wedding flotilla come to bring her to her bridegroom, Henri d'Orléans, second son of the French king.

Even in an age of graceful compliments, no one called the young bride beautiful. She had celebrated her fourteenth birthday four months earlier and was considered of average height for her years. Her skin was fair and rather sallow, her hair dark and abundant, her lower lip a little heavy, in contrast with the thin upper lip and strongly marked, determined eyebrows. Her nose and rather prominent eyes bore the marks of the House of Medici. But if she was not beautiful, she was charming and extraordinarily gracious, qualities highly valued in Renaissance Italy. If she inherited something of the Medici arrogrance, it did not show.

Adversity and uncertainty had—strangely, in so young a child—given her poise and an independence that masked itself as docility. In the first fourteen bewildering and perilous years of her life, she had learned that safety—and success—often depended on patience, humility, and a meticulous effort to please. From her childhood, she had come to recognise that while her position made her of immeasurable importance, of herself she was of little account. With her keen intelligence and steady acceptance of reality, she had acknowledged the fact without rebelling against it. The complexity of her role had, apparently, stunted neither her mind nor her ability to take pleasure in the life offered her. That it may very well have stunted her ability to respond to simple and pure affection was a fact that would not have occurred to her contemporaries or, indeed, to Caterina herself. In fact, personal affection was offered her so rarely throughout her life that there was little need for her to learn how to cope with it.[1]

Her father was Lorenzo de Medici, grandson of *Il Magnifico*, as he had been called with both pride and animosity. Lorenzo, however, had little in common with his magnificent grandfather. Although heir to something of *Il Magnifico*'s pride and desire to achieve, he lacked both the will and the ability to attain his goals. In March, 1518, at the age of twenty-six, he travelled into France to complete his marriage to Madeleine de La Tour d'Auvergne, a marriage arranged by his uncle Leo X, anxious to cement his friendship with France. The wedding took place at the château of Amboise, which François I, with his passionate love of the new architecture, was to make one of the most renowned of the royal residences. At the end of May it was an ideal setting for a wedding, and François, who loved to impress, made the most of it. From the terraces the Loire could be seen stretching in blue, unbroken peace. The fruit trees were in blossom, and the terraced slopes lay smooth and green. The great hall was hung lavishly with tapestries, some depicting feats of war, others feats of love—both were, for François, the marks of greatness. Music and light were everywhere. Each course in the elaborate wedding banquet was served with a fanfare of music, while the silver plate, embossed with the arms of France, winked in the glow of innumerable candles. The dance that followed was, if anything, more sumptuous than the banquet. Seventy-two demoiselles, the most graceful the French court had to offer, dressed in the costumes of Italy, Germany, and France, began the dance that lasted until well after midnight.[2]

For eight days the celebrations continued, giving the guests ample time to observe the bridegroom and his wife. Lorenzo, it was clear, lacked the strength for such unbroken festivities. Even his trip to France had been made slowly and, according to one observer, "with great difficulty." The same observer noted it was not simply Lorenzo's unhealed wound that left him pale and exhausted. The bridegroom, he disclosed, had recently been suffering from a "shameful disease" that had poisoned his blood. The gossip was unfortunately true, and when the twenty-seven-year-old duke led his bride back to Florence, he had less than a year to live.[3]

Of Madeleine, not a single contemporary has anything but praise. Although she was described during the wedding feast as "brilliant," the adjective is used only once. Generally, she is characterised as pretty, gracious, virtuous, and wise. They are, in a sense, but the banalities of Renaissance praise, yet somehow with Madeleine they have the ring of truth. It is, however, Goro Gheri's phrase that best evokes the fragile and courageous bride of sixteen years. *Gentilissima madama* he calls her with respectful admiration.[4]

When Lorenzo and his bride arrived in Florence towards the beginning of September, Madeleine was already pregnant. Gay, affectionate, she was charmed by life in Florence, endearing herself to the people by wearing Italian dress, responding with obvious pleasure to their interest. "It was her aim to please and she succeeded," commented a later biographer.[5]

A few days after their arrival Florence gave the bride and groom a reception so elaborate that the city merchants ran out of silk and messengers were sent in haste to Venice and Lucca to purchase material for the nobles' gowns. It was one of Madeleine's last moments of gaiety. Six weeks later it was clear that Lorenzo was seriously ill, and five days before Christmas he was carried by litter to Sassetti, high on Monte Montughi, where, it was thought, the fresh, clear air would reduce the young duke's fever and cure his infection. Here he spent Christmas, looking over the white mountaintops and suffering recurring bouts of fever. Towards the end of January he seemed to be responding to the "cure," and there was talk of bringing him home to Florence. The "cure," however, was only temporary, and by early spring it was clear that no recovery was possible, for Lorenzo, already debilitated by syphilis, was now a prey to galloping consumption. In April he began the painful journey to Florence to be with Madeleine for the birth of their child. If they loved each other, the moment of their meeting must have been one of great anguish and great joy; if they did not, the frustration of their lives must have been close to unendurable.

On April 13, in the great Medici palace on the Via Larga, built by Cosimo the Elder, *la gentilissima madama* gave birth to a baby girl. Gheri's first report was that the infant was healthy and that the duchess had not suffered unduly from her labour. Three days later he noted the duchess had a slight touch of fever, but he was assured by the women who attended her that this was an ordinary consequence of childbirth. On April 18, however, Lorenzo was told that his wife of just a year was mortally ill. Ten days later she was dead. In a mixture of grief and resignation, Lorenzo, feeling the tenuous balance of his own life, wrote to Cardinal Bibbiena:[6]

> Having received such a blow to my soul and to my happiness, I do not know how
> I shall ever be content again. Even though I know that death is a normal thing and
> that we must all take this step in whatever time and manner it pleases Almighty
> God, still I suffer great grief at having lost my beloved companion. Nevertheless, I
> try to surrender myself to whatever pleases the Divine Majesty.

Lorenzo's trip from Sassetti to Florence had been his final effort; with the
death of Madeleine he could fight no more. On May 3 he received the last sacra-
ments, and the following morning he died. He was buried with great ceremony—
if not great affection—beside his wife in the tombs of his ancestors at San Lorenzo. Always arrogant, he had returned from France a little too autocratic for Florentine taste. His long absence had increased the foment and spirit of rebellion
within the city, and now, when Florence most needed a leader to set it in order,
the single sprig of the Medici line was an infant of twenty-two days, lying, as the
poets made haste to say, "in her cradle between two coffins." Orphaned so suddenly, the child seemed peculiarly fragile and vulnerable.

> A solitary branch becomes green with a few leaves;
> And I am in suspense between fear and hope
> Whether winter will spare it to me, or tear it from me[7]

wrote Italy's famed Ariosto.

Three months later it seemed Caterina's cradle would become her own coffin
as she lay dangerously near death. Her Mantuan contemporary, Baldassare Castiglione, whose book *Il Libro del cortegiano* was then being read in all the courts
of Europe, wrote in grief to the Pope that the infant had little chance of recovery.
Castiglione, however, was not privy to that enormous resilience of body and
mind that was to bring Caterina through innumerable duels with death, until
sheer exhaustion conquered her at the age of sixty-nine. This time she recovered
and in October was sufficiently well to be brought to the papal court where her
great-uncle ruled to 1521, when he was succeeded by Adrian VI.

Like all high ecclesiastical manoeuvres in the Renaissance, the elevation of
Giovanni Cardinal de Medici to the Papacy had been a political move. He was a
man who avoided extremes, playing the game of Roman politics as those who
had elected him had anticipated. Some saw in him a generous, good-hearted
man, a devoted patron of the arts, captivated by the pleasure of the good life.
Those less enthusiastic, repeated that he had been heard to say at his election,
"Let us profit from the Papacy since God has given it to us." His response to the
pale infant who was now held out to him, swathed in layers of petticoats and
dresses,[8] was indifferent. This infant was still too young to be of use to him.

He appointed Giulio Cardinal de Medici to be her tutor and placed her in the
care of Clarice Strozzi, her maternal aunt. How the Duchessina—as she was now

called—spent the years from 1520 to 1527 is not entirely clear. Evidence indicates, however, that she may have remained at Rome until 1525, when she returned to Florence. Although her aunt was a hard taskmaster, Catherine seems to have been genuinely grateful for those years when Clarice and her husband, Filippo Strozzi, made a home for her. Sometimes she was a member of the Strozzi household in their newly built palace; at others she was joined in the Medici palace by her half brother Alessandro and her cousin Ippolito. Clarice was an austere woman who believed in disciplined learning, and she kept Catherine at her books, yet what the child learned from the life around her reached far deeper than the abstract ideas about which she read. Italy, more than ever, was in ferment, and while Caterina was too young to follow the intricacies of politics, she felt the pulse of Florence change.

Upon Pope Adrian VI's death in 1523, another Medici was called to the Chair of Peter. This time Catherine's tutor, Giulio de Medici, assumed the title of Clement VII. Florence mourned his departure, for the four years of his administration had been firm, constant, and relatively peaceful. He was replaced by Silvio Passerini, Cardinal of Cortona, a stubborn, autocratic man who lacked the skill and vision for the difficult task of keeping Florence from revolt. By 1527 his effort to dominate Florence until he could prepare Caterina's brother Alessandro for the task was met with open rebellion.[9]

The spirit of insurrection at Florence was, of course, no more than a microcosm of the turmoil and confusion pervading all Italy. The Holy Roman emperor Charles V, despite his pious avowals that he desired nothing so much as a united and tranquil Christendom, continued his aggrandisement in Italy. In 1526 Clement VII, in an effort to protect himself from Charles, had signed an alliance with François I. Yet when, a year later, the imperial forces cut and burned their way through Lombardy, François was deaf to the Italian cries for help. "He does nothing but speak kind words," wrote the Florentine ambassador in contempt.[10] Florence, however, by some strange miracle, was bypassed in the thundering march south, while Rome, the Holy City, the seat of Christendom, was vanquished by the imperial forces with a brutality even the barbarian invasions had not exceeded. The German mercenaries had been promised plunder, and they took it wherever they found it—in churches, palaces, convents. Many of them were believers in the New Religion, which saw Rome as the great whore of Babylon. To sack it satisfied not only their lusts, but their religious convictions as well. "They have sackyd and spoylyd the towne and slayne to the nombre of 45,000, sparing neither state nor sex," an English agent wrote to London.[11]

When news reached Florence that Rome had been taken and the Pope driven into hiding, the city seized its chance for rebellion against the Medici. With this open revolt, Caterina's childhood ended. For the next three years she lived in peril, anxiety, and mistrust. At the age of eight she was given a bewildering insight into her own value. For as both sides fought to control her person she recognised that though she might be despised or hated, her presence added immense power to those who could gain her.

Alessandro and Ippolito had been able to slip northward to Lucca, but the revolutionaries intended to make sure that the one remaining Medici hostage remain in their hands. Although initially Clarice Strozzi had been able to cow the insurgents into letting Caterina remain with her in the Medici palace, she was soon moved to the relative safety of Poggio. Displeased with this, the rebels ordered her to be returned to Florence to live in the republican atmosphere of the Dominican convent of Santa Lucia. This, too, however, proved to be but a temporary measure, and two days after Christmas, to protect her from the plague-infested section of San Gallo, she was taken, heavily veiled and guarded, across the city, to the Murate, a Benedictine convent with the full mellifluous title of Santissima Annunziata delle Murate.

The Murate, where Caterina was to spend the next eighteen months of her life, has been variously described. To consider it a "prison," with its high walls, inner courtyards, and narrow entrances, is to miss the significance of religious architecture. The enclosure which protected the religious from the street life around them in no sense deprived them of a satisfying life of their own. The Medici, who had always been generous patrons of the Murate, had enriched it with paintings and statues. The fierce religious austerity that would leave monasteries denuded of beauty, their blank white walls unadorned except for the single uncompromising symbol of the cross, had not yet conquered Florence. Savonarola, it was true, had already preached his fiery gospel of self-denial, but he had been more openly accepted by his fellow Dominicans at Santa Lucia than in the sophisticated Benedictine environment of the Murate. He had, in fact, levelled his denunciations at these nuns who, he contended, lived so far from that austere denial to which he had reduced the Christian faith. Unintimidated, however, they continued faithful to their Benedictine tradition of scholarship, hospitality, and quiet, reflective prayer. They were reputed to "sing like angels," and on the great feasts their church was crowded by citizens who wished to share the beauty of their worship.

Into such an atmosphere was welcomed, with great cordiality, the Duchessina. "She is a little girl of eight years old with a very gracious manner," noted Sister Giustina Niccolini in her chronicle.[12] It was here that the following May Caterina received news of the death of Clarice Strozzi, who had been the one constant and devoted presence in the nine turbulent years of her life. Here, too, she learned of the increasing danger to Florence which was now exposed to enemies on every side. Imperial forces continued to roam Italy, and the French king, despite his promises, did nothing. "What will become of her?" asked a Florentine patriot, weeping over his native city. When it was learned that the Pope had made a peace with the emperor that excluded Florence, the fury grew. Clement, his Medici blood incensed by the continued turmoil in the city, was determined to subdue it at any cost. He was not above using force to gain his end, and soon imperial troops, swelled by papal soldiers, began their march northward. The Florentines were ordered to surrender without quarter. Their answer was inevitable: They prepared for war.

Already the Medici arms had been pulled down and broken. Now the statues of the two Medici Popes, Leo and Clement, were mutilated. The special messengers sent into France, begging for help for Florence in this "her gravest danger," achieved nothing.[13]

The only movement came from the valley of the Arno, where the imperial army pushed towards its goal. But the people through whose lands they passed, aroused by a sense of betrayal, determined to make it a costly victory. They set fire to their barns and fields and killed their livestock, preferring self-destruction, if by this measure they could retard the enemy a single moment. But nothing stopped these brutal soldiers, many of whom had already fed on Rome and carried its gold around their necks. They marched through the burning fields, taking their own savage revenge on anything they found alive. By October 24 they were encamped around Florence; five days later the guns began in earnest, and the fortifications which Michelangelo had constructed behind San Miniato began to tremble. Throughout the winter and into the following summer the siege continued, for nothing—neither famine, plague, nor bloody death—could force the people to surrender.

Protected only by the grey walls of the Murate from the indescribable horrors of a city under siege, Caterina celebrated her eleventh birthday. Three months later the Duchessina suddenly became a subject of renewed importance. During the months of siege there had been a resurgence in favor of the Medici, and the rebels now saw the young Medici in their midst as a source of dangerous influence. They feared that her presence at the Murate was stirring up the nuns in favor of the Medici and that they, in turn, were infecting others. At a time when Florence was being prepared for a siege unto death, they could not afford false sympathisers.

Silvestro Aldobrandini, secretary to the Signoria, the governing body of Florence, was sent to bring Caterina back to the republican atmosphere of Santa Lucia. But the Duchessina, usually so docile, refused to go. Dressed in a religious habit, with her hair cut to indicate her profession of virginity, she announced she intended to stay at the Murate and become a nun. When the secretary insisted, she wept. Aldobrandini, loath to use force in so delicate a situation, returned to the Signoria. On July 20, however, he came again to the Murate. This time he was adamant, for he knew that of the possible fates suggested for the Duchessina a return to Santa Lucia was the kindest. The radicals, now in control, had already suggested that she be put in a bordello instead of a convent or that the soldiery might enjoy her. How directly Caterina was aware of the threats that hung over her it is impossible to know; but this time, tearful but obedient, she followed Aldobrandini into the courtyard, where a little mule awaited her, and rode with him to the cloister on the Via San Gallo.

It must have been a terrible journey, for no longer protected by the cloister walls, she saw at last what war had made of Florence. The fairest city in the world had become a grotesque. The city of domes, of churches with their columned loggias, of the famed Campanile with its aspiring thrust had become a place of jagged wounds. Hunger, lean and pale, had crept into corners where guns would never have found their way, and plague had inevitably followed. The bodies of those who died in battle were summarily disposed of, but down the narrow city streets bodies stretched or huddled in doorways, clothed only with the dry skin of famine. It was often hard to tell the living from the dead, and in fact, there was little to distinguish one from the other, except that one had ceased to suffer.

It was not a long journey from the Murate, along the Via Ghibellina and north to the Via San Gallo, yet for Caterina it was long enough to last a lifetime. The hot July sun had drained the streets of colour, and what she saw was enscribed so clearly on her memory that it charted the course of her life. She saw war plain, without decoration, without idealism. War, she found, was not the tapestries or frescoes that decorated the palace of the Medici; war was an etching whose acid bit into those profound places of her being where nothing else had ever found its way. That nightmare journey to the Via San Gallo determined her lifelong horror of war and shaped her constant resolution for peace at any price. It was what would compel her later to ride from one end of France to the other, to sit countless hours at the conference table, to risk the contempt of those for whom war still had a romantic ring. That insistent resolution, "We must have peace," must surely have been born during those hot summer hours when nothing could free her from the sick, sweet smell of death or erase its hideous sight from her imagination.

Her welcome at Santa Lucia could scarcely have been cordial. Here she was less honoured charge than prisoner of war. It was her first experience of living in an atmosphere of undisguised hostility and suspicion, and like her journey through the charnel streets of Florence, it must have marked her for life. Here her gracious manner charmed no one. She was a Medici, and that was enough to condemn her. Fortunately, her stay was of short duration, for the city's stubborn will to survive was broken at last and Florence capitulated on August 12, 1530. Within weeks Caterina was on her way to Rome and the safety of the papal court.

Clement VII stepped out of his usual rigid reserve to greet his niece with what an observer described as a "truly paternal welcome," adding that the Pontiff's eyes were filled with tears of relief and joy in seeing this young niece so calm of manner and so wise-spoken. But a papal embrace was hardly sufficient to negate the months of terror, and the same observer noted significantly, "Yet she cannot forget the terrible way in which she had been treated."[14]

With her arrival in Rome, a new phase of Caterina's life began. She was approaching a marriageable age, and those suitors, some of whom had been waiting in the background since her birth, began to step forward. There was no lack of choice; it was simply a question of where she might be made most valuable for her uncle. James V of Scotland was favoured by her maternal uncle, the Duke of Albany; England suggested the Duke of Richmond, the natural son of Henry VIII. In Italy there was Guidobaldo della Rovere, a marriage that would unite two important Italian houses. There was also Federigo Gonzaga, Duke of Mantua, whose scandalous life, it was said, made him unacceptable, or Francisco Sforza, Duke of Milan, who was considered a little too old and poor to provide an advantageous match. From France there were the Duc de Vaudémont, brother of the Duc de Lorraine, and last, Henri, Duc d'Orléans, second son of the French king. It was a wide and disparate field of choice.[15]

Caterina, of course, had no part in the negotiations. She continued her education and perfected her talent to be obedient, to be charming, and to please. She also, it would seem, fell in love with her cousin Ippolito. Her childhood devotion had matured into romantic affection for this handsome young man, ten years her senior, whose portrait by Titian hangs in the Pitti Palace. Here he is painted in full uniform, the mulberry velvet giving a dark cast to his skin and a shadowy mystery to his eyes. It is easy to believe, as one studies the portrait, that he was "but little inclined" to the ecclesiastic state for which he was destined. He had already been given the cardinal's hat, but, reported the Venetian ambassador, "it is being whispered that the cardinal intends to put his hat aside to marry Caterina." He noted even more significantly that Caterina trusted no one but him and discussed her personal affairs with him alone. "She loves him tenderly," he concluded.[16] His statement does not stand alone. It seemed to have been common belief that Caterina loved her cousin. That either of them ever seriously considered marriage seems doubtful. Caterina, at least, was not the stuff of which Juliets are made, and Ippolito gives the impression of being moved more by the romance of love than by love itself.

In any case, marriage negotiations were moving ahead in quite a different direction under the practised hands of French and papal diplomats. By 1533 negotiations were in their final stages for a marriage between Caterina and Henri d'Orléans, François I's second son. This union, as envisioned by François and Clement, was to influence all Europe: It was to clip the claws of the emperor by uniting two powerful forces against him and thus secure the Papacy against imperial encroachments; it was to give France the right to certain Italian lands which it had been coveting for more than a century; it was even, François hoped, to cajole the Pope into a favourable hearing on Henry VIII's divorce.

In May, 1533, Caterina received news of the final settlement at Florence, where she had been living since the preceding spring. Two months later an official pronouncement stated that Clement would embark for France for a diplomatic meeting with François I and to bring his niece to her prospective husband. Although, according to the English ambassador, it was the French king who was "right hot and diligent" for this marriage, yet from the beginning François assumed the typical air of condescension that made it patently clear he considered the honour to be all on the side of Caterina. Although Pisa, Livorno, Reggio, Modena, and Parma were to be settled on the bride, although her trousseau was of fabled Florentine workmanship, and a fortune in diamonds and pearls was bestowed on her by the Pope, in French eyes none of this was of equal value to the privilege of marrying into the royal family of France.[17]

To the French, the Duchessina herself was even less impressive than her dowry. Vasari, who had been commissioned to paint her portrait while she had been at Florence and who had rhapsodised over her in lyrical style, had noted in a letter to a friend that Caterina had a quality which no paint brush would ever capture and yet which was the most important quality of all.[18] It is a vague allusion, part, perhaps, of Vasari's golden rhetoric, but as time was to discover, the young bride who sailed into Marseilles beneath the golden fleur-de-lys of France did indeed possess a quality which was to make her one of the most extraordinary women of Europe. That quality, still blurred by adolescence, had not yet clearly defined itself; it would, actually, remain unused and unfulfilled for another twenty-five years. It was a quality of statesmanship which, though not always successful, was to keep France alive until the skilful hands of Henri IV could unite it in a steady peace. This most invaluable part of her dowry was one of which even Caterina was still unaware. She knew only those lessons life and her masters had already taught her: to be docile, to be obedient, to be charming; to be grateful for the privileges that were given her; most of all, to face life with the realistic appraisal that she would always be somebody's pawn. Perhaps experience had already given her the faint glimmer of one other important reality: that to be in the background need not mean to be without power.

On September 1 Caterina left Florence still in the care of those faithful guardians, Filippo Strozzi and her distant cousin Maria Salviati. At Poggio she was met by her brother Alessandro in whose company she travelled north to Pistoia, where Guillaume du Bellay, the emissary of the French king, joined her retinue.[19] Six days later, she arrived at the clean-washed harbour of Spezia, where twenty-seven French ships awaited her. Florence could have offered nothing more magnificent. Her own royal galley was decorated with crimson damask. Awnings of purple velvet had been erected to protect the bride from sun and rain. Over all were embroidered the dazzling golden lilies of France. It was a time for sunshine in northern Italy, and the sky was of that deep, cool blue which travellers continue to remember when their recollections of Italy's man-made glories have dimmed. The early autumn breeze was crisp and free, and the Bay of Spezia glittered with fire points, caught and tossed from wave to wave. Here the Duchessina embarked, travelling westward along the coast, before crossing to Villafranca, where she was to await her uncle's arrival.

A month later the entire fleet set sail. On October 12 the French and papal galleys came in sight of the harbour of Marseilles. Their welcome was immediate and exhilarating. All the church bells were set ringing, and the huge cannon guarding the city sent off their salvos. Boats, filled with noblemen and musicians, left the docks to circle about the fleet. Anne de Montmorency, marshal of France, under whose direction the reception took place, welcomed them warmly into his own palace. The following day the Pontiff made his solemn entrance. Robed in his white pontifical vestments, Clement was carried high above the crowd in his ceremonial *sedia gestatoria*. Preceded by a white palfrey carrying the Corpus Domini, he travelled through the noisy, congested town, followed by his full retinue of cardinals and bishops in their scarlet and purple. Among them, in full ecclesiastical dress, was Ippolito de Medici, recently returned from a papal mission in Hungary.

On October 23 Caterina made her own entrance into the city, and three days later the contract of marriage was officially signed. On October 28 the Pope himself officiated at the marriage ceremony, giving the wedding ring to the spouses and blessing them with the full majesty of his papal benediction. The bride was dressed with unparalleled magnificence. Her brocaded gown was trimmed with ermine, its bodice of violet velvet cut according to the Florentine style. Her dark, abundant hair was woven with jewels, and on her head was her ducal crown. The sheer weight made the Duchessina stumble, but it did not impress the French who continued to feel that France had little to gain by marrying royal blood to a merchant's daughter. She could not be so rich as she was reputed, and certainly she was not beautiful. If anything, the portraits that had preceded her had idealised her. When later François was reputed to have said—despite the dowry he had bargained for so sharply—that she had come to him "completely naked," he simply affirmed the attitude of his people.

A month later Clement, satisfied with the promises exchanged with the French king (although Clement was never to keep his) and content the marriage had been consummated (thus closing the door to the possibility of annulment), departed for Italy. Filippo Strozzi, along with a party of attendants, was left in France to take charge of the Duchessina's affairs. Ippolito returned to Rome with his uncle, taking with him the Barbary lion which François had given him and with which he later had his portrait painted. Caterina was never to see either him or her uncle again. Two years later both Clement and Ippolito were dead.

With their departure the weeks of festivities came to an end, and Catherine—as she now became—was left to discover the role she was to play in this large and complex court. It was clear where the center of power lay: François was a king who ruled. Having been called from his birth "My king, my Lord, my Caesar" by his ambitious and dominant mother, he had been groomed from the beginning for his royal role.[20] Although the portraits that have come down to us do not reveal a handsome man, they reveal a man of intense dynamism, a man of alert charm who knew how to win as well as to dominate. He was a big man, with wide shoulders and a powerful chest. No doubt he thought of himself in the mould of Castiglione's courtier: warrior, statesman, patron of the arts. A few years later the Venetian Matteo Dandolo was to write of him that he was recognised as a great hunter of both deer and women, a magnanimous king whose gifts—especially to the women of the court—knew no limits. He praised his spontaneity, the gaiety of his expression, the cordiality of his manner. "I have never heard it said that anyone left him dissatisfied," he concluded. Dandolo was exaggeratedly kind, for François displeased many. As he grew older, there was less tolerance for the restlessness that shifted the court from one royal residence to another, for his preoccupation with hunting, sometimes at the expense of state affairs, and especially for his indiscriminate love affairs. Brantôme, generally indulgent to members of the Valois family, later wrote, "King François loved too wildly and too much; for being young and free, he became involved first with one, then with another, for in that time a man was not considered much of a gallant unless he whored every place without distinction."[21]

By 1533, however, the king's youthful excesses seemed to have quieted in favour of a steady passion for one woman, Anne d'Heilly, Duchesse d'Étampes. Queen Eleanor, whom he had married as part of the political settlement with Charles V following the French defeat at Pavia, never claimed his affection. If, as some observers claimed, she looked like an "Andalusian madonna, stiff and solemn in her heavy robes," it is easy to see why she never won her husband's interest. She, in her turn, must have stiffened against the public humiliations to which he subjected her. An English agent writing to Henry VIII noted that on the very day on which Queen Eleanor was to make her solemn entrance into Paris, François rode to the house where his mistress lived and "set her before him in an open window, talking two hours with her in the sight of all the people."[22]

François, despite his tendency to sexual domination, had a remarkably liberal attitude towards the place of women at his court. He was never satisfied by mere beauty or sexual response. The learned woman was very pleasing to him. Far from feeling threatened by the intellectual conversation of the women of the court, he was flattered by it. A less liberal contemporary was reputed to have condemned the king for having a "court of women" who influenced politics to the detriment of the country. It is an exaggeration, undoubtedly, for François charted his own political course, yet it provides an interesting insight into the tone of the court in which Catherine was to find her place.[23]

Catherine, happily, was not without her contemporaries at court, for Madeleine and Marguerite, the king's two daughters by his first wife, Claude, were still at court, and with the latter Catherine formed a lasting friendship. The most important influence, however, was the king's younger sister, Marguerite d'Angoulême, wife of the King of Navarre. Marguerite, often called the pearl of princesses, was an extraordinary woman with her free-ranging mind and her absolute devotion to her brother. It was Marguerite who endorsed and encouraged her brother's interest in the arts, Marguerite who brought in the first of those religious reformers to discourse upon their theologies in the little academy of the court, who introduced such men as Clément Marot, whose translations of the Psalms into French were to become so inflammatory during the later religious wars. Although her marriage limited her visits to her brother's court, yet she found time to direct the studies of the young demoiselles whose education was still incomplete. Under her guidance, Catherine studied mathematics and the art of poetry, improved her Latin, and began an arduous introduction to Greek. Several years later Pierre de Ronsard, who was just beginning his literary career, wrote of Catherine's achievement:

> What princess has achieved so well
> The skill of mathematics;
> What princess understands so well
> That great world of painting,
> The ways of nature
> And the music of the heavens?[24]

It is hard to imagine Catherine trimming her native pragmatism to a wholly academic life, yet she was apparently the brightest of the demoiselles. Her intelligence was obvious, although that intelligence had not yet found its natural channel. She was trained to discipline—most of all, she was highly motivated. Since her father-in-law took pleasure in the scholarly achievements of the young ladies of his court, then she would shine in scholarly achievements. It was the old goal of pleasing now put to a different end.

One is sometimes inclined to forget that the unassuming Catherine of the French court had grown up in an atmosphere of both scholarship and cultural riches which her adopted country was sedulously imitating. When Ronsard, in his verses, spoke of that "great world of painting," he had touched on the ordinary climate of Catherine's early years. She had grown up in an Italy alive not simply with genius but genius experienced and appreciated. She had lived in the city of Giotto's Campanile, Brunelleschi's extraordinary dome, Ghiberti's famed bronze doors of the Baptistry. Within her lifetime, Andrea del Sarto, Michelangelo, Raphael, Leonardo da Vinci all had made their contributions. At Rome she had knelt in the chapel where Michelangelo had recently painted his story of the Creation and passed through the quarters which housed the Laocoön and the Apollo Belvedere. She had seen the great Medici tomb at Florence where her uncle Giulio and her father were to be idealised. She had lived in close contact with the works of Masaccio, Botticelli, Ghirlandaio. What France looked at longingly as something still to be achieved, Catherine had already experienced as part of her Italian heritage. She had had her portrait painted by Vasari, and Niccolo Machiavelli, on finishing *The Prince*, had dedicated it to her father with the flattering but vain hope that he would be the saviour of Florence. This sophistication of taste undoubtedly pleased François, who had already expended a fortune in wooing such Italian artists as Andrea del Sarto, Leonardo da Vinci, Il Rosso Fiorentino, and Primaticcio to France.

In Catherine's third year at court an event occurred that shifted the course of her life. François d'Angoulême, eldest son of the king, died suddenly on his way to join his father at Valence. The circumstances were so sudden and of such grave consequence that poisoning was immediately suggested. His cupbearer, an Italian, Sebastiano de Montecuculi, who had been in contact with the emperor, was accused and, despite the meagre evidence, put to death. The king's grief was immense. "None of you has the courage to tell me my son is dead," he raged at the hesitant messenger.[25] It was more than grief over a firstborn; it was chagrin that by this unjust dealing of fate the throne of France would pass to the king's least-favoured son, Henri d'Orléans.

Despite his reputed tolerance for divergent ideas, François had little tolerance for men. He expected them to conform to his own image. Henri d'Orléans, unfortunately, did not fit the mould. Although he had inherited his father's physique and his love of warlike deeds, where François was built with the strength and subtlety of steel, Henri's metal was massive and unyielding. His mind lacked both the quickness and the penetration of his father's. Ideas did not interest him, except insofar as they could be translated into action. He was not stupid. He had been well educated by the noted Humanist Benedetto Tagliacarne. He had an excellent memory and was soon proficient in Latin, Italian, and Spanish. Later he was inspired by his mistress to try his hand at love poetry, which, although highly conventional, indicates an ear trained to music and metaphor. He lacked his father's gaiety, his facile expression, his spontaneity. His own more constant, methodical temper might, in some ways, make him a better ruler, but it would never win him that immediate devotion his father, at the crest of his popularity, could evoke.

There had never been any love lost between father and son. François never attempted to hide his preferences, and Henri was not one of them. Henri, in his turn, never forgot that his father, in order to gain his own freedom after his capture at Pavia, had agreed to send his two young sons into Spain as hostages. Those dark terrifying months of his childhood when he had suffered the loneliness and rigour of a Spanish prison were very hard to forgive. He had been only seven years old when he had been shut up in the dark prison at Madrid. When he emerged three years later, the handsome little French boy with the rosy cheeks had become a taller boy, pale, silent, half-shy, half-sullen, who could not be drawn from his moodiness even by the gift of freedom. Although his older brother, who had shared his imprisonment, was vocal in his tale of ill-treatment and his consequent hatred of everything Spanish, he had adjusted spontaneously to his return to France. The road home for Henri was to be much slower. Although there is no description of him at this time, a few years later Dandolo observed: "[He is] rather big . . . neither fat nor thin, but so well built that it seems that he is all muscle. . . . However, his nature is rather sombre and taciturn. He laughs or makes any sign of laughing very rarely so that most of those at court say that they have only seen him laugh once."[26]

With the elevation of Henri to dauphin, Catherine's place at court changed perceptibly. As wife to the second son, her role had been one of comparative unimportance. As wife of the dauphin, however, she would someday be queen, and the responsibility for bearing children for the throne of France fell on her with its full weight. And with it came the terror of sterility, for in the three years of their marriage, Catherine had not become pregnant. At first, this gave no concern; her age might well account for the difficulty. "Time," murmured the court doctors who were consulted. But time worked no miracles, and those who had always opposed this Italian union now talked secretly of repudiating the marriage and sending this useless and unworthy bourgeoise back to Florence. When the dauphin acknowledged the paternity of a child born to a young Italian girl, it became reproachably clear where the curse of sterility lay.

In the next few years neither the humiliating examinations of doctors with their painful remedies nor the strange spells and potions prepared by folk medicine remedied Catherine's sterility. With concern Dandolo wrote to the Signoria at Venice in 1542, "The most high dauphine seems well in everything except those qualities concerning the ability to bear children, for not only has she not done so to date, but I doubt that she will ever do so."[27]

Dandolo's words carried the ring of death, and Catherine, for the first time in her adult life, repudiated her passive obedience and assumed the initiative in her own fate. She went, we are told, to the king, offering to accept whatever he would decide for the good of the kingdom. She would go or stay, according to his pleasure. Should he consider her presence an obstacle to the good of France, she would either retire to a convent or, if the privilege were granted her, remain to serve her husband's new wife. It could hardly have been a more humble offer, nor could it have been more subtly directed at the king's ego. Had she fought, had she objected, had she even outlined a feasible plan, she might well have ended her days in Italy. Instead, she put herself trustingly in the hands of her wise (and loving) father-in-law.

The results were magical. He would not permit her to go; he wished her in France. With those words, the only power in the land had spoken in her favour. Even should her husband wish to reject her, he was powerless to do so. The gossips in the court were silenced, and Catherine, quiet, overtly submissive, had taken her first step to power. Small wonder the observant Venetian ambassador Lorenzo Contarini could write that year, "Although she is not beautiful, she has a certain wisdom and an extraordinary prudence; there is no doubt that she would be very capable of governing." It is the first mention of Catherine's possible role in political life.[28]

The fear of sterility was not the only suffering under which Catherine was labouring in these years. Her husband, withdrawn, silent, indifferent to her, had fallen in love with a passion that was to last a lifetime. His mistress, Diane de Poitiers, was a woman almost twenty years his senior, a woman whose beauty and influence have given rise to more legend than truth. The dramatic story that she had, in her youth, given herself to François I to win the king's pardon for her father is totally unfounded. In addition, it is psychologically unlikely. Diane was not a woman given to self-sacrificing gestures. Married at an early age to Louis de Brézé, grand sénéchal of Normandy, it was her good fortune to be widowed in ample time to become the dauphin's mistress. At first glance, it seems an unlikely liaison, but Diane was a woman not only of immense beauty but of immense common sense. To be mistress to the silent, melancholy boy who would one day hold the sceptre of France was a role of great value. As for the dauphin, whatever other satisfactions the affair offered—and there must have been many —there must surely have been an element of maternal security. One expects that out of Diane's immeasurable sophistication, she offered a comforting embrace to the young man, an embrace less demanding than youthful passion, and far more steady. For more than twenty years Diane de Poitiers lived at court, supporting the king, nursing Queen Catherine when she was ill, devoting herself to the care of the royal children. For despite the ominous prophecies of the Florentine ambassador, there were royal children. In the years between 1544 and 1556 Catherine gave birth to ten children, seven of whom lived to maturity.

The first was born at Fontainebleau on January 20, 1544, and named François in honor of his grandfather. It seemed for the first few days that the ordeal of birth might have been too much for the infant, whose respiration was at first impaired.

Within a week, however, he seemed brighter and stronger, and on February 10 he was baptised. Marguerite d'Angoulême, with her usual felicity of phrase, caught the temper of the event when she wrote to her brother that "the joy is greater than that at the birth of your first-born for this was been longer awaited and less hoped for."[29] Ironically, no one mentions Catherine at this moment of triumph. At last she had performed the miracle expected of her. She had given birth not simply to a child, but to a male child—a fact of unparalleled importance in a country where the Salic Law, prohibiting women from the throne, still obtained.

The birth of his grandchild was one of François I's last unmarred joys. The final years of his life were clouded by his own increasing ill health and by the death, in the fall of 1545, of his youngest and most beloved son. Charles had been made in his father's mould: proud, audacious, and gallantly charming. At his bedside the king, it was said, fainted with grief.

Although disappointment and sickness had aged him suddenly, yet François still retained his kingly bearing. The Venetian Marino Cavalli wrote of him in 1546: "The king is now fifty-four years old. His bearing is entirely regal so that even a stranger who had never seen him or his portrait would be able to say simply by looking at him, 'That is the king.' "[30]

Yet life was becoming stale and flat for him. His blood no longer raced towards love or war. He grew pensive and melancholy, restless and dissatisfied with what the court offered him. At times he withdrew into solitude, unwilling to see anyone except his sister Marguerite. His wife, whose response to him had never been satisfying, had already withdrawn into her own seclusion, seeing only her priests and the Spanish ambassador. After a visit to Plessis-les-Tours, François gave orders for a progress through his kingdom, but the brilliance of such progresses was over. He wandered for a while from castle to castle, weary, finding satisfaction only in the hunt. Marguerite had once written of her adored brother:

> On earth, he is like the sun in heaven:
> Strong, courageous, wise, and valiant in battle
> . . . yet in his grandeur
> He is kindly, gentle, humble
> He is strong and powerful and full of patience
> Either in prison, sadness, or adversity.[31]

The verses were no longer true. The king's patience and courage, like his body, had grown feeble and inconstant.

Late in January he received word of the death of Henry VIII of England. The news must have touched a nerve, for the two sovereigns, so close in age, had followed parallel courses. At least he was spared the humiliation of the English monarch, who in his last days had become so badly crippled he could neither walk nor stand, depending on "mechanical contrivances" for moving his royal person. In March, 1547, determined to celebrate Mardi Gras, François travelled to his château at Loches. Here, however, his pain became unendurable, and he left for St. Germain to see his court physician, Ambrose Paré. He stopped overnight at Rambouillet and in a last burst of physical strength took part in the chase. When he returned, he knew he was dying.

Unlike Henry of England, who, it was said, considered it an act of treason to speak of the death of the king, those who surrounded François spoke openly of mortality with him. Accounts of his dying are, of course, festooned with pious rhetoric: He made his confession, asking his confessor to read him the Gospel account of the repentance of Mary Magdalene; he asked pardon openly for his faults—especially that of waging war too lightly; he admonished his son to "conserve the purity of the Catholic faith." Such is the traditional account of the death of Catholic kings. His folly, his caprice, his arbitrary decisions and aggressive wars were submerged in that last avowal of sinfulness and the final groping towards the crucifix. Not all judgements were so kind, however, and one of François' councillors, the Marshal de Tavannes, often biting in his comments on the vices of kings, observed, "Women more than his age caused his death. He enjoyed some good fortune and suffered much that was bad. He advanced some people without cause and used them without consideration."[32]

Capricious as he was, however, when François I died on March 31, three of the four most powerful women in France wept with an uncontrollable sense of loss: his mistress, Madame d'Étampes, who knew her role had come to an end; Marguerite d'Angoulême, whose brother had long been her only star; and Catherine, who recognised she had lost a protector and, insofar as François could sustain the part, a friend.

Just two months after his death François' casket was lowered into the royal tomb at St. Denis where two of his sons already lay. The officers of his household, following the prescribed ritual, cast their broken sceptres into the grave, as the herald cried, "King François is no more. Long live our gracious sovereign Henri II whom God preserve."

Chapter II

On July 25, 1547, Henri II was crowned in the Cathedral of Reims.

Kingship apparently agreed with Henri. The cloud of disapproval under which he had lived during his father's reign was dissolved, and with it some of those negative traits which had made many mistrustful of the dauphin's ability to reign. The tendency to melancholy, reported Dandolo, was gone. "He has become gay," he noted, his usual paleness replaced by a healthy glow. His strength and energy had burgeoned. True, he was slow of speech, yet conversely, he was firm in his opinions. Though less intellectually agile than his father, he was also less capricious. "Often these are the men who succeed best," commented Cavalli hopefully.[1]

On his deathbed, François had given his son a number of injunctions. It was at once apparent, however, that the new king intended to pursue his own policy. The reign of François I was over.

Immediately after his death, the unpopular Madame d'Étampes, reportedly crying, "O earth, swallow me!" had made for her litter and, in the protection of her brother, had fled to Limoges. Queen Eleanor, freed at last from her distasteful role in France, had left for the more congenial environment of Brussels, proclaiming, "God knows how I have been treated and the way in which the king has used me."[2] François' trusted councillors were left without a place in the new government, while the disgraced Constable Montmorency was reinstated. Most of all, Diane de Poitiers emerged as the most powerful figure at court. St. Mauris, the Spanish ambassador, wrote in code to the emperor: "As for the king, he continues to submit himself more and more to Silvius [Diane], to whom he makes himself a slave, a thing which his people greatly lament." He no longer held audiences after dinner, St. Mauris observed, nor was he available during the morning. "The worst is that the king lets himself be led and does everything that Silvius and his lords advise, which drives the people to despair." It is not wholly the ambassador's prejudice speaking, for other contemporaries also noted this tendency on the part of the king to let himself "be led on leash," to accede too easily to the demands of those who pleased him. "It must be acknowledged," Tavannes was to write later, "that this is the reign of the Constable, of Madame de Valentinois [Diane], of Monsieur de Guise, rather than his own."[3]

Tavannes' accusation oversimplified the problem, however. It was a far more complex situation than that of a weak king manoeuvred by a strong coalition, for there was no harmony among the three masters who led the king.

Anne de Montmorency, already in his fifties, had spent his life in the service of France. He was a man of great energy, endurance, and loyalty. Unfortunately, a keen intelligence was not among his gifts, and his advice and strategies had often led to disaster. François I, annoyed at his bungling, had dismissed him from court. But to Henri, endowed with the same ponderous mind, he symbolised order, security, and personal devotion. They were men cut from the same cloth. Confident and at ease in their armour, they had limited ability at the council table. They both had suffered imprisonment for the former king and felt, no doubt, something of the same resentment that their pains had won such short-lived gratitude. They were drawn together by their mutual bitterness that the golden king, who had asked so much of them, had been so leaden-hearted in their regard. They were drawn together even more, perhaps, by the young king's need not simply for an elder statesman, but for a father. To this need, Montmorency responded with a profound devotion that was both possessive and exclusive. Any relationship with the king which detracted from his own he found intolerable. Inevitably, he feared Diane and despised the Guises.

The Guises—a cadet branch of the House of Lorraine, which for centuries had been an independent kingdom—were still considered outsiders by many Frenchmen. It was due to the supreme genius of Charles, Cardinal de Lorraine, and his elder brother, François, Duc de Guise, that within a dozen years the House of Guise would become one of the most powerful families in France. Of the two brothers, there is no doubt the cardinal was the leader. Although still in his twenties when Henri came to power, he had already made his mark. Where the constable was likely to seek solutions in action, the young cardinal sought them in diplomacy. Handsome, astute, eloquent, he resembled the new architecture that had abandoned the thick walls and dungeons of the feudal period for the polish of a more sophisticated era. As a churchman he was to be nonpareil in France. His brother François, though not his equal in eloquence or wit, had his own power and a military skill which was to win him the epithet *Le Grand*.

These were the two opposing forces that sought to lead the king, forces of immeasureable strength and ambition. Between them stood Diane, of whom a contemporary historian would later write, "No woman in France of her condition had ever before amassed so much."[4] Within a year after Henri's accession, the duchy of Valentinois became hers, along with the château at Chenonceaux. The crown jewels were placed in her hands, and in the following years subsidies the treasury could ill afford were made over to her. Despite her age (she was nearing fifty), Diane's beauty remained unmarred. The milky glow of her skin, her features at once soft and classical, the high, firm breasts, the exquisite grace of her neck had not lost their loveliness. Supremely confident, she used time to her advantage, letting herself be painted as she had in her youth. When her hair began to grey, she did nothing to hide it but let its silver add something gentle and wise to her beauty. Age did not frighten her. Her dress remained as simple and as elegant as ever, the black and white of her gowns acting as the perfect mounting for the king's jewels, which she wore not in defiance but as her right.

The enmity between the constable and Diane—Madame La Sénéchale as she was called—was thinly veiled. He was jealous of her influence, and she knew it. The tension was increased by Montmorency's continued friendship with the queen. From the beginning, he had shown himself to be Catherine's advocate. Even during his years of exile they had corresponded. He had been tireless in suggesting remedies for her sterility and encouraging her hope during those ten long years of humiliation. It was to him, as her most trusted friend in France, that Catherine wrote of her first hope of pregnancy. "I want very much to write to you to tell you that there is hope that I am pregnant," she wrote in June, 1543, "for I know that there is no one who will be happier than you."[5]

Diane, far subtler than the constable, betrayed no jealousy; instead, she used her charm to manage what came to be called a *ménage à quatre*, a ménage composed of the king, the queen, the constable, the mistress. It was a bizarre combination, but it was to all their advantages to see that it worked.

If Catherine had felt humiliated by Diane's presence before, now that she was queen and thus so much more in the public eye, her humiliation must have increased a hundredfold. In those first months of celebration in honour of the new king, Diane's emblem was everywhere. She was Diane: classical image of the moon and the chase; symbol, at once, of fertility and chastity. "When I would wish to celebrate thy name / I would say only: Diana is thy name," rhapsodised Ronsard in an ode in her honour.[6] She rode with the king on all his triumphs, keeping her place, yet claiming power far beyond any the queen could boast.

When, the following September, Henri made a flamboyant entrance into the wealthy and cosmopolitan city of Lyons, it was the beauty of Diane that shone in those thousands of torches lighting up the city "as though in the day." Of the queen's entrance, the Spanish ambassador wrote belittlingly: "It is indeed true that little could be seen when the queen made her entrance, because night came on. . . . [The] people say that, as she is not good looking, the king gave orders that her pageant should be kept back until a late hour, so that Her Highness should pass unnoticed."[7] It is a cruel observation, made crueler because there is no reason to doubt it.

The classical allegorists of the day had cast Catherine in the role of Juno—goddess of wives, acquiescent and heavy-wombed. Garbed in the full majesty of queenship, she was in ironic contrast with Diana, the huntress, slender, swift-footed, and always a step beyond men's achieving. Marino Cavalli's observation that the king "is not at all given to women, for his own is enough for him," was patently naïve. The court gossip was closer to the truth—and far more bitter—that it was Diane who from time to time persuaded the king to go to his wife's bed.[8]

The signs of the king's devotion to his mistress, which had been kept in check during his father's lifetime, came to full flowering in the years following François' death. He responded immediately to Diane's request for the royal château at Chenonceaux. The most famous gardeners of Touraine were employed to plant the musk roses she loved, to tend the fruit trees, to give the necessary care to such rarities as melons and artichokes. The vineyards were dug and carefully nurtured because Diane had a fondness for their red wine. A bridge was begun, to connect the château with the left bank of the Cher; an Italian parterre was fashioned. Inside the château, every extravagance of marble, enamel, and tapestry was assembled. Most of all, the king began to order those intricate designs that linked the initials "H" and "D" in an eternal memorial of his love.

The château of Anet, west of Paris, which had come to Diane through her first husband, now felt the full power of her golden hands. The old feudal buildings were refashioned in the new Franco-Italian style. Philibert Delorme, already famed for his architectural genius, was given carte blanche to re-create a world of beauty. When he finished, his work was called the Paradise of Anet. It was a work rich, alive, inventive, part traditional, part new. A staircase led to the gardens, and in the center of the parterre, two fountains played, symbolising immortal life. Anet was a triumph of taste and a monument of egocentricity: The walls of the château were hung with tapestries worked especially for Diane; stained glass depicted the mythological deeds of the classical Diana; enamels commemorated Diane and Henri; and the fountain of Diana, with its nude goddess, celebrated the exuberant grace of her body. There was also a special set of apartments, set off from the ordinary life of the château and kept "for a very special guest."

It is apparent from the notations of the various ambassadors that the "special guest" spent as much time there as he could. Here Sir John Pickering, having been granted a royal audience, noted in awe that it was "a wonderful fair and sumptuous house . . . as princelike as ever I saw." Here Henri sometimes brought his ministers, occasionally his wife, and at least once the young dauphin, who wrote in childlike excitement over the wonderful, huge bed in which he had slept.[9]

When affairs kept the king from Diane, he wrote to her—simple love letters, such as any boy in the first flush of love might write. There is nothing either sophisticated or regal about his expression. Whatever Diane's feelings for her royal lover, his for her were unequivocal. When he heard she was ill, he was upset. "I beg you to tell me the truth about how you are," he pleaded. And when she responded, he wrote at once, humbly, deferentially, "My love, I thank you very humbly for taking the trouble to send me news of you, which gives me more pleasure than anything else in the world; and I beg you to keep your promise to me, for I cannot live without you." When he was detained at Fontainebleau by state business, he wrote, "I think you can imagine how little pleasure I find here in Fontainebleau without you, for being away from her on whom depends all my happiness, it is very hard for me to find any real joy." She was his joy, and joy made him articulate. The sullen, silent boy, whose father had despaired of his ever learning the graces of a courtier, found his tongue at last, to write verses to his mistress. Although there is little lyric grace to them, the miracle is that he wrote them at all:

> Alas, my God, how deeply I regret
> The time I have wasted in my youth,
> For now how many times I have been spurred on
> In having Diane for my only mistress.[10]

Diane, however, shrewd enough to recognise that such love is rarely lasting, set about to make herself indispensable in more practical ways. She busied herself to an extraordinary degree with the royal children. By 1550 there were four children in the royal nursery: two boys (François and Charles) and two girls (Elizabeth and Claude). In the next three years, Catherine would give birth to three more children: Edouard Alexandre, who later became known as Henri; Marguerite; and Hercule, who after the death of the dauphin assumed the name François. It was Diane who attended their births, supervised their nurses, concerned herself with their illnesses. In fact, it is her letters, rather than Catherine's, that provide the details of their childhood: Claude has a cough, the dauphin is weakened by recurring bouts of diarrhoea, the nurse must be changed because there is a suspicion her milk is not good.[11] In addition, she assisted the queen in every possible way. For Catherine, the ubiquitous presence of her husband's mistress must have bit deeply into her pride, but Henri, in his infatuation, saw nothing but the limitless goodness of the woman he adored. In January, 1550, he gave her an outright gift of more than 5,000 pounds in "gratitude for the good and commendable services which she has performed for our dear and well-beloved queen." "There is no telling to what the grandeur and power of the Duchesse de Valentinois will come," wrote Leone Ricasoli to Florence.[12]

Two years later Diane was able to make herself more indispensable than ever, for that March at Joinville Catherine fell ill with scarlet fever. The disease was often fatal, and Catherine came perilously close to death. Despite the contagious nature of the illness, Diane never left her, and when, finally, Catherine recovered, the doctor assured her it was Diane's unflagging and intelligent care that had saved her life. It was a burden of gratitude that weighed on her like lead.

That April Catherine celebrated her thirty-third birthday. She had been married for more than eighteen years, and she had borne six children, five of whom were still living. It was during those years that the Venetian ambassador, Giovanni Capello, could report that she was "loved and respected" and that she merited to be so "for her personal qualities and her cordiality. . . . The whole kingdom is of this opinion," he concluded.[13] It was one of the few times in Catherine's life when she was not a sword of contradiction. Were it not for the bitter presence of her husband's mistress, these might have been very happy years. While there was no question of her being beautiful, she carried herself with Florentine elegance. Again it is Capello who observes, ". . . she has a handsome figure and her skin is very fine; as for her face, she is certainly not beautiful, for her mouth is too big and her eyes too prominent and lifeless. . . . She dresses richly and with very good taste."[14]

She was a fitting counterpart for her husband, who during the early years of his kingship had developed a style and graciousness far exceeding his father's hopes for him. "Comely and breathing the very air of majesty," Contarini had said of him as he approached his mid-thirties. The handsome forehead, the lively black eyes, the dark skin and large dominant nose gave him a look of steady endeavour. "He is always very cordial and listens to everyone in the most courteous way. . . . He is very noble-minded, and it can be seen that he wishes to expand his state," concluded the Venetian.[15]

Like François I, Henri saw in Italy a golden harvest for French enterprise. Already considering Naples and Milan his rightful possessions, he saw French connections between France and Italy further strengthened by François de Guise's marriage into the famous and powerful family of Este, which had long ruled Ferrara and Modena. The assassination of Catherine's half brother Alessandro and the subsequent usurpation of Florence by Cosimo de Medici brought Florence as well into the range of French interests.

Although during her first years in France Catherine was markedly quiet concerning Italian affairs, she was never indifferent to her fellow Italians. From the beginning, she had been looked on as the patroness of the growing number of fuorusciti—those political exiles who flocked to France for asylum. Discreet and reserved, she nevertheless worked tirelessly—and successfully—for their advancement in France. Although there are few letters to Italy extant from this early period, it is obvious that many in Italy considered they had in her a powerful advocate. When, in 1547, she became queen, her Italian circle grew, and the Sienese literary critic Claudio Tolomei wrote to her, "It is hard to imagine the joy that the largest part of Italy has felt at your happiness; for it seems to them that this good fortune is theirs as well."[16]

Writers, artists, ecclesiastics, bankers, soldiers, having fallen on evil days in their own country came to France to win their fortunes and to influence Italian policy in their favour. Most were not disappointed. Luigi Alamanni, renowned for his imitation of Vergil's *Georgics,* became Catherine's maître d'hôtel, while his wife was appointed her personal maid. Lesser-known figures amassed wealth and position in Paris or Lyons. Those closest to Catherine's heart, however, were the four sons of Filippo and Clarice Strozzi, who had served her from her infancy in Florence. Through Catherine's influence, Piero and Leone were given significant military posts, Lorenzo found his place in the church, and Roberto set up a banking firm in Lyons. Arrogant and foolish though they often were, Catherine would hear no wrong of them.[17]

In 1552 Henri's military interest in Italy reached its height. While Henri attacked the emperor Charles in the Low Countries, French troops successfully entered Piedmont on their way to assist the Sienese and Florentines against their oppressor. In his absence, Henri officially appointed the queen regent of France. Although he seems to have been ambivalent in his conception of her role, Catherine's understanding was straight as an arrow. For the first time in her thirty-three years, she was in a position to judge, to make decisions, to assume responsibilities. For the first time, that keen and circling intelligence had found its natural channel. Catherine was born for the world of political action. She was shrewd, she was dedicated, and she had a perseverance that would outstay many an adversary. While Henri rode off to take Toul and Metz against the emperor, Catherine remained at St. Germain-en-Laye learning to rule. She bent herself to this art as she had once bent herself to the study of Greek, methodically, unswervingly, and with an overwhelming determination. "I assure you," she wrote the constable, "I am going to be a past master at it; for from one hour to the next I study only this."[18]

It was not her personal limitations that shackled her, but rather the limitations of her power. Uncertain of the scope of her authority and suspicious lest something be kept from her, she perused the document confirming her regency. At once she perceived where the trouble lay, and as a member of the court reported, "she said to me, smiling, that in some places she had been given too much and in others too little."[19] It was, unfortunately, a plight that was to hobble her for much of her political life. Despite the ambiguity of her position, however, she did a fine, practical job—meeting with the king's Council; keeping the ambassadors close to St. Germain, where they could be kept informed about matters of state; warning the Cardinal de Bourbon about possible uprisings in Paris; urging that funds be raised for the maintenance of the king's army.

Perhaps she hoped, by her total devotion to the task he had left her, to win her husband's love. Her letters during these months are larded with expressions of her love for him: "To please the king," "to be in his good graces," "to serve him in any way I can." To the constable she wrote, "Please take good care of the king, for you know the painful and dangerous sickness that is going around this year." During this period, when her husband was subject to danger and death, she wore only mourning, insisting the women of her household do the same. Yet it was to Diane rather than Catherine that the king wrote. Frustrated by Henri's failure to answer her letters, she redoubled her letters to Montmorency, begging for news of the king. When, towards the end of June, the constable wrote enquiring about her health, she answered with something like acerbity, "You have inquired about my health. I must tell you that it is not the water that has made me sick so much as not having news of the king, for I am beginning to think that you and he and all the rest have forgotten that I am still alive. There is nothing which could make me so ill as to feel that I am outside his good grace."[20]

Meanwhile, the war continued throughout 1553 and into 1554 with few decisive moments. Although the king had taken Toul and Metz, he had been unsuccessful in his siege of Strasbourg. In the northeast the constable took Brussels and Dinant, but then retreated through Cambrais and Calais. In Italy the royal forces were even less successful. In the summer of 1554 they were vanquished at Marciano, and Catherine's favourite, Piero Strozzi, was seriously wounded. The following spring Siena capitulated to the Spanish, and in February, 1556, the Truce of Vaucelles was signed, which, while not a defeat for France, fulfilled few of the hopes for which the campaigns had been started.

Although Vaucelles brought military conflict to an end, it only increased the rivalry between Guise and Montmorency, who had assumed opposing views of foreign policy. Guise was enamoured with his vision of a French empire in Italy; Montmorency was stubborn in his desire for peace. Paul IV, even more outraged than Guise by this sudden truce, which left him at the mercy of Spanish aggression, continued to plead for French help. Finally, late in 1557, Guise was sent back across the Italian Alps with a sizeable army, ostensibly—as the Venetian ambassador wrote—"to succour the Pope." Catherine, though generally slow to show open interest in Italian affairs, was patently in favour of this move, and that December she wrote to the Duke of Ferrara: "I have long desired to see the goodwill in which the king has resolved to send the Duc de Guise . . . which gives me hope that with the help of God I shall see the king in Italy, as I have wished, and that your greatness will be increased with his."[21]

Her hopes were never to be realised. After a difficult winter crossing of the Alps, Guise made his way through the Milanais and into Rome. Here his reputed military genius foundered. Delayed by both the weather and what he irately called "bad faith" on the part of the Pope, he did not leave for Naples until April. Four months later the news of the sudden and disastrous defeat of the French at St. Quentin put an end to all his Italian aspirations and brought Guise home in desperate haste.

The bewildering defeat at St. Quentin had been brought about by a coalition of two ancient enemies: Spain and England. It was inevitable that Mary Tudor's marriage to Philip of Spain should have repercussions throughout Europe. In England it had not been a popular union, and the queen's sudden declaration of war against France was not a popular cause. Spain, so long England's enemy, now purported to be its friend, coercing it into enmity with France, whose friendship was of the greatest practical importance. To many Englishmen, this sudden Spanish alliance seemed only a ruse whereby Spain could put England to its use. It was the coercion of Philip, they maintained, far more than the dangerous presence of French ships off the coast of Scotland, that led the queen to her decision.

French intervention in Scotland was a persistent issue. The fact that the regent of Scotland (Marie de Guise) was a member of the House of Guise made French concern in Scottish affairs inevitable. This concern was augmented when, in 1548, to protect her from the turmoil within her own country, Marie de Guise's daughter, the five-year-old Scottish queen Mary Stuart, was brought to France as the affianced bride of the dauphin. For the next ten years, she lived at court under the care of her uncles, the Duc de Guise and the Cardinal de Lorraine. From the beginning she was greeted as some divine child, flawless in body and spirit. "She is the most beautiful child I have ever seen," Henri II was reputed to have said when she arrived in October, 1548. Four years later the cardinal wrote that she grew daily in goodness, beauty, and wisdom and that "the king has taken a fancy to her," while she, in turn, knows how to deal with him, "like a woman of twenty-five." Long before the conclusion of her marriage with the dauphin, Mary Stuart, pretty, intelligent, imperious, and under the careful tutelage of her uncles, was swaying the balance of the court. "The Queen of Scots and her house . . . bear in this court the whole swing," wrote the English ambassador in the winter of 1551. "The credit of the House of Guise in this court surpasseth all others," he continued. "For albeit the Constable hath the outward administration of all things . . . yet he is constrained to sail and many times to take that course that he liketh never a whit."[22]

By 1557 the constable's power and reputation had further diminished. Many disliked the way he had made war and equally disliked his attitude towards peace. His failure at St. Quentin completed his ruin. No one had anticipated the capture of St. Quentin. The French considered it invincible, so much so that when the Venetian Giacomo Soranzo asked the king about the condition of the city, the king replied in full confidence that the Admiral de Coligny, the constable's nephew, who was responsible for it, had just written to him giving him "every assurance" and telling him to be "under no apprehension. . . ."[23]

That such confidence was misplaced became obvious as the imperial forces began to batter the citadel. Despite Coligny's brave assurances, St. Quentin surrendered and the town was brutally sacked. Part of it was set on fire; all of it was mutilated and defaced. "Women and children gave such pitiful cries that it would grieve any Christian heart," wrote the Count of Bedford, who had taken part in the siege.[24]

With St. Quentin taken, there was nothing to stop the imperial forces from marching south to Paris. "Should they choose to march towards this city," wrote Soranzo, "they could come by the straight road without finding a fortress to detain them for long." The Parisians were wild with terror. They fled the city, carrying their possessions with them, travelling as far as Orléans, men whipping their horses forward, women carrying their babies and pushing their children ahead of them. The horrors of St. Quentin had made them irrational with fear. So real was the possibility that Paris might fall to the enemy that the king sent to St. Denis to have the jewels and royal ornaments removed, and then ordered a solemn procession to Notre Dame, in which the whole court, garbed in black, bereft of jewels and ornaments, took part.[25]

Most frightening of all, no military leader was left to rally the demoralised French forces: Gaspard de Coligny had been taken prisoner; Montmorency, badly wounded, was also in enemy hands. The court withdrew to St. Germain, having sent the dauphin for further safety into Touraine.

If France were to survive, it would need both money and a strong military leader. Henri had already sent messengers to Italy ordering the immediate return of the Duc de Guise. This surprised no one, for Guise was unquestionably France's strongest captain. The king's manner of coping with his financial need was less expected. Catherine, whose only role in government had been the ambiguous months spent five years earlier as regent, was now charged with the task of confronting the Paris Parlement and obtaining from it the funds necessary for carrying on the war.

It was, as far as we know, the first time Catherine addressed a large assembly, but at once she revealed a style uniquely her own. She came in full majesty, surrounded by the princes of the court, her ladies, the attending cardinals, yet it was a muted majesty, grave, solemn, dressed in mourning. France, it suggested, was close to death, and only the action of the Parlement might save it: The king needed 300,000 francs if France was to emerge from its struggle victorious. Recognising the emotional state of the Parisians, she played on their fears, their sense of hopelessness, their broken pride. "Her Majesty spoke with such earnestness and eloquence that everyone was moved," wrote Soranzo. She neither threatened nor demanded; she begged. Parlement, surprised and flattered, responded at once. "And," continued Soranzo, "the queen thanked them in so sweet a form of speech that she made well nigh the whole Parlement shed tears from emotion." The contemporaries who commented on this occasion noted not simply the queen's arguments, but even more her manner. "She humbly asked," they observed, impressed by the deference and modesty with which she addressed them. "All over Paris nothing is talked of but the prudent and gracious mode adopted by Her Majesty in this business," Soranzo concluded.[26] Italian though she was, her anxiety and concern for France were unquestionable. The simple black dress, the lines of fatigue in her face, her unabashed tears evoked their trust. She won the money the king needed; even more important in the long run, she won—temporarily at least—the affection and regard of the people of Paris.

Two months later Guise arrived from Italy, and the imperial forces, delayed by the exaggerated caution of the Spanish king, lost their chance to seize Paris. With the arrival of Guise, the French troops took heart. It was part of his glory as a military leader to draw men to him, to inspire them to believe in victory despite the odds. Now he hoped to retaliate for St. Quentin by capturing the English-held seaport of Calais. For more than a hundred years, the English had held the port, boasting France would never regain it until iron and lead floated like cork. Now, as Guise pushed north, forcing the imperial troops to withdraw before him, the boast proved false. By the end of December, the Pale—the 100 square miles surrounding Calais—was under attack, and on January 7 Calais itself surrendered.

The recapture of Calais had been a French dream for years. The news rejuvenated France and exalted the man who had accomplished it. "I came, I saw, I conquered at Calais," wrote the poet Du Bellay in tribute to Guise's victory. But although Calais was a triumph that raised French morale and Guise supremacy, it was not sufficient to turn the war into a French victory. In the following months, it became clear that the defeat at St. Quentin was a blow from which France could not recover. Its treasuries were drained, and its credit so disastrously undermined that it was no longer possible to borrow money. Many of the nobility were financially ruined, and the soldiers, deprived of their pay, were deserting in droves. Obviously the war could not be continued under such circumstances. It was simply a question of choosing the most advantageous moment for overtures of peace.

The following November negotiations had already begun when news arrived of the death of Mary Tudor. Increasingly unpopular with her people because of her Spanish marriage, yearning for her husband's return from Spain, Mary had clung tenaciously to the hope that she was pregnant and that her pregnancy would bring Philip back to her. The final realisation that she was not pregnant but mortally ill was the dissolution of her final dream. By the beginning of November it was clear she was close to death; on November 17 she died, to be succeeded by her half sister, the pale golden-haired Elizabeth, then in her twenty-fifth year.

Philip pushed shrewdly for peace, for with the death of his wife and the accession of his shrewd Protestant sister-in-law, he could no longer count on English support. In fact, Spain was as close to bankruptcy as France, but this Henri II did not know when, at the end of March, 1559, he agreed to the unfavourable terms of the Treaty of Cateau-Cambrésis. The treaty was unpopular both at home and abroad. "O wretched France," wrote the governor of Piedmont, "to what loss and to what ruin have you been reduced."[27] His cry expressed the popular sentiment, for it seemed to most Frenchmen that by its terms France had lost much of what it had worked so hard to gain. Their warrior-king, with his bright schemes for tripping up young Philip of Spain, of pushing the boundaries of France north into the Low Countries and south into Italy, had, instead, drawn them into the net of a Spanish victory. The few voices raised in favour of the peace were unheard. Such a defeat as François I had brought on them at the Battle of Pavia they could accept, but now they had not been so much defeated as outwitted. Frustration and mistrust, as chill and distorting as fog, lay over the French countryside.

No one suffered more from the peace of Cateau-Cambrésis than the king himself. It seriously weakened his people's confidence, and the old accusations were reiterated: Henry was too easily gulled by the councillors who surrounded him, too easily influenced by those he loved. He had been led into a disastrous war by some and into a disastrous peace by others. He was, as had been feared, a man too easily "led on leash." There was never a doubt that he was a king sincerely devoted to his country and its people. He was a good man, moderate, neither as capricious nor as libertine as his father. But his heavy, methodical mind was no match for the sharp intelligences of his favourites. During this period a pasquinade appeared which portioned out the blame for France's sorry state:

> The Cardinal de Lorraine ruins everything
> The Duc de Guise loses everything
> Madame de Valentinois grabs everything
> The Cardinal de Sens ratifies everything
> The Court of Parlement concedes everything
> The Cardinal de Chatillon listens to everything
> The king endures everything—
> And the devil carries away the day![28]

It is significant that in this popular attack on court figures, the queen is not mentioned. Actually, Catherine was never to be more universally appreciated than in those years. Parlement still remembered her plea made so movingly and so deferentially. In Paris there was the feeling that it was the queen who had "saved France." She was universally praised as "wise and prudent," and the Italian poet Pietro Aretino, usually so vitriolic over the pretensions of princes, wrote glorifying Catherine and proclaiming, "You alone are queen." It is, perhaps, a subtle insinuation that Diane, now nearing sixty, could no longer maintain the full power of her charm. Even at her summit, Diane had never won the people's love; now the Venetian ambassador wrote to the Signoria that Catherine's graciousness and kindness had captivated everyone. "She is so much loved that it is almost unbelievable," he observed.[29] The years of deferential service, of quiet obedience had achieved their goal. She had, it was true, no passionate admirers or zealous partisans, but neither did she have mortal enemies. She had steered her course, insofar as she could, in the way of peace. She had been impelled less by weakness or timidity than by an instinctive belief, confirmed during her childhood in a besieged city, that open hostility can end only in destruction.

This desire to placate opposing forces was one in which her husband had no share. He was, essentially, a man of rigid categories, who rarely asked questions beyond the immediate evidence. Perhaps it was this quality that made him an efficient captain and—to a point—a capable king. He was a man with a mind for establishing boundaries and honouring them; it was his misfortune to be born in an era in which boundaries were shifting and old classifications crumbling. That they could not be put together again by force and resolution was beyond Henri's ability to understand.

Of all the problems he had inherited from his father's reign, the gravest and most far-reaching was the restless spirit of religious reform. It was more than forty years since Martin Luther had posted his controversial theses at Wittenberg, and the intervening years had proved the folly of Leo X's initial judgement that this was merely an "issue for monks." During the lifetime of François I, the number of reformers in France continued to grow in the face of government opposition. John Calvin, following Luther's lead, had been forced to flee from orthodox Paris and, ultimately, from France. Such exile accomplished little. Books dealing with the new theology, despite edicts of repression, were secretly sold. Monks left their monasteries, bishops were suspected of heresy, and even the king's sister Marguerite was said to be "tainted." François, however, had a certain intellectual curiosity that made him ambivalent in his attitude towards the New Religion. Although he had no desire to see his kingdom rent by heresy, yet he took a kind of academic pleasure in listening to certain "suspect" preachers and saw nothing dangerous in his sister's patronage of Clément Marot and his vernacular translation of the Psalms. Yet despite his own far-ranging ideas, one of his dying exhortations to his son was to maintain the purity of the Catholic religion.

Heedless of so much that his father requested, Henri was unswervingly loyal to this one command. He had none of his father's breadth of vision, which had enabled François I to absorb conflicting ideas. Though generous and loyal to those who shared his viewpoints, Henri was marred by that inflexibility that frequently scars the narrow-minded. He saw no solution to heresy except repression, and when such repression failed, he never questioned his position, but only its implementation. It was beyond him to understand that the very severity he endorsed was fuel for the fire.

It must be acknowledged in his defence, however, that the problem encountered by Henri II was far broader and more penetrating than it had been during François I's lifetime. By 1555 the reform was of epidemic proportions. Significant assemblies with strong and persuasive preachers existed in such cities as Troyes, Bordeaux, Bourges, Rouen, Blois, Angers, even in Paris itself. La Rochelle, with its dangerous proximity to Protestant England, had become a strong-hold of the new faith, and in the provinces of the southwest, the Religion, as it was called, had attained its major strength. Here, in fact, lay the greatest political danger, for the kingdom of Navarre was in open support of the heresy. Its current rulers were Henri's cousin Jeanne d'Albret (daughter of Marguerite d'Angou-lême, who had died in 1549) and her husband, Antoine de Bourbon, First Prince of the Blood. For some time they had been reputed to provide hospitality to ex-iled preachers, and in 1555, Théodore de Bp.m.ze, a leader of the movement and one of its most persuasive preachers, wrote in elation, "The king and queen [of Navarre] begin to taste something of the truth."[30] Three years later Antoine was being exhorted by Calvin himself to assume the leadership of the Religion.

Had Calvin had more personal contact with Antoine de Bourbon, he might have been less anxious for him to assume such an important position, for An-toine, though gifted with charm and enthusiasm, was to show himself during the next few years markedly inconstant. Vain, ambitious, visionary, his head always full of conflicting schemes, he would use his royal blood to secure himself a pow-erful position at court; he would become the devoted leader of the Huguenots (as the French Protestants became known); he would intrigue with the King of Spain and win back some of the ancient boundaries of Navarre; he would cast his lot with the Guises and win a kingdom in Italy. In fact, he did nothing. Enamoured with his own grandiose daydreams, he never recognised that frequently he was not the manipulator but the manipulated.

Heresy in high places constituted a peril against which the king had no suitable weapons. He had, at the beginning of his reign, set up the *Chambre Ardente* to deal exclusively with cases of heresy. During the next ten years, he set in motion a series of repressive edicts, but fortunately for the reformers, the edicts were im-plemented only sporadically. While the heretics knew they had no friend in the king, they counted on the fact that he was generally more interested in foreign aggression than domestic affairs. With the Treaty of Cateau-Cambrésis, how-ever, foreign wars were at an end, and the king had ample time to reflect on mat-ters at home.

The most immediate of his domestic problems was to make the treaty itself seem less unpalatable. If Cateau-Cambrésis had any saving clauses, they were those providing for the marriage of Catherine and Henri's daughter Elizabeth to Philip II and Henri's sister Marguerite to the Duke of Savoy, Philip's ally.

Elizabeth de Valois had just celebrated her fourteenth birthday. Of all the Va-lois children, Elizabeth alone was without blemish. Small-boned, graceful, per-fectly proportioned, with a mass of black hair and dark—almost Spanish—eyes, she seems to have displeased no one. "You would have said that she had been created before the beginning of the world and reserved in the very thought of God until it was His will to unite her to her husband," rhapsodised Brantôme.[31] She was intelligent, obedient, and gifted with a sense of diplomacy beyond her years.

Despite the obvious differences between them, there appears to have been a depth of understanding between Catherine and her eldest daughter that was not diminished by their years of separation. Perhaps Catherine saw, mirrored in her, the image of her own experience. She, too, at exactly Elizabeth's age had been sent into a foreign marriage as a means of bringing peace to hostile countries.

Her husband, however, had been but a boy little older than herself; her daughter was to marry a man twice her age who had already buried two wives. Elizabeth, of course, had never seen Philip. She was told he was handsome, well built, quiet, and reserved, looking more Austrian than Spanish with his blond hair and blue eyes. Henri, curious for a glimpse of his son-in-law, urged him to come to Paris, but Philip replied that the kings of Spain were not accustomed to going to get their wives. The marriage would take place by proxy, with Philip represented by Fernando Alvarez de Toledo, Duke of Alba.

In mid-June the Spanish retinue arrived, and on June 22 the actual marriage ceremony took place. It was a rich celebration, calculated to impress the Spaniards and to raise French morale. Elizabeth's gown was stiff with precious stones, and her small head bent beneath the weight of an imperial crown, set with jewels and adorned with thin gold loops, from which hung an immense diamond. Alba, though usually a man of simple taste, now in token of his role was dressed in brilliant plumage of red, yellow, and black. The wedding took place at noon, and following it, Elizabeth was solemnly proclaimed Queen of Spain. Six days later, the marriage contract between the king's sister and the Duke of Savoy was signed, and the following week was devoted to festivities of every kind: balls, dances, masques, the full panoply of royal entertainment.

High on the list were the days of tourney in which the French king intended to demonstrate the skill and endurance of the French in feats of arms. Henri, though still a powerful figure, looked older than his forty years. His hair had begun to grey, and despite the hours of disciplined exercise, he had grown corpulent. Now, however, in the courtyard of the Tournelles, he showed his skill to great advantage. One by one he defeated his opponents. It was not until the third day that a young lord, the Comte de Montgomery, captain of the Scots Guard, held his own against the king. Unwilling to leave the contest at a draw, Henri compelled the count to a final contest. Twice they circled and missed each other; at the third try, they clashed, their lances splintered, and as the crowds began to cheer, they saw the king reel, slip over the pommel of his saddle, and crash to the ground. Montgomery's splintered lance had, by a freak of timing, pierced the king's visor and penetrated the brain. The king, dazed, tried to stagger to his feet; Catherine, seeing the blood drip through the broken visor, fainted. The galleries were in pandemonium as Henri, supported by his attendants, was freed from his armour and carried to his rooms in the Tournelles. It was impossible to tell whether he was alive or dead, for, as they carried him from the field, the terrible wound in his head was covered and the great body lay perfectly still.

Ten days later, on July 10, shortly after midnight Henri II died. The unlikely prophecy of the seer Nostradamus, made four years earlier, had come true: The "young lion" had overcome the "old one"; he had lost an eye "in single combat" and as a result had died a "cruel death."[32]

When Henri had been carried from the field, the doctors, while admitting the gravity of the wound, had not considered it mortal. That night Montmorency had written to Elizabeth of England describing the accident, but assuring her that although the wound was severe, "The first and second dressing appeared . . . to give good hope that the result will be satisfactory."[33] The doctors' initial optimism had been short-lived, however, and the king's death came as no surprise.

During the ten days following his injury Henri had been locked into the circle of his pain, drifting in and out of consciousness, but never lucid long enough to carry on the business of the kingdom. The "eminent surgeons" who came to the royal bedside probed the wound and removed what they could of the splinters from Montgomery's broken lance. The king, always a brave soldier, endured the agony with only a single cry of pain. Still dissatisfied, the doctors examined the heads of several criminals, lately executed, in order by this lesson in practical anatomy to determine how deeply injured the brain might be. But, observed the Marshal de Vieilleville, who claimed to be present, "It was in vain."[34]

The royal marriages had drawn many to Paris, especially among the nobility, and the crowds who waited for news of the king's condition were far larger than normal. The sudden shift from gaiety to mourning was more than the citizenry could cope with, and the Parisians, usually so volatile, were silent and uncomprehending at this sudden mystery of death which had struck their strong, life-loving king. As Henri's condition became known, the grief and anxiety of those surrounding him grew. Diane, whose colours he had been wearing during the fatal tourney, brazened out her own fears and the hostility of many at court, claiming, "As long as there is a single breath of life in him . . . I am still invincible." Yet her anxiety was all too clear as she paced the corridors, asking again and again, "Is the king dead?" knowing that when he died, her place and glory would perish with him.[35]

Of those who waited out the long ten days, no one was more deeply involved than the dauphin. François was now in his sixteenth year, yet everything about him was underdeveloped. He lacked his father's stature, and it seemed to those who now watched him that he lacked his courage as well, for the thought of the king's death threw him into a paroxysm of terror. Nothing had prepared the sallow adolescent for the kingship thrust on him so brusquely. As dauphin François had always recognised that someday France would be his to govern, but the burden had come to him too suddenly and too soon. His young wife of fifteen months, in so many ways his superior, was unable to console him, for Mary Stuart, white as death, seemed bemused by the sudden turn of events. The days of uncertainty had exhausted them both as they waited in fear and bewilderment for a royal crown to be passed to them.

Two days before his death the king ordered that the marriage of his sister Marguerite to the Duke of Savoy be postponed no longer, and at midnight in a darkened chapel and before a few silent witnesses, the union took place. The year many had said would go down in history as the year of marriages had turned into a year of death. Catherine attended the ceremony, clothed in black, her eyes heavy-lidded with fatigue and weeping. The oppression of anticipated death made her mute. During one of the king's lucid moments, he sent for her, wrote Vieilleville, and she, in "floods of tears," stood by the royal bed, promising to execute the orders her husband gave her. Knowing he was dying, Henri bade Catherine leave him; but the moment of parting was more than she could endure, and she would have swooned had not Vieilleville caught her and helped carry her into her own room.[36] It is a wonderfully dramatic scene, but, unfortunately, Vieilleville is not a reliable witness.

Undoubtedly Catherine was weakened by a grief she could not have feigned, yet, like the dauphin, part of her grief must have stemmed from fear, for she could have had few illusions that her eldest son was either wise or strong enough to guide a kingdom—especially a kingdom so far from domestic peace. François was not unintelligent; he might be trained for the task before him; he might, indeed, become a king of note—if there were time. But on the morning of July 10 time was at an end. The king was dead. The dauphin was declared king, and within moments the lassitude of waiting which the court had experienced for more than a week was turned into a storm of activity. There must be no pause in the chain of events, no moment at which the throne was vacant.

Hardly had the body of the former king grown cold than France was set upon its new destiny.

Thrust Towards Power

Make yourself mistress, and do not attend to the advice
of your evil counsellors.

—MICHEL DE L'HÔPITAL

Chapter III

Although the days preceding her husband's death had been days of deep personal anguish for Catherine, they must also have been days of shrewd political planning, for when Henri II died in the early hours of July 10, there was not a moment's hesitation on the part of the court: At once, François was taken by carriage from the Tournelles to the Louvre, in the company of those indispensable uncles, the Duc de Guise and the Cardinal de Lorraine. No one doubted what this meant. The persistent war between Montmorency and Guise had been won by the House of Guise. The constable, advanced in years but still a powerful figure, was ordered to remain with the body of his former master. It was a new twist to the old saying "Let the dead bury the dead."

Montmorency was more than able to interpret his mission: he was to be excluded from the government as he had helped exclude the former favourites at the death of François I. He had no recourse but to submit, for in addition to the feudal enmity between his house and that of Guise was the change in attitude of the queen mother. After so many years of apparent friendship, her affection had cooled, and now, like many others, she was inclined to blame him for the unsatisfactory terms of Cateau-Cambrésis. When the constable received word from the young king that he would not be retained in power, he accepted the decision without demur. "[He] bent before the wind," wrote Tavannes, "as someone in a boat lets the waves carry him off his course rather than be submerged."[1] Putting on the best face possible, he asked that, because of his years, he be given permission to retire to his country home at Chantilly. The permission was readily granted, for his presence would have been an embarrassment to the Guises—and possibly even a threat. Montmorency was still a powerful man with five able sons and three powerful nephews; if they, with their Huguenot sympathies, were to league with the Princes of the Blood (Antoine de Bourbon and his brother Louis de Condé) the Guises might find their power seriously threatened.

It was this the English ambassador Nicholas Throckmorton suggested in the report written to Elizabeth on July 11, summing up the sudden shift in court personnel: ". . . it is gathered that the Constable and his shall even now at the first be excluded from all doings, and that the house of Guise is like to govern all about the King, who is much affected toward them: but what is like to become of this State and the Government cannot be known until the coming of [Antoine de Bourbon] the King of Navarre, who is hourly looked for.''[2] Throckmorton's final sentence struck at the heart of the problem: The task of governing the kingdom, which had been preempted by the Guises, in actual fact belonged to Antoine de Bourbon and Louis de Condé as Princes of the Blood.

As soon as he realised that the king's death was imminent, Montmorency, in an effort to stave off a coup on the part of the Guises, had sent a message to Antoine, begging him to hurry to court. It was, one would have thought, the moment for which the King of Navarre had been waiting all his life. To be at court—and not simply as a poor relation but as regent of France—to have the young king dependent on his advise, to be in the seat of power, to direct, to command.

Antoine, having frequently preened himself with false importance, now seemed unable to recognise his potential greatness. From all sides people sued for his favour: The Calvinist preachers begged him to wipe out popish idolatry; the disaffected nobles implored his political leadership; the Huguenots saw him as the champion of religious liberty. Even across the Channel, Elizabeth and her ministers assessed with satisfaction the value of having a professed Huguenot as regent of France. Perhaps it was the burden of this sudden and unexpected importance, as well as fear of betrayal, that delayed Antoine. Whatever the cause, his journey north from Béarn was slow, and by the time he arrived at court it was obvious to everyone he had arrived too late.

His indecision had given the Guises all the time they needed. When he arrived at St. Germain-en-Laye on August 18, they were secure in the saddle. By their orders the palace guard had been doubled to protect the young king from all intrusion. The fact that Antoine had come with an imposing retinue was a grave error of judgement, for it aroused not admiration but further hostility. Instead of a princely welcome, a series of humiliations awaited him. No adequate suite had been prepared; François, who was out hunting, had left no plans for his welcome; Catherine, when he was finally brought to her, continued speaking to the cardinal and the Duc de Guise, hardly acknowledging his presence. Yet Antoine, despite the obvious affronts, maintained his affable smile, greeting old friends, embracing the Guises, making his usual contradictory statements, explanations, promises.

Antoine seemed incapable of understanding that his tendency to compromise any principle in his effort to curry favour actually compromised his own advantage. The Huguenots soon began to lose faith in him. His course was too tortuous for their single-mindedness. They wanted a leader who would be unyielding in their interests, not a temporiser. In bitter disappointment, the Huguenot polemicist François Hotman wrote "Navarre has miserably betrayed all our hopes."[3] They were beginning to look to Navarre's younger brother, Louis de Condé, or Montmorency's nephew, Gaspard de Coligny, for their leadership.

At court, Antoine fared no better. No longer a dangerous threat to those in power, he was now reduced to a simple embarrassment, yet he seemed in no hurry to depart. What he hoped to gain by lingering is not clear. The Guises were firmly established in the seat of power. The queen mother, whatever her private emotions, continued to ally herself with the "uncles." Montmorency and his friends were gone from court. Still Antoine lingered. Finally towards the end of the year, he was entrusted with the mission of conducting Elizabeth de Valois to her Spanish husband. It was obvious to all what had prompted the request. "They wanted to get him out of the way," wrote the Italian historian Enrico Davila.[4] Antoine, however, accepted the charge with alacrity, hoping his mission would bring him face to face with Philip of Spain, with whom he might negotiate a successful settlement over the disputed territory of Navarre.

On September 18, 1559, François was crowned King of France, the second of that name, in the Cathedral of Reims. He had made his solemn entrance three days earlier in a torrent of rain and wind. According to custom, he was mounted on a white palfrey and was greeted at the gates of the city by a young maiden who offered him the official keys. The weather made it difficult to attend, and the demoiselle's light voice was almost lost as she greeted the new sovereign:

> O most Christian king, flower of nobility
> Hope of our peace and our tranquillity. . . .[5]

No contemporary speaks of the coronation as one of outstanding splendour. The ritual, performed by the Cardinal de Lorraine, was carried out with meticulous formality, but a note of jubilance was lacking. For all the triumphal music of the *Te Deum*, there was still a hint of the tragic lament of the old king's death: *"Pleurez, France la desolée, pleurez."* Many wise courtiers, as they watched their pale young king, felt there was still reason for grief. Some whispered that François had winced when the crown was placed on his narrow head and that during the ceremony he had been heard to murmur that it was too heavy. Even the tall, lyric grace of the new queen was not without mar, for a few weeks before it had been common gossip among the ambassadors that Mary Stuart's health was failing. "The young Queen is suffering from consumption; she has not long to live," the Tuscan ambassador Ricasoli had written to Florence.[6]

The French court, with its love of beautiful women, took pride and pleasure in having the queen's throne graced by a girl reputed to be one of the most beautiful in Europe. Her beauty was such that it "eclipsed the sun," Brantôme later wrote, adding, "and as for her soul, it was incomparable."[7] Before this "goddess in human form," Catherine de Medici had slipped into a less ostentatious role but one that fitted her like her own supple Italian gloves: She would be from now on *Regina Madre*. It was not an uncomfortable role for her to assume; she had always been more secure as mother than as wife. There had been nothing Diane de Poitiers could do to contaminate her motherhood. Her marriage, tainted almost from its beginnings, had had one thing the seductive beauty of Diane had not been able to touch: her children. Diane, despite her sixty years, was still unquestionably beautiful. In the days following the king's accident, her vitality had contrasted sharply with Catherine's deep grief. The queen's eyes, always heavy-lidded, had grown increasingly swollen with weeping and sleeplessness; her body, already tending to flatulence, had become slow and unresponsive, while her unadorned black mourning, relieved only by a small ermine collar, made her skin more sallow than ever. The Venetian ambassador Girolamo Lippomano described in some detail the mourning queen in his first audience after the death of Henri II:

> She was in her room which was entirely draped in black; not only the walls but even the floor was covered. There were no lights except for two candles burning on an altar draped in black. The bed was covered in the same way. Her Majesty was garbed in the most austere dress: a black robe with a long train which had no ornamentation except an ermine collar. . . . The queen mother answered in the name of all, but she did so in such a feeble voice that it was difficult to understand her. . . . For in addition to the weakness of her voice in these circumstances she had a black veil on her head which covered her completely even to her face.[8]

This excess of grief which "astonished" those who witnessed it was soon tempered by time, by politics, and by Catherine's religious philosophy. Just a month after the death of her husband, she wrote to her cousin the Duke of Florence of the necessity of "conforming myself to the will of God and accepting everything as coming from His hand, bearing in mind the uncertainty and instability of everything on this earth." Her letter to Elizabeth of England was couched in the same religious rhetoric, affirming that her sorrow was so extreme it would have been unendurable had not God sustained her with "His power and grace."[9] In fact, it was the exigencies of her political position as well as the less tangible support of God's grace that foreshortened her mourning.

There is little evidence of how Catherine occupied herself in the days immediately preceding Henri's death, but on the morning of July 10 it was obvious she had taken her own political stance. She made no effort to assume royal power herself but, instead, allied herself with the Guises, subordinating herself to their "wise counsels." Her motives for doing so have been variously defined. Ambition, fear, naïveté—they were undoubtedly all present to some degree. One thing is clear: although the law of the state dictated that the power of regent be invested in the First Prince of the Blood, Catherine gave short shrift to such a course. To vest such power in a man so inconstant as Antoine, a man now further disadvantaged by his formal profession of the New Religion, would have seemed sheer folly to Catherine's practical mind.

The Guises, conversely, were powerful, intelligent, consistent in action, and—perhaps most important of all—already at hand. True, they were not universally liked. Their arrogance had sometimes offended their peers, their ambition was legendary, their religious position made them unacceptable to the Huguenots, yet no one could question the influence they wielded both in France and beyond its borders. Although there were many who disapproved, no one was surprised when, by the beginning of August, all military matters were confided to the Duc de Guise, while matters of state and finance were entrusted to his brother the cardinal. "They completely possess our young king," the contemporary jurist Étienne Pasquier wrote mistrustfully, "and all affairs of state pass through their hands." Ricasoli was still more blunt in assessing Guisard power when he wrote to Florence in early August, "The Cardinal de Lorraine is both Pope and king, wielding an authority greater than any that has ever existed in this kingdom."[10]

Those who looked with suspicion at their massive power were not without cause. While it was true that the duke had recently won Calais for France and that the cardinal had championed French interests during the Council at Trent, yet they had interests and concerns that might not always be consonant with the interests and concerns of France. As early as 1559 many Frenchmen were frightened by the overt cordiality between the Guises and the King of Spain, so much so that the contemporary historian Jacques-Auguste de Thou went so far as to accuse them of having already "broached" an intrigue with Spain which would disadvantage France."[11]

Their involvement with Scotland could be even more dangerous. Now that Mary Stuart was Queen of France as well as Scotland, French concern with events in Scotland inevitably increased. As the regent, Marie de Guise, faced increasing opposition from the Scottish reformers, France increased its military aid. This measure did nothing to improve relations between England and France, and 1560 was filled with prickly warnings from Elizabeth to remove this foreign threat from her back door. With the power of Spain growing along its borders, France could not afford to have England as an enemy, yet it was clear that if the Guises had their way, their sister would be helped in every way in her battle against the Scottish rebels.

This strong opposition to the reform in Scotland was clear evidence of what the Huguenots might expect while the Guises were in power. As Throckmorton had noted in a letter to Lord Burghley, there had been little mourning among the reformers in France at the death of Henri II. Instead, they felt a sense of relief and anticipation, for the queen mother seemed far less intolerant than her husband. In addition, Antoine, who, they expected, would assume the regency, was already looked upon as the probable leader of the Huguenots. Their disappointment was bitter indeed when François II made it immediately clear that government affairs would be entirely in the hands of the most conservative family in France. It was evident the members of the Religion could expect no mercy from the crown.

Bèze's recital of the persecution in France during these days is undoubtedly exaggerated: prisoners led away on every hand—"men, women, children, people of every class"—their houses abandoned to pillage "as though it were a city at war."[12] Yet the fact was that commissions were being sent into the provinces "for the persecution of religion," and at Paris, Anne Du Bourg, an esteemed member of the Paris Parlement, despite his years of service to the state, languished in prison for heresy. Du Bourg's imprisonment, one of Henri II's last official acts, had shocked and displeased many, for Du Bourg was a man of position and integrity. With the death of the king there was hope that he would regain his freedom; instead, his condemnation to death was confirmed.

If the Guises thought by such measures to intimidate the reformers, they soon found they had achieved the opposite. As the day for Du Bourg's execution approached, the resistance grew. On December 18 Antoine Minard, one of Du Bourg's judges, was shot in the streets of Paris, and a threat was directed against the Cardinal de Lorraine: "Be careful, Cardinal, lest you be treated à la minarde." The rebellion soon spread beyond Paris, and Thomas Killigrew, Throckmorton's secretary, wrote in his report: "Garboils at Lyons, Paris, Gascony, and other places. . . ."[13] No threats of violence, however, were able to save Du Bourg, who died with constancy on December 23. To his coreligionists, the fact that he suffered on the very eve of Christmas brightened the lustre of his martyrdom.

Earlier that fall the policy of increased repression had led the Huguenots to write to the queen mother, assuring her their religious position was in no way meant to indicate disloyalty to their sovereign. Following Du Bourg's death, they wrote again:

> We protest before the Divine Majesty and Your Majesty that we have never wished—nor do we now—to attempt anything against Your Majesty; we wish, indeed, to live and die in the homage, service, and humble obedience which we owe to you. As for the forces which have been called to your attention, they are only for your service. Thus, we have armed ourselves in order to oppose the tyranny of the Guises who have never attempted anything except to increase their own power at the expense of your ruin and all those who belong to you.[14]

This was far more than the statement of simple, religious men who sought only the right to worship according to their consciences; rather, it bore out La Planche's observation that the Huguenots were of two classes, religious and political—the latter determined to oppose Guise usurpation of powers they maintained belonged rightly to the Princes of the Blood. This letter, written towards

the end of 1559, indicates in embryo the position the Huguenots continued to espouse during the entire course of the religious wars: They were royalists, loyal to
the established government, their armies having no other end but to "protect"
the king from those subtle court factions, headed by the Duc de Guise and his
brother the cardinal. Even when tempers were at their height, following the execution of Du Bourg, it was not the king or the queen mother at whom the
crowd's anger was directed. Rather, the royal family was cast in the role of victim, hopelessly manipulated by a power too strong for it.

It was certainly hard to look at the young king and not be moved by pity. The
crown placed on his head at Reims was, in every sense, too heavy for him. The
periods of lassitude he had always suffered had become more frequent. His pallor
had grown so extreme Killigrew had repeated the current gossip to Elizabeth: "It
is very secretly reported that the French King has become a leper."[15]
Catherine, too, was cast in the role of victim. Quiet, inexperienced, and of the
weaker sex, she had, it was assumed, dissipated her power by her dependence on
the royal uncles. In fact, there is little evidence of Catherine's reactions during
those first six months. Her letters are scarce, and the references to her in contemporary memoirs and letters infrequent. It is not difficult to conjecture, however,
that they were months of both loneliness and anxiety. She had relinquished the
title of queen to a girl who, with the arrogance of youth and royalty, was reputed
to have called her mother-in-law a shopkeeper's daughter. She watched her son
in his constant battle against ill health; even more painful, she watched while this
same son—who but a few months before was reputed to "do nothing except what
she wishes"—was drawn beyond the circle of her solicitous love.[16] She was no
match for the adroit management of the House of Guise. She who was to spend
her life in an "eternal quest" for peace now watched passively while battle lines
were drawn. The Guises were in the saddle, and they were master horsemen. It
must have been Catherine's deepest regret to recall it was she who had held the
stirrup.
In the last months of 1559 she seemed to be losing everything. Her husband
was dead, her eldest son had journeyed beyond her, and in December, she bade
farewell to her beloved daughter Elizabeth. Elizabeth, of all the Valois children,
seemed most capable of eliciting love. During her years as Queen of Spain, she
won the hearts of the Spanish people, who called her affectionately Isabel de la
Paz, and insofar as Philip could let his heart be won, she won the heart of her
husband. Following her betrothal, it had been conceded she should remain at the
French court for six months longer, since she had not yet celebrated her fifteenth
birthday. By the end of November, however, plans were completed for bringing
her to the Spanish border. At the same time Marguerite de France, younger sister
of Henri II and close friend of Catherine, was also leaving court to join her hus-

band. To lose at once both her favourite daughter and her friend of twenty-five years was a bitter blow. A little of her grief was dissipated, however, by the reports of Sébastien de L'Aubespine, the French ambassador at Madrid, who wrote of Philip's conspicuous happiness at the anticipation of Elizabeth's arrival.[17]

Catherine spent a lonely Christmas at Blois, made anxious by the unrest spreading across France. The smoke from Du Bourg's execution lingered far longer than anyone had anticipated. Throughout January the atmosphere grew more acrid as other Huguenots were delivered to the flames. Paris was seething, and special measures were taken to keep order. "Factions in religion are springing up everywhere," Throckmorton wrote to his queen on February 4.[18] But the Guises, intractable in their position, refused to nullify any of the repressive legislation despite the warnings that surrounded them.

For the Huguenots the situation had become insufferable. Already letters had gone to Calvin asking if in such circumstances an insurrection would not be justifiable. Calvin, however, more moderate than many who sought his leadership, would not sanction such a measure unless this was necessary to "maintain the Princes of the Blood in their rightful positions . . . and only if this is sanctioned by Parlement." He was adamant in his stand that it was "better to perish a thousand times" than rise against lawful government.[19] Calvin's pacifism in the face of their unjust persecution did not sit well with the Huguenots. From their vantage point, action seemed imperative, not only for their own safety, but for the good of the kingdom.

Thus was set in motion those abortive plans and tangled motives which later became known as the Conspiracy of Amboise. From the beginning, its lack of competent leadership doomed it to failure. The logical leaders—Antoine and his brother—ostensibly took no part in the insurrection; indeed, they later denied any knowledge of it. The leadership was assumed by Jean de Barry, Sieur de La Renaudie, an adventurer of questionable motives, who sometime earlier had taken refuge in Switzerland following an unsuccessful attempt at forgery. Here he became a member of the Reformed Religion and a candidate for the proposed conspiracy. In a venture demanding prudence, strategy, and discretion, La Renaudie was notably ill qualified. When Calvin met him in Geneva, he described him as "a man full of vanity and presumption," adding, "I did everything I could to divert him from this folly."[20] It was La Renaudie's doom that he could not be diverted.

The plans were completed at Nantes in the first weeks of February. Their success was dependent on secrecy, yet word of the plot was soon leaked to the Guises. The château at Blois where the court was then gathered was no place to sustain an insurrection, and towards the end of February the court left Blois and made its way by slow stages down the Loire to Amboise. It was here that Catherine, convinced a continued policy of repression would lead to civil war, assumed the initiative for the first time. She sent for the Admiral de Coligny, who had joined the Religion two years before, and together with the mild chancellor François Olivier, they discussed possible solutions to the impending danger. Although widely divergent in temperament and ambition, the three found themselves in accord on one point: France must not be drawn into civil conflict. Their resolution was formulated in the Edict of Amboise, which distinguished between "religious Huguenots" (those seeking religious toleration and their basic rights as citizens of France) and "seditious Huguenots" (those who were active enemies of the state). The latter would be persecuted for what they were; the former would be recognised and granted amnesty by the crown.

Such policy ran directly counter to the Guises' program of total repression. For the first time since François II had assumed the throne, they found their power shaken. To oppose the edict would simply reenforce the bond between Catherine and Coligny and thus strengthen the House of Montmorency. Even worse, it would lend credence to the Huguenots' accusation that the continued persecution was the work of the Guises and not of the royal family. They had little choice but to acquiesce, and on March 2 the edict was sent to Paris to be registered by Parlement as quickly as possible. Unfortunately, the compromise came too late to influence La Renaudie and his conspirators.

Once the court had changed residence from Blois to Amboise, a more practical man would have rethought his plans, for Amboise was close to impregnable. That La Renaudie continued to believe in the possibility of success is sufficient evidence of his naïveté. Built originally by the counts of Anjou, the château rose from sheer rock on the right bank of the Loire. With its high towers, it dominated a view of the river for miles on the north, while on the south, it was protected by the forest of Amboise. For a sizeable group to approach Amboise undetected was close to impossible, even with the most elaborate planning. The group that converged on Amboise in mid-March of 1560 had none. Badly equipped and badly directed, they wandered through the forest—a dozen or so together—assembling more by accident than design. If their later testimony is to be credited, even the purpose of their enterprise was cloudy. Some believed they were simply asking for an audience with the king to present their grievance and sue for a meeting of the Estates General. One or two believed they were to kill both the Guises and the king. Most maintained, however, that their goal was to seize the cardinal and his brother and so "free" the king.[21]

The enterprise failed before it had begun. On March 11 two of the captains were captured by the king's men at the castle of Noizay near Tours, where they had established a headquarters. In the following week various other bands of conspirators were intercepted near Tours or wandering in the forest of Amboise. Some few were put to the torture in order to extract information; but in general, the spirit of conciliation that had been induced by Catherine and Coligny still prevailed, and most of those taken were sent back to their homes with no more than a threat of future punishment. "Ill-disciplined and worse armed. . . . Poor country fellows, not knowing what to do," Michel de Castelnau described them in his *Mémoires*. [22]

On March 16, however, the climate was changed by an act of overt aggression. Shortly before dawn a group of more than 100 horsemen rode into the courtyard at Amboise. Some boatmen on the Loire, seeing them through the pre-dawn mist, alerted the château, but despite all the elaborate precautions, the king's guards were singularly unready to cope with the attack. Had the attackers been sure of their own strategy, the Conspiracy of Amboise might well have succeeded. As it was, they seemed as bewildered as their foe. After firing their pistols haphazardly, they remounted and headed back the way they had come. Throckmorton, describing the scene to Queen Elizabeth (whose money, it was rumoured, had partially armed the conspirators), wrote, "Whereupon there was such alarm and running up and down in the court, as if the enemies encamped about them had sought to make an entry into the castle and there was crying, To Horse, To Horse!" [23]

It was this abortive attack on the royal château that changed the climate at Amboise from tolerance to strict justice—and beyond. The verbal admonitions the first captives had received were now replaced with torture and death. The cruelty exercised at Amboise has become legendary, for it reached beyond justice into spectacle. The day after the attack on the château François, convinced now that mercy was a useless instrument, elevated the Duc de Guise to the position of lieutenant general of the kingdom. For a moment Guise had slipped in the saddle, but now he was erect again, more powerful than ever. Catherine, meanwhile, had to bear the chagrin of failure. She had set herself on the side of mercy, and mercy had betrayed her. She had spoken in favour of the Huguenots, and at the very moment of her patronage they had attacked her. She would be slow to take that way again. Most humiliating of all, she had lost her advantage to the House of Guise. Thus ended the first clash in that lifelong duel in which neither side was ever to gain a decisive victory.

No climate is so suited to cruelty as fear, and for months the French court had been living in fear and uncertainty. At the beginning of March Perronot de Chantonnay, the Spanish ambassador, had written to the Bishop of Arras, "The affairs of this kingdom are in such confusion that one cannot hold anything for certain," an observation underscored by Throckmorton who commented, "They do not know whom they can count on or whom they should distrust." [24] The Cardinal de Lorraine, it was noted by his contemporaries, was peculiarly susceptible to fear. Unlike his brother, he was no soldier. His weapons were his wit, his eloquence, his arrogance. The threat of physical violence was new to him, and he met it less nobly than one might have expected. When, at last, he was in a position to avenge himself for those long months of terror, he did so without mercy. It was the cardinal rather than his military brother who demanded the full penalty of the law. One can also recognise his hand in the *lettres de cachet,* determining the policy towards the rebels, which advised "have neither pity nor compassion on any of them."[25]

It is difficult to sort out truth from legend in the accounts of Amboise. Those who were eyewitnesses to the events were far too partisan to see them objectively. The account given by the Huguenot Agrippa d'Aubigné in his *Mémoires* is undoubtedly exaggerated. There could hardly have been the hundreds of heads affixed to poles which he claims to have seen and which, at the age of eight and a half, he vowed to avenge.[26] It is not so much the numbers that died (although they were substantial) as the attitude of the persecutors that made the deaths at Amboise less execution than massacre.

One need not believe the legend of a white-lipped Mary Stuart, forced to look on the executions until she fainted. Even less must one give credence to the whispered accounts of sadistic pleasure enjoyed by the women of the court. It is enough to follow the sober accounts of the ambassadors: some torn on the wheel, some decapitated and their heads spiked at the corners of the château; large numbers sewn into sacks and drowned in the moat or the nearby Loire. Even the graceful wrought-iron balustrades which flanked the windows of the château carried their human dead. The atmosphere of peace and formality that had characterised Amboise was gone. The slow reaches of the Loire, brimming with the first spring rains, the greening of the lush shrubbery along the banks of the river served only to magnify the horror on the hill. The boatmen who traversed the river, long before they saw the corpses that dangled from the windows, smelled the sick-sweet smell of decay. Amboise was polluted with death, and the royal family was advised to leave before plague broke out.

One man among the victors did sicken and die at Amboise—from remorse, it was said, rather than disease. The chancellor Olivier could not sustain the sight of those cruelties for which he felt himself partially responsible. "Pierced with remorse and compunction," a contemporary wrote, "he fell ill with extreme depression." When the cardinal, hearing that he was dying, came to visit him, Olivier (so the account goes) turned away in despair, murmuring, "Thou wicked Cardinal, not only are you damned but you have damned all of us as well."[27]

Amboise had settled nothing. It had, instead, heightened the hostilities and complexities of the groups contending for power.

The Guises, always anxious to weaken the power of the Princes of the Blood, now attempted to cast the major responsibility for the conspiracy on Condé and Antoine. Yet despite the tortures to which they put the prisoners, they were unable to secure sufficient evidence to incriminate the Princes of the Blood. Although some had named Condé as the *chef muet*, the silent leader, there was no proof to substantiate the charge.

Condé continued to deny any implication, while Antoine—who had never left his lands in the south—assumed a stance of bland innocence. Condé, with none of his brother's ability to temporise, could not brook the suspicion with which he was surrounded and, in April, demanded a hearing by the king's Council. Fiery and impatient, he recounted his noble birth, his loyalty to the king, his manifold services to the crown in both peace and war, concluding, according to the Spanish ambassador: "I know that it is said at court that I was the leader of the conspirators against the person of my king and sovereign lord. Never has anything like this entered into my thoughts, and I declare, with the king's permission, that whoever has said this has maliciously and falsely lied."[28] It was, of course, a charge directed at the Guises. Having declared his innocence, Condé at once left Chenonceaux to take the road south to Béarn.

Six months earlier he might have found his departure hindered, but the Guises had lost face during the conspiracy. The hostility against them had increased, and they were no longer so confident of their power. When, towards the end of March, the king had written of the suppression of the conspiracy, the Huguenots had replied that it was a delusion to think such an enterprise so quickly ended: "As long as the king is a minor and does not govern the kingdom himself . . . this enterprise will never be crushed, for there will always be attempts to establish justice over the tyranny, cruelty, greed, disloyalty, ambition, and the unendurable pride and avarice of the House of Guise."[29] As proof of their declaration, Huguenot uprisings continued in Limousin, Agenais, Périgord. François Hotman published his venomous attack on the Cardinal de Lorraine in *Le Tigre,* and in Paris the cardinal was hung in effigy. The Guises, fearful not only for their prestige but for their bodily safety, moved cautiously from place to place, often accompanied by an armed guard. "These changes," Chantonnay wrote to Philip, "are a sure sign of fire."[30]

The Spanish ambassador's position during the spring of 1560 was a delicate one, for the relations between his master and the House of Guise were ambiguous in the extreme. Although Philip wished to aid the Guises in the suppression of heretics, he was reluctant to increase their power. A France that boasted a queen wearing the triple crowns of France, Scotland, and England was distinctly contrary to Philip's taste, yet this was obviously the direction in which France was moving. As early as November of the preceding year, Killigrew had written to Elizabeth that the young king and queen had made their formal entrance into Châtellerault under a canopy of crimson damask with the arms of England, France, and Scotland embroidered on it, using the title *Franciscus et Maria, Dei gratia, Rex et Regina Franciae, Scotiae, Angliae, et Hiberniae.* The following spring another despatch was sent to England describing Mary Stuart's presumptuous conduct: "She has entitled herself Queen of England by her own speech, by her ushers, by writings and seals and by inscriptions in all her triumphs and heralds."[31] This was obviously the work of those aspiring uncles who knew the use to which their niece could be put. The Conspiracy of Amboise, however, temporarily diminished the Guises' concern with Scotland and England, and Marie de Guise was told that she must be satisfied with French arbitration rather than French arms.

Catherine had never been comfortable with heavy French involvement in Scotland. In all her audiences with Throckmorton, she had protested that her friendship and affection for England were unwavering. Amity and peace, she assured him, were her deepest desires for both their countries. Throckmorton, however, always distrustful, listened to Catherine with suspicion. Now, although he conscientiously reported Catherine's assurances of friendship to England, he added warningly, "They use this fair language to bring the [English] Queen to lay down her forces."[32]

Throckmorton had overstated the case. Catherine did, in actual fact, prize friendship with England, nor did she intend to sacrifice this friendship because her daughter-in-law wore the crown of Scotland and was being taught to aspire to that of England. It is difficult to assess the relationship between queen and queen mother. The accounts that have come down to us indicate no overt friction. They were—unavoidably—often in each other's company. They sat beside each other at court functions; they received the ambassadors together, Mary often deferring to Catherine during the audiences. None of this, however, indicates anything resembling affection or trust. They chose their words and channelled their emotions. To sing, to dance, to charm, to dissemble—these were the arts in which they had been trained. Catherine, being older, was perhaps more deft.

Following Amboise, Catherine found herself in a stronger position than at any time since her husband's death. The more hostility and distrust encircling the Guises, the more she was in a position to determine her own policies. The wheel of fortune had turned. For eight months it had held the Guises high; now their fortunes had dipped, and Catherine had her first chance to play a role at which she was to become increasingly adept—that of opportunist. She had never believed in the merciless persecution of the Protestants; she had never believed in alienating the Princes of the Blood. Such measures would inevitably divide, and a divided France would make her fair prey to any enemy. Now, for the first time, she was given the opportunity of working out the balance of power that was to form the focus of all her political strategies. "She is uniting the Princes of the Blood and the Huguenots," wrote the Comte de Tavannes, "in order to check the authority of the Guises."[33] This, essentially, was her policy.

When, at the end of March, Olivier died, his death left open the most important post in France: the chancellorship. This time Catherine saw to it that it was filled by a man whom she, not the Guises, could number among her advocates.

In an age of violent partisanship, Michel de L'Hôpital charted a course extraordinarily free of passion and self-interest. He was no temporiser, he curried no favour, and he was a man of unassailable honour. Catherine could not have chosen more wisely. There was little opposition, not even from the Guises, perhaps because they felt there was little to fear from such a high-minded man as L'Hôpital. He was a noted Humanist; his Latin was elegant; he was erudite; he was a poet. It seemed too much to ask that he be an astute politician as well. They soon found, however, they had misjudged the new chancellor.

Towards the end of May the pressure against the Huguenots was eased by the Edict of Romorantin. Catherine had already learned that overt sympathy for the Huguenots was a dangerous position. Romorantin was something far subtler. Although its specific wording did not broaden the base of religious liberty, its intent was to spare the Huguenots actual persecution. While the edict clearly demanded the repression of "seditious assemblies," it left the way open for liberty of conscience. Had the leaders on both sides been as passionately devoted to peace as the queen mother and her chancellor, it might have worked. As it was, the summer of 1560 was aflame with violence. From Troyes, Bayonne, Agen came accounts of churches burned, statues destroyed, priests molested. And for every act of atrocity attributed to the reformers, there was the reciprocal violence of the Catholics. To the foreign agents who observed the events, it was clear these were more than local disturbances. Guido Giannetti, a Venetian in Elizabeth's employ, used the term "religious wars."[34]

L'Hôpital had already advised that an open council in which these religious issues could be freely discussed was the only way to peace, yet Pius IV hesitated in approving such a measure. He feared what might occur in such a national council and, instead, repeated his intention to reconvene the general church Council of Trent. France, however, with little faith in Trent and impatient with Roman deliberation, sent an invitation, under the king's seal, stating: "All prelates and members of the Gallican church shall assemble within six months at the designated place in order to confer on all things, and together to reform the ecclesiastical state and restore it to its former splendour."[35] Meanwhile, an Assembly of Notables (members of the royal council, officers of the crown, Princes of the Blood) was convoked at Fontainebleau in mid-August. Catherine, although hopeful such an assembly might alleviate the mounting tension, was under no illusion that a few days at the conference table could end the kingdom's deep divisions. On July 28 she wrote to L'Aubespine that they had arrived at Fontainebleau "to come to some resolution about our affairs and to establish some order," but added realistically, "As you can imagine, this is not the work of a day or even of a month."[36]

Of the notables who gathered at Fontainebleau, the Princes of the Blood were markedly absent. Once again, Condé and Antoine had chosen to absent themselves, when their presence could have been of prime influence. At the death of Henri II Antoine had ignored the urgent summons of Montmorency; now he had ignored the pleas of the queen mother. Catherine, attempting to increase the royal power by balancing Bourbon against Guise, was moved to bitter frustration. Two weeks before the assembly opened, she wrote personally to Antoine:

> For more than a year now, I have suffered in seeing this poor kingdom afflicted with one calamity after another . . . and now witnessing those major affairs in which the king my son finds himself concerned . . . it seems to me that all his true servants can find no better means of acting . . . than to assemble together . . . assuring myself that since you are the first by reason of blood, you will also be the first in the devotion you have always shown to my lord.[37]

But Antoine, usually so impressed by flattery, did not move out of Béarn.

Indeed, he could ill afford to do so, for in the summer of 1560 the Princes of the Blood were engaged in a plot that came close to costing their lives. In late June, Condé, cocky, tempestuous, and chafing under the humiliations he had suffered, met his brother in Guyenne. He would no longer brook that *tyrannie Guisienne* to which he had been treated at court. It was not hard to find among the hotheaded Gascons other lords who shared his feelings. One of these was Ferrières de Maligny, who had been involved in the conspiracy of Amboise. This congenital revolutionary now put himself at the head of a group which planned to seize Lyons. Lyons was a wealthy city, a centre of foreign enterprise, a city often called the crossroads of Europe. It was, as well, a city in which anti-Catholic feeling ran high. With Lyons in their grasp, they would have the ideal position from which they could march towards Paris and "vindicate their rights."[38]

Both Bèze and Hotman spent part of that summer at Nérac-Bèze, preaching the evil of everything not in accord with the purity of the Gospel, and Hotman, stirring tempers against his prime target: the House of Guise. Maligny, meanwhile, with more than 1,000 men, was headed for Lyons. What none of the conspirators realised was that the Guises, with their elaborate system of spies, were kept meticulously informed of events in the south. As the assembly at Fontainebleau was drawing to a close, Jacques de La Sague, a courier employed by the Bourbons, was, by order of the Guises, detained and searched as he left Paris for the south. The letters he carried were sufficiently incriminating to put him to the torture. Like most men, vanquished by pain and fear, he revealed what he knew of the plot. At once the Vidame de Chartres, to whom La Sague had delivered letters, was arrested. The Lyons enterprise was, of course, immediately countermanded, and Maligny was again forced to flee the scene of an abortive conspiracy.

Before La Sague's capture, a messenger had been sent south to inform Condé and Antoine that the king wished them at court. He was instructed to tell them they "might come with the utmost Safety, and should be as free from Danger as if they were in their own Houses, or any other Place they could desire."[39] When the extent of the uprising was revealed, however, the king's tone changed. Angered that those closest to him by blood and dignity should twice within a year be implicated in a revolt within an already disturbed kingdom, he assured his ministers he would tolerate no more. Once again the princes were ordered to court. The king was no longer issuing a request but a command. "I know very well how to make him recognise that I am king," François wrote, referring to Antoine. Still hoping that the invocation of royal authority would be sufficient to intimidate him, François wrote a few days later: "If he comes as a subject ought to come to his prince, then we shall receive him and make him welcome; if not, we shall attack him and let him feel that it is I who am king and that I have the power and means to make myself obeyed and to punish those of my subjects who are so bold as to deny me their obedience."[40]

For François, the matter resolved itself into a simple matter of royal authority; for the queen mother, the problem was more complex. The balance of power she had been perfecting for the last six months would be necessarily destroyed if the Bourbon princes were involved in an uprising. The folly of Antoine and Condé would become the strongest weapon of the House of Guise, and the Guises themselves would be perilously close to reclaiming that position of power they had lost after Amboise.

The suspicion that fell on the Princes of the Blood inevitably shadowed the House of Montmorency with which they were closely linked. The constable, who had come well armed to the meeting at Fontainebleau, rose "in choler" at the ungrounded suspicions cast at him. There was a tempestuous scene with the queen mother in which, as Chantonnay reported, some "foul language" was used. The constable accused Catherine of "wanting to rule at any cost" and of surrounding the king with men who were "universally hated."[41] The queen mother winced at the unmerited rebuke. If she wished to rule, it was—as she reiterated until the end of her life—only that her sons be protected and France be brought to peace. As for deliberately keeping the Guises close to the king, this was far from her desires. She feared their power; she feared their influence over François that diminished her own. Unable to rid the court of them, she had worked tirelessly to undermine their power. If their star had risen again, the fault was not hers, but that of those two mad egotists in the south who were setting France afire.

In the south, there was chaos, for the two princes could agree on no course of action. Not only had the attempt at Lyons failed, but the simultaneous uprisings in Languedoc, Provence, Dauphiné had also been unsuccessful. In September their younger brother, Charles, Cardinal de Bourbon, arrived to persuade them to return to court and vindicate themselves. Obviously, they considered the pressing command to come to court a trap, yet failure to obey the king's summons would make them rebels to the crown. Antoine, irresolute to the point of caricature, now found himself in a dilemma a far more decisive man would have found difficult to resolve. While his cardinal brother was persuading him that he had no recourse but to return to court, Calvin was urging that he become the leader of the reform. "This leader must diligently reunite his forces," wrote Calvin to Bèze. ". . . There is a rumour that they are beguiling him with false caresses in order to subdue him, which seems to me highly improbable because things have reached the point where they admit of no reconciliation."[42] At precisely this point, however, Antoine decided reconciliation was possible.

Undoubtedly the influence of his brother the cardinal and the continued reassurances of the queen mother were prime factors in his decision. Condé, less tractable, was rumoured to have said that he would go to court only on condition that he be "well accompanied." Catherine, annoyed by his bickering and frightened at the thought of a hostile force in Orléans (where the court now sat), replied that "it was not proper" to make a show of strength where the king was in residence. Consequently, on September 17, Antoine and Condé, sparsely attended, left Nérac. Although there were many along the way who would have liked to have swelled their retinue, the Guises' surveillance made this impossible. When, at the beginning of October, the princes stopped at Poitiers, they were besieged by crowds of malcontents clamouring for them to espouse their cause. Catherine, fearful lest such episodes might weaken Antoine's resolution, wrote repeatedly to express her disappointment that his journey had been so often delayed and assuring him of a cordial welcome at court.

Towards sundown on October 30 Antoine, with his reluctant brother, entered Orléans. They were, as Catherine had promised, "expected." The squares of the city were barricaded and flanked with soldiers. The palace had doubled its guard. The princes were not permitted to use the ordinary entrance but were forced to dismount and enter through a narrow wicket gate. The contemporary historian Nicolas de Bordenave remarked that they were treated "not as relatives but as criminals." This was but the beginning of their humiliation. As they made their way through the courtyard and into the audience chamber, they were greeted perfunctorily by those stationed "to avoid any uprising or tumult." Here Condé was told to wait, and Antoine entered alone to greet the king, whom he found surrounded by those protecting forces the Cardinal de Lorraine, the Duc de Guise, the Cardinal de Tournon, and the Marshal de St. André.[43]

A year of kingship had done little to strengthen François. He seemed almost too frail to stand erect. His eyes, always weak, now watered constantly; his pallor, too, seemed more marked. As he was seen amid the tall well-made figures of his Council, it was easy to understand the recurring rumours that the king had not long to live. The boy who had such a passion to be a man was never to succeed. Although there was gossip from time to time that his young wife was pregnant, there was nothing to substantiate it. The evidence is rather that her young husband was incapable of fatherhood. The verse written of him by a contemporary poet is highly ironic: "I was sparing of wine, of Venus, of vice." Sobriety was not difficult for François, for he had no appetite for those "fleshly pleasures" considered the taste of kings. In every aspect, his powers were stunted. He lacked the strength and intelligence to oppose the Guises. Nowhere is this clearer than in his attitude towards his Bourbon uncles.

In place of the "grateful reception and warm welcome," which Giovanni Michieli, the Venetian ambassador, said was expected, there was hardly a welcome at all. Antoine, with his ability to shift with the wind, tried to adjust to this unexpected situation. "He made a number of very humble bows . . . with his knee to the ground," Michieli continued. The king, however, barely acknowledged this homage, indicating only that his uncle should make the same obeisance to his mother.[44] Catherine was no more gracious than her son. The warm protestations of trust and affection that had drawn the princes to Orléans had disappeared without a trace. Even when Antoine was led into the more intimate atmosphere of the queen mother's chamber, the tone did not change. When Condé was brought in, he was treated even more coldly than Antoine.

Antoine, who had talked his way through so many crises, found it hard to believe his charm would fail here. But his explanations—that he had come to court at the king's command, that he had brought his brother in order to clear his name of suspicion, that it would be easy to disprove the charges—fell on deaf ears. Without further discussion, Condé was taken into custody and led from the room. Antoine, bewildered at this unexpected turn and frightened for his own safety, looked accusingly at the queen mother, whose promises of safety had been so earnest. She made no explanation beyond the simple declaration "It is the will of my son." At once Michele Suriano wrote to Venice: "This arrest has caused the greatest commotion and consternation in the Court, as no one desired or expected it."[45]

The Guises, of course, desired it. Whether or not Catherine desired it is difficult to say. That it was her "plot" from the beginning—that she had all along determined on the death of Condé and the virtual imprisonment of Antoine—is hard to believe. Undoubtedly she had drawn them to court in order to terminate the possibility of revolt. Perhaps, too, she felt they could extricate themselves from the charges of sedition and that some "bargains" might be struck between Guise and Bourbon. The woman who had been contemptuously labelled the shopkeeper's daughter was not averse to the Florentine art of bargaining.

Condé's imprisonment now provided the atmosphere for a reign of terror. Two more arrests were soon made: Antoine's secretary and Condé's mother-in-law were accused of complicity in the Amboise affair. Condé's wife, Eléanore, with a certain flair for melodrama, reputedly threw herself at the king's feet, begging him tearfully to spare her husband or at least to let her see him. Despite her wild outbursts, the king remained unmoved, "telling her Publickly," as Castelnau observed, "that her husband designed to usurp his Crown and take away his Life."[46] Condé's case moved forward rapidly. On November 17 Throckmorton noted in his despatch: "The Prince [Condé] was taken before the Council who committed him prisoner . . . he will soon be sent to Loches, the strongest prison in France. The King of Navarre [Antoine] goes at liberty but is as it were a prisoner.''[47] On November 26 an improvised tribunal was assembled, and despite Condé's refusal to be judged by other than his peers, he was found guilty of treason. It was a crime that carried the death penalty, and Condé's execution was set for December 10.

Chapter IV

By the first week of December the Prince de Condé had been forgotten in the turmoil caused by the king's mortal illness. In the third week of November François had returned home from hunting, complaining of a violent earache. Soon recurring chills and fever confined him to his room. The Guises, aware of how little it would take to start an uprising, did what they could to keep the seriousness of the illness secret. The king, it was said, was but suffering a temporary malady, the result of excessive exercise and the sudden unseasonable cold.

Not even the discretion of the Guises, however, could long keep the gravity of the king's condition from the court. Soon the ambassadors were noting that François was suffering from a lump behind his ear "as large as a walnut," that his ear was discharging a black, pussy substance, that he was "weak and languid" and often unable to speak. "The king is seen to be in so much distress that he is almost out of his mind," wrote Suriano to Venice.[1] The purgings and bloodlettings the doctors prescribed only weakened him further. For a little while he found relief when the tumour was pierced, but the inflammation soon spread beyond his ear to the brain itself. On November 29 Throckmorton reported to Elizabeth, "Great lamentation is made at the Court, for they mistrust the King will not recover."[2]

The king's room, darkened and silent in an effort to relieve his intense pain, admitted few visitors. Mary Stuart, despite her own frail health, did what she could to nurse her husband. His mother never left him, even eating her meals in the royal antechamber, where she was sometimes attended by the Cardinal de Lorraine. All audiences were cancelled. In such an atmosphere of secrecy, rumours were bound to grow, and soon it was being said the king had been poisoned by some wicked Huguenot—by his barber, who had poured a deadly substance into his ear; by his cook, who had poisoned his dinner; by a servingman, who had slipped a potion into the royal glass. To the king, weakened by dysentery and the fiery pain in his head, it mattered little who was responsible for his death. He had no strength left for enmity. By December 5 he had slipped into a semicoma; the following day, probably towards evening, he died.

From the moment of his death the political activity silently at work for weeks surfaced. The Venetian ambassador, watching the sudden shift in tone, commented compassionately, "Soon the death of the late king will be forgotten by all except his little wife. . . ." As once, in the twinkling of an eye, Mary Stuart had displaced Catherine de Medici, so now after seventeen months of queenship, she herself was displaced. Undoubtedly, she wept for a lost crown and an uncertain future, but it is not too generous to believe that she wept as well for the loss of a close and affectionate companion who, for a short time, had been her husband. It is foolish to predicate either romance or passion of their marriage, but Mary and François had spent their short lives together. There is no reason to believe the sobs her contemporaries noted were anything but sincere. Brantôme, at any rate, did not question them and wrote later of Mary's "divine beauty" hidden beneath the white garments of her "mourning and grief."[3]

Catherine's grief was more measured. Towards the end of November she had written to her sister-in-law the Duchess of Savoy that although her son was in great pain, still she hoped that God would not "visit such terrible misfortune upon me as to take him from me entirely." A week later, however, she knew her hope was vain. On December 6, the day after his death, she wrote of her sorrow in this new loss which "pierced her so deeply" that it would be unendurable, except that it is "the will of God, which disposes of us all as He wishes." It is the same conventional piety she had used sixteen months earlier at the death of her husband.

In her letter to her daughter Elizabeth, however, one glimpses a little of the loneliness and fear she hid from her contemporaries and, from time to time, even from herself:

> And so, my dearest daughter, commend yourself to God, for you have seen me as happy as you are now, with no thought of ever having any sorrow except not to be loved as much as I wanted by the king your father—although he honoured me far more than I deserved. Yet I loved him so much that—as you know—I was always in fear. Yet God has taken him from me, and still, not content with that, He has taken your brother, whom I have loved as you well know. And now I am left with three small children and a kingdom divided into factions, so that there is not one in whom I can completely trust.[4]

In fact, Catherine might have numbered four small children, for the new king, Charles, was but a child himself, a boy of ten, described as full of nobility, gravity, modesty, courage—but, as the Venetian ambassador commented, "not very robust." His two younger brothers, Henri (aged nine) and Hercule (aged five), gave more promise of a long and healthy life than the new king. Some about court were already whispering that Charles, like his brother François, had not long to live.[5] Even had he been more robust, his age would have precluded the strength necessary for kingship. He was still a child, and Catherine knew, from both her Machiavelli and her own bitter experience, that a child on the throne creates those "troubled waters" in which ambitious men fish to their own profit. This time she was determined her own grief and uncertainty in the face of death would not paralyse her. She had erred dangerously, at her husband's death, in placing the preponderance of power in the House of Guise. This time she was determined that the power of the state would be vested in her and that the ambitions of Guise, Montmorency, and the Princes of the Blood would thus be kept in balance.

Her first formal step was taken within hours after her son's death. On the evening of December 6, 1560, after a perfunctory religious service in the king's bedchamber, the Council was convened. A year and a half earlier these men had intimidated her. In the meantime, she had taken their measure. She knew what flattered them; she knew what threatened them. The Cardinal de Lorraine was a man more perceptive than his brother, a diplomat, singularly sensitive to his own honour, whom Suriano described as "unequalled for dissimulation." His brother was the soldier, fearless, resolute, impetuous. They shared one quality: an insatiable ambition. To counterbalance this force, Catherine recalled the constable. Despite his seventy years, Anne de Montmorency was still a fighter, with a steady mind and a soldier's body. It was Catherine's hope that he would provide a checkmate to the ambition of his avowed enemies, the Guises.

Of the three Bourbon princes, only one concerned her: Antoine, King of Navarre. Condé was still in prison, and Charles, Cardinal de Bourbon ("a pious man with good intentions"), posed no threat. Antoine, however, as First Prince of the Blood, would have to be managed carefully. Antoine was then nearing his forty-fifth year. Despite his greying beard, he was still a handsome man, tall, robust, with a charm his brothers lacked. "He is very civil to everyone," wrote Michieli, "without pomp or ostentation; he is very free in his manner which is very French. His generosity is such that he is always in debt."[6] It was the portrait of a man on whom the gods had smiled, but, despite his gifts, there was a weakness at the core. He was a fickle and inconstant man, whose ambitions contradicted each other. It was precisely this underlying irresolution in his nature that Catherine played on for her own purposes.

Catherine had not waited for her son's death to work out her new policy. She had spent the preceding week in a series of subtle political moves, assuring the constable of a place in the new government, shearing the power of the Guises, dangling golden promises before the vain and gullible Antoine. When the royal Council met, Catherine, without struggle or manifest opposition, assumed the regency. She announced that to be of the greatest help to her son, she would keep him with her "and help govern the state as a loving mother should."[7] Antoine would be first councillor and perhaps lieutenant general for the king's forces. Despite her original promise of sharing the regent's power with him, she retained possession of the royal seal, indicating that Antoine would assist her, but never overrule her.

Her letters to her daughter Elizabeth during these days reveal her state of mind: "It is my first aim to have the honour of God before my eyes and to conserve my authority, not for myself, but in order to preserve this kingdom for the good of all your brothers." It was not a purpose with which Antoine could take issue. He agreed, with that excessive docility that made him the despair of those who counted on his leadership. Ten days later Catherine wrote triumphantly to her daughter that although the laws of the kingdom demanded that while the king was a minor, the First Prince of the Blood must rule with the mother, this was no cause for anxiety since Antoine was entirely in her hands. "He is completely obedient to me and has no authority except what I permit him," she concluded.[8]

On December 9 a letter bearing the signature "Charles IX" was sent to the provinces, the sovereigns of Europe, and the ambassadors. It stated that during the minority of the king his mother would act as regent, "supplying by her wisdom for the limitations of his age." It was in every sense a coup—peaceful, almost imperceptible, but a coup nonetheless. Sometime earlier, fearing the power of the Guises and their harsh treatment of those who opposed them, she had asked counsel of L'Hôpital. Make yourself mistress, he had advised, and do not depend on evil councillors. She had successfully followed his advice. The Duc de Nevers stated an accepted fact when he wrote, "The queen mother is now the most powerful of all."[9]

On the same day that the official letter declaring Catherine's regency was sent out, the heart of François II was laid to rest. Sealed in a small lead casket covered in gold, it was brought to the nearby Cathedral of St. Croix. His wife, no longer of use or importance, still wept, writing her verses of loneliness and regret. As for the others, there was little time for sorrow. Catherine was already beginning to show that tendency which was to grow with her years—the tendency not to look backward, to see the past as dead. The living had no debt to the dead; their debt was to the living.

Throckmorton, who had watched the shifting fortunes at the French court, first with suspense and then with a certain amusement, wrote to the Privy Council in England: "Since the late King's death, great love is made between the great here."[10] The "great love" was, of course, a matter of expediency. Antoine and Montmorency had had their moment of reconciliation, chiefly motivated by their common fear of the Guises. Then Antoine, under Catherine's coercion, had in turn embraced the Guises, assuring them that he bore them no ill will—an extraordinary statement when one recalls that they had been largely responsible for his public disgrace and his brother's death sentence. For the time being a certain exterior harmony had been established, and Catherine's leap to power was an accepted fact.

Catherine, though grateful for this period of peace, had no illusions that her move was universally popular. There had been among the Huguenots a sense of relief and elation at the death of the stern François II, and Calvin had written triumphantly: "God has suddenly appeared in the heavens and He who pierced the father's eye has now struck the ear of the son." Part of their elation, of course, originated in the belief that Antoine, as First Prince of the Blood, would assume the regency. Although Calvin already suspected his inconstancy, he now exhorted him to religious leadership, assuring him that God had ordained him to be a "father . . . to all the poor faithful." Antoine, however, had no intention of risking his present position in order to uphold a religion to which he had but a minimal commitment. Calvin found it inconceivable that a man of noble birth should concede his rightful position to a woman like Catherine. "To consent that a widow and a foreigner and an Italian to boot should rule," he wrote, "will not only redound to his [Antoine's] own great dishonour but to such prejudice to the crown that he will be everlastingly blamed."[11]

Calvin was not alone. There were many within the French kingdom who resented Catherine's common origins and especially her Italian blood. Even those who approved of her wondered how long she could succeed in holding France together. Shortly after François' death, Suriano wrote to Venice:

> This is the present state of France: a very young king without experience or authority; a Council rife with discord; all power residing in the hands of the queen, a wise woman but frightened and irresolute and always merely a woman; the King of Navarre, a very noble and courtly prince but inconstant and with little experience in public affairs; as for the people, they are all divided into factions.[12]

On December 13, just seven days after the death of the king, the Estates General, which had been announced the preceding summer, opened in Orléans. It was the first public appearance of Charles as king. He sat, raised as high as possible and surrounded by the members of the royal family, at his left, his mother; on either side, his brothers and his sister Margot, not quite eight, but already showing the promise that would make her one of the most beautiful women of the kingdom. At first glance, there seemed to be no king here—only three small boys, extravagantly dressed for a part in some pageant, with their mother near at hand to give them their cues. In fact, this was the family portrait Catherine always cherished. Had it been possible, she would always have kept her children near her skirts, for until the end of her life she continued to believe she could solve their problems, cool their feverish impulses, even save them, perhaps, from their own mortality.

The peaceful family portrait was to be short-lived, however, for the dissenting factions, having found a forum, were soon in open discord. "There is an old folly," Étienne Pasquier shrewdly wrote, "which runs in the souls of even the wisest Frenchmen, that there is nothing which comforts the people more than these assemblies; on the contrary, there is nothing that leads to more harm."[13]

L'Hôpital himself opened the Estates. His address stressed those qualities of reconciliation he felt were of primary importance. It was a long speech and so softly spoken that many of the delegates heard but snatches of it. Those who caught the full substance, however, found little to please them. His conciliating attitude to the New Religion angered the solid Catholics, while it left the Huguenots dissatisfied with its fluid generalizations. Far more disquieting, however, was the fact that beneath the mild voice and conciliating phrases was an unyielding confirmation of royal supremacy. The king was supreme—and the king was to rule through his Florentine mother. With the help of the Council, she would formulate policy, bestow favours, make decisions. The single prerogative of the Estates was to find ways of raising money for the crown.

The opposition began at once. Both the nobility and the third estate asserted the right of the Estates to determine the course of action when the king was a minor. The regency, they maintained, belongs by right to the Princes of the Blood; it cannot be preempted. Catherine, secure in her victory in the king's Council, now found herself facing defeat from an unexpected quarter. During the recess declared by the chancellor she worked to develop a strategy that would characterise her personal statesmanship. Recognising the difficulty of dealing with the Estates as a whole, she determined to deal singly with their leaders. Throughout her life, she would continue to deal with individuals, always reducing warfare to single combat. She would never become a general, but as a duellist she became close to invincible. She began now to conquer the Estates as she had conquered the king's Council, winning their leaders one by one.

She lifted Condé's death sentence and set him at liberty, directing him to return to his lands in Picardy. Condé's pardon had two objectives: to rid her of a troublesome and erratic opponent and to win the gratitude of the Bourbon family, who were responsible for much of the opposition. As for Antoine, who as First Prince of the Blood had the strongest right to oppose Catherine's regency, he continued his passive acceptance. With their leaders mollified by personal gain, the opposition of the Estates was dissipated, and on December 21 Catherine's absolute power as regent was formally proclaimed. When the Duc de Guise returned to Orléans after a short absence, Guise le Grand found not only Catherine securely established but himself replaced by a man twice his age, with whom he had been at enmity all his life. He stormed; he railed; he retired to his rooms half crazy with anger and humiliation.

It was the dangerous fact of Catherine's strategy that for every ally gained, she strengthened the opposition by creating a bitter enemy.

After a month of fruitless discussion, centred largely on the kingdom's perilous financial state, the Estates—which had not met in full regular assembly for more than seventy years—were prorogued. A small group was appointed to reconvene in May to consider further the question of finances. Meanwhile, the royal budget had been trimmed. Salaries were cut and pensions reduced. François' funeral had been almost that of a poor man, and all his horses, his hunting dogs and falcons were disposed of. It was very little, but perhaps it would act as a token of goodwill.

As for the religious question, it seemed more unsolvable than ever. Although the chancellor had attempted to establish a conciliating tone during the Estates, nothing had confirmed his position. Philip, apprehensive of Catherine's tendency to compromise, had sent his ambassador extraordinary, Juan Mauriquez de Lara, "to make Catherine see reason." "Concerning religious affairs," his instructions read, "you must speak to Queen Catherine very clearly and frankly, encouraging her on our part to the greatest care and vigilance in matters pertaining to religion, so that she will never permit these new ideas which have taken root in her kingdom to grow and flourish."[14] Mauriquez's position was supported by the Bishop of Fermo, recently arrived from the Pope, as well as Sebastiano Gualterio, the resident Nuncio. They were a powerful trio, whom Catherine had no desire to alienate; yet neither did she wish to alienate the French Huguenots. By way of answer, she instructed her ambassador, L'Aubespine, to explain to Philip that she had no desire to implement heresy, but that the course of total repression that had worked in Spain was ineffective in France. "For more than twenty or thirty years," she concluded, "we have tried cautery, hoping by that means to cut away the contagion, but we have seen by experience that these violent measures only make it grow and multiply."[15]

In fact, Catherine had shown little favour to the Huguenots beyond disagreeing with the brutal measures sanctioned by Philip's ambassador, yet this mild forbearance gave them hope. Early in February, 1561, Calvin wrote from Geneva: "Our hope is growing from day to day because the harshness of the queen is becoming softened. . . . If she keeps her promises, our church will progress far and wide."[16]

Many in France, of course, felt that the Religion had spread quite far enough, blaming its growth on the initial blunder of taking it too lightly. Suriano, appraising the religious situation, wrote to Venice:

> At first it was only a game; they affixed papers which they called placards at the corners of streets. . . . But the game caught on and spread into many parts of the kingdom. The King, observing the evil, tried to cope with it by threatening decrees and severe sentences. . . . Thus fear kept the people in line until the time of Henri II. But this King was too busy with his wars, and so neglected the evil. . . . Thus the poison spread secretly; it reached the court and many of the most important men in the kingdom so that by the time it was discovered, it had done irreparable harm.[17]

Even as he wrote, he explained, the houses of many in Orléans were freely open to the Preaching and psalm singing, with the inhabitants openly discussing the

New Religion and speaking freely against the Catholic faith. Were it not for François' untimely death, Suriano continued, he might have been able to stem the evil; as for Charles, Suriano had little faith in what the new king could do, "for being so young, he is forced to rule through the will of another."[18]

The other was, of course, Catherine, and Suriano had no faith that she could or would stem the evil of heresy.

Neither Suriano nor Calvin quite hit the mark in his evaluation of the queen mother's religious position. She was concerned with neither orthodoxy nor heresy as ultimate values, but rather with a kingdom at peace within itself and secure from foreign aggression. Her dilemma in the months following the Estates—and indeed during the remainder of her life—was to determine what religious policy would best serve these ends.

In early February the court left Orléans with a sense of relief. Orléans, though a beautiful city, had brought them nothing but sorrow and anxiety since their arrival in October. The queen mother, with her son, took up residence at Fontainebleau. During the next few years mother and son were rarely separated, for Catherine had already established that pattern of conduct on which Suriano commented: "She keeps her son under her thumb; she does not even let anyone but herself sleep in his room. She never leaves him."[19]

Had Catherine hoped to find at Fontainebleau a surcease from the troubles of Orléans, she was disappointed. Antoine, who during the Estates had shown himself both loyal and docile to her will, now acted with that sudden caprice which made him the despair of his friends. During the third week of February he disrupted a meeting of the Council by demanding more power for himself, the public vindication of his brother Condé, and the dismissal of the Duc de Guise, who, he maintained, was responsible for the dishonour caused his family. Suriano, observing the havoc created by this unexpected move, noted, "He is constantly shifting from right to left; siding with the Catholics out of fear of the Pope, with the Huguenots in order to win himself a party here in France, with the Lutherans in order to fashion some ties with Germany. This inconstancy has its own purpose, but it reveals a very weak and irresolute character."[20] In his weakness, Antoine showed himself both arrogant and stubborn. If his demands were not met, he threatened, he would leave court.

Catherine's dilemma was obvious: If Antoine left, he would join Condé, and together they would constitute a formidable enemy, yet to demand Guise's withdrawal would create an enemy of equal power. She argued to no purpose that Guise's position demanded his presence at court. Antoine made no reply but continued the preparations for his departure. The situation was made more desperate by Montmorency's decision to join him. On February 28 Catherine watched helplessly while they made ready to leave. It was Charles who saved the day, running into the courtyard and begging the constable, in memory of his father, whom he had served so faithfully, and in honour of all his own great deeds for France, not to abandon them. While Montmorency could turn a deaf ear to Catherine, he could not resist the son of his warrior-king. Silently, he dismounted and returned to the palace. Antoine, uneasy without the constable's support, also capitulated, but not before he had been promised that the royal seal would be handed over to him and that Condé would be invited to court to vindicate himself.

"Thanks be to God, I am at peace again," Catherine wrote to her daughter Elizabeth, but it was to be short-lived peace. In the next few months the battles would follow one another without respite. Catherine, aware of how nearly she had been vanquished, renewed her efforts to conserve friendships on all sides. Knowing Philip would condemn her for conceding too easily, she wrote to her ambassador in Madrid, "Leniency was used very lavishly, but you must believe that under the shadow of this, I will use every means so that nothing will be changed which concerns the honour of God and the good of the kingdom."[21] The sentence is deliberately deceptive. Philip is to be led to believe that her "leniency" is a deliberate policy of velvet glove and iron hand. In fact, Catherine's "leniency" cloaked something far less volitional—her weakness.

That weakness was to become increasingly apparent in the spring of 1561.

At the beginning of March, Condé arrived at Fontainebleau for his "vindication." An air of hostility preceded him, for even before his arrival there had been a squabble concerning the size of his escort. Once at the château, he retired at once to his brother's rooms, refusing to greet either Charles or the queen mother while Guise was with them. Montmorency offered to act as mediator, and for two hours or so, slowed by age, he made his way back and forth, carrying "messages of honour," until some resolution could be reached. Condé finally agreed that he would "meet" Guise but would not speak to him; Guise retaliated by forbidding Condé to look at him. The fate of France was ultimately solved by a "dry nod" from Condé and a "curt acknowledgement" from Guise.

On March 13 Condé swore before the Council that he had never conspired against the king. The Council accepted his word and reinstated him. Only the most simple-minded could have believed the ensuing amity was any more than a verbal truce. The following day Throckmorton wrote Cecil, "There have been lately some jars between the great parties about the Prince of Condé's matter, but all were made friends again to outward show; nevertheless, in most men's opinions some great matter will follow shortly." So ominous had the atmosphere become that the day before Condé's departure the guard had been doubled and a proclamation issued forbidding anyone to carry arms. Throckmorton's prophecy was fulfilled when, on March 17, Condé left Fontainebleau for Paris "full of threats."[22]

Two days later threat became fact when word came to the court that at a meeting of the Prévôté of Paris, that body with direct jurisdiction over the city, the queen mother's right to the regency had been disputed. The assembly had disavowed the confirmation made at Orléans, insisting that, by law, the regency belonged inalienably to Antoine, who did not have the right to renounce it. Should he refuse to exercise this duty, then it would pass to Condé. The queen mother's role was to be restricted to the simple care of her children. The action clearly bore Condé's stamp.

Antoine, buoyed up by his brother's action, immediately demanded his "rights," insisting again that Guise be removed from court. Guise, enraged that his position was questioned for the second time in a month, reacted with his own threat of violence. "There is no one in the world strong enough to chase me," he averred. "Before I leave, 40,000 men will die at my feet."[23]

For once, Catherine was on Guise's side. Her first impulse was a categorical refusal of all of Navarre's demands, but as she listened to reports that the Huguenots were massing and that hundreds of horsemen had gathered around Condé, she feared lest her resolution propel them into civil war. If she could find a way to conciliate, she would take it. For four terrible days she negotiated; at the end her regency was reaffirmed, Antoine conceded that Guise could continue at court, and Catherine acceded to the remainder of Antoine's demands. On March 25 a letter went out from the king to the governors of the provinces countering the rumours of dissension and assuring them of the "total union, accord, and perfect understanding between the queen, our most honoured lady, our dear and beloved uncle, the King of Navarre, our present lieutenant general, and our dear and beloved cousins . . . all Princes of the Blood."[24]

A few days later Catherine wrote to L'Aubespine in Madrid of the "fools" who would have "deprived me of the government, leaving me only the simple charge of taking care of my children." But, she continued, "Thanks be to God, all these things are now peacefully settled . . . and I hope we shall stay clear of all these brawls in which I have been involved since the death of my son. . . . Let me tell you frankly that I have been in great trouble here," she concluded.[25] Once again she had tacked to avert shipwreck, but she had been saved by only the narrowest margin.

She had done her best to make her concessions seem a matter of largesse, but it was obvious they were the decisions of weakness, not of strength. As Catherine stood between the crossfire of Guise and Bourbon, her weakness had been laid bare. "They have put a bridle on the queen," the Duchesse de Guise wrote to a friend towards the end of March, and another contemporary observed: "The queen has finally proved that she is only a woman."[26] Although her negotiations had had an immediate success, her conciliatory attitude towards the Bourbons had further alienated the Guises. In a letter to her daughter Elizabeth at the beginning of April, she accused the Duc de Guise and his brother the cardinal of continuing to foment division. Worst of all, she contended, they were spreading rumours that she was "not a good Christian."[27]

Many believed at this time that Catherine was seriously involved in the New

Religion. Her continued leniency towards the members of the Religion had caused large numbers of Huguenots, who had taken refuge in Germany and Geneva, to return to France to practice their religion more openly. In Rouen the reformed cult was publicly celebrated; in Beauvais the Cardinal de Châtillon had been threatened; in Bayeux Catholic churches were destroyed. Throughout the south (Nérac, Agen, Lectour, Cahors, Béziers, Carcassonne) the Religion was stronger than ever. "There is not a single city in all the kingdom which does not have its pastor and evangelical church and where one does not worship either under the sky or in a temple," wrote a contemporary.[28] Everywhere the Huguenots were demanding the right to public worship, maintaining that private homes could no longer contain them.

Even the court was "contaminated." Preaching had been held openly in the apartments of Condé and the Admiral de Coligny. Antoine went sometimes to mass, sometimes to the services in his brother's rooms. It was soon rumoured that the queen mother occasionally led the king himself to the Preaching and that she had "tried to instruct him in these new opinions." It was certain that she had surrounded herself with women who had been "infected" and that even the bishop she favoured, Jean de Monluc, had been influenced by heretical opinions.[29]

Zealous Catholics could not tolerate such ambivalence. Their response was an alliance to counter heretical forces. On Easter Monday Montmorency invited the Duc de Guise and the Marshall de St. André to dine with him. At the conclusion of the meal, burying the enmities that had separated them for years, they united in a "common goal": the preservation of the Roman faith in France. It was the birth of the Triumvirate and the seed of that Catholic League that would divide France for the next thirty-five years. Their mutual support emboldened them, and that evening Guise warned the queen mother that if she continued to "drink at two fountains," she would be responsible for the ruin of France. The following day Guise and Montmorency left court.

With their departure, it was impossible to keep up the pretence of unity. Fontainebleau, Catherine's idyl of harmony, had been violated. She had left Orléans, believing she would leave behind the contentions she found so unendurable. But the journey had been for nothing. Factions and feuds had pursued her into her enchanted garden—Guise with his arrogant accusations, Antoine with his petty points of honour. Fontainebleau had lost its magic. Although she continued to give orders to begin the spring planting, to attend the orchard, and to stock the pools with fish, her mind was grappling with the best way of ensuring her son's authority.

She decided on his immediate anointing at Reims, trusting in this symbolic rite to sustain his power.

Chapter V

On May 3 the king's retinue left Fontainebleau and two days later arrived at the château of the Duc de Guise in Nanteuil. Undoubtedly Catherine hoped, by bestowing on Guise the favour of his sovereign's presence, to mitigate his hostility; instead, the visit only widened the rift. For Catherine, perhaps foolishly, put a dangerous question: What would you do, she asked, should the king change his religion? "My whole family, my numerous friends, and I myself are determined, should such a thing occur," the Duke was reputed to reply, "to oppose it. You would find us to be the strongest defenders of that faith which has been preserved by all the former kings since the first who embraced Christianity. Therefore, Madame, be very careful of what you do, for you may find yourself surprised."[1]

Ten days later the Cardinal de Lorraine anointed Charles in the Cathedral of Reims. It was not a ceremony that exalted the king. The state of the royal treasury permitted few luxuries. Many members of the court absented themselves because their consciences no longer permitted them to attend the mass. Lorraine's sermon seemed less congratulation than threat. Primarily, however, it was the young king himself who diminished the sense of royal spectacle. He was dwarfed, not only by the columns and vaults of the cathedral, but by the men surrounding him. Even the ceremonial robes, which should have enhanced his dignity, served only to emphasise his youth. Charles was not yet twelve. Although he was tall for his age, his narrow shoulders were already stooped. His thin neck, always a' little curved, now bent dangerously under the weight of the crown. Some said he cried during the ceremony. Although there were many who praised him, describing him as a "wonderful child," having all the "promise" of a great king, promise was not enough. "They need here a very firm king who will act even before people realise what he is about," wrote the Venetian Giovanni Correro. "On the contrary, there is a timid, reserved young prince who does not dare to say yes or no without the consent of his mother."[2]

Although the coronation had not reflected royal magnificence and power as

Catherine had hoped, it had provided a semblance of unity and induced Guise to return to Paris "for the honour of God"—necessary elements if the assemblies Catherine had planned for the coming summer were to succeed. One thing the Estates of Orléans had taught the queen mother: Large assemblies generally foment dissension and settle nothing. Consequently, her strategy for the summer of 1561 was carefully calculated: The Assembly of Parlement would devote itself to a consideration of the political status of the New Religion; a modified Estates would settle the question of the king's debt; clergy of both religions would meet for a "free and open" discussion of their differences. Even Catherine's critics concede that this effort to distinguish the religious issue from the political was one of her most astute moves.

The proceedings of the Assembly at Paris held no surprises. Guise and Montmorency assumed a defensive position; Coligny made an impassioned plea for the reform; Antoine's speech, confused and ambiguous, generally placed him on the side of the Triumvirate. The Assembly of the Clergy, opened by Charles on the last day of July, was another matter. It had been condemned in advance by Philip, the Pope, and even by the Sorbonne, which objected that such an assembly ran counter to obedience to Rome. Catherine listened—she was even reputed to have smiled—but she did not submit. Her goal was a meeting in which both sides could talk freely. Even when the Sorbonne warned that it was already heresy to listen to heretics, she remained obdurate.

During the first three weeks of August the Roman clergy who composed the second estate assembled at Poissy to discuss matters of church abuse and reform. Towards the end of the month the Protestant delegates began to arrive. On August 23 Calvin's representative, Théodore de Bèze, arrived at St. Germain-en-Laye. Already a legend for his persuasive preaching and high moral life, he surprised many at court by his sweetness and charm and, in turn, was gratified by his welcome. "I arrived here at court two days ago," he wrote to Calvin, "and I can assure you that I have been very well received by all the most important people."[3] The amity was only temporary, however.

On September 9 the delegates of the reform joined the Roman clergy assembled in the Benedictine monastery at Poissy. Charles himself opened the session (despite opinions that a child should not be present at such discussions), explaining, "What I would like, and the reason I have decided to bring you here, is that you should reach some conclusion so that my subjects can live in peace and union with each other. This is what I hope that you will do. . . ."[4]

Despite the eager avowals that everyone wanted this peace and union, from the beginning there was little effort at conciliation. When Bèze attempted to explain the Protestant theology of the eucharist, the cry of *Blasphemavit!* rose in the hall. When Lorraine rose to answer, he was met with disdain. His eloquence failed to impress the Huguenots, one of whom commented scornfully that his talk was so feeble "even a child would laugh."[5] On September 17 many bishops, arguing that nothing could be accomplished in such an assembly, made plans to return to their dioceses. The Protestants, however, who saw in the conference their one hope of recognition, were not to give up so easily. It was suggested that small "private" groups replace the larger conference, but the Catholic opposition brought even this to a halt. "The prelates and the ministers no longer converse, and are likely to depart without resolving anything,"[6] wrote Throckmorton prophetically.

With their departure France found itself in greater turmoil than before. The queen mother's quiet tolerance had made the Catholics angrier and the Huguenots more confident. "I assure you," Bèze wrote to Calvin, "our queen is better disposed towards us than she has ever been." Such statements only increased the hostility of the Catholic powers. In an effort to placate Spain, Catherine had Charles write to Madrid that he had been "forced by the necessity of the time and the insistent demand of all the estates of my kingdom to permit the ministers of the reformed churches—as they call themselves—to assemble here."[7] It was humiliating that the King of France should be obliged to justify himself to another sovereign, but France could not afford to alienate Philip.

Philip, however, was not placated and secretly offered military aid to the French Catholics. The offer was tantamount to a threat of war. It was more prudent, Philip explained, to extinguish the fire in one's neighbour's house rather than wait until one's own house is in danger. When, two days later, Catherine gave audience to Chantonnay, she confronted him angrily with Philip's interference. Surely, she remonstrated, it was "very strange" that the King of Spain should offer to send troops into another country without their being requested by the ruler of that country. "Do you think that I sustain the heretics?" she asked bluntly. "If you do not favour them, you do temporise," Chantonnay replied with the arrogance that would soon make him intolerable to Catherine.[8]

Philip's influence was far-reaching. Reports reached Catherine of Spanish intrigue in Italy and Germany and of suspicious movements of Spanish troops near the frontier. Throckmorton was soon writing to Cecil: "There is some secret whispering that there is a league concluded betwixt the Emperor, the King of Spain, the Pope, the Duke of Florence, and other states in Italy and Germany to repress the Protestant religion."[9] Catherine, left without financial support, could only advise vigilance, unable to increase the garrisons.

Tensions increased in November, when Montmorency and the Guises announced they were departing for their own lands, unwilling to stay at a court where the Reformed Religion was openly practised by such professed Huguenots as Condé, Coligny, and Antoine's wife, Jeanne d'Albret. The rumour was spreading that even the young king was "infected," having reputedly told his aunt that when he grew up, he would no longer attend the mass.

Perhaps it was this rumour that sparked the bizarre scheme to kidnap the king's younger brother. Shortly before the Guises left court, the Duc de Nemours, a member of their entourage, called aside the ten-year-old Henri, Duc d'Anjou, to warn him that neither he nor his brothers were safe from the evil plans of the Huguenots and offering to take him into Lorraine, where he would be secure. Anjou, bewildered, replied that he did not think his mother would like him to leave his brother the king. Nemours pointed out that it was, after all, for his own good, recommended he think it over, but tell no one. The following day the young son of the Duc de Guise—himself only twelve—confided to Anjou that they could get him out a window at midnight, smuggle him into a waiting coach, and take him into Lorraine "before anyone was aware." Anjou, frightened and perplexed, divulged the scheme to his mother. At once Catherine had the palace guard reenforced and the windows overlooking the park walled up, "so that her son was confined as in a prison," observed Suriano. When she confronted Nemours and Guise, they explained urbanely that the "plot" was only a "high-spirited prank" that Catherine—always prone to ungrounded suspicions—had magnified.[10]

Catherine was not reassured. A few days later she wrote, describing the episode: "The child came to tell me, but I was so astonished that I could hardly believe it. . . . All my life I have loved M. de Nemours as dearly as any prince in the kingdom. I can hardly believe that he would do something so much to their [her sons'] disadvantage." The incident had both shocked and terrified her. She had known the Guise faction would do whatever they could to manipulate political events, but that they would venture to touch the members of her family had never occurred to her. That her children might be deliberately harmed brought a new terror, closer to the bone than anything she had felt before.

Christmas at St. Germain was very cold that year. Money was scarcer than ever, and the court was neither brilliant nor numerous. The royal children had been in ill health, and the king had frightened everyone by complaining of earache. "There is small joy in the Court, being Christmas," Thomas Shakerly wrote to England."[11]

In January a small assembly was convoked at St. Germain to arrive at some legislation for dealing with the Reformed Religion. L'Hôpital set the liberal tone when, in his opening speech, he indicated that it was possible to be a citizen of France while remaining outside the Roman persuasion. In the absence of the Guises, Bèze and Coligny had a free hand in helping draft the edict, which was to be the most liberal religious legislation France was to have for the next twenty-six years. For the first time the Huguenots were given permission to worship in public. Although there were limitations, Bèze was persuasive in convincing his coreligionists to accept the edict, lest in demanding more they lose everything. The Catholic opposition was scattered. Although Montmorency made a speech of violent denunciation and the Cardinal de Tournon called it *sceleratissimo,* the Nuncio found it "reasonable," and Spain was unusually quiet. The opposition came, unexpectedly, from the Paris Parlement, which vowed its members would die rather than register such an edict.

Catherine was equally determined they would accept it. The contemporary diarist Claude Haton provides a vivid, if hyperbolic, account of Catherine's clash with Parlement. The queen mother was so furious, he wrote, that "she went at once to Paris and came close to riding into the palace, horse and all" to show how determined she was to get the edict registered. "Even when she entered the room," he continued, "her anger had not yet cooled . . . and she began to plead and weep just as women do when they are angry." The dramatic scene did little, however, to coerce Parlement, for, at the end, the president cautioned her, saying, "Madame, you and your children will be the first to regret this, for it is the means by which the crown and the kingdom of France will be lost to them."[12]

In fact, Catherine seems to have been far more reasonable in her presentation than Haton gives her credit for. She explained that these measures were taken only in order to keep France from ruin, begging them to treat the dissidents more gently for the sake of all and avowing her own Catholic faith. Even so, the Parlement remained obdurate. The edict was not registered until the beginning of March. By that time it was too late; France had moved to the brink of civil war.

It is one of the paradoxes of history that the course of events is often determined not by the strong but by the weak. So now, Antoine of Navarre, vain and empty-headed, found himself the pivotal man in France. In whatever direction he leaned the scales tipped, and with the new year came a new direction. The Guises, aware of how his presence would strengthen their cause, set out to woo him. What the solid weight of possessions was to most men, the whisper of promises was to Antoine. He could be made to dance by the mere tinkle of music. The music provided by the Guises, though faint, was highly seductive. They suggested that Philip might be inclined to return the territory now constituting Spanish Navarre or that a kingdom such as Sardinia or Tunisia might be made available to Antoine. There was even the hint that an annulment of his marriage with the declared Huguenot Jeanne d'Albret might be arranged in favour of a marriage with that goddess among princesses, the widowed Mary Stuart, niece of the Guises. They were dreams that glittered wonderfully, and Antoine mistook them for gold. By the beginning of 1562 he had abandoned all ties to the Huguenots and had cast his lot with the Triumvirate. "The King of Navarre is all Spanish now," Throckmorton wrote in disgust to the English queen.[13]

On February 12 Antoine had a violent scene with Catherine in which he demanded that Coligny and his brothers be dismissed from court. Although he threatened that Spain would back his claims, Catherine refused to be cowed. She would not send Coligny from court. The balance of power had shifted so far that Coligny was now the only man on whom the queen mother felt she could depend. L'Hôpital, it is true, she trusted and liked, but L'Hôpital lacked power. Coligny was at once soldier and administrator, a man of unquestionable integrity, yet practical enough to admit the necessity of compromise. For some time the Huguenots, wary of Condé's tempestuous decisions, had turned for leadership to the steady vision of the admiral. To choose a Huguenot leader over the First Prince of the Blood was a perilous decision and indicates how desperate Catherine had become.

Coligny's response to her trust was one for which she was totally unprepared: He would prefer, he said, to leave court and return to his château at Châtillon. He made no explanation except his personal desire to be with his wife at the term of her pregnancy.

There has never been a satisfactory explanation for Coligny's decision. He was not a man who avoided confrontation; he was not a man to shift his allegiance easily. Perhaps he feared his continued presence at court might plunge France into war with Spain, although to abandon Catherine at such a moment would be equally ruinous. Even Bèze, who would have known more of Coligny's motivation than most, wrote to Calvin in perplexity: "The admiral and his brother have just left before the fury of that madman, the King of Navarre. . . . For my part, I would have much preferred that they remain here firmly until the end. But those who know better than I the secret workings of this court have judged otherwise."[14]

The day after Coligny's departure Catherine and her son, warned of the growing hostility in Paris, left St. Germain-en-Laye for Montceaux, where they hoped to find some safety from their troubles. There was to be no respite, however, for here, on March 8, the first garbled reports of the "episode at Wassy" reached them. The first news was that Guise had been attacked by the Huguenots; the second, that the Huguenots had been massacred by Guise's command. History has never made clear who initiated the incident, but the conclusion was unambiguous. Guise's men were both armed and trained; the Huguenots were simple village people gathered for religious worship. Whether or not they were a "tumultuous crowd," as Haton described them, they were no match for their adversaries.

In the speech Guise made before the Parlement the following month, he alleged he had been on his way to court, in the company of his family, when he had been attacked. He maintained he had never given orders for the killing that ensued. It is probable his statements were true, but they did not change the fact that 180 unarmed Huguenots were killed or wounded. The Catholics persisted in calling Wassy an "accident," the Huguenots, a "massacre." In either case, it was an inflammatory act that propelled France into open conflict. "If one can judge these things," wrote Étienne Pasquier, reflecting on the episode, "I would say that this is the beginning of a tragedy which we shall see played out in our midst to our own expense—and God grant that it shall touch nothing more than our purses.''[15]

It was, of course, a vain wish. In the thirty-six years of civil war that were to follow, France was to be touched in every nerve. Its countryside was to fall prey to foreign forces; its fields were to lie fallow or be turned into muddy battlefields; its rivers were to be polluted with dead, its churches to be destroyed—their statues mutilated, their stained glass windows sent crashing to the ground. Most of all, its people were to be set against one another. Many Frenchmen could have written as did the Huguenot François de La Noue: ''I found myself siding with those of the Religion, and yet I must admit that on the other side I had a dozen friends who were as dear to me as my own brothers.''[16]

Catherine, whose childhood had been spent in the terror of civil war, understood better than most the conflict that was being precipitated. In an effort to avoid it, she sent to Nanteuil, where Guise had withdrawn, asking him to come to see the king at Montceaux. It was a royal summons, but Guise ignored it. He had gathered St. André and Montmorency at Nanteuil, and together they were preoccupied in charting the course of the Triumvirate.

On Monday, March 16, in midafternoon, the Duc de Guise, riding in honour between Montmorency and St. André and accompanied by several of his brothers, entered Paris through the St. Denis gate. He had, Throckmorton reported, more than 3,000 horsemen in his train. Catholic Paris was out in thousands to cheer the ''heroes of Wassy.'' ''The people shouted in the streets,'' wrote D'Aubigné, '' 'Long live Guise,' just as they would have cried, 'Long live the king!' ''[17] Guise le Grand, they were sure, would rout the Huguenots and bring order to France.

Paris was close to insurrection, for Condé, with his own sizeable retinue, was also in the capital. Catherine, in despair at the thought of what such a clash would mean, sent word from Montceaux, begging both groups to leave the city. The Triumvirate replied at once that such a course of action was impossible since their duty to the king demanded they remain. It was the answer Catherine had expected, for since Guise's refusal to obey her request to come to Montceaux, it was obvious he considered himself master. It was for such a crisis that she had counted on Coligny. Now, desperate for any help that would check the power of the Guises, she turned to the Prince de Condé. Although it was her only recourse, it was a step that would cost her dear. Between March 16 and 23 she wrote a series of letters to Condé, imploring his assistance. She assured him she believed in his loyalty to the king and urged him to trust that whatever she did was motivated solely by her desire to bring peace and tranquillity. ''I see so many things that grieve me,'' she wrote, ''that were it not for my trust in God and my assurance that you will help me save this kingdom in spite of those who wish it lost, I would be still more upset.''

Condé was, as always, gallant. "Madame," he replied, "please believe that there is not a man in France who is more desirous to see you in peace and happiness than I."[18] The gallant answer lacked substance, however, and Catherine found her confidence misplaced. On March 23 Condé left Paris as Catherine had requested, but instead of taking the road to Fontainebleau, where the queen mother had now taken up residence, he went east towards Meaux, where he issued orders tantamount to a declaration of war.

Condé's actions played perfectly into the Triumvirate's hands. His call to arms made him a declared rebel, and Guise, now the champion of France, moved quickly to "save" the king from his "enemies." On March 26, Antoine and Montmorency arrived at Fontainebleau, accompanied by close to 1,000 horsemen. They had come, they announced, to bring the king to Paris. Catherine knew well that with the king in Paris royal power would be at the mercy of the Triumvirate, but she was powerless. Neither pleading nor bargaining was to any avail. They wanted the king's person, and she had no grounds for compromise. She could accompany them or follow them, they told her; the choice was hers.

Good Friday, the traditional day of death and bereavement, was spent in useless struggle. It was a new suffering to find herself so bereft of hope. It was the anguish of her childhood relived, those days when the Duchessina had been taken from refuge to refuge, never knowing whom she could trust, never knowing how serious the proposals were—to hang her outside the city walls; to kill her; to leave her to be raped by the soldiers. Then her terror had been limited to her child's imagination and her child's innocence. Now it knew no bounds. It was no longer a question of her own safety; it was the safety of her son and the future of France that were at stake.

On March 31 the king, accompanied by his mother, left Fontainebleau by litter for Paris. The Triumvirate had succeeded in every detail: The king and the queen mother would soon be safely in Paris; the Huguenots would be labelled the enemy of France and of the king, and the Triumvirate would assume the role of saviour. So successfully had the element of coercion been masked that the Nuncio wrote naïvely that the queen mother's fear of Condé and his armed followers had forced her to withdraw from Fontainebleau.

Although Catherine and her son were, in fact, prisoners, it was to her advantage—as well as to the Triumvirate's—that this fact never be overtly acknowledged. Thus, Guise, in order to offset the rumours he had curtailed Catherine's liberty, left her relatively free to conduct affairs, and she used her "freedom" to reopen negotiations with Condé. Condé, however, aware of the queen mother's position, disregarded her injunction to disarm and, instead, issued a manifesto, explaining that he had been impelled to take up arms "in defence of the royal authority, of the government of the queen, and of the tranquillity of the realm."[19] Three days later, on April 11, the Protestant lords signed a Treaty of Association, which had for its purpose "to maintain the honour of God, the peace of the kingdom, the liberty of the king under the government of the queen his mother." Catherine, horrified by the possibility of an armed revolt, sent Monluc, the Bishop of Valence, to Orléans to assure Condé that neither she nor the king was a prisoner and to beg him to prove his loyalty to the crown by putting down his arms.

Condé was not a subtle man, and he failed to understand Catherine's precarious balance. He was sensitive of his honour, and Catherine's repudiation piqued him. Less than a month before she had begged his help; now she questioned his loyalty. This sudden shift exasperated him into further indiscretion. He still had the letters Catherine had written him in mid-March, and he now made them public. Although in no place do they overtly ask for Condé's armed assistance, their very ambiguity permits such an interpretation. According to Condé, whatever action he had taken had been initiated by the orders of the queen mother. It was a charge close to treason, and Catherine was terrified. "The queen was so furious at the ignominy of being calumniated in this manner," wrote Santa Croce, the Papal Nuncio, "that she has said publicly that these people are all crazy and insane and that she intends to treat them as such."[20] Anger was her only means to brazen out the charges, but it was far from successful.

Catherine had lost credibility on all sides. Condé insisted it was because of her he was in arms; the Catholics accused her of "hobbling from side to side," of changing her religion and attempting to change that of her children. In an effort to regain Catholic confidence, she wrote angrily to her ambassador in Spain: "I have never either in fact, or in desire, or in my manner of life changed my religion; I have clung to it for forty-three years now." At the same time she denounced the Huguenots, accusing them of using her to mask their true aims. "In order to cover over what they are doing," she wrote, "and to draw more people to their cause, they have announced that what they do was for the service of the king, my son, and by my consent."[21]

It was to Coligny's brother, Odet de Châtillon, that she expressed the full measure of her resentment, hoping he might be able to persuade Condé to disarm. "I am very upset," she wrote, "that it will be said throughout Christendom that it is I—although I have been so concerned about the honour of this country—who am responsible for ruining it. For I think that the truth is—and I say this with regret—that it is those who counsel Monsieur le Prince [Condé] who are responsible for ruining this kingdom—and everyone says that the admiral is his sole councillor." The king, she pointed out, wished "no other arms but the love and obedience of his subjects," warning that to bear arms against the express command of the sovereign was to be guilty of treason. Her letter ends with a single, bleak statement, more notable because it stands in such contrast with the hopeful platitudes concluding so many of her letters: "I do not see any great hope. . . . I see rather the manifest loss of this whole kingdom."[22]

Despair, however, was a disease to which long exposure would make her immune. At the beginning of May she was again trying to negotiate a conference with Condé, while responding gratefully to Philip's offer of help. She would far prefer to make concessions to Condé than to accept Spanish help, for she had no doubt that Spain would use the troubles in France for its own aggrandisement. Condé's intransigence, however, continued to make negotiations impossible. Far from conciliating, he now issued a condemnation of the Triumvirate, in which he declared them enemies of France and of the king.

When, therefore, on June 1, Catherine received word that Condé had agreed to an interview, she was surprised and overjoyed. Less than a week later they met near Toury, a village between Étampes and Orléans. Catherine was accompanied by Antoine; Condé had brought the admiral, as well as an armed group "of brave and lusty young gentlemen," dressed à la Huguenot. They seemed strangely out of place in their long white coats—"according to the old manner"—with full sleeves covering their armour. They waited at a distance of 800 paces from Catherine's retinue. The atmosphere was more that of an impending battle than a peace conference. From the beginning there seemed small hope of success, for Antoine was intransigent and Condé arrogant. Tempers flared, and Catherine's plea, to "have compassion on the king's youth and on France," went unheeded.[23]

Antoine, with his usual folly, had issued an edict banishing all Protestants from Paris under pain of death. The result was a new storm of brutality against the Huguenots, and Condé declared there was no room for compromise while his coreligionists were treated so savagely. The accusations of brutality were, of course, equally violent on the Catholic side. Guise wrote to the Duke of Württemberg that he would weep to see the indignities heaped on the clergy, and Ronsard turned his verses from love to patriotism, asking Bèze how he could preach "A Christ, blackened by smoke, helmeted like a warrior, with his cutlass dripping with human blood." "There is small hope left now for any composition but such as the sword shall force," Throckmorton wrote to his fellow ambassador in Madrid.[24]

Catherine's return to Paris was cheerless and slow. She was forced to travel by litter, for she had suffered a bad fall from her horse near Étampes. Yet hardly had she settled at the Bois de Vincennes than the possibility of another meeting with Condé sent her travelling towards Orléans, again in a litter, for she was still in severe pain. From Étampes she wrote with unflagging optimism of that great hope she had in the fact that Condé had evinced "an extreme desire . . . to see me."

Three days later she felt her optimism had at last been justified. Still limping badly, she had met with the Huguenot leaders on three consecutive days. At the end, Condé, soothed perhaps by her conciliatory tone or moved by her obvious effort to sacrifice whatever she could in the cause of peace, agreed to withdraw his army and enter into serious negotiations for peace. So certain was Catherine that she had succeeded that she instructed Throckmorton to inform his queen at once that France would soon be at peace. She had spoken too quickly. The other Huguenot leaders, less impressionable than Condé, refused to honour his promises.

On June 30 Catherine admitted she had been misled. "They made me suffer the humiliation of being carried away in spite of myself; and of making me understand what little account they make of me and what a poor recompense they give me for all the pain that I have taken to keep them from being cut to pieces. . . . But I have at least this consolation," she wrote to the Paris Parlement, "for I believe that I will be justified before Our Lord and all the world for having done all that I could."[25] It was not clear who had won, Condé or the Triumvirate, but it was clear that Catherine had lost.

France was about to be destroyed by its saviours.

This final breakdown in negotiations forced Catherine to the side of the Triumvirate. There was no doubt they were her masters now, and the contempt surrounding her on her return to Paris was palpable. The Huguenots were furious. Even Bèze, once so reasonable, was now urging Condé to finish "a work begun by God," and Coligny and his brother Andelot were talking of the sack of Paris—a sack to be carried on not by Frenchmen but promised as a reward to German mercenaries. "*There* is something to attract them," wrote Hotman with satisfaction. There was death in the air, not simply in the minds of men, but even in the atmosphere. A contemporary, catching the tone of that dark summer, noted in his diary:

> Mark how disturbing this time was, with the endless rains so that the poor could not harvest their wheat which flowered its stalks . . . it was hardly possible to tell if it were winter or summer because the sky was always like dusk and all the roads filled with slush as in the middle of winter. . . . The plague which has infected Paris for such a long time has increased because of the weather, so that France is afflicted with three scourges of God: plague, famine, and civil war.[26]

Inevitably, the civil strife had drawn foreign powers into the conflict. By fall, Spain was standing solidly behind the Triumvirate, and England behind the Huguenots. Elizabeth was never quick to offer English resources, but assured by Throckmorton that it was to her interest to do so, she sent a veiled promise to Condé. "The aunt is very willing to help her nephew," Condé was told.[27] Three weeks later the Treaty of Hampton Court was signed. By it the Prince de Condé was lent 100,000 crowns ("for succouring the Prince against the hate his enemies bear to the word of God"), promised 6,000 men and, in return, made over into English hands the French port of Havre de Grâce.

When the terms of Hampton Court became known, it was decried as the basest treason. While it was true that according to the treaty, Havre de Grâce was to remain in English hands only temporarily, even this could not explain the Huguenots' making territorial concessions to a foreign power. England continued to insist that it was a "friendly neighbour," wishing to do all it could to "save" the king from those internal forces infringing on his power. In a paper entitled "Why the Queen Puts Her Subjects in Arms" and published at the same time as the Hampton Court Treaty, it was affirmed. "She [Elizabeth] desires only to keep peace with the King; and finding his person is in the possession of those who use it to stir up a war in Christendom, she has thought it necessary to arm part of her subjects and not to suffer the King to be misused."[28]

Meanwhile, troops, intended for the Duc de Guise, were massing from Savoy, Ferrara, Florence. Many of them wore the white cross on a red ground, indicating their allegiance to Spain. The fact that they had come by Catherine's order only deepened her despair. What she had feared for months and worked so hard to avert had come to pass: France had become a battleground for foreign forces. Although Elizabeth maintained she acted only "to succour that Prince so oppressed by his own subjects," Catherine found the increase of English troops in the north too dangerous to go unchecked. Despite the inadequacies of men and money, she ordered an attack on the key city of Rouen. [29]

On October 15, after several assaults, the city capitulated. Catherine, who had come to Rouen to lend support to the besiegers, found herself more deeply disturbed than she had anticipated by the brutality and waste of war—not simply the waste of human lives, but of the irreplaceable glories of an ancient city. The years Rouen had spent under English rule, following the Hundred Years' War, had only strengthened its pride in its French heritage: Here was the *Gros Horloge*, one of the largest and perhaps the oldest clock in Christendom; the cathedral more than 300 years in the building; the churches and bell towers dotting the city; and most of all that monument to French pride and endurance—the *donjon* where Jeanne d'Arc had been examined and from which she had been brought out to die at the stake. It was a costly heritage, and Catherine ordered that "this beautiful city" be spared as far as possible from destruction and plundering. What she asked was, of course, impossible. The art of war was to destroy. On October 26 she wrote that Guise's forces had been victorious, but that the "beautiful city" had been sacked.

A few days later Charles entered as king of the city his soldiers had conquered. There was little glory in his entry, however; a pall—like that of defeat—hung over the victors.

The Most Christian King entered Rouen the day after its capture [wrote the Venetian diplomat Barbaro] but not as the Kings of France were in the habit of entering a city for the first time. Instead of passing under a baldachino through streets richly adorned, his Most Christian Majesty rode over dead bodies stripped by the soldiers. His victory, too, differed from other victories, in that instead of adding to the greatness of his Kingdom, it would have a contrary effect—a thing much to be deplored.[30]

Among the leaders injured at the siege of Rouen was Antoine de Navarre, who had received a bullet wound in his shoulder. Although at first Antoine's wound seemed slight, the surgeons were unable to control the infection, and a month later he was dying. For a man who had veered so repeatedly between two religions, the rite of death was difficult. Some contemporaries reported that at the end he asked his Huguenot physician to read the Gospels to him; others, that a monk was in attendance, maintaining him in the Roman faith. Nabonne cynically explained that both were there—one praying louder than the other, while Antoine's restless spirit turned, as always, first to one, then to the other.

With Antoine's death, the responsibilities of First Prince of the Blood devolved on Condé. To have a declared rebel in such a major position was a frightening prospect. It was no doubt this fear, rather than any personal affection for Antoine, that caused Charles to write to St. Sulpice, "You can imagine my regret, anxiety, and grief in losing him in such a turbulent time." Although Catherine tried to use Condé's new eminence to cajole him into peace negotiations, her efforts were unsuccessful. Condé, suspicious of anything Catherine might propose, hedged, hesitated, turned upon his word. "Everything here is cloaked by mysterious fears," wrote Suriano. "One does not know the projects or plans of anyone. It seems as though every member of the Council keeps his own counsel."[31]

When Condé learned that fresh Spanish troops had been sent to join the Duc de Guise, his suspicions were reaffirmed. He saw no alternative but open war, and on December 19 the opposing armies met in the fields outside the Norman town of Dreux. Throughout the afternoon Catherine waited with her children in the château at Rambouillet, twenty-five miles distant. Later she confided to Monluc she had lived those hours "in terror" wondering what their fate would be should the Huguenots win. The first reports were disheartening: The Triumvirate forces had been thrown off-balance by the first violent shock of the Huguenot cavalry. By nightfall, however, it was clearly a victory for the Catholic party, although both sides had sustained heavy losses. Both the Marshal de St. André and the constable's son, Gabriel de Montmorency, had been killed; Condé had been taken prisoner; the constable, whose horse had been shot under him, had been captured. The final victory was clearly due to Guise. "He behaved like a great and valaint [sic] captain," Throckmorton conceded, adding, "The victory is to be ascribed to him alone."[32]

Dreux was a victory that brought no amelioration. It had simply sharpened the hatred between enemies; it had increased Spanish power in France and exalted the Duc de Guise. As for the common people on whose land the war was fought, they were—like Catherine herself—caught in the vise of opposing powers. "Normandy was so harassed by both Armies," wrote Castelnau in his memoirs, "that the whole Country was waste, and the poor Inhabitants reduced to the utmost Misery . . . for the People conveyed all their Goods and Cattle into great Caves, which that Province abounds with, and likewise retired there themselves, like savage Creatures in the last Despair."[33]

With the death of St. André and the capture of the constable, the full power of the Triumvirate was vested in Guise. While, on one hand, Catherine was grateful for the victories he won, on the other, she feared this monopoly of power. If she had her way, he would use his energies to procure peace rather than continue the war. Her effort to bring the captured Condé and Guise together for this purpose proved futile, for imprisonment had made Condé more intransigent than ever. After a few hours of hopeless wrangling, she had him returned to strict captivity, while Guise departed to besiege the Huguenot stronghold at Orléans.

Catherine's fears of how Guise might use his unlimited power were short-lived. On February 18 she received word that the duke had been mortally wounded by a paid assassin immediately identified as a Huguenot. Catherine's reaction to this news must have been, at best, ambivalent. With Guise dead, the Triumvirate would no longer exist, and the Catholic party would be leaderless. It was impossible to conjecture what this might lead to: possibly, a rapprochement with the Huguenots; possibly, still more vengeful fighting, if it were proved that Huguenot leaders were responsible for the attack on Guise.

Catherine left at once for Guise's headquarters outside Orléans. He was conscious when she arrived and able to tell her the details of the attack. The preceding evening he had crossed the Loiret, accompanied by an aide. He had sent his pages on ahead to tell his wife to "cover the table," for he would soon be home for dinner. In the dusk he noticed a man in a tawny cloak. The duke returned his salute and continued on his way. He had gone no more than ten paces, however, when the man discharged his pistol, hitting the duke in the right shoulder. Before he or his aide could move, the assassin, "well mounted" on a "fine horse," had fled. His "fine horse" did him little good, however, for in the dark he lost his way in the forest and was apprehended the following day close to the scene of the attack. When questioned, he stated that his name was Poltrot de Méré and that he was a former servant of Admiral de Coligny.[34]

Méré's declaration was all the bitterly bereft Catholics needed—proof positive that the admiral was responsible for their leader's death in revenge for what had happened at Wassy. Such a deed confirmed what they had always known: that Coligny and his brothers were lying traitors, treacherous Frenchmen, who had first sold their country to England by the Treaty of Hampton Court and who had now cunningly and cravenly rid themselves of the one man capable of crushing them. But as Méré was examined further, the admiral's complicity became less clear, for Méré changed his evidence from one interrogation to the next. At first, he laid the responsibility squarely at Coligny's feet, averring that he and Bèze had "promised him heaven" (and a sum of money) if he would rid the world of this "enemy of the Gospel." In the next interrogation, however, he said he had not confessed the truth, that Coligny had had no complicity in the deed, and he alone was responsible. Actually Méré's testimony had little influence on public opinion, for no Huguenot would believe Coligny was involved in so cowardly a deed, and no Guisard would believe he was not.

From the outset it had been clear Guise would not recover. For six days he lingered, and during that time Catherine came to see him daily. It was strange that Guise le Grand should be consoled in his last hours by the woman he had so often opposed and humiliated. He had once thought to triumph over her, but now they both knew she had nothing to fear. Guise lay silent, weakened by pain and fever, the jagged scar that had won him another epithet, *Le Balafré*—Scarface—taut and dark against his pallor.

On Wednesday, February 24, the first day of the Lenten season, Guise died. The queen mother's own bed was covered with black damask, and there the body of the duke was laid. The following day Catherine wrote to her sister-in-law the Duchess of Savoy, "We have suffered a great loss in this man, for he was the most powerful captain in the kingdom." Witnesses reported that the royal family were profoundly moved at the duke's death. "The King wept long and tenderly," wrote Barbaro, and "the Queen, looking at the body when she sprinkled it with holy water, fell fainting to the ground and was carried from the room."[35]

It is hard to believe Catherine wept for the man who had made her weep so often. She had not been insincere when she had said he had been the kingdom's most powerful captain or when she acknowledged that France had suffered a great loss. There had been much to admire in Guise—his valor, his endurance, his military prowess—but for Catherine, he had been a symbol of contradiction. No matter what direction she had taken, his foot had been out to trip her up. Even when he stood at her side, she could not trust him. "The death of the Duke will make some great turn," the English ambassador wrote to his queen. "The Papists have lost their greatest stay, hope, and comfort. Many noblemen and gentlemen followed the camp and that faction rather for love of him than for any other cause."[36] Catherine undoubtedly hoped he was right, for if he were, there might be some hope of peace.

Civil Tumult

Take and govern this poor vessel
And in spite of the tempest and the merciless effort
Of the sea and the gale, lead it to a safe harbour.
— Pierre de Ronsard

Chapter VI

A few months earlier, Ronsard, in a poetic description of the evils of the time, had invoked Catherine:

> Alas, Madame, in this time when a cruel storm
> Threatens Frenchmen with pitiful shipwreck;
> When hail and rain and the fury of the heavens
> Have stirred up the sea by contrary winds
> And when the twin stars no longer cast their light;
> Take and govern this poor vessel
> And in spite of the tempest and the merciless effort
> Of the sea and the gale, lead it to a safe harbour.[1]

Ronsard's plea touched Catherine's own deepest longing, and in the first week of March she resumed the task of saving France from the "cruel billows of war." This time it was Montmorency and Condé whom she brought together for that purpose. Montmorency had never been as obdurate as Guise; Condé had now lost something of his bluster. The Catholics recognised their leadership was imperilled; the Huguenots knew they lay under the stigma of Guise's murder. Consequently, the negotiations went far more rapidly than Catherine had anticipated, and by March 13 the peace was spoken of as already accomplished.

The preamble, drawn up by L'Hôpital, recalled the evils of civil war, pleaded for reconciliation, and indicated his hope for future peace lay in a general or national council and the coming majority of the king. All former condemnations of the Huguenots were abolished. Everyone was free to return to his property, his office, etc. All foreigners must leave the kingdom. In addition to liberty of conscience, restricted liberty of worship was granted. In fact, the Peace of Amboise was a truce rather than a peace, for according to L'Hôpital's preamble, nothing could be permanently settled until a free council was held. Here lay its weakness. It asked that everything be different without implementing the necessary changes. It asked that those who hated each other yesterday love each other tomorrow, without providing a rationale for doing so.

The Peace of Amboise was the first of Catherine's ineffective treaties, based on the untenable assumption that all men prized peace as she did. The queen mother had been an apt pupil in the four years since her husband's death. She had learned hard and fast, but she had not yet come to the practical realisation that the L'Hôpitals of the world are impotent against the greed, the egotism, the fanaticism of human nature. It was still a guileless queen who wrote in her own hand to Montmorency, "Thanks be to God; the peace is made."[2]

Even in her first exultation, Catherine knew there were many quarters where the peace would not be popular. During the remainder of March and into April she was busy with letters and instructions to be sent to her ambassadors in Madrid, Rome, Vienna, explaining "the need and necessity that compelled us to make this peace." Although both Philip and the Pope were restrained in their formal responses, Pius IV indicated his vexation. "For over fifteen months," he expostulated, "they had the means to apprehend the leaders of this gang, but instead, they were forced to make this shameful peace." None of these halting measures would bring peace, he reiterated. That could only be accomplished by the "free, general council," which was then meeting at Trent.[3]

Despite such criticism, Catherine was determined the peace would work. Not only was it a domestic necessity, but it was the only means of driving the English from French soil. Elizabeth's avowal that the presence of English troops in France had been only to protect the king against his enemies at home had little validity now that peace was established. On April 30 Charles wrote her, "You have given us to understand that in taking possession of Havre, you intended only to save these places until the . . . establishment of peace. . . . We now ask you to act in accordance with that sincerity which you have always avowed and to remit into our hands the city of Havre."[4]

No one, of course, believed Elizabeth would relinquish so valuable a port without a struggle. Slow to become involved, Elizabeth was tenacious with what she possessed. She gave short shrift to the diplomats who had been sent from France to negotiate. Doubtless, she was counting on the truth of the reports that France was still too busy with domestic turmoil to risk conflict with a foreign power. They were comforting reports, but they were contradicted almost at once by warnings that the queen mother was determined to regain Le Havre at any price and that the king had already indicated that he intended soon to "draw nigh to Normandy."[5]

By the middle of May it was obvious that despite the ruinous state of the country, France intended to go to war. On May 27 the king (looking "weak and poorly" despite his "bright, intelligent eyes") held a Lit de Justice in order to procure the necessary moneys. The royal debt was staggering—50,000,000 pounds.

L'Hôpital concluded his plea for help by exhorting the assembly: "Act as poor sailors must who, in the midst of a storm, throw part of their goods into the sea in order to save the rest."[6] Catherine had already informed Jacques Matignon, governor of Normandy, that the decision had been taken to recover Le Havre "either by love or force." She had written to Lyons, asking for 200,000 pounds of powder, and given orders to the Comte de Brissac to march towards Le Havre with two regiments.

Elizabeth, aware that Le Havre was in poor condition to withstand a siege, continued to negotiate for a peaceful settlement, assuring the queen mother she would surrender Le Havre, provided the terms of Cateau-Cambrésis were maintained, whereby Calais was to be returned to her. If Catherine hesitated, it was only in order to gain time to strengthen the French position. Shrewdly, she used the continued threat of English interference to unite the dissonant French factions. Thus, she gave France a common cause, and soon, as one contemporary wrote, "From here to Bayonne everyone is shouting: *Vive la France!*"[7]

On June 25 the court left Vincennes for Normandy, travelling northwest through Nantes and arriving at the little town of Gaillon on July 18. Catherine was pleased with the forces she brought. She was pleased with the unity a common enemy had given them, pleased with Condé's eagerness and with the vigour with which Montmorency—despite his years—was entering battle.

Elizabeth, meanwhile, was receiving news of nothing but tragedy. In mid-June one of her agents had written Burghley that the plague had become so bad in the English camp that they were losing 200 men every week. By July Warwick, who had command of the English forces, informed Elizabeth: "Our flour and biscuit are all spoiled and the soldiers are on the point of mutinying."[8] He begged her to send help if she expected them to hold Le Havre. At once a fleet set out from England; but contrary winds held it near Portsmouth, and it could not put to sea until the end of the month. When, at last, shortly after noon on July 31, it hove into sight, Le Havre had already capitulated. The ships intended to help the English withstand the siege now had no other purpose than to carry the defeated soldiers back to England. So anxious to return to English soil that they stumbled over one another to get to the waiting ships, they carried and dragged their sick and wounded with them. Castelnau records they left 3,000 dead behind them, and several hundred who lay in the captured city dying of plague.[9]

For the French, the siege had been far less costly, and Catherine wrote delightedly to Jean Evrard de St. Sulpice, her newly appointed ambassador in Madrid:

> God has given us the grace to succeed in the enterprise of Le Havre . . . this very day I hope to see this place in our hands . . . they are already beginning to embark and I hope that in a little while they will all be in England, and that, considering the loss they have suffered of between four and five thousand men, they will not be in such a hurry to return.[10]

For the first time in several years, France had had an experience of national purpose and national success, and Catherine now gave symbolic substance to this feeling of unity by a ceremony in which Charles announced his majority. On August 15, 1563, in the château of Rouen, Charles gathered his court around him. Earlier he had celebrated his thirteenth birthday. He was tall for his years, but unhealthily thin, his long neck giving the impression of even greater angularity. Accompanied by the chancellor, grave-faced and solemn in his black velvet robes, he received the homage of his brother Anjou, fifteen months his junior but with a vitality and affability which contrasted markedly with the young king's constraint. He received his mother, raising her from her knees, embracing her, and assuring her that despite his majority, hers was still the power to command.

This was precisely as Catherine wanted it: The glory was to belong to her son. Hers was the power to counsel, to influence, most of all, perhaps, to bargain in all those enterprises where the heart of the matter was concluded not in the throne room but in the marketplace. While she was at hand, the king need never descend from his dais. *L'affetto di signoreggiare,* a desire to dominate—undoubtedly— but of a very special kind.

A month later France came close to losing its queen mother. In mid-September Catherine suffered so severe a fall from her horse that her life was despaired of. Her horse had fallen on top of her, but she was assisted so quickly that at first it seemed she had suffered nothing more than an injury to her arm. Soon, however, the pain in her head became so intense that she could not move. No remedy relieved her, until, as she related, "a small opening was made in my head, near where the pain was worst, which caused such improvement that the pain was immediately assuaged." It had been a sobering experience, and the Florentine ambassador had written anxiously, "On the queen's life depends the salvation of the kingdom."[11]

Perhaps it was this sudden brush with death that caused Catherine to write the curious (and undated) document entitled "Advice given by Catherine de Medici to Charles IX for the Policy of His Court and for the Government of His State." It is a document typical of Catherine's practical attitude towards the business of kingship. She seemed far less concerned with principles of monarchy than with the day-to-day management of court events, which, she was convinced, is what determines a people's satisfaction with their king. It is no waste of time, she assured her son, to conduct a levée as did his father, for it is important for the court to see the king and have an opportunity of speaking with him. As for his daily schedule, he should attend mass, then have his dinner, followed by a little walk "for your health." He should also arrange several times a week to "ride out" on horseback so that the people may have the pleasure of seeing him. He should also make certain he provides time each week "for the young people." François I, she reminded him, maintained that there must be a ball at least twice a week in order to keep the French happy and make them love their king. Finally, she wrote, "it is of prime importance that all your subjects—both far and near—feel that you will take care of them."[12] What she was recommending to her thirteen-year-old son was a concept of king as father which, throughout his life, remained as alien to Charles' temperament as it was akin to her own.

Now, in order to bring Charles before his people, she initiated plans for a royal progress through the kingdom. Her advisers encouraged her, hoping the king's presence might help appease the bitterness that still existed between religious sects. Catherine also hoped to improve foreign relations by meeting personally during the progress with Philip and the emperor Maximilian. She had already written to Philip in October, 1563, suggesting that such a meeting not only would give her great personal pleasure, but would augment the friendship and glory of their countries. A month later she wrote her ambassador at Vienna asking him to discuss a possible meeting with the emperor Maximilian. The Pope encouraged Catherine, interpreting her proposal as a move away from the Huguenots and hoping that it would result in a "league for the extermination of heresy."[13] Catherine's concerns were far more domestic: She had marriage plans for her children. She wished to solicit the goodwill of her neighbours, and she had great confidence in her abilities to persuade vis-à-vis. If Pius wanted to band the Catholic powers together for war, Catherine wanted to band them together for peace.

Meanwhile, the court had moved on to St. Maur and then to Fontainebleau, where Catherine enjoyed six weeks of relative tranquillity. She had hardly known such a period since Henri's death, and she used it to indulge in a series of unprecedented entertainments. She gave lavish suppers, arranged balls, presented masques, and organised tourneys. Nothing was lacking—except, perhaps, the money to pay for it all. For six weeks she indulged, without restraint, in what she would have liked to have had all her life: a brilliant court. She had inherited the Medici passion for splendour, and she had a special gift for presenting those elaborate masques where music and spectacle dazzled and awed. Even in the midst of such a court, however, she never sought the limelight. She dressed quietly—always in black since the death of her husband. Never seductive, she had lost her figure in the cares of childbearing, and the extreme court fashions did nothing to flatter her. For Mardi Gras that year she had commissioned Ronsard to compose a *bergerie*—a pastoral in which all the royal children took part and in which Catherine played the part of the shepherdess. It was a symbolic role, surely, as she stood with her shepherd's crook in the midst of her children, guarding, directing, defending. *La Bergère*, the Good Shepherdess, who would bring all her sheep into a single fold—who desired nothing so much as to ring them with her protective influence.

Before the court left Fontainebleau to begin the royal progress, Catherine received disappointing news. The emperor felt such a meeting as she proposed might be misconstrued and lead to further discord. Philip, too, had his reservations. On February 19 a new ambassador replaced Perrenot de Chantonnay, whose arrogance Catherine had found intolerable. Don Francis d'Álava, though described as "the type of the perfect ambassador," soon showed himself to be formed in the same mould as his predecessor. At his first private audience Catherine expressed her deep desire to see Philip and her remorse that he did not seem to share her desire. Álava, however, quick to turn the recrimination back on Catherine, replied, according to his own report: "It is not the king, my master, who should be blamed, but you, Madame, for you don't want to reveal what will be treated of. . . . The king, my master, could not consent without knowing what the results might be." When he continued, pointing out Philip's doubts concerning the wisdom of her actions during the past year, she replied, ruffled, that things would be in a far worse state had she done otherwise, demanding, "What does Philip want?" "Everything would be very simple," Álava concluded, "if Your Majesty did not favour certain unworthy people with your confidence." It was, of course, a call to rid herself of the admiral and to lean more heavily on the House of Guise.[14]

Catherine, however, refused to be badgered. Her preoccupation at the end of February was to set in motion the royal progress. On March 13 the court left Fontainebleau, journeying east to Montereau, a pleasant town at the confluence of the Yonne and the Seine. The visitation of their king was to be a costly business for the towns that welcomed him. He travelled throughout his domain not with a retinue of a few hundred soldiers, but with thousands of attendants of every kind. It was, as one contemporary described it, "a travelling city"—the gentlemen of the king's household, the pages, the Swiss Guard with their fifes and tambourines, the Scots in their kilts, archers on foot and on horseback, hunters with their leashed hounds, falconers tending their hooded birds, grooms and coachmen, muleteers to take care of the litters, wagon men to see to the unwieldy wagons loaded with draperies, kitchenware, and silver vessels; in addition came the cooks, fruiterers, salad chefs and bakery chefs, carpenters, goldsmiths, leatherworkers and spurmakers, tailors, and barbers. In all, 8,000 horses accompanied the king on his progress.

The first city to feel the full glory of the king's presence was Troyes. Prosperous, proud of its ancient heritage, essentially Catholic, Troyes was equal to the task. For Charles' entrance, the city was decked in tapestries, with the king's device, *Justitia et Pietas*, prominently displayed. The king's white mount was perfectly paced, and Charles, dressed in blue and silver, a long white plume extending from his cap, played his part with graciousness and ease. He was always to look more regal on horseback, where his superb horsemanship showed to advantage. In the city square the worshipful crowds were held back while a group of "satyrs," mounted on goats and asses and led by a unicorn decked with ivy, welcomed the king with classic symbolism. Catherine, it was reported, did not ride with her son but watched, delighted, from a window.

The court remained at Troyes for three weeks. During that time Charles had time to enter fully into all the services of Holy Week and Easter—washing the feet of the poor, offering his gift at the altar, venerating the cross of Christ in public procession. It was an excellent beginning for a journey which intended to demonstrate beyond doubt that the king was a Catholic in thought, word, and deed.

The days in Troyes, however, were devoted to more than religious ceremonies; they were days of intense diplomatic negotiations with England. Since the capitulation of Le Havre the preceding July, sporadic efforts had been under way to conclude a peace treaty between England and France. It was a thorny business: Elizabeth held out for the full terms stipulated by the Treaty of Cateau-Cambrésis; France maintained these no longer obtained since England had broken the treaty by investing Le Havre. Both queens recognised, however, that it was the sheerest folly to continue a war that not only depleted their own treasuries but made them fair game for their enemies. On April 12 peace was agreed to: Le Havre and Calais would remain in French hands, and France would repay, not the 300,000 crowns originally stipulated, but 125,000, in ransom for the hostages held since Cateau-Cambrésis. The following day Catherine, triumphant, with Throckmorton on her left and Thomas Smith, the new ambassador, on her right, accompanied Charles to the Cathedral of Troyes to celebrate the peace "in the Catholic manner."

With peace formally established, the court left Troyes, travelling north through Châlons-sur-Marne and east into Bar-le-Duc, where the king assisted at the baptism of his sister Claude's first son. On May 15 the travelling city set out again, this time following the Marne south into Langres and then on to Dijon.

It was the beginning of June when the court left Dijon to travel by boat down the Saône to the small city of Mâcon. Here, waiting for them, was Antoine de Navarre's widow, Jeanne d'Albret. Although she was never physically robust, there was something unyielding about the tall, spare figure and angular features of the Queen of Navarre. In every way her husband's opposite, she was fearless and uncompromising in her convictions. Less impetuous than Antoine, she had responded slowly to the New Religion, but when she did, it was with an unwavering dedication that lasted a lifetime. Sent from court in 1562 at her husband's instigation, she linked herself more wholeheartedly than before to the Huguenot cause. With Condé's support, she turned her small domain into a Huguenot kingdom. Unable to intimidate her, the Pope finally sent a *monitum*—a formal warning—demanding that she appear before the Inquisition for questioning or suffer excommunication. For more than eight months Jeanne had been living with this threat of excommunication, realising that to appear in Rome might cost her her liberty, while to refuse would undoubtedly cost her her kingdom.

During these months of anxiety Charles and Catherine had upheld her cause, less out of personal devotion to Jeanne than because they saw in such papal threats infringements on their royal privileges. If Pius could arbitrarily confiscate the kingdom of Navarre on a point of religion, it would set a dangerous precedent. Both Charles and Catherine had written at once to Rome, denouncing the act as "contrary to the traditional rights and privileges of the Gallican church . . . and prejudicial to the authority of His Majesty." Although Jeanne wrote in gratitude to Catherine, she made no move to obey the queen mother's injunction to rejoin the French court and distance herself from the Huguenots. When Jeanne finally met them at Mâcon, she came obdurately accompanied by eight Calvinist ministers and a protective guard of several hundred cavalry.[15] Despite the warm exchange of letters between Catherine and Jeanne during the preceding winter, the meeting at Mâcon was constrained. If Catherine had hoped to win Jeanne, as she had sometimes won her husband, by kind words and promises, she had misread her royal cousin. Jeanne was as intransigent as her husband had been malleable. Angry at Jeanne's obduracy and fearful the king's silence might be construed as approval, Catherine advised Charles to forbid all Preaching in the city. Jeanne continued to disobey his regulations, and by the time the "travelling city" reached Lyons in mid-June it was a city at war with itself.

No city in France could absorb more diversity than Lyons, a city of great wealth and enormous sophistication. It was proud of its ancient Roman tradition, proud to have been one of the first Christian communities in Gaul, proud that it had been sanctified by the blood of martyrs. Yet its pride was not a monument to the dead, but a living thing, which made the city turn to the sun wherever the sun was to be found. For all its strong Catholicism, Lyons offered a relatively secure home for the Huguenots. No man was alien in Lyons, for its streets were noisy with Germans and Venetians, Turks and Spaniards. Lyons was rich, gay, confident, free.

The reception it offered its king was more flamboyant than anything Charles had yet experienced. Here were the Milanese merchants in their short black velvet capes, the Florentines with ornately embroidered violet doublets, men from Lucca accompanied by their Moorish pages, German lords with velvet hats and cloaks of fine black taffeta. Charles himself was dressed in green velvet, his bonnet ornamented with a high white plume and his supple leather boots giving shape to his spindly legs. Behind him rode that "perfectly handsome young prince," his brother Anjou, glorious in crimson and gold brocade, and his cousin Henri, son of Jeanne d'Albret and inheritor of Navarre. Of the three young princes, Navarre was by far the most robust; his early years in the mountains around Pau had given him a hardiness that made his Valois cousins look pale and delicate by comparison.

Ten days later the royal image was further gilded when the peace between England and France, agreed to at Troyes two months earlier, was solemnly ratified in the Cathedral of Lyons. At the same time, England honoured Charles by receiving him into the Order of the Garter. Lord Hunsdon, who bestowed the garter, was delighted with the ceremony and expressed but one regret—that the garter itself was unsuitably large for the king's thin leg. "[I] wish," he wrote, "that the King's garter had been better considered, for it is neither rich nor fair; and besides it is so great as he can neither put it on nor wear it."[16] But those who gathered in the ancient Cathedral of St. Jean saw only the glory of their king, heard only the oath of peace pronounced between the two crowns, and the triumphal *Te Deum* with which the ceremony closed. Nowhere was peace more valued than at Lyons, for its commerce could flourish only in harmony. Charles was toasted and cheered as the figure of eternal concord, the young promise of hope. The ceremony was a dramatic triumph for the young king.

When the curtain had fallen on the public pageant, however, the domestic tensions within the court remained. Jeanne d'Albret was at their vortex. Although she had assured Catherine of her gratitude for her support against the Pope, such gratitude did not soften her own religious position. At Lyons she had allied herself with the Huguenot community, taking not only her attendants to their meetings, but her ten-year-old son as well. In his ten years, Henri de Navarre had lived a life of checkered loyalties. Forced to remain with his father when Jeanne had been sent from the court, "in disgrace," two years before, he had done his best to remain faithful to his mother's religion. Ultimately, he had been coerced into adopting the religion of the court, but it was obvious his allegiance lay with Jeanne. Catherine, annoyed by his tenacity and infuriated that Jeanne should repay her protection by such clear defiance, now forbade Henri to live in his mother's apartments or to accompany her to the Preaching, swearing further that she would have anyone beheaded who did not attend mass. Thereupon Jeanne demanded permission to leave court and return to Navarre with her son. Catherine, fearful of what Jeanne might do, refused both requests. Jeanne, if she wished, could take up residence in Vendôme, but the young Prince de Navarre was to remain with the court. Although Catherine had originally set out to win Jeanne's friendship, it was apparent by the summer of 1564 that she had, instead, made an implacable enemy.

The days at Lyons, begun so triumphantly, had been blighted. In addition to the discord within the court, the plague had struck the city with unusual ferocity. Soon the hospitals were overflowing, and a "city of tents" sprang up to accommodate the victims. Bodies sometimes lay in the street all night until a cart came lumbering by piled with corpses, which were eventually dumped into the river. Sir Thomas Smith, writing to Burghley, asserted that London, even at its worst, had never seen the like, continuing, "Sometimes ten and twelve corpses [are] lying in the streets . . . some naked, and there they lie till night or till the deputies for those matters, clothed in yellow, come. . . . A great number they cast into the river, because they will not be at the cost to make graves." The results of such measures were inevitable and soon Smith wrote in disgust: ". . . the Rhône men dare eat no fish nor fishers lay their engines and nets, because instead of fish they take up the pestiferous carcasses which are thrown in.''[17] When a woman accompanying Jeanne d'Albret succumbed to the plague, the court grew panic-stricken and, on July 9, left Lyons, taking the road south into Dauphiné.

The discord in the kingdom which Catherine had sought to stem by her son's presence only increased through the summer months. More and more—especially after the clash with Jeanne d'Albret—the Huguenots saw the king's progress, not as a means of bringing peace, but as a means of strengthening the Catholics and stamping out the Huguenots. Months before, Bèze had warned the ministers of the "evil meaning of the queen mother and the cardinal [de Lorraine]."[18] Now, at Roussillon, Charles gave evidence for such suspicions by signing an edict forbidding the exercise of the Reformed Religion within ten leagues of the court. The Huguenots interpreted the measure as a sign that Catherine was giving way before foreign pressure.

In fact, Catherine was again engaged in that double game by which she hoped to maintain the independence of the crown. While she tried to win Catholic confidence by assuring the Nuncio she would continue to take new steps in subjugating the Religion, she was simultaneously engaged in negotiations for a possible marriage of the king to the Protestant Queen of England!

By mid-August the court had moved into Provence, fatigued and nervous with the excessive heat and the growing atmosphere of distrust. At Valence the plague had preceded them. The flowers and tapestries and speeches of welcome were oddly at variance with the houses where the plague-stricken lay, the whitewashed boards barring their doors and windows, carrying the stigma of death.

While at Valence, Catherine received news of near death from another quarter. From Madrid came letters from St. Sulpice telling her that her daughter Elizabeth was not expected to live. After hours of unbearable agony, St. Sulpice explained, Elizabeth had been delivered of two premature female children. The Spanish doctors (never of great reputation in France) did what they could, resorting to bleeding, to cupping, to plunging the young queen into baths; but her haemorrhages continued, and her fever rose until she passed into a coma.

Catherine was inconsolable. "My only comfort," she wrote at once to St. Sulpice, "is to hear the news hour by hour," begging him to spare no cost in sending messengers to her. By some miracle of endurance, Elizabeth triumphed over the barbarities of Spanish medicine, and a month later the ambassador was assuring the anxious mother that Elizabeth "is doing very well, although she is still very weak, pale and thin, because of this long and severe illness."[19] In fact, Elizabeth was to live for another three years, twice more enduring the terrors of pregnancy in an effort to provide Philip with a male child.

Typically, Catherine had not permitted her anxiety over Elizabeth to slow the king's progress. Despite Charles' ill health, she kept the court moving south through Mondragon, Orange, Caderousse, and, finally, into Avignon. Only Avignon—a city under papal rule—did not bear the scars of religious conflict.

Paradoxically, however, Avignon showed less joy at its king's presence than many other towns, fearing, perhaps, that the troubled court might stir up conflict where none had existed.

When, on September 23, Charles made his solemn entrance, the Avignonais were not impressed. Exhausted from the long months of travel, the king looked pale, thin, almost listless. The long journey was taking its toll in many ways. Avignon, long-used to papal luxury, found their king "poorly equipped." "The King is marvelously in debt," the English ambassador wrote in the beginning of October, continuing, "all men are vilely paid, and the realm poorer than some men would think, not only of money, but also of credit."[20] When Catherine tried to raise money by proposing a tax on paper, she was flatly refused: The king's servants might go threadbare, but the people would be taxed no more.

There were few joyful moments in the following months. The court was heading into winter. Already the winds from the Alpilles had begun to buffet the caravan, and soon rain and snow made the rivers impassable. On November 6, they arrived in Marseilles, where, thirty-one years before, Catherine, resplendent in purple and gold, had married into French royalty.

In those thirty years the face of France had changed. The state which had been the envy of Europe was now poor, wasted, a prey to domestic discord and foreign aggression. The preceding year Marc-Antonio Barbaro had written to Venice in summation of the state of France:

> This is the condition in which I found the kingdom of France at my arrival. I recognised from the beginning that the administration was without order, that justice was violated; I saw the mortal enmities, the passions, the caprices of men of power; the opposing interests of princes which shifted from one occasion to another; I saw religious troubles, the disobedience and turbulence among the people, the rebellion and godlessness among the great; I saw everything turned upside down.[21]

Barbaro's vision was in substance the same as Catherine's, for they both had the practical sight of the shrewd Italian observer. It was a terrible vision. Yet if despair touched Catherine at all, it was only a momentary presence, immediately dissipated by her incorrigible hope. Throughout her life she held (often tenuously) to the belief that the existing order is never beyond remedy. Her task was always to find the cure. Passive acquiescence was so foreign to her temperament that when, later, she met it in the person of her son Anjou, she was incapable of recognising it for what it was.

By the beginning of 1565 the court had had its fill of journeys and yearned for a return to Paris; Catherine, however, maintained her plans for another twelve months of travel. She, too, was tired, frustrated by the winter delays, anxious over reports of street fighting in Paris, but she still hoped to arrange a meeting with Philip somewhere in the south of France.

Although earlier negotiations had come to nothing, St. Sulpice, who was now in charge, pushed hard, suggesting to Philip that when he and his queen were at Valladolid, they might continue north for a meeting with the French sovereigns. Philip, for whom caution had become a way of life, answered typically that the proposal deserved "serious thought," concluding, "I must consider it."[22] Although Philip seemed inclined towards such a meeting, the Duke of Alba, whom he had placed in charge of his negotiations, showed little enthusiasm, blocking St. Sulpice's suggestions at every turn. Ultimately, Alba conceded, and Bayonne, a town on the southwest border, was agreed to as the place of conference.

Philip's personal presence at the conference continued to be a moot point. Catherine, assuming that grateful optimism was often the closest way to victory, wrote cordially to him in February: "I hope that this will not only bring great happiness to the king and me but that it will be for the well-being and conservation of all Christianity." The next few months were filled with Spanish vacillation. Sometime in March, Catherine received word that her daughter was again pregnant and could not, therefore, be subjected to a long journey. By the end of March, however, Elizabeth's pregnancy had proved false, and Catherine was assured that her daughter would spend Holy Week in Valladolid and then travel north to Burgos and on to Bayonne.[23] By then the queen mother had resigned herself to her son-in-law's absence.

As plans for the conference continued, the king's progress resumed—out of Carcassonne, north into Toulouse, Montauban, Agen, and finally to Bordeaux, where the court spent almost a month. By the end of April they began the last southward lap of the journey, stopping for some time at Mont-de-Marsan and Tartas and then travelling slowly through the cool green mountains into Dax, with its curative waters. The last portion of the journey was made by boat from Saubuze down the Adour. On June 3 they arrived at Bayonne, where they found Alba already established in the finest house of the city. Bayonne was a pretty town, small, relatively insignificant, with no ambition to greatness, and strained to the breaking point by the dubious honour of playing host to these two travelling cities. They would like to see their king, but they had little affection for their Spanish neighbours.

Soon after the king's formal entrance, Charles and his mother left for Hendaye, which had been set as the formal meeting place. Here, at the mouth of the Bidassoa, amid heat so intense that several soldiers, weighed down by their armour, died of it, the queen mother awaited her daughter. From the promontory of Hendaye, Catherine could see, for the first time, the country of Spain, a country that was to continue to fascinate and frustrate her to the end of her life. Now, despite her fatigue and her concern over Charles, whose constitution could not endure excesses of heat and cold, her mood was one of joyful expectation. She would see her daughter again, and she would, she was sure, despite Philip's absence, work out something to the advantage of France.

The meeting of Elizabeth with her brother and her mother was accompanied by extreme emotion on all sides. The queen who advanced across the pontoon bridge, erected to span the river, looked older than her years. Although only twenty, she had twice been close to death. Her pregnancies had drained her of life, and a recent attack of measles, although not scarring her, had left her pale and sallow. If she had lost something of her adolescent beauty, she had gained "great grace." "She is gifted with an unusual spirit and extraordinary courtesy," wrote Giovanni Soranzo, the Venetian ambassador. "Everyone considers her wise and prudent with a manner which in everything is far beyond her years." In Spain, she was reputed to be almost a saint, winning the love of both her husband and her people. And yet, noted Soranzo, despite Philip's reputed love and respect, he gave her little that would make her happy. Many of her days she spent alone, scarcely leaving her apartments, rarely seeing her husband "as she would like." But, concluded the perceptive Venetian, "she hides her feelings . . . indicating that she desires only to please the king, wanting only what he wants." Elizabeth's life, it would seem, was a melancholy echo of what her mother's had been.[24]

Elizabeth's royal entrance into Bayonne lacked nothing, for Catherine had determined that the ceremonies would manifest not only a certain family solidarity, but the glory and wealth of France. She entered the city by candlelight, riding a white palfrey which Charles had had brought from the famous stables of Tournelles. The harness had been an extravagant gift from her husband, reputed to be worth 4,000 ducats. For the next two weeks the Spaniards were treated to an endless round of processions, masques, balls, tourneys, suppers. Ronsard, once again called into service, apostrophised the events:

> O happy age, worthy to be called
> The golden age, if ever there has been one,
> Where the Spaniard in loyal friendship
> Loves France so that the two become one.[25]

The poet was permitted his hyperbole, but he did not blind Alba's keen Spanish judgement. If anything, the extravagances of Bayonne increased his sense of French folly, for the evidence was clear that France was in perilous straits. If the family group gathered at Bayonne portrayed a country at peace, the reports coming constantly from Tours, Blois, Pamiers indicated a country shaken by violence and unrest.

It was precisely this internal dissension that Alba hoped to build on for the interests of Spain. Philip had made his instructions explicit: The conferences were to deal primarily with the religious issue. In order to confirm the Catholic faith in France, the Protestant cult must be forbidden, its ministers expelled, and the decrees of the Council of Trent made public. Philip's ostensible religious purpose, however, masked his concern over the deeper political issues. The New Religion inevitably kindled the fire of revolt; it must, therefore, be extinguished in France lest the fire catch in the Low Countries or, worse, in Spain itself. Underneath Alba's high moral eloquence, this was his dominant purpose.

Catherine, despite her confidence in her power to beguile, had small chance with Alba. He was primarily a soldier: tall, stiffly erect—despite his fifty-five years—his face sallow and emaciated from the hardships of war and elongated by his black beard. His eyes, too, betrayed the soldier—alert, restless, vigilant. Insensitive to blandishments, he was at odds with the queen mother from the beginning.

Alba's hostility was no surprise, but Catherine was unprepared for the subtle change in her daughter. She had always been proud of Elizabeth's intelligence; of all her children she had the most subtle political sense. Now, however, she found that sense used against her. "My daughter, you have become very Spanish," Catherine complained to Elizabeth. To which her daughter replied, "I am Spanish, I admit it; it is my duty; but I am still your daughter just as I was when you sent me into Spain."[26] The last phrase contained a subtle rebuke: In whatever way Elizabeth was now "Spanish," it was the ineluctable result of accepting the role her mother had decreed for her.

When Alba finally brought the conference to the issue of religion, Elizabeth continued to be "Spanish," helping her husband's emissary rather than her mother. Although Alba found Catherine more evasive than he had anticipated, he finally managed a direct question: "Since the Peace of Amboise, has religion gained or lost?" he asked. "It has gained," she replied unhesitatingly. The dialogue grew heated, until in exasperation Alba cried, "This wicked sect must be banished from France!" Still Catherine evaded the issue, unwilling to discuss a possible resumption of war. When he criticised L'Hôpital's religious position and questioned Catherine's wisdom in retaining him as chancellor, she retorted, "He is not so bad as you think." "But," Alba remonstrated, "you cannot deny that he is a Huguenot." "No, he is not," the queen mother answered. The argument became two against one when Elizabeth rejoined: "Even during the lifetime of my father, he was considered a Huguenot. As long as he is chancellor, the Catholics will be oppressed and the Huguenots favoured."

Catherine had been ready for Alba's attack, but not for Elizabeth's contradiction. She was embarrassed and bewildered. Alba, of course, finding his own position strengthened by Elizabeth's attitude, wrote in satisfaction to Philip: "Her Majesty is acquitting herself perfectly of this office." Yet even with both Alba and Elizabeth allied against her, the queen mother would concede nothing: She would not admit that toleration had brought anything but harmony to France; she would not agree to accept the Council of Trent; she refused absolutely to put France at war again.[27]

It was not at the council table that Alba scored his victories, but in his secret enclaves with the Catholic lords. He flattered Monluc into believing his actions could determine France's fate; he roused Montpensier into a tirade against the Huguenot leaders, ending with the threat that the religious issue could best be settled by "cutting off the heads of Condé, the admiral, Andelot, Rochefoucauld and Gramont." He coaxed from Bourdillon the statement "If he [the king] wait any longer [to move against the Huguenots] not only will the faith be lost, but the crown itself." By the time the conference was over, Alba had coerced several prominent Catholic lords into acknowledging Philip as "the true father of French Catholics." It was a significant step forward in Spanish policy.[28]

As for Catherine, her gains were hard to evaluate. Her joy at seeing her daughter was mixed with anxiety over Elizabeth's "Spanish" position, she had failed in her goal of seeing Philip face to face, and she had found Alba a poor substitute. The marriages she had suggested (her daughter Margot—now twelve—to Philip's son, Don Carlos; her son Anjou to Juana of Portugal) had failed to meet with Spanish approval. Far from strengthening the French position in either foreign or domestic affairs, the Bayonne conferences were to cast a shadow from which Catherine never escaped. Whatever prestige the queen mother gained was insignificant compared with the mistrust the conferences had stirred at home. The emperor Maximilian had been right when he protested that any effort at a meeting of Catholic sovereigns would stir Protestant suspicions. Despite Charles' letters, assuring them that the conference was motivated solely by "tears of blood and natural love," despite Catherine's protests that these talks would in no way compromise the toleration that had been granted, the general feeling of mistrust grew. The Huguenots, as Castelnau reported, were "prodigiously alarmed."[29]

What happened at Bayonne between Catherine and Alba, what secret promises were exchanged, what secret pledges were given, has long been a subject of speculation. In a sense, what happened at Bayonne is less important than what contemporaries *thought* happened. And the Huguenots had no doubt they had been betrayed. "There was a resolution taken at Bayonne . . . to destroy those of the Religion in both France and the Low Countries," Turenne wrote categorically in his memoirs. The evidence for such a betrayal is slight; most of it sustains Catherine's avowal that she was inflexible in her resolve to maintain the Huguenots.

At the beginning of July, however, Catherine wrote Philip assuring him of "the zeal we have for our religion and the desire to see everything contribute to the satisfaction of the service of God" and concluding with the veiled allusion: "[I am] assured that the queen my daughter will explain to you all the other resolutions we have taken together for the maintenance and strengthening of our friendship, a matter so private that she would never dare to talk about it to anyone else."[30]

Catherine's interpreters have sought vainly for conclusive evidence of what this deeply private matter could be. Some have suggested a kind of limited massacre, following Monluc's advice that the religious problem could be settled if the Huguenot leaders were disposed of. Others have seen in it the first pledge of that "Matins of Paris"—that great St. Bartholomew's Day Massacre that would take place in the summer of 1572. There is insufficient proof for either interpretation. It is far more in character to see this ambiguous pledge as one more piece of mystification by which Catherine vainly hoped to keep Philip on her side, without sacrificing any of her internal policies.

Indeed, on the same day she wrote so enigmatically to Philip, she also wrote to Montmorency in Paris, urging him to rigorous observance of the edict of toleration in order to allay the suspicions of those "unquiet souls" who feared the results of the Bayonne conference. She then concluded with a characteristically misleading statement: "During these interviews, we have concerned ourselves solely with gestures of affection, of banqueting, and good living, and in the most general terms of each one's desire for continued friendship between us."[31] If, on the one hand, she hoped to make Philip content by hinting at high promises, she hoped equally to content Montmorency by assuring him the conferences had never gone beyond the shallowest kind of exchange.

It seems extraordinary that Catherine, so astute in many of her judgements, could not foresee that her efforts to play the friend to opposing forces could end only in failure. Yet even failure was unable to enlighten her, and throughout her life she clung to a course of action that ultimately spelled her doom.

Chapter VII

The king's progress after Bayonne lost whatever lustre it had had. Huguenot hostility was palpable as they travelled north. In Angoulême they were warned of a conspiracy against the king ("a tumult as at Amboise"); at La Rochelle, despite an elaborate welcome, there was an air of suspicion and coldness. Even Blois was under Huguenot influence, with Condé and Jeanne d'Albret openly holding Preachings. In an effort to prove her goodwill towards the Huguenots, Catherine overreached herself and, despite the remonstrances of the Catholics, refused to interfere, provided that the services were "held in secret."

A prime source of friction between Catholics and Protestants was Coligny's complicity in the murder of the Duc de Guise. At a confrontation between the admiral and the Cardinal de Lorraine, Catherine pleaded for reconciliation, asserting that France would never enjoy "general peace" until "particular quarrels" were settled. Lorraine maintained that he bore "neither hatred or vengeance" but was determined to "see justice done." Coligny countered by reaffirming his innocence. Finally, after two weeks of highly charged rhetoric and "investigation" (although the conclusion must have been apparent from the start), Coligny was declared innocent, and the king "sentenced" both men not to "speak ill of each other." The conventional embraces were exchanged, and the feud was ostensibly ended.[1]

The two months the court spent at Moulins were largely devoted to business. An Assembly of Notables had been convoked at the direction of L'Hôpital, who hoped to institute a firmer system of justice. One idea governed him: Everything must be carefully established under law and edict. No one, nothing must be exempt from the code of justice. To men of integrity, L'Hôpital, the idealist, seemed to chart a perfect course; to the cynics, he seemed to fly too high. His principles were too speculative, too abstract to influence a France immersed in the problems of daily existence. "It is all very well, but it will all go up in smoke," commented the pragmatic Álava.[2]

The conferences at Moulins drained both Catherine and Charles of their remaining energy, and the last lap of the progress was perfunctory. Leaving Moulins in mid-March, they journeyed south into Auvergne, then north again through Bourbonnais, Nivernais, and within six weeks reached the final haven of St. Maur. They had been en route for twenty-six months and had covered approximately 3,000 miles.

The king had "shot up two fingers" during the months of his travels, but he had grown no more robust. The English ambassador noted how "slender" he still was with his "great knees and ancles [sic]," ill-proportioned to his spindly legs. His intelligence, observed Smith, was "good for his years," yet no one who had seen Charles during the months of his journeyings was impressed by his royal character. He was now sixteen, already an adult by Renaissance standards. "It is high time the King were a man," wrote an English agent to Throckmorton with manifest dissatisfaction.[3] In nothing had the royal progress achieved Catherine's hopes for it: The people had not been impressed by their king; the Huguenots had become more restive than ever; the Catholic lords had drawn closer to Spain. As for Spain itself, despite its protestations of friendship, it became in 1566 a source of even greater discomfit to France.

While the court was at Moulins, it had received word that a French expedition to Florida sponsored by Coligny—already alert to the importance of colonisation—had been massacred by the Spanish. "I am beside myself," Catherine wrote in anger to her new ambassador in Spain, the Baron de Fourquevaux. When she questioned Álava, he protested with righteous indignation that it was the French who were to blame for intruding on territory already staked out by Spain. "Trading is free," she retorted, warning him that she expected some reparation for "so cruel and inhuman an act."[4] Despite her anger, she feared the consequences of a complete break with Spain and hastened to assure her daughter that although this action had deeply distressed her, it would not cause a rift in the friendship between "our two houses."

In the coming months friendship with Spain was to be further challenged by events in the Low Countries. The Low Countries, under the influence of the Reform, found Spanish domination increasingly repressive and were determined to free themselves politically and religiously. Philip found their aspirations intolerable. They were an insult to his divinely constituted kingship and a threat to the economic security of Spain. Towards the end of 1565, determined to crush any revolt, he ordered Alba to raise an army out of Sicily, Naples, and Milan. Catherine, aware that the easiest access to the Low Countries lay through France, wrote anxiously to Fourquevaux, "I beg you to keep your eyes open and see what you can find out.[5] The prospect of an army of 10,000 men under Spanish command making its way through France set the Huguenots on fire with anger and fear, and Coligny admitted openly that should Philip actually enter France the kingdom was doomed. Charles, with unexpected resolution, refused Spain's request for safe passage, explaining that the Huguenots might openly oppose such a foreign army, a possibility which, for all their sakes, he could not risk.

Philip read Charles' refusal as a Huguenot victory, well aware that if Coligny were strong enough, he would not only bar Spanish troops from France but actively aid his coreligionists in the Netherlands. It was an irritating possibility, and Philip attempted to parry it by warning Catherine that France would suffer great misfortune if she continued her liberality towards the Huguenots.[6]

Catherine and Charles remained adamant, however, and Alba had to lead his army up from Genoa through Savoy and Franche-Comté, careful to skirt the eastern border of France. As rumours of the size of this army reached Catherine, she began to wonder if the Huguenots were right in warning her that Philip's aim was not simply the Netherlands, but France itself. Her panic was contagious, and during the early summer Coligny, Condé, and Montmorency with his sons and nephews came to court to offer themselves and their men "for the service of the king." Instead of accepting the offer gracefully, Charles, inclined to be short-tempered and suspicious of the Huguenots' motivation, reminded them angrily that they had no men to offer, for "any Frenchman was the king's to command."[7] It was a foolish response, indicative of that caprice which was to rule so much of Charles' later behaviour.

More and more during the summer of 1567 both the king and the queen mother found themselves at odds with those of the Religion. There had been "bitter bickering" between the admiral and the queen mother, who charged him with stirring up trouble by sending 60,000 crowns to the Protestants in the Netherlands. Later that summer Condé had increased her annoyance by circulating rumours that the king intended to revoke the edict of pacification. Yet with it all, Catherine was forced to mask her anger lest she alienate them further. Correro had, indeed, touched the nerve of Catherine's attitude when he wrote to Venice:

> The queen . . . dares not manifest to the Huguenots the least distrust; she pretends not to notice what they do, tolerating them with infinite patience, receiving them cordially, favouring them with apparent affection. Thus, . . . she hopes to appease and satisfy them and little by little dispel that turbulent spirit which she is inclined to attribute rather to ambition and a desire for revenge than to any religious sentiment.[8]

What Catherine could not recognise and what made the events of the following September such a bewildering surprise to her was that she could not "satisfy" them. She failed to realise that by the Bayonne conferences she had thrown away all chance of maintaining the Huguenots' trust. It had been her one flagrant error, but its consequences were irreversible. They were convinced that they had been betrayed and Catherine was, at least in part, to blame. She failed to realise that those mysterious hints and half promises with which she was so prodigal satisfied no one. Again it was Correro who diagnosed her weakness. *Liberalissima di pa-*

role, he wrote of her. She was "too free with her words" which ultimately won her not confidence, but mistrust.

They were sad and bewildering days for Catherine, for all her efforts to "satisfy" had been fruitless. France was again moving towards war—and the thought terrified her. Fear, however, was a luxury she could not afford, and she tried to maintain her usual assurance. Correro, seeing under the surface, observed sympathetically, "I know that more than once she has been found crying in her person of the king—not out of any malice toward His Majesty—but in order to deceive those who would judge the state of affairs by the expression on her face, she will appear outside with a tranquil and joyous countenance."[9]

In September, 1567, the Huguenots held a synod at Coligny's château at Valéry. It was an inflammatory meeting, for Condé, always a master with flint and tinder, had all he needed to start a fire: The queen mother obviously could not be trusted; the king treated the Huguenots like scum; the Cardinal de Lorraine was again high in favour; restrictions against the Religion were increasing. Had Condé no further evidence of danger than this, it would have been enough. But during the meeting at Valéry came news that Swiss soldiers, under orders from the crown, had crossed the frontier into France and that the two popular leaders of the Netherlands cause—Counts Egmont and Hoorne—had been condemned to death by Spain. It was proof positive of everything they had feared: Their religious rights, their liberty, their lives all were at stake. Their anger, coupled with Condé's natural impetuosity, led them to immediate action. They would seize the person of the king—not out of any malice towards His Majesty—but in order to save him (and themselves) from the machinations of the King of Spain and his "Spaniardizers."

One of the first hints of trouble was picked up by Sir Henry Norris, who wrote to Leicester on September 13 of the "appearance of civil tumults," which he had noticed. The court, then assembled at Montceaux, had also been apprised of some suspicious activity, but Catherine dismissed it lightly. "There is a rumour here without much substance that those of the Religion wish to make some disturbance, but it is only a question of a little uneasiness that they feel," she wrote to Fourquevaux.[10] The rumour was sufficient, however, to cause the court to move from Montceaux into the town of Meaux. Meanwhile, Condé had set up his initial plans: Germany was asked to send reiters to assist their coreligionists; the Huguenots were advised that they would be expected to contribute the necessary money and that able-bodied men were to mass for war. Without hesitation, he moved his men out of Valéry towards Montereau, where they would remain until it was time to head towards Meaux.

By September 24 the court, stunned and frightened, had recognised that this was no local skirmish but a well-mounted revolt. At once the Swiss were urged to march quickly out of Château-Thierry and come to the assistance of the king. At Meaux the royal party divided on whether to remain at Meaux or try to get the king safely to Paris. It was Amboise over again, but this time they were playing against professionals. Those who favoured Paris won, and before daybreak the king, the queen mother, and other members of the court, flanked by the Swiss Guard, moved east towards the capital. As it grew lighter, they caught a glimpse of the rebel cavalry, who, however, retreated before this superior force.

Charles, if one can believe the contemporary accounts, was seized with rage rather than fear and at one point rode to the head of his troops, brandishing his arquebus. The constable rushed after him, warning, "Sire, you cannot risk your person in this way." For the queen mother, however, the journey was sixteen hours of unalleviated fear. When finally they arrived in Paris that evening, she could write only, "Thanks be to God, we have escaped."[11] "I cannot describe to you," wrote Barbaro to Venice, when the court was finally settled at the Louvre, "the fear involved in the flight from Meaux, as well as the hesitations at Montceaux where to stay was unsafe, yet to leave was also dangerous, and, in addition, there was the peril braved in travelling to Paris. Finally, there is the total confusion which has reigned over this city for the last few days."[12]

The Huguenots were exhilarated by their initial success. Although they had not seized the person of the king, they had the Catholics on the run. They had successfully occupied Orléans and Soissons and had cut off the capital from its sources of supply. Their very ruthlessness worked against them, however, for the peasants, watching them burn the crops and set the windmills on fire, fled towards Paris, taking with them sufficient foodstuffs to keep the city from feeling the pinch of the blockade. Condé, meanwhile, continued to assert he meant no harm to the king but wanted only to rescue the realm from Spanish threats and restore it to its former liberty.

Condé always sounded the notes of a high and noble purpose, but when, the following month, it became known that Condé had had coins minted with the inscription "Louis XIII by the grace of God, First King of the faithful of the Gospel," a discordant note spoiled his high and gallant call to justice. Although Catherine was angered, she was not surprised by Condé's presumption. While others spoke of him as a religious leader, she was inclined to see him motivated by Bourbon ambition rather than Huguenot piety. When she was told that he was called by some the Huguenot King, she commented drily, "The man has gone mad."[13]

Mad he may have been; but it was a madness shot through with charm and purpose, and the Huguenots responded to him eagerly. Towards the end of October an English agent could appraise the situation: "The forces of those of the Religion are very great and well and prudently led, so that it is almost impossible for the King to know their plans. . . . The object is the ruin of the House of Guise and so to get the government of the King and the management of affairs. . . ."[14]

On November 10, after a final effort at compromise, the king's army under the direction of the constable, engaged Condé's forces at St. Denis. After fifty years of royal service Anne de Montmorency now had his final opportunity to prove himself a loyal soldier of the king. He had outlived three sovereigns and served them well. Twice he had been sent from court in disgrace to make way for temporary favourites, yet when he was needed, he returned without demur. No man could have been guilty of all the conflicting faults of which he was accused: He was too stubborn a Catholic; he was too sympathetic to Protestants; he stirred up trouble by his allegiance to the Guises; he was disloyal to the crown by favouring his Châtillon nephews. Certainly the constable was not without faults: He was ambitious, sensible of the slightest rebuff, expecting royal honours for all his sons. No small passion, however, could ever override his larger passion for France. Now in his seventy-fourth year, dressed gloriously in a red gold-embroidered doublet, he manifested the ardour for battle that had characterised his youth.

The Battle of St. Denis was of short duration. It was midafternoon before the opposing forces were in place. During the remaining hours of daylight, Huguenots and Catholics were locked in an inconclusive struggle. The first news brought to the royal family gathered at the Louvre was of the mortal wounding of the constable. With his face slashed in several places and a bullet lodged in his back, he was carried from the field to linger for two days before he died. It seemed ironic that having fought in so many foreign wars and for so many "glorious causes," he should die in a small, bitter battle, fighting an enemy that included his beloved nephews.

With his death, Catherine's first link with the court of France was gone. It was Montmorency who had brought her to Marseilles for her wedding, Montmorency who had been in charge of the ceremonies of those first few weeks. He had helped her through the difficult years of her sterility, and while she had resented his friendship with Diane de Poitiers and, later, his association with the Guises, nonetheless, he was a comforting monument to the old order. Yet it was Charles, not Catherine, who expressed this sense of loss: "You can imagine the regret that I feel and the need I have of him in such a time," he wrote Fourquevaux. "For I have greater need than ever of his skill, his experience, and his great strength. These are the things which are ordinarily not found in one man. . . ." An even greater tribute was the legend inscribed on the receptacle which contained Montmorency's heart. "Here lies the heart which was our confidence, a heart of valour, a heart of honour . . . the heart of three kings."[15]

Despite the death of the constable, the battle at St. Denis was generally conceded to be a royal victory, although it was in no sense the glorious triumph Catherine's letters indicated. Writing to Philip on November 14, she described the enemy slinking away in the night, in mortal dread of the royal army. "This victory," she continued proudly, "is not only of concern for our peace and well-being but for all Christianity." And Charles, assuming his mother's tone, wrote that the Huguenots had left "in such haste and disorder . . . that it might best be described as a rout."[16]

Although the case was overstated to impress Philip, it was true that the Huguenot forces were fatigued and disappointed and that a decisive royal victory seemed possible. Unfortunately, the royal army lacked leadership. Following Montmorency's death, Anjou had been appointed lieutenant general. Although Anjou was a popular figure, his appointment was received with misgiving, for many felt the times demanded a more experienced soldier than a boy who had but recently celebrated his sixteenth birthday. Anjou was the most gifted of Catherine's sons. His healthy complexion, broad shoulders, and reserves of energy contrasted sharply with his older brother, and Charles bitterly resented the contrast. With his passion to be a warrior-king, he was restless and vexed at the hours he was forced to spend at the Council table. When Anjou, obviously his mother's favourite, was given the generalship of the army, a task for which Charles yearned, his rancour grew. It was the first overt sign of that enmity that would separate her sons throughout their lives and that would embroil Catherine in the microcosm of domestic war.

Catherine, so secret in so many of her manoeuvres, was transparent in her affection for Anjou. On November 23 she wrote the first of those letters, with which her correspondence is full—a letter of pure maternal devotion with a tone never quite reproduced for her other children:

> My son, I have been so happy to hear from you; but I fear that you must be a little tired from this first march which has been very long. . . . I beg you to remember what you have promised—to conduct yourself so that your health will not suffer, so that you will be able to win the honour and reputation which you so much desire.[17]

Catherine's role as *Regina Madre* is never clearer than in her dealings with Anjou. While with her queen's hand she signs the paper that sends him to war, with her mother's hand she pulls him back to the safety of her maternal love.

It was soon apparent that Anjou was unequal to his task. Instead of a royal victory, there were rumours that both the Protestant army and the German reiters were travelling unimpeded through Champagne. Philip, quick to sense new trouble, offered at once to send troops into France. "He was ready to go himself at the head of all his forces to reduce the Huguenots and set His Majesty at liberty," reported Castelnau.[18] Throughout November and into December, Spain continued to urge the French royal forces towards battle, reminding them that the heretics must be "plucked up by the roots." For a while everything worked towards Spain's advantage: Anjou fumbled in the field; the king negotiated for Spanish forces; the Huguenots were weakening. Everything was going very well, wrote Antoine Cardinal Granvelle, provided that the queen mother could be kept from "making some shaky bridge."[19] The "shaky bridge" to which Granvelle alluded, was, of course, peace with the Huguenots. Álava, the Spanish ambassador, exerted his full pressure to hinder such a step, but despite his coercion, Catherine continued to affirm that peace was to France's best interests.

It had become increasingly clear that Anjou could not manage his army, and at the beginning of the year Catherine, informed of new bickerings among the leaders of the king's forces, rode to Châlons to exert her own leadership over the dissenting factions. A fortnight later she returned to Paris, weary, cold, disconsolate, and unsure that she had accomplished anything worthwhile. Whatever course she chose, she found her way blocked by hostility. Especially in Paris, the atmosphere of distrust was dense. An episode from the legend already growing about her recounts that one night as she rode in the king's company through the Paris streets, she turned to say something to him. Out of the dark, a voice came mockingly, "Sire, do not believe her, for she will never tell you the truth."[20]

By the end of January, 1568, the movement for peace had gained momentum. There were no victories in the field, and there was no money at home—the promises of Florence, Venice, Rome had grown cold. The Huguenots, too, had grown impoverished and demoralised. England was loath to help men in revolt from their king, and the German reiters were animated only by self-interest. "Both parties begin to wax very weary of these wars," Sir Henry Norris wrote to England that winter.[21] Despite the coercion of the Papal Nuncio, the threats of Álava, and the opposition of the Sorbonne, Catherine was determined on peace. At first, the king himself opposed his mother's plan, and on February 27 Giovanni Petrucci wrote to Florence, "His Majesty is very bloodthirsty by nature . . . and in the presence of the queen, when peace was proposed to him, he replied: 'You want to force me to make peace. But I will not keep it, because I want to punish my enemies; and I will remember those who are now trying to persuade me.' "[22] A month later, despite the king's initial opposition, the peace was signed at Longjumeau.

At Chartres, Condé at once gave orders to disband his army, and the Huguenots began to return to their homes. In the cities normal activities were resumed. In the country the peasants looked at their wasted fields and burned houses. France had been in open conflict for little more than six months, but the wedge had been driven so deep no paper peace could mend the breach. The preceding summer Haton had described in his memoirs a "great wind" that had swept France. It was a wind stronger than had ever been felt. Even in the memories of the oldest men, nothing like it had ever been seen before. It bent everything before it, leaving the wheat—beautiful and golden—lying in the fields. The land was so dry and the wind so tempestuous that it was impossible to harvest the grain. It lay rotting in the fields, and that year there was no harvest. Some said it was God, touching their lands in punishment for their sins; some said it was the devil, taunting those who had made bargains with him. Perhaps it was simply the winds of war, for no one who understood the force of war could believe that what had been done at Longjumeau could quiet the storm.[23]

It was a peace doomed from the beginning. Neither side felt it had had sufficient voice in framing it and, consequently, felt no obligation to keep it. Coligny found it "bloody," Lorraine, "shameful." Even the chancellor, always the protagonist for peace, pointed out that the peace could not succeed until both sides laid down their arms. Within the royal family, the peace caused continued dissension. The king, despite his initial opposition, now avowed that he would see it enforced. Anjou, however, was of another mind. His taste of military command had whetted his appetite. He enjoyed giving orders in the field; he enjoyed putting down the king's enemies. What chance would he have for glory if there were no armies to lead? He vigorously opposed this easy capitulation to the Protestants. As a result, he soon gained the reputation for being a merciless defender of the Catholic cause and a devoted supporter of the Guise faction. Six weeks after the peace was signed, Norris wrote to England: "M. d'Anjou has kept his chamber, having uttered most despiteful words against them of the religion, saying that he hoped to march upon their bellies. . . . The jealousy . . . before advertised has again appeared between the King and M. d'Anjou."[24]

Even Catherine, whose peace it was, spoke apologetically of it to Correro, explaining that no alternative had been open, that there are sometimes circumstances which require one to "go against oneself in order to avoid a greater evil." Nostalgically, she reminded the Venetian ambassador of those happy days when everyone could walk safely through France, noting that now the royal family could not move without being guarded. "Even in this room," she continued (and here, says Correro, she lowered her voice conspiratorially), "there are perhaps people who would like to see us dead and would kill us with their own hands." But she then concluded with a touch of that imperious belief in her destiny that was often her only consolation: "God will not permit this; our cause is His and that of all Christendom. He will never abandon us."[25]

Yet the evidence was strong that France had already been "abandoned." Pillaging and armed conflict continued as though no peace had been signed. In the south, Monluc, goaded by his animosity for Jeanne d'Albret, pursued his ruthless policies against the Huguenots, and at Toulouse the Catholics continued their murdering and sacking. In retaliation came news of altars profaned, statues mutilated, old priests beaten, religious tortured and mocked. Although Condé had obeyed in disbanding his army, his disbanded army proved as destructive as a functioning one. Restless, unpaid, and enured to atrocities, they travelled through France, responsible to no command, terrifying the countryside.

In the midst of the tumult Catherine fell ill. For weeks she was confined to bed with what her son vaguely called "catarrh" but what, in a letter to Cardinal Granvelle, is more accurately described as pleurisy. It was accompanied by fever, violent headaches, and haemorrhaging. For days she lay close to death, with her fever rising so high that her attendants had to change her nightgown five and six times during the night. She kept to her bed well into May. It was May 17 before Norris wrote Cecil, "The Queen Mother is now well recovered. If she had died, this Court had stood in perilous state."[26] Although Charles, meanwhile, had taken up the reins of government ("commanding as king"), he lacked the power to enforce his decrees. When, towards the end of the month, Catherine was again able to see to affairs, it was too late to save the shards of peace.

Throughout the summer complaints from the Huguenots increased. Henri de Navarre, Jeanne d'Albret's son, now coming into manhood, wrote, protesting the conduct of Monluc in Guyenne and begging the king that he himself be placed in charge of this government, which was his through rightful inheritance. In July Condé, who after the peace had travelled into Picardy, wrote in anger: "We have to witness our own deaths, see our women violated, young girls snatched from their mothers and fathers. . . ." Catherine's placating reply, "Let us assure you that our intention is to keep the edict in its entirety," was worthless. If it did not indicate double-dealing, it at least indicated powerlessness.[27]

In August Condé's anger and mistrust were further aroused by a warning that the queen mother had mounted a plot to surround him in Noyers, a little town hidden in the mountainous region of the Morvan. Whether or not this had been Catherine's plan, as Tavannes' memoirs claim, it was the final blow that led Condé to publish a manifesto declaring war. Again he protested that he took up arms only in the interest of his king and against those—especially the Cardinal de Lorraine—who cared for "neither God nor country," but only for their own "interests and wealth." "Thus," wrote Castelnau, "the mask was thrown off and both parties made preparations for war again."[28]

This time everything seemed in favour of the Huguenots. La Rochelle, now their headquarters, was a strong city, strategically placed. Their leaders were vigorous, able, experienced. They could incite the people to both a sense of religious mission and anger against their "persecutors." Their opponents, by contrast, seemed strangely irresolute. They were a bankrupt people—lacking not only money, but mutual trust, a common goal, a determined course of action. Most of all, perhaps, they lacked consistent leadership. Charles, despite his childhood promise, lacked the ability to focus the energies of the court in himself. Now in his nineteenth year, he had borne the title of King of France for more than eight years. During those years he had sometimes evoked compassion, sometimes hope, but rarely a genuine feeling of respect. In the summer of 1568 a protracted illness made him more than ever unequal to his task. It was not a desperate illness, but a lingering and recurrent fever that left him weak and listless. It was, no doubt, the beginning of the pulmonary disease that would cause his death. On August 23 the Florentine ambassador reported: "The king has been ill

Catherine's marriage by proxy

François I of France

Diane de Poitiers, mistress of Henri II
Musée de Château Anet

Henri II of France,
son of François I,
husband of Catherine
Musée Condé, Chantilly

François de Guise, uncle of
Mary Stuart, antagonist of
Catherine
Musée du Louvre, Paris

Constable Montmorency, contemporary of François de Guise and Henri II
Musée Condé, Chantilly

François II and Mary Stuart

Charles IX of France, son of Cathe[...]
Musée Condé, Chantilly

Elizabeth of Austria,
wife of Charles IX
Musée Condé, Chantilly

Henri III of France, son of Catherine
Musée Condé, Chantilly

Louise de Vaudémont, wife of Henri III
Bibliothèque Nationale, Paris

Alençon, son of Catherine, suitor of
Elizabeth of England
Musée Condé, Chantilly

Elizabeth of England
Pinocoteca de Siena, Italy

for some time; he is very weak." Shortly after, Catherine wrote joyfully to Montpensier of the "complete recovery of my son," only to admit the following week that he was again suffering from fever. "The king is sick," Petrucci noted anxiously.[29]

The king's health, however, was not the only cause that kept the court irresolute in pursuing the war. They were desperately in need of money. Sometime earlier Lorraine had written to Philip, "I swear before God, I don't know what the king will have to eat next month."[30] Spain, however, made no effort to help, and Lorraine attempted to win support from Rome, assuring the Pope that the victory of the Catholic party in France would be for the good of all Christendom. In response came the papal permission to use the revenue from church lands, on condition that the edict of toleration be revoked.

For the cardinal and the members of his party, it was an ideal solution, but for such men as François de Montmorency (who had succeeded his father) and the chancellor, it was intolerable. L'Hôpital refused to affix the royal seal, and there ensued a scene that shattered the court. The cardinal, enraged, accused L'Hôpital, as well as his wife and daughter, of being Calvinists. The chancellor, still controlled, arose to reply, when Lorraine flew at him and would, reported the English ambassador, have "taken him by the beard," had not Montmorency stepped between them. "The Cardinal," continued Norris, "in great choler turning to the Queen said that he was the only cause of the troubles in the realm. . . . The Chancellor replied contrariwise that the Cardinal was the original cause of all the mischiefs that had chanced as well to France within these eight years."[31]

The scene was more than a moment's regretted anger. It was the summation of years of hostility. Hitherto, L'Hôpital, so gifted with reason, had absorbed personal enmity for the sake of France. Now he saw that one man's devotion to peace and reason was not enough to stem the tide. His presence would change nothing. He might, for a moment, raise obstacles, but they would be swept away in the current of opposing passions. "Even the king no longer received him with a friendly countenance," De Thou noted in his history.[32] He was growing old, and the thought of a quiet life on his estate was very pleasant. He begged permission to retire, and the king accepted the seals from him, while continuing him in his position as chancellor. L'Hôpital had conceded, and in due time, the king's new edict was promulgated: All public worship, except that of the Catholic faith, was forbidden, and all ministers exiled from France on pain of death.

On October 4, the royal army, led by the eager Anjou, took the road for Orléans. His departure had been heralded by a solemn religious procession, in which the king had participated, his head uncovered and a lighted candle in his hand. But it was Anjou, not Charles, who was the luminary. The contrast between them had grown more marked since Charles' recent illness. He had been bled so often that his veins had collapsed and his arm had grown swollen and inflamed.

Anxiety and suffering had left their marks. Although there was little more than a year between the brothers, they seemed almost of two generations. Anjou was the image of the warrior-prince. It was rumoured that the Cardinal de Lorraine had said he would look very handsome in the royal crown.

Shortly after the departure of the army, Catherine received news for which she was totally unprepared: Her daughter Elizabeth had died in childbirth on October 3. The previous spring Fourquevaux had informed her of the queen's pregnancy, and as usual, she had written a letter full of maternal advice: that moderate exercise would be good for Elizabeth, that she should walk about and not be confined to bed or her chambers, as was the Spanish custom—"for these people would like her never to take a step except in a litter or carried in her chair," she ended disapprovingly.

Despite her mother's advice, Elizabeth's health declined. She was taken with dizzy spells; she sometimes lost consciousness; her pulse fluctuated abnormally. For a while she tried to conceal her condition, having suffered too much from Spanish doctors to wish to entrust herself to them again. By fall, however, she was confined to bed, and by the end of September she knew she would not recover. Catherine, unaware of the seriousness of her daughter's condition, continued to write letters of advice—cautioning Philip against giving his wife too much to eat and not letting her get sufficient exercise. "Only two meals a day and nothing in between except a little bread," she recommended, unaware that Elizabeth was far beyond the power to walk or eat.[33] In midmorning of October 3 Elizabeth, after hours of labour, was delivered of a premature child which lived only long enough to be baptised. Four times she had endured the terrors of childbirth but had never succeeded in giving her husband a male heir. This time she did not outlive her child.

Charles had received the news on October 18 but could not bring himself to break it to Catherine until the next morning. When he did tell her, she said nothing but, after a moment, rose and withdrew in silence into her own chambers. When she returned several hours later, she was dry-eyed, reported the Venetian ambassador, although her sorrow was in her face. She took her place at the Council table, saying, "God has taken away every hope I have in this world. . . . But I will dry my tears and I will devote myself entirely to the cause of the king my son and that of God."[34] The sentiment, if not the words, is certainly authentic. In such perilous times, she could not afford to be the desolate mother. She must be primarily the political leader. Even in her grief she was aware of the political consequences of Elizabeth's death. An important link with Spain had been broken which must be reforged as soon as possible. Thus, her letters consoling the bereaved Philip also edged open the door for marriage negotiations between the Most Catholic King and her beautiful and talented daughter Marguerite.

By the middle of November she was actively engaged in this newest marital endeavour. Perhaps nowhere does Catherine more perfectly match her legend as a "scheming Florentine" than in her instructions concerning this marriage. Writing to Fourquevaux of the sadness she felt in the loss of Elizabeth, she immediately added, "But as a mother I would like to see, if possible, her sister in the same place," not, of course, for her own sake, but for "the good of this kingdom and the preservation of peace between these two kings." Soon, she advised him, he would be joined in Madrid by the Cardinal de Guise, who was being sent to express the condolences of the king on their mutual loss. "But," she warned, "do not say anything about what I have told you, until he speaks about it to you."

The following week her instructions were still more precise and more secret: Manage things, she advised him, so it will not appear the overtures are coming from us, "for young women ought to be asked for by men and not go offering themselves." She was sure Fourquevaux would find some "underhanded ways" of manipulating some of Philip's servants. "Above all," she concluded, "you must win over one of these three: the cardinal, the Prince of Eboli, or the confessor."[35]

It was a correspondence with the aroma of the Italian market rather than the French court. It was, ultimately, an abortive cause, for Margot, though not quite seventeen, was dancing high to the intoxicating music of her first affair. Her partner was Henri, the young Duc de Guise, son of Guise le Grand, who had inherited his full share of his father's pride and magnetism. Philip's spies were, of course, quick to inform their master. There was no place for such moral levity in the chambers of the Catholic king and Catherine's hopes of putting Margot in her saintly sister's place were over.

There was little that Catherine could take comfort in as 1568 drew to a close. Elizabeth was dead; Margot had compromised herself. In the field nothing of note had occurred. It was a bitterly cold winter, and neither army was prepared for the months of snow and ice and the inevitable face of famine. "The soldiers die daily," Norris wrote Burghley the day after Christmas.[36] Some among the king's Council—notably François de Montmorency and his brother Damville— had begun to talk of peace, but Lorraine remained obdurate in pursuing war. Compromise with the heretics was impossible, he pointed out; they had already made the mistake of one "shameful peace"; they could not afford another. This time Catherine declared herself on the side of war, even accepting Philip's offer of Spanish help. Undoubtedly, England's attitude was a factor in moving her in this direction, for while Elizabeth was assuring the French ambassador "that she would never do anything which could offend the king," the evidence was clear that the Huguenots were receiving help from across the Channel. "She [Elizabeth] furnishes our rebels with ammunition, artillery, money and soldiers;

she takes our ships, imprisons our subjects," Lorraine wrote Philip in an effort to stir him to equal assistance. "We must have money," he continued, "for it is the nerve of war."[37]

Despite Lorraine's plea, no help came from Spain. The decision to accept Spanish aid had been reached by Catherine with the gravest anxiety, and she was angered by this further humiliation of waiting like some poor cousin upon Philip's arbitrary decisions. In January she wrote in annoyance to Fourquevaux: "From now on we must be helped by something other than words and promises." But Alba, who commanded the Spanish troops, hesitated, explaining that Spain had need of its soldiers in other parts of the kingdom, that his men were tired and in need of rest, that travelling in such bad weather was very difficult.[38]

No one could contradict his plea of bad weather, for France had rarely suffered a worse winter. The trees, covered with ice, rose like ghosts from the wasted countryside. Day after day the sun rose pale and cold in a sky heavy with snow. Throughout the provinces the passage of troops could be traced by the charred remains of houses and frozen corpses. "The poor are left with nothing even to cover themselves," the Venetian ambassador noted. The soldiers were no better off. While Châtillon wrote to England begging for shoes for the Huguenot soldiers, Norris at the same time wrote to Elizabeth that the king's army was in "great want of all things necessary."[39]

While the court was at Metz, Catherine was seized by one of her long bouts of fever. There had been a subtle change in the queen mother after Elizabeth's death. Her eyes were often swollen, as though she had been crying; it cost her a great effort to retain her composure. She seemed suddenly older, less resilient, less hopeful. The winter had been very long, so long that it was hard to believe in spring.

In mid-March, however, with a shock that roused the court, came the news of a great royal victory at Jarnac in Poitou. It was close to midnight when the messenger arrived in the king's chamber, rousing him from sleep with the words "Sire, I bring you good news." "The king threw himself immediately on his knees," wrote the Tuscan ambassador. "He thanked God with great humility and devotion."[40] Pulling on his hose and throwing a cloak about his shoulders, he went at once to his mother's chambers, where, despite the objections of her attendants, he woke her to tell her that Condé was dead and the victory was theirs. The whole city of Metz was aroused, and the king, now fully dressed, went at once to the cathedral and in the glow of the torches and the pealing of bells the citizens sang the *Te Deum, à la royale.*

Jarnac was an important, if not a decisive, victory, and Anjou was dazzled by his own success. In the letters he wrote confirming his victory, he portrayed himself as the destined leader of the Catholic cause. "It has pleased God by His holy grace so to favour the holy, Catholic, apostolic and Roman religion and the justice of the king's cause . . . I have broken through their army and chased them before me at a gallop for more than two leagues,'' he wrote to the Duke of Urbino.[41] With the news of Anjou's victory, a sudden surge of life swept through the countryside. Catherine found herself suddenly better, her old energy momentarily restored. Anjou, on whom she doted, had brought the first breath of spring.

One royal victory, however, was not enough to defeat the Huguenots. The death of Condé had shaken them, but the manner of his death stirred them to anger. Badly wounded, he had been captured and then summarily shot. After his death, his body was ignominiously carted about on an ass as a public spectacle. Finally, disfigured and disgraced, his corpse was left on a stone slab like a common criminal. Such indignities as these the Huguenots would not easily forget.

Despite Catherine's initial surge of hope, by May the queen mother was again bowed beneath ill fortune. Although Anjou had emerged from Jarnac a hero, he lacked the leadership to sustain his troops: His own soldiers were deserting for lack of pay; he was at odds with Lorraine and Aumale; he feared that the admiral was massing troops in Saintonge and that the enemy was about to besiege La Charité. Everywhere the Huguenots seemed on the point of success. ''I see myself in peril of losing the reputation that I have just acquired,'' Anjou wrote to his mother, with that touch of petulance that would mark his later life.[42] This was enough to put Catherine on the road to join her son at Limoges. From here she wrote to Charles on June 9, assuring him they had not lost heart, nor would they lose any occasion to put an end to all these miseries. Meanwhile, reported an observer, she walked daily through the camp, talking to the soldiers, trying to reanimate their courage. Another observer noted that the queen mother in her desperation had had recourse to magic. Some of the wax figures of her enemies had, indeed, melted away. Three formidable Huguenot leaders had died in a short space: Condé, Andelot, and Deux-Ponts. Only Coligny—apparently indestructible—remained.

Chapter VIII

With Condé's death, young Henri de Navarre assumed the nominal leadership of the Huguenot party, but it was Coligny in fact who guided and directed. Catherine's hostility towards the admiral had the sharp edge of confidence betrayed. She had recognised his gifts of leadership; she had believed him when he professed loyalty to the crown; she had braved the anger of the Guises to keep him at court, where, she felt, he rightfully belonged. His recompense was to mount an army against the king. Such betrayal of trust evoked Catherine's implacable hatred. In June, 1569, Coligny was condemned by the Paris Parlement for the crime of treason "against God and the king" and sentenced to be degraded from his rank as a member of the nobility and hanged in effigy. Sometime later the Parlement further decreed a reward of 50,000 gold crowns to anyone who would deliver Coligny—alive or dead—to the king. Such threats, however, only increased the admiral's stature among his coreligionists, and in early September Burghley wrote: "Coligny is the leader of the Huguenots, although nominally it is Navarre and young Condé. In France, the power of the admiral surpasses that of the king."[1]

With Anjou's stubborn victory at Moncontour in October of that year negotiations for peace were reopened. It was an obdurate struggle that would drag on for six months, each side knowing that eventually it must concede something, but determined to drive a hard bargain. By the end of July it was obvious that despite the menacing stance assumed by Spain and the Papacy, peace would be made. "They are all going to the devil," Álava wrote in disgust to Philip.[2] When peace was concluded on August 8, 1570, at St. Germain-en-Laye, the Huguenots won the right of total liberty of conscience, of the public exercise of their religion wherever it had been permitted before the war, of general amnesty, and of four towns as places of surety. The Huguenots received it "with the utmost joy and satisfaction," for it granted them more than they had hoped for. The Catholics, however, found it no more acceptable than that signed at Longjumeau two years

135

before. Monluc, one of the fiercest of the Catholic lords, wrote, "We have fought and fought again but notwithstanding, they have such good credit at the king's Council that the edicts are always in their favour. We will win our [rights] by arms."[3] Neither side had great faith in the durability of the peace, for the basic issues had not been resolved. This is the weakness Henry Norris pointed out in his letter to Elizabeth: "Although this peace procures a certain community and civil policy amongst the meaner sort drawn partly thereunto by weariness of the wars, yet does not the same bring any firm reconciliation betwixt the nobility, so that the original case and spring of the war still continues."[4]

Catherine, however, availed herself of the temporary lull to engage in the subject dearest to her heart: her children's marriages.

Five years earlier, during the course of the royal progress, she had made her first tentative overture for a marriage between Charles and Elizabeth of England. Throughout the winter and spring of 1565 she had given explicit instructions to her ambassador Paul de Foix, telling him to assure the English queen that she would find everything about Charles—"both his body and his soul"—to her liking. Catherine was unabashedly eager. In view of Charles' youth, Sir Thomas Smith, the English ambassador, found such haste unwarranted. When Charles avowed he loved the English queen, Smith answered, unfortunately perhaps, "At your age, Sire, one does not yet know the meaning of love."[5] Although Charles blushed at the rebuff, he continued his avowals. Even the observation that Elizabeth was over thirty and Charles only fifteen did not dissipate his ardour. "I find no fault" he assured Smith. "I would she could be as well content with me as I with her age."

But Elizabeth was not to be so content, and, in a private audience with De Foix, she confessed that "she feared it would go as it did with Mary and Philip of Spain," adding that she "would prefer to be dead than to be scorned and abandoned." In July, De Foix finally conveyed to Charles and the queen mother Elizabeth's profound regret that her principal advisers had counselled her against this marriage because of "the great disparity of age."[6]

With Elizabeth's refusal, Catherine began negotiations in another quarter, writing to Fourquevaux to enlist Philip's help in her "great desire . . . to see the King my son married to one of the daughters of the emperor."[7] Despite Catherine's eagerness, it was to be more than two and a half years before these negotiations were concluded. It was, however, a marriage worth waiting for, for contemporaries are agreed that there were few princesses in Europe who could compare with Elizabeth of Austria. "One of the best, the sweetest, the wisest, and the most virtuous queens who has ever reigned," wrote Brantôme in a burst of enthusiasm.[8]

On November 27 the marriage of Charles IX of France and Elizabeth of Austria, daughter of the emperor Maximilian, took place amid "great pomp" in the cathedral at Mézières. Despite days of icy rains, the path from the king's lodgings to the church was covered with carpeting, and the town was richly hung with tapestries. The bride, pale and tired from weeks of travel, was clothed in white satin and silver cloth, with a cloak of violet velvet trimmed with speckled ermine and embroidered with fleurs-de-lys. Her crown—"of immense value"—was a circle of diamonds, rubies, and emeralds.[9]

The bride on whom all this luxury was expended was just fifteen. She was graceful and well proportioned, grave and sober in manner. Since she knew little French, she tended to be quiet. Catherine must have found her a marked (and comforting) contrast with her other daughter-in-law, the tall and dominant Mary Stuart. The bride had been in France barely three months, however, before she came close to death. Catherine had early enured her brood to the hardships of travel, but days of lurching along frozen roads, when even furs and pillows were inadequate against the cold, had been too rigorous for Elizabeth. "She has been so sick that we have almost despaired of her," wrote Catherine to Fourquevaux towards the end of January. "It was caused by the long travel and bad weather which we have had, both in her journeying into the kingdom and in that we have had since her arrival."[10]

With Charles successfully married, Catherine was free to devote herself to the marriage of her second son, Anjou. Once again she turned to Elizabeth of England. The preceding May she had mentioned the possibility to the English ambassador, who replied he thought his mistress would be "happy" to "talk" about it. That fall Catherine sent one of her trusted Italians, Guido Cavalcanti, to England to pursue the subject, which was put under serious scrutiny by Elizabeth's statesmen. Her chief adviser, Lord Burghley, drew up a series of papers dealing with "The Commodities that may follow upon the marriage with the Duke of Anjou," "Things needful to be fully considered," and "Reasonable demands to be required." The weight of the proposal seemed mostly on the credit side: Spanish power would be diminished; the Pope's "malice with his bulls and excommunications vanish away in a smoke"; Calais would be restored; Anjou would bring with him a good income. The chief item on the debit side was the question of religion. For Elizabeth herself, however, the question of age was still an issue; she feared, she told La Mothe-Fénelon, the French ambassador, that she had arrived at that age where she would be married not for herself but for her kingdom.[11]

In general, however, Catherine was encouraged by reports from England. It was Anjou, not Elizabeth, who began to set up obstacles. On February 2 Catherine wrote in exasperation to Fénelon, "My son has made me tell the king his brother that he does not wish to marry her even if she would wish it. . . . I have not been able to win him over in this, although he is obedient to me."[12] For the next few months Anjou continued to vacillate. Although the king and the queen mother were eager for this English alliance, the ultra-Catholic party, led by the Cardinal de Lorraine, was solidly opposed. It saw the match as a strategy of the Huguenots to diminish Anjou's power at home and win for themselves greater support from England. "You can be assured of this," wrote Cardinal Pellevé, "Monsieur will never be king; he will be only the husband of the queen."

For a young man of Anjou's ambition, such a warning was sufficient to deter him. Sir Thomas Walsingham, the newly appointed ambassador to France, wrote to Burghley: "The Pope, the King of Spain, and the rest of the confederates . . . seek by what means they may to withdraw him from the same." One of the means employed was the suggestion of a marriage between Anjou and France's former queen, Mary Stuart.[13] Such a possibility must certainly have exercised a fascination for Anjou. Although he had not seen his sister-in-law for more than ten years, his memory of her must have been of someone clever, beautiful—and partially French. These were all qualities of immense value to a Valois. In addition, Mary Stuart was a heroine such as the old romances described: forced from her rightful country and now held captive in a foreign land. Such a marriage would make him a hero twice over; in addition, it would give him the right to the crown of Scotland and—if his uncle the cardinal was right—perhaps, in due time, to the throne of England.

These were at best but shadowy baits, however, and what was near at hand was his mother's coercion and his brother's anger. The enmity between the brothers had grown steadily with Anjou's popularity. Charles, it was clear, wanted his brother out of the kingdom. Knowing his ambition, he refused to take seriously Anjou's pious scruples over a marriage to a Protestant queen, suspecting his hesitation stemmed from a desire to gain power in France itself. In July Charles "fell into a rage" and threatened his brother in front of the English ambassador. Walsingham lost no time in describing the scene to Burghley:

> "You allege conscience to be the cause," [Charles had cried], "but I know it is a late pension offered unto you by the clergy who would have you still remain here for a champion of the Catholic faith. I tell you plainly, I will have no other champion here but myself; and seeing you have such a desire to remain here on such respects, it behooves me the more narrowly to look to you. . . ." Upon this Monsieur retired into his cabinet and spent one half day in shedding tears. . . . The King is loath to have him here and Monsieur is afraid to be here. . . . The Queen Mother never wept so much since the death of her husband.[14]

Even his brother's threats did not change Anjou's mind, however, and he continued to affirm he could never marry into England until he had formal assurance he would be able to practise his religion.

Elizabeth, meanwhile, unable to believe that a marriage so advantageous to France could stumble on the issue of religion, continued to treat both the former ambassador De Foix and the ordinary ambassador, Fénelon, with charming good humour. She was pleased with the two portraits of Anjou brought by Cavalcanti and commented to Fénelon: "This is only a pencil sketch, a little smudged; but there is in the face an air of dignity and of serious maturity which makes me very happy, for I have never wanted to be led to the altar by a child."[15] By September, however, she had grown restive, finding that she was unable to sidestep the religious issue as she would have liked. She was weary of Anjou's obduracy, suspicious of De Foix's good faith. Ultimately, it seemed the concessions were to be all on her side. When De Foix took his leave for France, she turned petulantly to one of her ambassadors, saying, "We have accomplished nothing, for M. de Foix, not being satisfied with our responses, has done everything in his power to lead us to do things as he wished them done."[16]

Catherine's renewed protestations that their desires were "not growing cold," that "the king and I desire this infinitely" no longer aroused Elizabeth's confidence. Catherine, unwilling to acknowledge that her *mignon* might be at fault, wrote to Fénelon on September 28 that Anjou was "such a lover of his religion" that he could scarcely have acted otherwise, concluding, "We are very sorry that we haven't some other person like my son Anjou to offer her; but there is a very great difference between him and my son Alençon."[17] The statement can act as prologue for the most touching and ludicrous of the marriage dramas in which Catherine was to entangle her children.

The months of the marriage negotiations had been difficult ones for Anjou. Those who had accused him of using religion as a cloak for his real motivations were undoubtedly right. First of all, he was passionately in love, and the manifest charm and youth of Renée de Châteauneuf cast an unpleasant chill over his proposed union with the Virgin Queen. Even more, however, he was increasingly opposed to his brother's policies. Following the Peace of St. Germain, Charles appeared to lean more and more away from the interests of the Catholic party: He refused to join the Pope's Catholic League against the Turks; he granted two secret audiences to the Protestant leader in the Low Countries; he refused to take Philip's side in a question of sovereignty in Italy; most dangerous of all, he had encouraged Admiral de Coligny to return to court.

Tavannes, who was later to become one of the staunchest members of the Catholic League, no doubt came close to articulating Anjou's own thoughts when he wrote of the dangerous influence of the Huguenots on the king:

> They were determined to force Their Majesties into a war with Spain and to ally them with their own friends the English, they were involved in both foreign and civil war, they carried on intrigues in the court through the Montmorencys, they frightened the king and aroused his envy against the honour of his brother whom they planned to banish from France by a marriage with England.[18]

In fact, Charles was coming to realise that the goals of the Catholic party were not always in the interest of France. By 1570 it was clear, even to Charles, that Spain and Rome's primary concern was to find means of manipulating French internal policies to their own advantage. In times of real distress both Philip and Pius had shown themselves negligent in providing the help they had so generously promised. Charles saw no value in sacrificing his profitable treaty with the Turk to join in a religious crusade, nor did he wish to increase Spain's domination by backing Philip's claims to Siena. His goal was, above all, internal peace. He wished, as he explained in a letter to Fourquevaux, to "reunite his subjects in friendship and harmony . . . and to remove all signs of division." This was the goal determining his policy towards the Huguenots and especially towards Admiral de Coligny.[19]

Coligny had taken the initiative in his reconciliation with the crown, writing to Catherine and begging her to believe that there was no cause for the king to regard him with suspicion. "I would never do nor undertake anything against Your Majesty, even were I in a position to do so," he assured her. Despite his avowal of candour, it was, of course, a letter schooled in Renaissance diplomacy. His humble protestations of service did not quite explain away such treasonable behaviour as the Treaty of Hampton Court or the fact that he was even now called by many the King of La Rochelle. Some months later Coligny wrote again, begging Catherine to give no credence to those who were saying that he "threatened the king," reaffirming, "there is not a gentleman in France who more desires the well-being and peace of this kingdom."[20]

Although the admiral's protestations did not entirely allay Catherine's suspicions, his reinstatement was the easiest way of winning the Huguenots and thus assuring peace. By the end of July the Florentine ambassador wrote that the admiral had "regained the good graces of the queen," and on September 12, 1571, Coligny arrived at Blois at the king's invitation. Charles, whose tutor he had been, greeted him warmly, embraced him three times, and—according to D'Aubigné—took his hand, declaring, "Now that we have you, we are going to keep you." On Catherine's reception of the admiral there is no agreement, except that because she was sick, she received him in bed—"coldly," say some; "cordially," say others. Anjou made no effort to dissimulate his dislike. He, too, received the admiral from his sickbed, observing him silently, and, after a moment, turning his back, saying, "I consider him merely an old man."[21]

Although Coligny himself was unperturbed by such hostility, some at court grew nervous at what might happen to him. La Huguerye in his memoirs notes that one day Montpensier, meeting the admiral in a badly lighted hall, asked him, "What are you doing here all alone—it is very imprudent!" To which Coligny replied, "Am I not in the house of the king and on his word of honour?" "But," replied Montpensier, "the king is not always the master in his own house."[22] In fact, there were rumours abroad, not only in France, but in the courts of Madrid and Rome as well, that Coligny had been invited to Blois for the sole purpose of despatching him. To those who observed the king, however, this was manifestly untrue. His affection and respect for Coligny were marked—so marked the

Guises in annoyance left for their estates in Joinville, unable to watch "the murderer" of François de Guise treated so royally. Charles made no effort to keep them, believing, perhaps, in the prophecy Condé had made before his death—that there would never be peace in France while the Cardinal de Lorraine remained at court.

The shift in Charles' attitude is not easy to trace. He was now more than twenty-one, and more than half his life had been spent on the throne of France. During those years he had lost something of the affability of his childhood; he had become restless, impatient, suspicious. His ambitions outran his abilities. Admiration for his father was very strong in him, and he longed to lead armies and be a warrior-king. Instead, he was forced to bed by the fever that left him by turns agitated and apathetic, so that the ambassadors' reports were larded with notations that the king was ill. He grew resentful of his own weakness, of those who opposed him, even of those who advised him. He had had, it was reported, several unpleasant scenes with his mother. Charles had grown tired of Catherine's solicitude and domination and was determined to be his own man. He had also grown suspicious of the Guises and gave more and more credence to the rumours that Spain (assisted by the House of Guise) had secret plans to weaken France until he "would be forced to yield to anything the King of Spain would require."[23]

In defence, he tended to lean towards his mother's initial policy of using the Huguenots as a bulwark against Spanish power. For the first time, he began to listen seriously to the Huguenots' pleas to provide some assistance to the Netherlands. What better way to give Spain "something else to think about," as he put it to the Tuscan ambassador? It was, perhaps, the first overt reference to the possibility of France's becoming formally involved in what came to be called the enterprise of Flanders. With Charles' increasing disaffection for Spain and the Guises, the admiral's influence was to become predominant. At the beginning of August, Walsingham noted in his report to Burghley: "The King conceives of no other subject better than of the Admiral, and there is great hope that he will use him in matters of the greatest trust, for he begins to see the insufficience of others, some being more addicted to others than to him, others more Spanish than French, or given more to private pleasures than public affairs."[24]

Catherine found her son's latest policy extreme. While she had always maintained that the Huguenots should be integrated into the kingdom so that they would strengthen France, not divide it, she opposed any overt action that would bring down the wrath of Spain. Now she wrote constantly to Fourquevaux, instructing him to assure Philip that Charles had no desire for a rupture, that it was only rumour he was allying himself with the Huguenots for an invasion of the Netherlands.

Despite Catherine's efforts, war with Spain was an open topic in the fall of 1571. Coligny favoured war, and at the moment Coligny's voice was supreme.

The king, now a man, was prone to put his trust in other men rather than in a woman. She was not surprised that the admiral, so long a captain of armies, was deferred to in military matters; what came unanticipated was the affectionate relationship Charles formed with him. He called him father. The knife pricked dangerously close to the heart of her own vocation as *Regina Madre*. So totally had Catherine buried herself in her children's destinies that she seemed to have forgotten she had once existed apart from them. In some extraordinary way, Catherine had died with her husband, and a new woman had emerged after his death. She had hardly permitted herself the luxury of widowhood. This "poor foreigner who had no place to turn"—as she had once been described—had created for herself a new vocation, a vocation depending for its validity on her being the sole parent of her children. Now Charles, by a single word, had called that vocation into question. As queen she might have tolerated Coligny's political influence, but as mother a jealousy was excited in her that led to mortal enmity.

For the moment, however, she hid her feelings and continued to use the admiral to further her own peace plans—chief among them, the marriage of her daughter Marguerite to Jeanne d'Albret's son, Henri de Navarre. Although not yet nineteen, Margot—goddess among princesses, as Brantôme was later to call her—had already been the subject of at least two abortive marriage proposals. In addition to the hasty offer made by Catherine to Philip II, following Elizabeth's death, there had been lengthy negotiations to marry Margot to Sebastian of Portugal. This had been proposed, with apparent Spanish approval, at the conferences of Bayonne, when Margot was but twelve years old. Yet Philip, who had agreed to act as intermediary, had dallied, and six years later, Catherine still waited for some conclusive word. Piqued by this slight to the French royal house, she wrote sharply to Philip that she found the delays "very strange," that his "weak excuses" made a "mockery" of her and her daughter. Margot, however, was quite content with such delays, for, wrote Norris to Burghley, "if the young lady may have her will, she would choose rather to tarry in France than eat figs in Portugal."[25]

The more Margot learned of Sebastian, the less liking she had for him. He was reported to be sickly, eccentric—and deathly afraid of women. The Sieur de Malicorne, who headed the negotiations, described him as a religious fanatic, totally under the thumb of two Theatine priests. "He carries a book by St. Thomas in his belt," wrote Malicorne, "and runs from place to place until he wearies those who accompany him, so that he can be alone with his Theatines. He is spoken of as an erratic young prince of very little character."[26]

To Margot, Sebastian must have seemed a poor substitute for Henri de Guise, whose attentions she had been revelling in. But where Margot saw in Guise only a gallant young hero responsive to her charms, her brother sensed the manipulating hand of the Cardinal de Lorraine. What better capstone to Guise ambition than the marriage of the young duke to the king's sister? But here Lorraine had overshot the mark. The king and his mother, outraged at such presumption, had Henri de Guise summarily dismissed from court, and Margot—who had never been her mother's favourite—was subjected to a humiliating display of royal anger.

Enrico Davila, the contemporary Italian historian, said that the incident occurred at a royal ball. The Spanish ambassador, in his report to Philip, described an even more dramatic scene.

> About five o'clock in the morning, Charles, dressed in his nightshirt and accompanied by the Comte de Retz, came to his mother. After speaking together for some minutes, both of them sent for the princess. About a half hour later, she came, accompanied by Madame de Retz. Having sent away the countess, and leaving the count to guard the door so that no one could enter, mother and son pounced on Marguerite and struck her roughly. When they finished with her, her clothes were so torn and her hair in such disarray that the queen mother, fearful that someone would see her, spent an hour in rearranging her dress.

Within a few days Henri de Guise was married to Catherine de Clèves.[27]

Although there had been some talk of a marriage between Margot and the young Prince de Navarre before the conclusion of the Peace of St. Germain, serious negotiations did not get under way until the fall of 1571. In the beginning of that year Catherine extended an invitation to Jeanne d'Albret to come to court. Jeanne hesitated, writing Catherine, "I would like very much to come, but I am somewhat proud. I would like to receive there the honour and favour that I feel I deserve more than those who receive it."[28] Through the following months, the correspondence continued: Catherine soliciting her presence; Jeanne demurring for reasons of health, of business, of the state of her small kingdom. It was clear the Queen of Navarre hesitated at stepping into such a trap as her husband had once encountered.

It was not easy to allay Jeanne's fears; she had lived with them too long. That fall Petrucci noted in his despatches, "She fears, she hopes, she changes her mind, she does not know how to proceed, nor exactly what she wants."[29] Ultimately, however, she accepted Catherine's invitation and towards the beginning of December moved out of Béarn on the first lap of her trip to court. The weather was bitter, and Jeanne had not fully recovered from one of those heavy colds to which she was increasingly susceptible. As she journeyed north, she ran into increasingly heavy snows, and, once out of her own mountainous kingdom, there was less protection from the high winds sweeping the snow into sometimes impassable drifts. Everywhere trees lay cracked or bent to the ground with their heavy burden of ice. The cold was so intense, noted Haton, that "wine was frozen in its casks."[30]

For more than two months Jeanne journeyed north, forced to make frequent stops along the way. She left her son at Agen, where he was to remain until he received further directions. As she entered Touraine, her suspicions were aroused by a messenger from Catherine instructing her to go to Tours rather than Blois, where the court sat. Jeanne immediately perceived this as a deliberate insult, although, in fact, Catherine had been forced into this awkward adjustment by the unexpected arrival of the Papal Nuncio at Blois. It was inconceivable to house Michele Cardinal Alexandrini and Jeanne d'Albret together, especially since the Nuncio's mission was to put a stop to the proposed marriage.

For several months, the subject of a dispensation for Marguerite de Valois to marry a blood relative and a heretic had been an issue at the papal court. Catherine had instructed her ambassador, Ferals, to do whatever was necessary to obtain the dispensation, but Pius was obdurate, demanding that the bridegroom be converted "to the true religion" before the marriage. In November, Petrucci noted, "The Pope is determined not to grant a dispensation in this matter."[31] Cathrine's inclination to marry her children to Protestant sovereigns frightened Pius, who saw France (so long regarded as the "Eldest Daughter of Christendom") slipping away from the Catholic center towards the axis of Protestant powers. The Papacy, having already lost England, could not afford the disaffection of France.

Although Antonio Salviati, his Nuncio Extraordinary, was already in France, Pius now ordered Cardinal Alexandrini to the French court. His purpose: to influence Charles and the queen mother to terminate the marriage negotiations with Navarre, to resume those with Sebastian of Portugal, and to draw France into the Catholic League. Alexandrini, learning that Jeanne d'Albret was already on her way, accelerated his pace and slipped into Blois on February 7—just ahead of the queen of Navarre. For more than two weeks Alexandrini stayed on at Blois, cajoling, coercing, intimidating. When he left, neither Catherine nor her son had moved a hair's breadth.

On March 2 Jeanne arrived at Blois, and the marriage negotiations began. Although ill-matched in power, in goals, and in their means to achieve those goals, Catherine and Jeanne were not entirely alien. They had never been attractive women. Jeanne was tall, angular, with a prominent nose and thin, uncompromising lips. She had been the subject of two marriages: the first, later annulled, she had been forced into, at the age of twelve, by her uncle François I; the second, she had run to with the alacrity of love.

It was her misfortune that Antoine de Bourbon had been no match for her affection, her admiration, or, most of all, her fidelity. He had used her badly, letting her love serve him when it would and repudiating her publicly when it was to his advantage. Even if the ardour of her love had grown cold, her pride—and she had more than her share of this—was bitterly bruised. Later she wrote tersely of her husband that he had put "a thorn not in my foot but in my heart."[32] Long before his death he had left her to bear the full responsibility for her kingdom and her children. She had always been used to further other people's interests: first, by her uncle François I, then by her mother and her husband. Such exploitation had embittered her. The "smiling bride" of Châtellerault had grown gaunt and tight-lipped, rigid in her principles, suspicious, and susceptible to slights. When she faced Catherine across the bargaining table, she feared to be exploited once again.

The rotund figure of the queen mother was, in many ways, far less impressive than that of her adversary. She was shorter than the Queen of Navarre, and the "ample figure" noted even in her youth was now marked. Her skin was sallow, and her features seemed almost blurred when contrasted with the sharp features of Jeanne. There was little that was dynamic about her; even her eyes, with their strange opaque shield, belied her shrewd intelligence. She, like Jeanne, had been forced to hold together a kingdom and a family by her own resources. She, too, had been used, betrayed, exploited. She had spent her childhood in terror and loneliness. She had been married for the good of the Papacy and sent to a foreign country. For more than ten years she had had to live as queen in a court where everyone knew the king had found a more pleasing bed. She, too, had grown suspicious and mistrustful. But where Jeanne had grown rigid, Catherine had grown devious. Jeanne had become a profoundly religious woman—almost a fanatic. Catherine, too, had discovered a religion: Her creed was in her children and in their right to rule France; she would tolerate nothing else.

The opportunity to marry Margot to the inheritor of Navarre she saw as an unparalleled means for strengthening France. It would be a wedding of Huguenot and Catholic and, consequently, the end of faction, division, and civil strife. It would also be the end of Spanish hopes and English dreams. France need never again be pillaged by German reiters or papal troops. For such a goal, she was willing to fight by every means she knew. First, she must vanquish Jeanne's opposition.

According to the letters the Queen of Navarre wrote during March to her son and her ministers, Catherine's first means of attack was intimidation. Jeanne reported that her apartments were poorly furnished, she was spied upon and mocked. The queen mother "goads" her, Anjou tried to coerce her "with a mixture of mockery and deceit." As for the bride, she had been very gracious, but Jeanne was not permitted to see her alone. "I have remonstrated on three separate occasions with the Queen," she concluded, "but all she does is mock me, and afterwards tells others exactly the opposite of what I have said, with the result that they blame me."[33] Such overt intimidation does not seem like Catherine's usual attitude, unless Jeanne's obduracy had pushed her to the wall.

It was not only the manner in which she was treated that made Jeanne hesitant.

She was not a woman to compromise her religious convictions, and she sensed in the court a moral taint that made her turn away in revulsion. "Not for anything on earth would I have you come to live here," she wrote to her son, who still waited at Agen. "Although I knew it was bad, I find it even worse than I feared. Here women make advances to men, rather than the other way around. If you were here, you would never escape without a special intervention from God."[34] As for Margot, although her initial impression was pleasing, Jeanne noted that pretty as she was, she "spoils herself" with too much paint. More and more, Jeanne was disinclined towards the proposed marriage.

In the end, however, she was forced to concede, for Catherine held the trump card. At some point in the negotiations there was a very faint insinuation the Pope might be moved to consider Jeanne's first marriage valid, in which case Henri de Navarre, like any bastard, would forfeit all his inherited rights, including his position as inheritor of Navarre and First Prince of the Blood. It was a cruel and unexpected blow, one of those subtle and ruthless acts that won Catherine so much enmity and built up the legend of the cruel and wily queen.

On April 11 the marriage contract was finally signed by Charles, Catherine, and Jeanne. Word was sent for the bridegroom to travel north, and Jeanne, weary, anxious, defeated, left for Vendôme to rest and try to regain her vitality.

A month later she left for Paris to attend to the preparations for the wedding. It was obvious that she was seriously ill. The Duchesse de Nemours after seeing her wrote: "The Queen of Navarre is here; she is far from well, but very courageous."[35] By June 4 even courage would carry her no farther, and she was forced to her bed. Two days later Catherine, accompanied by Charles, visited her at her hotel. Catherine was singularly silent about this visit, which consisted, perhaps, simply of the conventional phrases of the sickroom. By then, it was clear Jeanne could not recover, and on June 9 she died. Her last night she spent in prayer, assisted by Coligny and Pastor Merlin, who read from the Psalms and the Gospel of John. After her death her body, clothed in white satin, with a cloak of purple velvet, was laid upon a simple black bed. The ceremonial for royalty was followed, insofar as Huguenot custom would permit, but much of the familiar Catholic ritual was missing. Margot, recalling the deaths of her father and her brother François and remembering the heavy smell of incense, the flickering shadows of the pale-orange candles, and the hypnotic drone of endless Latin verses, noted in wonder: "no priests, no cross, nor any holy water."[36]

News of Jeanne's death was not received with indifference. She had been a woman who evoked extremes—undying enmity or impassioned loyalty. The Catholics saw in the event the hand of God's justice, striking down an adversary. From Spain, Alba wrote triumphantly: "All Madrid rejoices that the Devil has got her at last."[37] The Huguenots meanwhile wept for their loss.

Despite Jeanne's obvious ill health, the accusation of poison was at once directed against the queen mother: She had treated the gloves of Florentine leather she had given to her; she had hired a servant to poison her food; she had bribed her Italian perfumer to tamper with her scent. Even when an autopsy indicated the slow progress of disease, suspicion lingered, limning one more line in the legendary portrait of the cruel and treacherous Florentine.

The Sinister Queen

Do not believe her, for she will never tell you the truth.
—Anon.

Chapter IX

Although Catherine was certainly not responsible for Jeanne's death, it caused her no grief. If anything, she was relieved to be rid of an intransigent adversary. With Jeanne dead, she was sure her son could be more easily coerced to the Roman religion and the question of a papal dispensation more easily resolved. At first, Rome, too, shared Catherine's optimism. In May Gregory XIII had replaced Pius V, and Ferals, who had known Ugo Boncompagni before he had assumed the tiara, assured Catherine he would be "cooperative." Gregory, however, turned out to be as obdurate as his predecessor. "All the decrees of the Church are contrary to what you are asking," he replied bluntly to the French ambassador. When Ferals objected that this was a matter of great public interest, Gregory turned aside, saying he had many affairs to attend to. Even Ferals' assurance that Navarre would undoubtedly become a Catholic immediately after the marriage, did not move the Pontiff.[1]

On July 3 Catherine herself wrote to Rome, extolling this marriage as the means of bringing that peace "which His Holiness so much desires." It was after all, she argued, "an ordinary request," which she was sure would be easily granted. Still Gregory remained intractable. If he felt that by such measures he could check Catherine, he did not know his adversary. Before the death of Pius V, Catherine had written to Ferals: "Remind the Pope that England is now separated from the Holy See because of a refusal of such a dispensation. . . . However, there is nothing of this kind to fear in France, for the king and my other sons are all very good Catholics." The menace was very clear, and she was capable of repeating it for the new Pontiff.

Charles, furious at Gregory's continued refusals, denounced the Pope as "that hypocritical old bigot" and threatened to have his sister married à la Huguenote if Gregory did not comply with the royal requests. On August 14, with the wedding only four days away, the dispensation had still not been granted. Catherine, determined the wedding would take place but not wishing to put either herself or her son in a position of acting in open defiance of the Pope, gave orders to stop any communication from Rome until after the ceremony. "You are not to allow any courier to pass, coming from Rome . . . until Monday be passed . . . taking care not to let them slip through secretly," she had ordered.[2]

The Pope's refusal to grant a dispensation made it difficult to find a prelate to perform the ceremony. The bishops of Auxerre, Châlons, Angers demurred, for they had no wish to act counter to the manifest wishes of the Holy See. Charles finally seized on the Cardinal de Bourbon, a nervous, vacillating prelate, whom he coerced by threats and vague assurances that a dispensation was in the offing. It would have been difficult for Bourbon, brother to Antoine de Bourbon and, therefore, uncle to the bridegroom, to refuse.

The month preceding the wedding was filled with uneasiness. At court tempers ran high. The negotiations with Jeanne d'Albret had been wearing. The Pope's attitude had been infuriating, and Charles, weakened in health, had less and less control of his temper. The weather increased the tensions, for Paris had rarely known a hotter August. People feared an outbreak of plague, as the city, crowded with thousands of visitors, staggered under the burden of new needs. Sanitation, always a problem, became more primitive. The Seine ran brown and sluggish; the air was heavy and threatening. Although the queen mother insisted this marriage would be the very "kiss of peace" for France, there was little gaiety in the atmosphere. Even the bridegroom's entrance into the city had had a sombre note, as he rode, still in mourning for his mother, between the gold and scarlet figures of the king's younger brothers, Henri d'Anjou and François d'Alençon.

Henri de Navarre, who had finally arrived in Paris in early July, accompanied by his cousin Henri, Prince de Condé, and 1,500 Huguenot horsemen, indicated only mild enthusiasm at the prospect of marriage. He was a young man of nineteen, small of stature, thin, wiry, with quizzical eyes, an embarrassingly large nose, and a wry expression about his mouth. He was already known for his penchant for women and the gaming table. Three years earlier Correro, who had observed him carefully, reported that he was "spirited, but carefully reared by his mother in the New Religion, and who, according to popular opinion, could become, if God does not remedy the situation, the scourge of our time."[3]

Not everyone took Navarre so seriously. In many ways, he seemed to be his father's son, and those who had known Antoine presumed the son would be as easily swayed. With three "conversions" to his credit, most people counted on a fourth. Navarre, however, held surprisingly firm, although it was obvious the situation would be much easier were he to nod in the direction of Rome. Even the marriage service was being adjusted because of his Protestant faith. Since no heretic could enter a Catholic church—even though that heretic be a member of the the Blood Royal—the wedding service would have to be conducted on the square outside the Cathedral of Notre Dame.

For weeks, workmen hauled and hammered the lumber to construct the great platform on which the service would be performed, as well as the gallery along which the royal couple would pass. Inside the cathedral the king's men hung the walls with tapestries, adorned the nave and the high altar with thousands of flowers and candles, raised the royal standards, and, with a singular lack of tact, set up the Huguenot standards captured at Jarnac and Moncontour.

On Sunday, August 17, the betrothal ceremony took place at the Louvre. The bridegroom signed the marriage contract and bestowed on his bride a diamond ring valued at 10,000 crowns. By dawn the following morning Paris was already astir, for although it was not a popular marriage among the conservative Parisians, it promised to be a grand spectacle. The wedding was scheduled for noon, but by the time the sun rose every window along the way had been rented and the streets were impassable with crowds of the curious, the disapproving, the hopeful—for there were many, besides the royal family, who hoped that this union would see the end of religious conflict. By ten o'clock the city aldermen and provosts in their short red robes, the king's archers and arquebusers stood at attention, keeping the crowds in place and forming a cordon for the royal procession.

After hours of waiting, in the heat of the noon sun, the crowd suddenly shifted spontaneously, then hushed as the sun caught the glint of metal on the weapons of the royal guard. Following them came the royal musicians, trumpets raised high to announce the bride's arrival. Then, along the length of the gallery, running parallel to the cathedral, walked Margot, straight and proud despite the weight of her robes. At her side was Charles, stooped and sallow, for although he was only two years her senior, he was already visibly marked with the mortal taint of his Valois heritage. The pale-yellow satin in which he was dressed only emphasised his unhealthy colour and emaciation. Next to him, Margot's energy was palpable. Her small dark head was erect under the weight of precious stones in her imperial crown, her body quick and alert to the pageantry about her. Margot's dress was of violet velvet, richly embroidered with fleurs-de-lys, and over it, despite the stifling heat, fell a royal mantle whose fifteen-foot train needed three princesses to carry it. Margot was already something of a legend of beauty, charm, and wit. She loved to glitter, and of her wedding day she wrote triumphally, "I blazed in diamonds."[4]

It was a cold flame, however, untouched by either passion or love. There was not a single breath of romance in this union which was to heal France. It was Catherine's political scheme from first to last. As for Margot and Henri, they seemed singularly uninterested in each other. Margot found her bridegroom rustic and ugly and—after a few days of intimate living—complained that he smelled. Henri, although marrying one of the most beautiful and talented women in France, seemed unresponsive and unimpressed. His mother had warned him to trust no one at this licentious court, and he seemed to have taken her advice.

It was rumoured Margot had argued tempestuously against this marriage, that she was still under the sway of her moonlight romance with the Duc de Guise, that during the ceremony the king had had to give a push to that small, wilful head to incline it to say yes to the marriage vows. In the end, however, she had given way, as she always had, to the intractable will of her mother, who had set her heart on this "marriage of two religions." The event was commemorated by a coin bearing the symbols of a lamb and a cross, with the legend *Annuntio vobis pacem* (I bring you tidings of peace). In the light of future events, it would be hard to imagine a more ironic commemoration.

For the rest of the week, all regular activities were suspended to allow the court to revel in four days of masquerades, balls, suppers, performances of musicians, poets, Italian comedians. This was primarily Catherine's marriage: she revelled in it. But despite all her efforts—and she spared nothing—she could not produce the air of gaiety such festivities normally evoke. The hostility between Catholics and Protestants, building for years, could not be dissipated by royal fiat. Although some of the surface hostility had been eased by the reinstatement of the admiral, the question of Spain and the Netherlands had brought a new dimension to the religious conflict.

The preceding July Charles had had a series of secret talks with Louis of Nassau, brother of William of Orange, leader of the Netherlands revolt, who had done his best to convince the king that Philip's goal was to "stir things up" in France until Charles, left without resources, would become prey to Spanish domination. Surely better to give Coligny what he asked for—permission to take French troops to help the rebels in the Netherlands. In April the Sea Beggars, as the rebels called themselves, had extraordinarily good fortune. While the Spanish were off guard, they took Brielle, Flushing, and, within a few days, had most of Middelburg in their power.

The victory encouraged Charles. Although he continued writing letters to Spain "so full of promises that if they are not kept one would never be able to trust anyone," he was simultaneously promising Louis of Nassau that he would help the oppressed people of the Low Countries. Catherine was scarcely more decisive. She, too, feared Spanish power, yet she did not wish to chance a possible defeat. With a certain masculine contempt, Tavannes wrote, "[She] fluctuates between peace and war, just like a woman who wishes and doesn't wish all at the same time."[5]

Actually, it is more accurate to say that Catherine fluctuated between ways of keeping the peace. War was never part of her decision. In fact, however, she found that her decision mattered less and less as the admiral became the star on Charles' horizon. "He does everything he can to make the king a partner in his evil intentions," wrote the Spanish ambassador, Juan de Zúñiga to Alba at the beginning of the summer.[6] To some extent, Coligny succeeded, for Charles agreed to send a secret force into the Netherlands under the command of the Huguenot leader Jean de Genlis at the beginning of July. Coligny, jubilant after a royal audience, exclaimed to his friends, "God be praised; all is going very well. Before long we shall have chased the Spaniards from the Low Countries," adding, "I would not even complain about my life, if I lost it in so good a cause."[7]

Meanwhile, Filippo Strozzi was ordered to keep a French fleet in readiness until the result of the expedition was apparent. Genlis, unfortunately, proved himself no master of his task. Having fallen into a Spanish ambush, his small force was cut to pieces by the Duke of Alba's son. Some—among them Genlis himself—were taken prisoner, and sufficient evidence was found to incriminate the French king in the rebel enterprise. "I have in my possession," wrote Alba's secretary jubilantly, "a letter which will astonish you; I have never seen anything like it in my life."[8] The evidence could scarcely be more damaging for Franco-Spanish relations, and Catherine now became forthright in her condemnation of Coligny's policies.

Coligny, however, was not easily intimidated. He believed in what his coreligionists were doing in the Low Countries; he believed that Philip was France's greatest enemy, and he refused to abandon his goal. The Venetian ambassador reported the admiral had informed the king that since he had "promised the Prince of Orange every help and assistance," he hoped the king would not take it amiss if he kept his promise "with the available friends, relatives and servants, and even with my own person should the need arise." Despite Genlis' fiasco, Coligny still hoped to bring France in on the side of the Netherlands. "His courage is invincible," wrote Walsingham to Burghley in admiration.[9] During the first week of August a Spanish agent wrote anxiously to Cardinal Granvelle, "Those who have just come from France say that there are great preparations going on. . . . The King of France is forever assuring us that he is taking no part in this game; but the admiral is with him every day. . . . I am very much afraid the French are fooling us."[10]

Coligny's access to the king was at this time unimpeded, for Catherine had left for Châlons to be with her daughter the Duchesse de Lorraine, who had been taken ill on her way to Margot's wedding. It was a crucial time for her to be absent, for Coligny used the days to push Charles irrevocably towards war. "The admiral has become as powerful as the Constable Montmorency used to be," wrote Michieli.[11]

When word reached Catherine of the continued preparations for war, she left at once for Paris. Her hostility towards Coligny had reached fever pitch. Although she had tried not to openly oppose her son's affection for him, she could never forget that Coligny had once deserted her when she had needed him desperately, that he had signed a treaty ceding French soil to a foreign power at Hampton Court, that, very possibly, he had hired the man who had murdered the Duc de Guise and thus stirred up civil war in France. More painful than all, however, was the recognition that he had deflected the affection of her son, taught him to unlearn the single lesson she had spent a lifetime teaching him: that she was the *Regina Madre*, the womb that had formed and nourished him, the source of his strength, the dominant love of his life.

So deep ran her hatred that she, perhaps, could not see its roots. She was not insincere when she maintained that her hostility was the righteous anger of a queen who saw an enemy within the state, a traitor who placed private interests above the public weal. That there was a deeper motivation, however, is clear from Catherine's actions. One need not accept the details of Tavannes' account of Catherine's meeting with her son on August 4 to recognise the level of her anger. Fearful of what was happening to the state and of her own diminishing influence, she spent her fury on her son:

> I can hardly believe, that after taking so much pains to raise you and to save the crown for you when both Huguenots and Catholics wanted to snatch it away, that after sacrificing myself for you and and taking so many risks that you would recompense me like this. You hide yourself from me, who am your mother, to take council with your enemies. You slip out of these arms which have sustained you in order to lean on those who would like to murder you. I know you are engaged in secret councils with the admiral. You want to catapult yourself into a war with Spain so that your kingdom will become the prey both of Spain and those of the Religion. Now that I have seen this, I ask only one thing: permission to withdraw from court and retire to my birthplace.[12]

Such is Tavannes' account, and while the rhetoric is not obviously fictive, there is no doubt that Catherine argued against the admiral and his thrust towards war. She bolstered her personal vehemence with arguments concerning the welfare of the state. She told Charles that she had heard the English were withdrawing their forces in the Netherlands and that without their support any aggressive action would end in failure. She repeated her well-worn caveats against the admiral, who had already given proof he would sell France for his own interests. Charles, always impressionable, now wavered in his allegiance. On August 9 a full meeting of the royal Council was held. To ease Coligny's mistrust, Charles invited not only statesmen but military men as well—Montpensier, Nevers, Tavannes. Yet despite the admiral's persuasive rhetoric, despite the closely argued report presented by Duplessis-Mornay, a young Huguenot recently returned from the Low Countries, the final decision made by the Council on August 10 was against war with Spain. The admiral, faced with defeat, acknowledged bitterly, "Since advice contrary to mine has prevailed, I have nothing more to say," but then, turning to the queen mother, he was reputed to have added those words which have been variously interpreted as simple regret or threat of future violence: "So, the king has decided not to undertake this war; God grant that another will not come upon him from which he will not be able to withdraw."[13]

Catherine had won. There was to be no war. Yet Coligny continued his agitation. He bitterly resented the Council's decision, not only for political and religious reasons but because of personal pride. He had promised help to his coreligionists, and the king's decision would force him to betray his word. Even during the Council meeting, he had declared he could not break his promise, and now he continued to raise troops and to spend long hours of debate with the vacillating young king. On August 11 the Prince of Orange wrote to his brother, "The admiral has advised me, that despite the defeat of the French in the past, he is again preparing about 12,000 arquebusers and 2,000 horse." And two days later the Venetian ambassador reported, "Three thousand Huguenots have recently gathered at the frontier in order to try to help Mons. . . . They say that the king has forbidden these troop movements, but we feel that he will not be any better obeyed than in the past."[14]

What on one level was a political and religious war between two major powers was, on another, a battle of wills for the possession of the irresolute king. There were even those who maintained that Catherine's intransigence was motivated primarily by her fear that war would curtail her power to govern. Although her motivation was certainly more complex than the desire for personal power, yet the death struggle between Catherine and the admiral cannot be minimised. In such an atmosphere of fear and hatred that union had taken place which history has named the Blood-Red Wedding.

There is always a depressing atmosphere in the days following a great event. The atmosphere in Paris, curious, anxious, hectic before the wedding, had now changed to sullen watching. The tapestries and banners were removed from Notre Dame. Within the cathedral the sickening smell of dead flowers mingled with the odor of torches and stale incense. Stronger than all was the heavy aftersmell of the thousands of sweating bodies that had packed the cathedral to attend the wedding mass. The streets of Paris, always dirty, were doubly so after the feast of wine and meat that had been served to the people in honour of the marriage. Stifling heat continued to oppress the city. Unhealthy mists hung over the bridges and quays. The atmosphere was heavy with an unfulfilled promise of rain.

Parisians were a close-locked group; they appraised strangers coldly and had no desire to share their crowded city with the Huguenot lords from the south. There was resentment in the area round the rue de Béthisy, where the Huguenots were lodged at the expense of the citizens; there was resentment at the Louvre, where many of the king's servants had been displaced to make room for the Huguenot nobility. Among the Huguenots, rumour had it that they had been relegated to one portion of the city so that the Parisians could more easily wreak their vengeance on them; among the Parisians, rumour had it that the Huguenots had massed for some treacherous action. Crowded beyond capacity, quick-tempered, intolerant, Paris was a tinderbox. The spark that kindled it was struck on the morning of August 22.

On that morning a meeting of the king's Council was held. At its conclusion Coligny emerged from the Louvre and, accompanied by a number of Huguenot lords, started towards his house on the rue de Béthisy. On his way down the rue de Poulies, he stopped for a moment to fix his shoe; as he did so, two shots rang out. Although doubled in pain, he nodded towards a window where smoke was streaming, and two of his companions ran to intercept the attacker. The bullets had lodged in Coligny's right hand and left arm. That they were aimed to kill there was no question. They would, no doubt, have hit their mark with perfect accuracy had it not been for that singularly timed and unexpected movement. Bleeding heavily but still in command, Coligny was helped to his house. While a messenger was sent to get the king's physician, Coligny listened to the report of the two men who had tried to apprehend the assassin. When they reached the room, they informed him, they had found it empty, although the smoking gun was still lying on a table. Investigation indicated that the house from which the shots were fired belonged to a Canon Villemur, formerly in the employ of the House of Guise. The would-be assassin was Charles de Louviers, Sieur de Maurevert, a former page of the House of Lorraine.

The name of Guise sounded too often in the tale to pass as mere coincidence.

Within an hour, the court knew of the attempted murder. Charles was informed as he played tennis with Charles de Teligny, the admiral's son-in-law. His reaction was more like that of a petulant child than a devoted friend. "What," he shouted, "Shall I never have peace!"

Catherine was informed of the event as she sat down to dinner. Without changing her expression, she rose silently from the table and retired to her room, where she remained closeted with her son for some time. Her conduct led Zúñiga to report to Philip that the attack on Coligny had been no surprise to her. Such reasoning, however, is illogical. If, in fact, as many of her contemporaries believed, Catherine's fine Italian hand had signed Coligny's death warrant, then the news that the admiral had been wounded was certainly not the news for which she was waiting, as Zúñiga suggests. If anything, she waited for news of the admiral's death. Had the shepherd been killed, the sheep might easily have been scattered. A wounded shepherd was an eventuality for which she could not have been prepared.[15]

Certainly Catherine had reason for wanting Coligny dead. He had already given evidence he would put his religious position before the welfare of his country. She was also jealous of the affection he evoked in her son and of his spiraling power, which inevitably diminished her own. For nine years, since the death of François de Guise, the House of Guise had encouraged her in every way to punish the admiral for his presumed complicity in the duke's death. Spain, too, fearful of what Coligny might accomplish in the Low Countries, had encouraged her to rid the country of such seditious leaders. On August 5 a letter had come from the Papal Nuncio in Madrid, suggesting, "If the Very Christian King intends to purge the kingdom of his enemies, the moment has come. In accord with the King of Spain, he could destroy those who remain, above all, now, while the admiral is at Paris where the people are very devoted to the Catholic religion, and thus it would be very easy to get rid of him forever.''[16] Coligny's assassination would not lack foreign support.

That Catherine was in some way implicated is hard to deny, although the measure of her complicity is difficult to determine. Many of her contemporaries felt she and Anjou were responsible for the plot, with the help of Madame de Nemours, widow of François de Guise. Whatever her implication, however, Catherine never intended the events which actually occurred, for the way in which the plot had literally misfired put them all in jeopardy. As for Charles, after his first expression of petulant anger, his reactions were those of a devoted friend. Ambrose Paré, his personal physician, was sent at once to the rue de Béthisy, and that afternoon, accompanied by his mother, his two brothers, and several Catholic lords, he himself came to visit the admiral.

If Catherine and her favourite, Anjou, were responsible for this attempted murder, the time spent in the admiral's room with the king must have stretched her power to dissemble to the breaking point. Coligny, propped up in bed, pale and drawn from the painful probings Paré had been forced to inflict on him, had never been so powerful. Although both arms were covered with bandages, he was more than ever the king's master. The wounds he had endured had elevated him from controversial statesman to religious martyr. Charles called him Father with deeper affection than before, avowing, "The pain is yours, but the grief is mine." Whatever Charles was later accused of, there seems no reason to doubt his sincerity here.

It is impossible to know how much Charles initially guessed of his mother's complicity. It is unbelievable that he did not have his suspicions. More and more, as the complex burdens of kingship increased, he had revealed a pitiful emotional imbalance, veering from spasmodic action to passivity. Restless, listless, apathetic, he would suddenly throw himself into hours of such violent exercise that he exhausted his small store of energy. Overwhelmingly sensitive on some points, he took abnormal delight in violence and bloodshed, needing the exhilaration of the hunt to stimulate his senses.

What role he played as husband it is difficult to know, for his wife, the gentle, self-effacing Elizabeth of Austria, has left no record. Only three people seem to have exerted a lasting influence on him: his mistress, Marie Touchet; the admiral; and his mother. For the first two he felt a genuine affection; for the latter, a child's ambivalent need to be bound to, yet free from a dominating presence.

By the summer of 1572 the smallest event could tip Charles' delicate balance. How, then, he coped with the suspicion his mother was responsible for the attempted assassination of the man he called Father is impossible to imagine. As for Catherine, not a word or gesture escaped to provide a clue to what she thought during those uncertain hours. She was like a city under siege, all life hidden behind those dark, impenetrable eyes.

The role the queen mother played in the events of the next forty-eight hours continues to be a mystery. Despite the wealth of contemporary accounts dealing with the St. Bartholomew's Day Massacre, few are based on anything more solid than hearsay, a hearsay made increasingly unreliable by the violent emotional bias of its recorders: Catholics, who saw the events as coming from the avenging hand of God, manifesting at last His divine wrath against heretics, or Huguenots, who inveighed against the most monstrous and cruel betrayal ever to have taken place since the beginning of the world. On one point, however, even the most divergent accounts agreed: The shadowy figure who set the enormous machine in motion was the Florentine woman—the Italian shopkeeper who had shown them time and again how she could shift and promise and then shift again. The legend of the sinister, unscrupulous, but powerful queen, who had brought to France a full Italian heritage of duplicity, had already taken shape.

Less than a year before she had welcomed the admiral to Blois, assuring him they could work together for the welfare of the state; now there seemed little doubt she had instigated his death, manipulating the mortal hatred of the Guises for her own purposes. But Coligny had not died, and on the evening of August 22 it seemed probable he would recover. The prospect was terrifying, for his power would be enhanced a hundred times by this abortive attempt on his life.

Already Navarre and Condé, surrounded by their angry followers, had been to the king to demand justice. Charles, deeply moved, assured them justice would be done, even offering to have the admiral moved to the Louvre to guarantee his safety. The offer was rejected out of hand, for to the Huguenots the Louvre seemed more dangerous than the public streets. They would stay where they were, they assured the king, who then promised them a guard for Coligny's house. Although tension gripped Paris, no serious incident had yet occurred, and Friday night, we are led to believe, passed quietly.

What secret drama was played between the wounding of the admiral on Friday morning and the beginning of the wholesale massacre in the early hours of Sunday has never been made clear. Time, events, characters shift and change, according to their narrators, slipping in and out, moving beyond historical fact into a surreal drama where the events are less clear than the atmosphere created by them.

How was the actual massacre planned, and by whom? How much, indeed, of the terrible events of August 24 was planned, and how much the result of blood lust and mob violence? Had there been a secret meeting in the cool green gardens of the Tuileries, presided over by Catherine, a squat dark figure, surrounded by her sinister Italians (Gondi, Birague, Nevers) and her beloved son Anjou? Was it here that the "spy" Bouchevannes came to inform them of what had been done at the Huguenot councils, of plans of reprisals against the royal family and the leaders of the kingdom? And was it here, consequently, that the plot to rid the kingdom of the Huguenot leaders was devised? The latter is attested to by more than legend, for in the collection of edicts and ordinances preserved from this period, one finds an item for the night of August 23 which reads "Royal order taken in secret council attended by the Queen Mother, the two brothers of the king, and several other private councillors which ordered the Massacre of St. Bartholomew."[17]

The legend is consistent in maintaining that the king was never part of the original planning. Charles, it maintained, was not brought into the plot until late Saturday night, when Catherine and her councillors presented it to him as a *fait accompli*. The image of the king in those last hours before the massacre is that of a puppet, a poor will-less creature, coerced by the mother he both feared and needed. Yet ultimately, it was not Catherine who convinced Charles but Albert de Gondi, who had once been his tutor. To the king's shocked refusal to order the admiral's death, Gondi responded by uncovering the "Huguenot plot" against the royal family. The thin, sallow face with its tired, veined eyes turned from one to another for contradiction, but instead they affirmed Gondi's intelligence. Charles was no match for them. And, says the legend, in a moment of fury and despair, he cried out, "God's death, kill them. Kill them all, so that none may come back to blame me," as he ran from the room, slamming the door behind him.

It is a dark and terrible scene: the room heavy with mists off the Seine and the acrid odor of burning candles; the young king livid with fear and exhaustion; his rival brother, Anjou, handsome and confident; his mother shrouded in malevolence and supported by her secret councillors. The truth is undoubtedly far less lurid than the legend, yet it is murky enough. In fact, Charles did give the orders which put the machinery of death into action. The mayor was sent for and warned that the Huguenots were planning an uprising. He was to take the proper measures to secure the city. The gates of Paris were closed, the boats chained along the river, the municipal guard alerted. The signal for the attack against the Huguenot leaders was to be the tolling of the bell of the church of St. Germain-l'Auxerrois, which had formerly called the royal family to prayer. It is not clear what hour had been decided on, but most sources indicate the massacre began long before dawn.

Meanwhile, the Duc de Guise was given the task of killing the man who had so inadvertently escaped his first efforts. In the rue de Béthisy, the guard posted by Navarre was easily hacked down and despite the efforts of Coligny's servants to barricade the door, a half dozen men of the Guise household gained access to the admiral. Defenceless, dressed only in his nightdress, with his arms hanging useless at his sides, he was run through in a moment. It took a little longer to toss him out of the window into the courtyard, where Guise and his uncle Aumale were waiting, for one of his bandaged hands had grasped convulsively at the windowsill and had to be pried loose. Just a few days before Coligny had written his young wife, "I would far prefer to be with you than to stay here any longer . . . but one must put the public good ahead of one's private interests. . . . Do not worry, for I assure you . . . I will do nothing that could cause a quarrel."[18] He had forgotten—or perhaps he had never sufficiently understood— that to be Coligny was in itself sufficient cause.

What happened after Coligny's death has been rehearsed in hundreds of accounts. The years of tension exploded, igniting the city in a wave of destruction that fed upon itself. Paris engaged in twenty-four hours of unparalleled carnage. The Holy Massacre had begun. Those closest to the admiral had no time to mourn, for they were at once dragged from their houses and run through in the streets. The dark, narrow alleys with their unexpected turns were ideal for the hunt, and as the Huguenots stumbled from their houses seeking some means of escape, they were clubbed down in the streets or dragged half-dead to the Seine.

Whole families lay together in the first light of dawn, for age or sex was no consideration. By noon the streets in some places were clogged with bodies and the Seine streaked with patches of blood. The captains had lost all control. Paris had become a devouring animal: cruel, irrational, uncontrolled. In terror, the mayor, Le Charron, made his way to the Louvre, begging that some action be taken to quell the mob. With a meaningless gesture, the king ordered that "all murders, looting, plundering, and rebellion be stopped at once."

Charles scarcely knew what he did during those nightmare hours, for he, too, had been infected with bloodlust. Since many of the Huguenot noblemen had been lodged at the Louvre for Navarre's wedding, the Louvre was to suffer its own carnage. No sooner had the *Marie* sounded than Navarre and Condé were disarmed and brought under guard to the king's chambers. As they waited, their companions were led systematically into the courtyard, where they were murdered with cold brutality by the Swiss Guard. Navarre and Condé, because of their position, were offered an alternative: death or the mass—and given three days to come to their decision.

By nightfall an exhausted Paris had grown quiet, although sporadic killing and looting were to continue well into the next day. As the still evening air settled over the city, the stench of dead bodies became unbearable. The signs of destruction were everywhere. Looted shops, some half-burned, stood empty, windows broken, doors swinging useless on their hinges. The Seine, now murky with blood, was dotted with bodies lying grotesquely along its banks. Corpses lay everywhere, many of them naked, for thieves had stripped them as soon as they fell. Paris was a morgue. It was the work of a people gone mad, a work from which France would not recover for years.

Even before the carnage was over, the responsibility for it was being laid at the queen mother's door. This was the work of the Florentine. Reared in the tradition of the bloody and treacherous Sicilian Vespers, she had now unleashed the Matins of Paris. This was the fruit of those conferences held at Bayonne seven years before. All those years she had waited and schemed until every detail was in place and she had only to order the ringing of the tocsin. This was the second Jezebel, subtle, evil, cruel. "The first one ruined Israel: The other has ruined France," ran a popular ballad. "By one the prophets consecrated to God were massacred; by the other, a hundred thousand of those who followed the Gospel were done to death."[19]

Whatever part Catherine played in the massacre, it seems clear she cannot be condemned for premeditation. Those who maintained that the massacre had been planned during the conferences of Bayonne reveal how little they understood the queen mother. Catherine was never a long-range planner. She had the mind and skill of an opportunist, alert to seize whatever chance presented itself. Sometimes her impulses were successful; frequently she had cause to regret them. It was fear rather than premeditated treachery that motivated her during those August days. Patient and persevering, she could not sustain fear. It unnerved her and made her foolish, often plunging her into ill-conceived and irresolute action. The attack on the admiral had tragically misfired, and terrified of the chain of events it might trigger, she had taken a desperate offensive.

Now at the Louvre she was left with the tragic aftermath. The years she had spent in arguing for whatever form of toleration would keep France at peace were all wasted. The symbolic wedding of Margot and Navarre, for which she had worked so unremittingly, now appeared as unforgivable duplicity. Navarre and Condé, still under guard, continued to protest this outrageous betrayal. In the courtyard the bodies had begun to stink. The king, for whose sake, she declared, she had undertaken her decision, could provide her with no support. The horror of the massacre had tumbled him beyond the borders of rationality. Lost in guilt and terror, he paced the Louvre in aimless rage, giving orders that could not be obeyed.

By Monday night some semblance of order had been restored to Paris. Catherine, however, was keenly aware that bringing the Parisians under control was only the first and smallest step in coping with the results of the massacre. Before her lay the enormous task of providing for the government of France and the monarchs of Europe a plausible explanation for the events of the day which would soon be called Bloody Sunday.

Chapter X

It did not take long for the news of the Paris massacre to travel. Variously described, variously interpreted, it was brought east into Germany, south to Spain, to Venice, to Rome. Théodore de Bèze received the news in Geneva. He was shocked beyond speech, for with Coligny reestablished at Charles' right hand and Navarre married to the king's sister, he had anticipated a period of toleration and peace. There had been half a dozen times during the prolonged religious wars when such a bloody deed had been anticipated—but not now. Shaken by sorrow and fear for the future, Bèze wrote to a coreligionist at Heidelberg: "These few lines that I write you, dearest brother, are for you and for all our friends. We are in mourning and lamentation. May God have pity on us. How often I have predicted this and how often I have worked to avert it. . . . Pray for the others among us who await a like fate."[1]

Bèze was right in assuming the massacre was not over. Long after Paris had returned to order, the carnage in the provinces continued. Toulouse, Bourges, Mons, Orléans all were to bear their bloody witness. As late as October 19 Filippe Cavriana wrote to Florence of the "continual plundering and persecution" of the Huguenots. Although he reported that Charles "was satisfied with the justice done to the leaders and wished to pardon the others," the king's will was not heavy enough to turn the scales. "The fury of the people has been unleashed," concluded Cavriana, "and thus egged on by cupidity for the goods of others as well as disdain for the edict, they have killed many and continue to kill them still."[2] Even the king's governors, men ostensibly loyal to the crown, used the prevailing chaos to wreak their own vengeance in the name of justice.

Bèze had good cause to tremble, yet the news he received in early October wounded him more deeply than the massacre itself: Navarre and Condé, the two young Huguenot leaders, had abjured their heresy and returned to the bosom of Rome. To the zealots of Geneva, such perfidy was unthinkable, but to the two young princes, confined and terrorised in the Louvre, it appeared the only sensible course. Perhaps even this harsh choice might have been denied them had it not been for Navarre's recent marriage to Marguerite and Catherine's pragmatism, which discerned that Navarre would be far more use to her alive than dead.

It was, nonetheless, a bitter and humiliating choice and one that, at the beginning, Condé could not stomach. Catherine, in an attempt to sweeten its terms, had dissuaded Charles from his threats and bullyings and instead had offered the princes position, wealth, influence if they would repent and return to the Roman Church. Actually, the princes found Charles' threats easier to handle than Catherine's bribes, for they wanted it clear to all that this was a forced conversion for which they could not be held responsible. Even the Spanish ambassador acknowledged this coercion and wrote to Philip: "As far as I am concerned, it seems that even if they wished they could not manifest any other attitude, for they are so dominated by these rulers."[3]

Condé's original cries of "Death rather than Rome" soon died away, and Navarre, who, according to the Tuscan ambassador Petrucci, "has always spoken as gently as a little lamb," acknowledged that the little lamb was ready to be admitted into the fold of Peter "and to serve the king in whatever way he can."[4] His request for a learned theologian to instruct him had been granted at once, and Hugues Sureau du Rosier—well known as a relapsed Huguenot minister—was brought from Orléans for the task. It was a peremptory instruction, however, for Charles was determined that the public recantation be incorporated into the formal celebration of St. Michael's Day.

On September 29, less than six weeks since he had been married before the doors of Notre Dame—unworthy to enter the sacred precincts—Navarre was led to a place near the high altar and close to the king himself. It was an ironic twist to find himself now clothed in white, his red velvet cloak amply studded with seed pearls, taking part in ceremonies he had been taught to abominate. Next to him walked Condé, despite all his protests, also caught up in the web of polity. As he walked to the altar, bearing his gift for the offertory procession, Catherine watched him closely. She had observed Condé twitch his cloak in anger, seen him bring his Protestant book of hours out of his long full sleeve in silent protest, but in Navarre's performance she could find no flaw. Politic and debonair, he had much of the charm—and perhaps the vacillation—of Antoine, his father. There seemed little of Jeanne d'Albret in this young man who could capitulate so easily. He seemed to bear no resentment for the events that had taken place in Paris only a month before; he seemed, indeed, hardly to recall them, although they had cost him, in one blow, all his dearest friends. The Venetian ambassador Correro had once warned that the young prince of Béarn "may well become the scourge of our time," but there was little the queen mother could discern in the thin, wiry young man offering his gifts at the altar to bear witness to such testimony.[5] He seemed no more than another weak Bourbon to be kept on leash until he might be put to practical use. Nevertheless, it was no small victory. Navarre, for all his external splendour, was in chains, and when he turned and bowed to her, as he returned to his place, those nearest heard the queen mother laugh aloud in triumph.

It was a triumph hardly won. Many things had gone wrong in those days following Bloody Sunday, and Catherine was not a bloody woman. She was not made of the stuff of Nero or Caligula, although Paris would soon be reading a pamphlet accusing her of being more cruel than either.[6] She was not even a Clytemnestra. If she was a strong woman, it was a strength she had learned for her own survival and that of her sons. In such interests, torture and death were sometimes necessary. But this time there had been too much death—too many bodies, too much blood. Paris should never have been turned into a charnel house. But if Catherine had the Florentine aversion for excess, she also had the Florentine talent for practical diplomacy. The massacre was now history; there was nothing she could do to change it. Her duty was clearly to paint the best possible face on a damning situation.

Charles could not recover from Bloody Sunday. No matter what his role in the massacre, no matter what his hostility towards his Huguenot subjects, he had never intended the full results of his deed. He had been told that a little bloodletting in a diseased member would strengthen the whole body, and he had believed it. Now, as he read his ambassadors' reports from Rome and Venice, Austria and Spain, he recognised that he had weakened his kingdom, not strengthened it. Charles, even at his peak, had never been politically adroit; in September, 1572, he was obviously no match for the task before him. It was Catherine who must assume the responsibility for royal decisions.

The initial explanation—that the massacre had stemmed from a feud between the warring houses of Châtillon and Montmorency—was discarded almost immediately. And when on August 26, Charles appeared before the Parlement, he assumed the full responsibility for the massacre, explaining that his action had been the only feasible course to defeat the Huguenot plot to murder the king, the queen mother, and the royal brothers. In Catholic courts (where Catherine expected no difficulty) such a tale would simply portray the perfidy and cruelty of the Huguenots in more lurid colours; in Protestant courts, such as Germany and England, the explanation would skirt the subject of religion and focus on the issue of royal authority and the crime of regicide. Neither England nor the German princes, for all their Protestant sympathies, could look tolerantly on the intended crime of lèse majesté. Thus, the letter Charles wrote to his agent Gaspard de Schomberg in Germany during the second week of September emphasised that the real explanation for the events in France had been "the wicked conspiracy which they had planned against my own person and against the queen my mother, my brothers and against my state."[7]

Yet the carefully worded letters from the queen mother and her son failed to convince either Protestant or Catholic sovereigns. Charles' father-in-law, the emperor Maximilian, summed up the feelings of many when he murmured,

"Too bloody, too bloody," adding, "When one wants to accomplish something, one can always find pretexts."[8] From Venice, Arnauld du Ferrier, one of France's most experienced and trusted diplomats, wrote with a candour few would have had the courage to use to the queen mother: "It is an undeniable truth that the massacres have spread throughout France, not only against the admiral and the other leaders of the Religion, but also against many poor innocent people, and this has very strongly moved and even altered the sentiments of those who were formerly devoted to your crown." Sometime later he wrote again, warning Catherine that events in Paris might cause Charles to lose the nomination for the Holy Roman Empire and, even more, had already diminished Anjou's chances for the throne of Poland—a throne Catherine had long been coveting for her second son.[9]

From Rome, however, came unequivocal praise. In the Eternal City, intolerance of heresy had become the dominant criterion for Christian kings, and Charles, sometimes suspect for his leniency, had now proved his right to his title as Most Christian King. The messenger who had brought the news to Rome had been highly praised, and the Pope had declared without hesitation: "Charles, King of France, holds his title as Most Christian not simply as an ancient title that belongs to his inheritance but with a new right which he has recently acquired and which he merits for destroying the heretics, the enemies of Christ."[10]

Well aware of Rome's preoccupation with heresy, Charles had, in his letter to Ferals, emphasised the religious motivation, an emphasis even more strongly underscored by the Duc de Montpensier, who had written to the Pope, praising Charles' "determination to annihilate all this scum." Gregory was quick to reply that he found the deed "a hundred times more pleasing than fifty victories like Lepanto."[11] Such praise as Rome's, however, carried a sting in its tail, and Catherine and Charles found themselves more in peril from praise than they had been from blame. Gregory's unqualified approval of the massacre soon led to the rumour that the Catholic powers (France, Spain, the Holy Roman Empire), led by Rome, were engaged in a full-scale conspiracy to exterminate heresy throughout Europe. The thought made Catherine blanch. France could ill afford the enmity with England such rumour would engender. She hoped to close the wounds caused by the massacre, not open them further.

Spain, like Rome, expressed unqualified praise for the events of August. "For me, it is the best and most joyous news I could receive at present," Philip had written. Jean de Vivonne, Sieur de St. Gouard, the French ambassador at Madrid, had reaffirmed Philip's own words. "Although of all the princes in the world he is most able to dissimulate," he had written to the queen mother, "yet he could not hide his pleasure in receiving news of this."[12] Catherine soon found, however, that at the court of Madrid she was being credited with far more than she could safely accept: She found herself accorded the dangerous quality of premeditation. Although she had written to Philip a few days after the massacre,

asking him to rejoice with her that "by the grace of God" they had "been preserved" from the "wicked hands" of those "evil rebels," Zúñiga was writing his
master a somewhat different story. Agreeing that most of what had been done in
Paris might have been done on the spur of the moment (*repentino*), yet he maintained the assassination of the admiral had been deliberate (*caso pensando*).[13] He
was loath to accept Catherine's explanation of simple self-defence.

On September 12 Zúñiga had an audience the queen mother found distinctly
disconcerting. He assured her that both Philip and the Duke of Alba were very
pleased that she had "put into operation" what they had "discussed at
Bayonne."[14] It could hardly have been a more damaging statement, for nothing
would discredit France more dangerously with Elizabeth and the German
princes—indeed with many Catholic princes—than the insinuation that the
bloody events of August had been in planning since the Bayonne conferences
more than seven years before. It was becoming more obvious what Du Ferrier
had meant when he had written to her in exasperation, asking how she could have
engaged in an action so contrary to her own interests and so apt for augmenting
the power of the king of Spain. To Du Ferrier's seasoned diplomatic experience,
Philip's enmity was far less dangerous than his "friendship." Even Cavriana,
less astute than Du Ferrier, had tempered his initial enthusiasm and was now seeing the less triumphant side of the coin. Writing to the Grand Duke of Florence,
he commented, "Spain is growing at our expense," adding, "Philip fills me with
distrust."[15]

Despite the distrust Philip engendered, there was nothing false in his expression of joy. The events in Paris had indeed, as he had written to Catherine, filled
him with happiness for without lifting his diplomatic finger, he now found himself in a most strategic position. Every despatch from France pleased him more.
Zúñiga reported that Charles seemed ill and restless, that both he and his mother
were "unquiet," adding, "Even should they find their table set, yet they would
not feel sufficiently confident to take their places at it."[16] For the young ruler of
France, Philip felt a growing disdain.

Charles, increasingly aware of how badly the news of the massacre was being
received, continued to shift his position in an effort to find creditable ground for
his action. One explanation was given to Philip, another to the Pope, a third to
Elizabeth and the German princes. It was not such dissembling that evoked
Philip's contempt, but that the dissembling was done so poorly. With every effort
to curry favour, Charles' position became more tenuous, and soon Zúñiga reported to his sovereign that he need not fear any alliance Charles tried to make, for he
was no longer trusted anywhere.

Philip now saw an unparalleled opportunity for a rupture between England and
France which could culminate in his own successful conquest of England. Tri-
umphantly, he wrote on the margin of a document concerning such an action:
"Yes, stir up the English against the French. Very good. I approve of this."

Shortly afterwards he wrote at greater length: "What really matters and what I want is the power to unite all Christian princes against England, with the goal of subjecting this island to the Catholic faith, exterminating heresy and compelling England to return to our holy and age-old religion; and towards this end, I will work fully."[17]

Philip's goal—to create trouble between England and France—needed little outside assistance. The massacre had done its work well. When, on August 26, Walsingham was summoned to court, it was the first time he had dared emerge from his rooms since the alarm had sounded more than forty-eight hours before. During those two days he had stayed behind bolted doors, opening them only to admit the stream of English refugees whose only safety lay in diplomatic immunity. When, on Tuesday morning, he followed a royal escort through the streets of Paris, where naked and mangled bodies still lay, he attempted to assess the results of such carnage for Anglo-French relations and to discover his own best diplomatic posture.

Once in the royal audience chamber, he listened in silence to Charles' speech, in which the religious element was carefully precluded and emphasis placed on the treachery and rebellion plotted by the "rebel" Huguenots against the royal family. The story did not ring entirely true to English ears, but Walsingham said little, aware he stood on shaky ground until he received instructions from Elizabeth. He lodged his complaint concerning the several English who had been killed in the massacre, he accepted Charles' expression of regret, and he returned home to write his report to the queen.

In the succeeding weeks, Walsingham's mistrust of the king's explanation grew, as the cruelty continued—less fanatically, less overtly, but still Huguenots continued to be knifed or strangled, their possessions seized, their homes sacked. What he saw now was not simply the destruction of a sect, but the ruin of a country. "Which manner of proceeding," he wrote to Elizabeth, "is by the Catholics themselves utterly condemned, who desire to depart hence out of this country, to quit themselves of this strange kind of Government, for they see here that none can assure themselves of either goods or life."[18]

In England, meanwhile, Fénelon waited anxiously for instructions from Paris, outlining what he should say to Elizabeth. London was burning with rumour, but Fénelon could say nothing until he had received his official instructions. Insulted, baited, threatened, he wrote desperately to the French court, "You would not believe how greatly moved everyone here is by this news . . . interpreting it diversely according to their own particular prejudices rather than according to the truth." When, at last, his official instructions did arrive, he was left to cool his heels while Elizabeth, determined to make a proper show of her anger, refused to give him audience. When, finally, she granted his request, she did nothing to alleviate his discomfit. "I found her in her private chamber," wrote Fénelon,

"accompanied by several of the lords of her Council and some of the principal
women of the court, all in great silence."[19]

Into that silence, Fénelon advanced. Elizabeth was in heavy mourning, as
were her lords and ladies. She did not speak, nor did she make any gesture of
welcome. Fénelon was cast less in the role of ambassador than of a murderer
come to ask pardon of the family he had injured. When, finally, the queen spoke,
it was not in anger, as he had expected, but in a tone "grave and sad," to ask
him, as he wrote later to France, "if it were possible that she should have heard
such strange news as that which was being made public about a prince whom she
had so loved and honoured and in whom she had put more trust than in all the rest
of the world."

Anger would have been easier to cope with, but Fénelon did his best, following his instructions, explaining the "wicked plot" against the royal family, the
necessity for immediate action, the sorrow of the king that the innocent had had
to suffer. When the queen shook her head and said she preferred punishment to
come through the normal channels of justice, he answered quickly, as he later
wrote to the king, "I begged her to consider that this was to hold the wolf by the
ears . . . that the irresolution of a single hour was enough to destroy your life
and those around you. . . .The suddenness of the danger did not leave the king
a single hour of reflection," explained the ambassador. "The urgent necessity
forced him to sacrifice the admiral's life in order to save his own." But he could
tell that the English ears that listened to his explanation were far from
convinced.[20] Elizabeth had no intention of absolving France so easily. Nor, despite what she might say in public, had she any intention of a complete diplomatic rupture. The stronger she felt the power of Spain, the more she needed France
to help her in her life struggle against the Catholic king.

Meanwhile, however, she intended to let the vacillating young king and his
Florentine mother squirm a bit before she made peace.

The day after Fénelon's audience Elizabeth had Burghley write to Walsingham, instructing him:

> And you may also say unto her [the queen mother], that she being of such wis-
> dom as she is, and having such experience as she had of the extreme hatred of the
> factions there against the Admiral, did not at the first, take order that the informa-
> tions should be examined and the Admiral and others of his party suspected,
> charged, tried, and so by order of justice proceeded, which had been honourable to
> the King, and good in the sight of God, and so either the guilty had duly suffered,
> or the innocent blood had been saved.[21]

Catherine, however, refused to be intimidated, and when, the following week,
Walsingham manifested shocked surprise that the decision had been taken to
forbid the Huguenots the right to practise their religion, she replied tartly, "Even

as your mistress suffereth the Catholiques of England." Catherine was well aware Elizabeth would not capitulate until it was to her advantage. Fénelon's pessimistic assessment of the situation in England came as no surprise. "I assure you, Madame," the ambassador had written, "that this recent accident . . . has made so deep a wound that it will take a most skilful surgeon and a most excellent balme to effect any immediate cure."[22]

Catherine, however, with her unquenchable optimism, was certain she had at hand just such an "excellent balme," in the person of her youngest son, François, Duc d'Alençon. When, the preceding January, marriage negotiations between Elizabeth and Anjou had broken off, Catherine had been quick to suggest that Anjou's younger brother might be even more to the Queen of England's taste. So anxious was she that her youngest son be considered that the English secretary Killigrew reported, with some amusement, she had stopped him during a court masque to assure him Alençon's living was greater than Anjou's. By mid-January Sir Thomas Smith had reached the conclusion such a match might be worth investigating and he had written to Burghley that Alençon was as rich in land and goods as Anjou, not so "tall and fair," but neither so "obstinate, papistical and restive like a mule. . . . As for getting of children," they had assured him that he is "more apt than the other."[23] Scarcely a week later Walsingham, never one to deal in false optimism, wrote encouragingly that if Elizabeth were seriously interested, he thought it possible to get Alençon to England on a visit.

The question of this visit was not immediately pursued. During the first months of 1572 Catherine had been engaged in those tooth-and-nail conferences with Jeanne d'Albret and had let her son's marriage wait upon her daughter's. To someone of less determination, the Paris massacre would have sounded the knell of such aspirations, but to Catherine, failure was never more than a temporary state. While she searched for more solid excuses for the massacre, she attempted to resume negotiations for a marriage between Elizabeth and Alençon. Even Elizabeth, gifted though she was with a certain brash determination, was startled by the queen mother's temerity. On September 28 she wrote to Walsingham: "But yet the King to destroy and utterly root out of his Realm all those of that Religion that we profess, and to desire us in marriage for his brother, must needs seem unto us at the first, a thing very repugnant in itself."

Catherine, nonetheless, won her point, for "repugnant" as Elizabeth avowed to find the proposal, she did not entirely reject it. Walsingham, meanwhile, was growing increasingly sceptical of these "fair speeches and friendly offers," concluding that he found it safer to have the French for enemies.[24] Yet despite Walsingham's misgivings, the wedge had been inserted, and the queen mother lost no time in driving it more deeply.

That same month Albert de Gondi, that "subtle Florentine," in whom Catherine placed such confidence, was sent to England with the three-pronged mission of asking Elizabeth to be godmother to Charles' newborn daughter, of concluding a treaty of friendship, and, if possible, of negotiating a loan. That he was also to learn what he could about Elizabeth's intentions to marry goes without saying.

Although Gondi was never a popular figure in France—Brantôme, among others, characterised him as "subtle, crafty, corrupt"—Elizabeth found him both intelligent and impressive.[25] Impressive he most certainly was, for he travelled with a magnificence few royal princes could exceed. "It is enough to make those laugh in their sleeves who knew the mother and father of this ambassador," wrote a hostile contemporary; but Elizabeth was charmed, found him a brilliant asset to her court assembled at Canterbury, and, when Gondi returned to France, it was with the Queen of England's renewed friendship, as well as her promise to act as godmother for the infant princess, Elizabeth-Marie. That he had not been able to procure a loan was unimportant compared to the offer of friendship which left the door open for further marriage negotiations.

Earlier in the month Catherine had instructed Fénelon to assure Elizabeth that Alençon remained her "faithful servant" and that both she and the king wished to deal with Elizabeth as sincerely and directly as ever, adding that "the death of the admiral and his adherents has done nothing to change this in any way." She continued, almost abruptly, with plans for bringing Alençon and Elizabeth face to face, suggesting that Elizabeth travel to Dover while she and Alençon would go to Calais or Boulogne and then, on some "fair day," arrange to meet at sea.[26] Elizabeth did not reply, and the proposed meeting never took place.

It is impossible to conjecture how the lines of history might have changed had Gloriana met the young man whom Catherine intended to bring in tow. Certainly, she would not have been impressed by his physical appearance. If anything, he looked younger than his eighteen years—Elizabeth herself was nearing forty. Alençon was already an embarrassment to the elegance of the French court. Baptised Hercule, he was mercifully delivered of his pretentious name following the death of his older brother François to become, in turn, another François. If we can believe his court companion the Comte de Turenne, he had in his childhood been personable enough—"dark like the Medici," with a certain Medici charm, but with his father's skill in games and tourneys in which he often worsted his brothers, Charles and Henri. "A gentle spirit," Turenne continued, "hating every form of evil and never showing the slightest anger."[27]

When he emerged from his chamber after a dangerous bout with smallpox, there was little left of the promising young prince. His appearance was totally changed: His face was deeply pitted, his eyes bloodshot and rheumy, his voice thin and reedy, and his nose almost doubled in size—"more fit to be drawn with a pencil than a pen," as one of the English agents graphically expressed it.[28] His spirit, too, had undergone a profound change. It is little to be wondered at, for when Alençon rose from his bed, he found he no longer had a part to play in that world in which handsome faces and virile bodies were given first prize.

He woke to find himself weak, graceless, and marvellously ugly. As the youngest of an aspiring family he had always been the least important; until now he had had sufficient confidence to master his disadvantages. Sometime earlier the Venetian ambassador Michieli, had written: "The Duke of Alençon is very young, but he has more grace and style than the others and a very good mind." Now he commented disapprovingly, "They make him a laughingstock."[29] No Valois could brook ridicule, least of all Alençon, who had felt its sting so suddenly. There had been no preparation for this change in his fortune, and he found his instinctive refuge in withdrawal. "He is a very silent person," wrote Cavalli, "nor is it easy to know what he thinks."[30]

This baffling reticence on the part of her youngest the queen mother found more difficult to cope with than his ugliness or his increasing irritability. Perhaps she feared Cavalli's assessment might be close to the mark. "It is said that he dissimulates an immeasurable ambition,"[31] the Florentine wrote. Catherine wanted her children to be ambitious—her most bitter disappointment was that often they did not seem ambitious enough—but she never wanted them to be independent. And Alençon, of all her children, did not need his mother.

Catherine was always passionately proud of her children, perhaps because they were the only proof she had of her own worth. When at fourteen she had been married to Henri de Valois, she knew that she had been married into France to beget children for France. The awkward adolescent who had brought her to bed had done so out of no love for her, but because his father, François, and her uncle Leo had deemed it profitable for their respective kingdoms. It was her womb that had been of value in their eyes. The years of her childlessness she would never forget, those ten long years when she had endured the practises of doctors and soothsayers and magic spells—and all to no avail. It is no wonder that when, in 1543, her first son was born, she felt a surge of triumph that coloured her whole life. Her maternity had been her victory, and it remained so until her death. She lived her children's lives because their lives were her own. In her, *l'affetto di signoreggiare* was more than a drive; it was a maternal vocation. Alençon, more than all her other children, was to place a checkmate on that vocation.

Even in the first months of the marriage negotiations with England, Alençon did not leave things in Catherine's hands; instead, he engaged in that secret diplomacy that was to mark his short life and, ultimately, bring him to his ruin. Alençon, while overtly accepting his mother's assistance, played his own game behind her back. Even while Gondi was reporting on his successful embassy to England, Alençon was sending an envoy of his own.

From the beginning, there is something ludicrous in the negotiations between Elizabeth and Alençon; it is more than a question of disparity of age, more than the ugliness of the intended bridegroom. The impression is that of real people in a make-believe setting. It seems more a sophisticated game than the business of reality. It is highly probable that for Gloriana it was never more than a game—never a game played in simple fun or in mere personal vanity, but a game with the exorbitant stakes of political power. It was Alençon's most suicidal fault to be in deadly earnest. Alençon, for all his chicanery, all his plotting and backstairs diplomacy, was, to his own peril, very easy to read.

The man Alençon sent to represent him with Elizabeth in December, 1572, indicated from the beginning the colouring the affair was to have. The Sieur de Maisonfleur had neither the vision to perceive nor the instruments to counter Elizabeth's cool pragmatism. He was a Huguenot who, following his narrow escape on St. Bartholomew's Day, had become fanatical in his religious dreams. His rhetoric was that of high-flown religious romanticism: Alençon was to be the Messiah, the new Moses, leading his people from the Promised Land, and Elizabeth, of course, was to be at his right hand. He was enamoured with himself in the role of secret agent, creating an unnecessary—and farcical—aura of suspense and mystery. It was Maisonfleur who provided the actors in the drama with their romantic names: Alençon as Don Lucidor; Elizabeth as Madame de Lisle; and Catherine, the villain of the piece, as Madame Serpente.

In this drama of religious chivalry, Maisonfleur saw himself as prime mover. When Elizabeth hesitated, he chastised her lack of moral purpose. "It were expedient, Madame," he once wrote, "that you thought less of this mere corporeal beauty, provided that the service of God be done." When Alençon hesitated, he admonished him with the thought that only he had the power to make Elizabeth overcome her distrust of France. "It is impossible to tell you the extreme distrust of Mde de Lisle in this matter. She has been so persuaded that the whole affair is a manoeuvre of Mde de la Serpente that it is almost impossible to make her lose this apprehension; for she says she has so often been deceived by all the race that she can no more put faith in aught that cometh from that quarter. . . . Come, then, Signor Lucidor!"[32]

But Signor Lucidor continued to hesitate, perhaps because he feared that Elizabeth might indeed repudiate him for his lack of that "mere corporeal beauty" which Maisonfleur dismissed so cavalierly, even more, perhaps, because he recognised that the clandestine discussions he had initiated without royal consent could never end with the marriage of two great European powers. If his relations with Elizabeth were to be anything more than a flirtation, there would have to be official negotiations.

Throughout Maisonfleur's "secret" negotiations, Catherine had charted her own course and not without success. Towards the end of the year she had instructed Fénelon to assure Elizabeth that Alençon continued to be her "devoted servant," describing enthusiastically his passage into manhood: "He has become very big and strong, so that now he is completely a man . . . he has changed very much from the time that she said that he would be taken for her son."[33] The following month she wrote to Worcester, who was to represent Elizabeth at the baptism of Charles' infant daughter, explaining that Alençon could not be present because he was engaged in the siege of La Rochelle, against the Huguenots, and then continuing, "He is very much changed—and for the best— since my Lord Lincoln came to France; his face looks much better and his beard is beginning to grow. He is as tall as his two older brothers. At the siege where his duty has called him, he is learning to command." Alençon's military skill failed to impress Worcester, who, on meeting Catherine, admonished her: "It is annoying that the King has employed him in a war against his own subjects. It would have been much better for him not to go; this would have been taken in better part by our Queen and, indeed, throughout England."[34]

Undaunted, the queen mother resumed negotiations through normal diplomatic channels and on February 5 wrote to her ambassador in England: "I beg you not to lose a single opportunity which you think could advance this matter, for, as I have written to you many times before, you will thereby do a very great service to this crown and to me in particular, as well as to my son, the Duc d'Alençon."[35] Throughout the spring of 1573 the game continued, with Catherine and Elizabeth now firmly established in the players' chairs. Although it was obvious Catherine intended to be the aggressor, all her attacks only left Elizabeth the stronger.

In this, as in so many other ventures, both diplomatic and military, Elizabeth gained the victory by the simple expedient of waiting. Catherine filled the time with a flurry of protests: Age, surely, need not be an issue now that Alençon had grown into manhood, nor should cult be an obstacle, for, she promised Walsingham towards the end of March, "My son will not exercise our religion except in private and with his most intimate servants, who are also French." As for the other reason that she had heard rumoured: She was certain that Elizabeth was far "too wise and prudent" to marry for "a handsome face," rather than for the good of her affairs. It was precisely this point, however, which Elizabeth returned to repeatedly in her instructions to Walsingham. She found Alençon's disfigurement "because of the smallpox" a "major difficulty." Maisonfleur's argument, that she "ought to be thankful for the advantages she has over him in beauty and wit," fell on deaf ears.[36]

On one point, Elizabeth was immoveable: She would accept no man for her husband unless she had seen him first. Although Catherine's former effort to have such an encounter take place had failed, she was eager to try again, and towards the end of April she wrote to Elizabeth that Alençon had already asked for a passport for England, "so that he may kiss your hands and make himself known to you just as he is."[37] With Alençon almost on her doorstep, however, Elizabeth once again withdrew, as she would later do in so many similar situations. She wrote Catherine in mid-May, cautioning that such an interview was not to be taken as a final settlement. Perhaps, she concluded, it might be better for Alençon to wait until a more definite arrangement could be made. But Catherine, nev-

er more intransigent than where the futures of her children were concerned, refused to accept Elizabeth's position and answered, almost humbly, that indeed
they in France would not be offended should the marriage not take place. By the
end of May, however, Catherine received news that turned her interests from
Alençon to his older brother. She learned that month that Anjou had been offered
the throne of Poland.

It was not an honour that had come unbidden. For several years Catherine, in
her unceasing efforts to find thrones for all her children, had kept her eyes on Poland. Sigismundus Augustus was growing old, and since Poland frequently elected its ruler from outside its own domain, it might prove an opportune crown for
Anjou. With this as her goal, Catherine had, in the fall of 1571, enlisted the help
of the Tuscan ambassador Petrucci to gain papal approval for her design. "Since
the Pope is always indicating that he loves him as a son," she wrote Petrucci,
"and that he would favour him in every way he could . . . then here is the moment when he can show this favour."[38] The specific result of these negotiations
is not clear, but at the beginning of 1572 Du Ferrier wrote triumphantly from Venice: "The common rumour here is that Monseigneur will get his part, Madame;
for if the voice of the people is the voice of God, as Scripture says, then he will
be elected king."[39]

Elated by Du Ferrier's opinion, Catherine continued her strategies. The Polish
mission was to be entrusted to Jean de Monluc, Bishop of Valence, who blended
the natural wiles of the Gascon with years of diplomatic experience.* Catherine,
however, was never satisfied with her official diplomats; she also needed her secret agents. Thus, she sent into Poland Jean de Balagny, Monluc's natural son,
who, in the guise of a travelling student, was to keep her unofficially informed.

Shortly after Balagny's arrival in Poland, Catherine received word of the death
of Sigismundus Augustus and immediately ordered Monluc to set out for Poland.
He had gone no farther than St. Dizier, however, before he learned of the tragic
events of August 24. The Paris massacre considerably impeded Monluc's journey; imprisoned in Verdun, threatened in Frankfurt, he did not reach Poland until
the end of October. When he finally crossed the border, it was to discover a land
desolated by plague. As he travelled through the bleak countryside, dotted with
deserted farmhouses, he came to realize that it was not simply plague that kept
people at a distance—it was, in addition, a strong anti-French feeling. Monluc
became increasingly aware as he travelled towards Warsaw that no Frenchman
would be given more than a grudging welcome since the tragic events of August.
Poland prided itself on religious toleration, and the Paris massacre had countered
one of its basic political tenets. Whatever Anjou's chances had been earlier, they
had diminished considerably by the fall of 1572.

As early as October the Papal Legate Giovanni Cardinal Commendone had

*Not to be confused with the fierce enemy of the Huguenots, Blaise de Monluc.

written to the Cardinal of Cuomo, "The news of the death of the admiral, which has been received from France, has upset the heretics here very much, and alienated many of those who were partisans of Monsieur d'Anjou."[40] Jean de Choisnin, Monluc's secretary, who later published his memoirs of those years, recalled the lurid reports that poured into Poland after the massacre: savage polemics, eyewitness accounts of atrocities, vivid pictures, "depicting every kind of cruel death." The worst of it all, recalled Choisnin, was that many pictures showed Charles and Anjou not only looking on, but indicating by their expressions that "they were sorry that the executioners were not more cruel."[41]

It was Monluc's task to counter the reports arriving weekly from England, France, Germany, Switzerland by explaining what had "really" taken place during those August days. His "True and Sincere Account of the Troubles of Paris" assumed the stance that had already been taken in France: An "insidious rebellion" had developed, which had to be quelled if the royal family were to escape with their lives. Whatever horrors were committed were not the work of the royal family, but of the frenzied Parisians—the mob. Surely, argued Monluc, speaking of Charles, we cannot believe that a kind and virtuous prince would suddenly turn into a monster of cruelty. As for Anjou, Monluc depicted him as the ideal prince: "easy of access, patient in listening, wise in answering." "Study this face," he continued, "can you perceive in these features, bearing the marks of kindness and goodness, the least trace of cruelty?"[42] The defence was well handled but it remained to be seen whether it was good enough to counter the frenzied attacks coming, especially, from the Huguenot strongholds of Geneva and Basle. Monluc himself seemed to have small hope, as he wrote bitterly, "This evil wind which has come from France has sunk the ship which we had managed to bring to the very entrance of the harbour."[43] He saw little point in remaining in Poland and waited, he said, only for those orders that would give him permission to return to France.

Such orders, of course, were never issued. Discouraging as the situation might be, Catherine could never admit defeat. The Polish Electoral Diet was not to take place until the spring; that left her an entire winter to plan and coerce. Catherine was convinced that by spring she could present a candidate for the Polish throne so winning, so strong, so competent in war and statecraft that no other candidate could match him. She was determined that Anjou was to win a crown.

While Monluc waited in Poland, Anjou, as lieutenant general of the king's forces, was preparing to enhance his reputation as a commander. Following the events of August, the people of La Rochelle had refused obedience to the king. By November the impasse was such that Charles declared war against them, declaring them "rebels, disturbers of the state, and unworthy of our good grace." Anjou was given power "to chastise them by every means in your power."[44] The task, which had looked deceptively simple to Anjou's youthful eyes, in fact proved formidable. On leaving Paris in early January, Anjou found himself in the midst of the worst possible weather: The rivers were flooding; the cold and damp were penetrating. Before the month was out, his army was afflicted with serious sickness, and Anjou himself taken with a debilitating nausea. Already they were short of money, and the 6,000 Swiss levied by the ambassador Pomponne de Bellièvre had not yet arrived. Anjou wrote to Charles, begging for help, but Charles did not reply.

In the next few months Anjou's dreams of glory dulled as he realised that this was not the open battlefield of Moncontour, where victory could be established in a matter of hours. To take La Rochelle would mean weeks of the inglorious drudgery of digging trenches in an attempt to undermine the citadel's solid foundations. He drove his soldiers hard, but there was little to show for their labours. Fearful of Charles' harsh judgement, he wrote at the end of February: "I beg you most humbly to believe me when I say I am losing neither time nor opportunity."[45] Yet of the eight assaults made on the city between February and June, none was decisive. Even the efforts to starve it into subjection were doomed to failure, for one moonlit night, four ships slid into the harbour and provisioned the city.

La Rochelle seemed invincible. The citizens, despite the threat of famine and death, clung to the hope of victory, even planting on May Day, according to their custom, an oak tree, symbol of life, "In order," as the chronicler wrote, "to show our enemy that this city will never be shaken."[46]

On the plains below, there were few signs of life. Here the dread disease resembling cholera and called *la colique de Poitou* ravaged the royal army. Étienne Pasquier's complacent comment, "There was never a better camp than that which was before La Rochelle," was obviously written by a man who had never seen the king's soldiers dying by hundreds in the freezing marshes.[47] With the spring rains the disease increased, and Anjou's army was less at war with mortal men than with hunger, mud, and sickness. For every man who died of his wounds, ten were struck down by dysentery. Anjou found himself, for the first time in his life, a prey to failure. He had wanted desperately to exhibit his prowess; instead, he had lost face on every side—or, more accurately, on every side but one: Catherine continued to believe in his eventual success and to encourage him by that belief.

On April 2 she wrote a letter of maternal solicitude and trust. Scolding him for signing himself "your most affectionate servant," she continued:

> I want you to be my "affectionate son" and thus to acknowledge me as the most devoted mother that ever a child had; so please, no longer use the word "servant," but rather that which you truly are to me. . . . I have indicated to you very clearly that I would prefer you to acquire reputation and glory rather than to have you with me—although that would be a very great happiness to me. But I am not the kind of mother who carries her children off just for her own enjoyment, for I would much prefer to see you the first in greatness and honour and reputation.[48]

The glory Catherine sought for her favourite became a fact when, on May 28, Charles and Catherine received the news that Anjou had been elected King of Poland. Catherine swelled with elation: The old prophecy, that all her sons would sit on thrones, was coming true! Charles, too, was gratified, though for different reasons. The rivalry between the two brothers had reached a peak following the massacre, and Charles had come to feel that he could never rest easy until his enterprising young brother was out of the kingdom.

As for the new king, there is little record of his response. His continued failure at La Rochelle undoubtedly curtailed his elation. His situation was at best ambiguous. On one side, he felt he must prove himself victorious to impress Poland with his military skill; on the other, he recognised that to conquer and subdue "heretics" would hardly be looked on with favour by a country that had made it clear that religious toleration was one of its essential principles.

By mid-June, however, the decision of victory or defeat was no longer Anjou's to make; by then it was obvious the royal army would never subdue La Rochelle. Both Charles and the queen mother pushed for a compromise peace, and on June 28 Charles wrote to his brother, "We must make peace, if we are wise." Once again Anjou felt duped. It had been Charles who had declared war, and now it was Charles who determined the peace. Yet Charles had never given him the powers he needed, never taken seriously his desperate requests for more men, more money, more arms.

It was a bitter prince who left Niort on July 8, two days after the peace was signed, to journey to Tours and then by flatboat down the Loire to Orléans and eventually to Paris.

Chapter XI

Anjou's election had been less difficult than Monluc had anticipated. When the Electoral Diet opened on April 5, on the vast plains southeast of Warsaw, the candidates had been narrowed to two: Archduke Ernest, son of the emperor Maximilian, and Anjou. Despite the forceful speeches made by Austria and the Papacy in favor of the archduke, they could not match Monluc's tempting promises. Not only did he extol Anjou's virtues, but he outlined the promises his brother, the Most Christian King, would make to Poland were Anjou elected: a perpetual alliance with France; a pledge to help Poland in any situation in which it was attacked; a profitable commercial treaty; a promise to send 4,000 arquebusers against their aggressive neighbours the Muscovites. In response, the crowd, "In great tumult," cried, *"Gallum, Gallum:* We want the Frenchman." When the official voting took place on May 9, the eve of Pentecost, the conclusion was assured. The archbishop, "shaking with joy," made the solemn proclamation: "We have for our king the most illustrious Duke of Anjou." The following day Monluc wrote jubilantly to Catherine: "Madame, I have done what I promised; you shall see Monseigneur king of this realm."[1]

Catherine, exhilarated, wasted little worry on how Monluc's elaborate promises could be fulfilled. Instead, she revelled in her victory, rejoicing, as her foreign ambassadors wrote, at the happy reactions to Anjou's election. In the first part of June she wrote Anjou in the full flush of maternal pride: "I hardly know how to thank God, for now I see you in the role I have always wanted for you. . . . I beg you now to use this for His service and for that of your brother who is happier than I have ever seen him in your good fortune"—and then, in her own hand: "We have had the *Te Deum* sung and bonfires made in Paris . . . and I beg you with all my heart to permit yourself from now on to be called king, as in fact, thanks be to God, you actually are."[2]

Charles also wrote his congratulations to his younger brother; he could hardly have done otherwise. But his letter, scarcely more than a few lines, was, despite his protestations of joy, stiff and constrained: "Dear Brother . . . I am so pleased that I hardly know what to say. I praise God with all my heart. Please pardon me, for my happiness keeps me from saying very much. I hardly know what to say."[3] It was, undoubtedly, a true statement of his ambivalence. The long tension between the brothers, growing month by month, was an open subject of court gossip. The Duc de Nevers, always the diplomat, had advised Anjou to try to conceal his feelings towards his brother and to "avoid occasions of anger."[4] It was a course Nevers, ten years older and far more practised, might have managed, but Anjou lacked the skill for such a game.

His position was made more difficult by the fact that something violent in Charles had been unleashed by the horrors of the massacre, and his rages had become more frequent and more irrational. Anjou's popularity only augmented the difficulty. He had had from childhood a charm and grace his elder brother lacked. Almost without seeking it, he found himself more easily loved, more spontaneously obeyed. The Florentine Vincenzio Alamanni summed up the situation adroitly when he wrote, "With the rank and authority conferred on him, he had become so powerful that it was better to serve him than the king. . . . God grant that one day he will not want to compete with the king." Antonio Salviati reinforced this opinion when, writing carefully in cipher to the Holy See, he warned, "Should these brothers remain as they are at court, everyone feels that it will be impossible to keep terrible quarrels from springing up among them."[5] Catherine, who remained throughout her life infatuated with the concept of peace, was having her first bitter taste of war in her own household.

On August 19 the Polish ambassadors arrived in Paris. The Parisians could not but be impressed, for they came in a kind of splendour at once imposing and bizarre. There were, in all, close to 200 gentlemen, each with his servants. Their coaches were drawn by six to eight horses with harnesses elaborately adorned with silver and precious stones. To the Parisians, they seemed the tallest men they had ever seen, made more regal by their beards and high-plumed bonnets. Their high yellow boots ornamented with metal, their curved scimitars, their bows and quivers, added to their formidable appearance. As they traversed the city by the rue de la Juiverie, they provided a fascinating spectacle for the Parisians, who leaned from windows and jostled in doorways, laughing and pointing at the foreign clothes and strange language. One diarist recorded that Catherine, in her annoyance at this display of bad manners, yelled at them to keep quiet.

Two days later the ambassadors came to the Louvre for their first formal audience with the king and the queen mother. De Thou recorded with amazement that they all spoke Latin, that many spoke German and Italian, and that some spoke impeccable French. On August 22 they had their official meeting with the new King of Poland. In their long robes of cloth of gold and multicoloured silk, they seemed more than ever to tower over the fragilely formed Valois. Adam Konarski, the Bishop of Posnan, made the formal speech of invitation in Latin, but Henri, aware of his linguistic limitations, replied as briefly as possible, leaving the Comte de Cheverny, who spoke Latin "like Horace himself," to continue more fully.[6]

When the conferences opened, it was immediately clear that the Polish concept of kingship differed widely from the Valois. The power vested in the Polish monarch was comparatively limited. "Powerless to do wrong, you will be omnipotent in doing good," they explained to the newly elected king.[7] It was not good enough for Anjou, however, who baulked at such limited power. Zúñiga, jubilant with the turn things were taking, wrote Philip that the Poles were beginning to learn how little Anjou really knew and that Anjou, on his part, was so displeased with some of the articles of the royal oath that he had almost reached the decision not to swear to them at all. "Thus," continued Zúñiga, "the Poles wish to impose such conditions on him that he would be reduced to the same situation as the Doge of Venice," and then observed tellingly, "Every day the duke has cried like a child and his mother has encouraged him and upheld him three or four hours a day."[8]

It was not simply the curtailment of his royal prerogatives that brought tears to Anjou; it was, rather, the thought of leaving France. Anjou was, at best, a provincial man, a man who loved what he knew, who needed the security of the familiar. He would never be a traveller, not even within his own kingdom. When, later, he governed France, it was his mother who travelled in his behalf; Anjou remained at home, reading the letters she sent, but rarely travelling far afield. Although a royal crown had enormous appeal for him, a crown in a foreign country could never be to his taste. He would prefer, wrote Cavalli to Venice, "a quarter of the crown of France to all the provinces of another kingdom."[9]

Despite his reservations, Anjou ultimately conceded to the stipulated conditions, and on September 10, assisted by his brother, he took the necessary oath. Three days later there took place the formal ceremony of the Decree of Election. The Grande Salle of the Palais de Justice was prepared for the occasion. The room was crowded to capacity as the Duc de Guise, in his role as grand master, led the Polish ambassadors to the table where lay the silver chest containing the decree. Again, it was Adam Konarski who spoke and Cheverny who replied. The speech—formal rhetoric though it was—said everything that delighted Catherine's ears and was sufficient to dispel the hostility that had arisen during the debates:

. . . having cast our eyes on all parts of Europe, and having with mature reflection considered what prince we would choose for our king, a prince who would be able to govern and who, by the gentleness of his nature, would be able to maintain in our country that liberty which is its custom, the senate and the large number of the nobility with common consent, with neither bribery nor dissimulation, have elected you King of Poland and Grand Duke of Lithuania.[10]

Despite the setbacks, the frustrations, the political conniving, Anjou was at last King of Poland, and Cheverny's final words raised the event from a carefully manipulated political issue to that divine realm which was so much a part of Catherine's political mystique. "Let us go now," cried Cheverny, "where the will of God and our faith call us!"[11]

The following day Paris turned out for the formal procession of the new King of Poland. From the Porte St. Antoine past Notre Dame and on to the Louvre the procession journeyed. Despite the heat of Indian summer, Anjou was dressed in full armour. The cavalry of Paris, the elders in their silk cloaks, the members of Parlement in their purple—all passed slowly through the innumerable *arcs de triomphes*, decorated with inscriptions praising the glory of Poland, the splendour of Anjou, and the devotion of both French and Poles to their kings. The crowds jostled and hung from windows to catch a glimpse of the three royal brothers, riding together in fraternal amity. Only the English ambassador noted the withdrawn look on Charles' face and the disdain he barely concealed.

That night Anjou was fêted in the garden of the Tuileries—that palace in which Philibert Delorme, at Catherine's command, had created some of the finest architecture of the French Renaissance. The entertainment had been entrusted to Ronsard and Jean Dorat, who had composed a classical masque that flatteringly depicted the royal family. The queen mother, with a helmet on her head and a halberd in her hand, was Pallas Gallica; Charles, holding an eagle and with a dragon at his feet, was Jupiter Servator; and Anjou, replete with lyre, quiver, and arrows, was Apollo Gallicus.

For once, Catherine had indulged her Italian taste to the utmost, and a member of the Polish delegation, who had never seen fantasy so sumptuously expressed, wrote in amazement to Poland:

> On September 15, the queen mother gave a marvellous banquet in her very beautiful garden. Here we saw sixteen nymphs who represented the sixteen provinces of France. . . . We saw a mountain at the summit of which a eunuch was singing with a wonderfully sweet voice, while a little further down, a woman sang, accompanied by a lute, lamenting . . . the departure of the King of Poland, and wishing him happiness.

Josefwicz had every reason to be impressed. Who, indeed, watching all this splendour, could believe that France was other than a very powerful and exceedingly rich kingdom? Catherine's entertainment—like everything else in her life—had its political point.[12]

Two weeks later the royal family left Paris for Fontainebleau, where they celebrated the Feast of St. Michael. By this time the Polish ambassadors were growing restive with the liberality of the French court: They had not come to Paris to be entertained, but to bring their elected king home. Anjou, however, felt no sense of urgency and continued on with his brother to the royal palace at Villers-

Cotterêts, where Charles could indulge his passion for hunting. The Polish delegates could no longer dissemble their annoyance. One of them reputedly left in disgust, and the Nuncio wrote to Rome, "There is growing ill humour on the part of the Polish ambassadors owing to the continual delays of their king."[13]

Anjou's natural reluctance to leave France was now reenforced by his brother's illness. Charles, who, even during the course of the summer, had been afflicted with sweats and haemorrhages, now became seriously ill following a hunting expedition at Vitry. For sixteen days the court lingered with their sovereign. On November 9 Zúñiga wrote to Philip, "May God keep him, for it would be a great misfortune to lose him." A day later Cavalli also wrote of the serious nature of Charles' illness, explaining it was not a simple fever as the doctors had originally diagnosed, but an eruption of blood all over his body.[14] It was obvious Charles would not be able to accompany his brother to the French border.

Catherine was beside herself with grief and anxiety. Were Charles to die while Anjou was in Poland, what would happen to the kingdom of France? It was a question being asked by more than Catherine, and one contemporary appraised the situation, saying, "With the king in this state of health, there is the possibility of losing France itself, for the Duc d'Alençon will miss no opportunity of manoeuvring things his way."[15] His way, of course, would be to assume the leadership of the nation, strongly assisted by the Huguenot faction, which already saw in him a possible Messiah.

For the time being, however, the king's health improved, and on November 12 the final parting between the brothers took place. Tears were shed on both sides, and Charles wrote to Du Ferrier in Venice: "I beg you to believe that our separation has been so grievous to us both that I have never felt deeper regret for anything that has ever happened to me; however, it is for his own good and the honour of our house that he is leaving and this gives me some consolation."[16] In the light of Charles' constant hostility towards his younger brother, such an expression of grief is suspect, but Anjou's tears were not to be doubted, for he was about to leave behind all he loved most.

For the next few weeks Catherine, Alençon, and Anjou continued their journey east. On November 25 they left Nancy, arriving at St. Nicolas-de-Port the following day. The few remaining days were spent in Blâmont, and on December 3, three months later than originally promised, Anjou took his final leave of his mother and of France. Whether, as legend says, Catherine whispered in her son's ear, "Do not worry; you will soon be back," is impossible to determine. It was not a difficult prophecy to make, for the signs of Charles' mortal illness were visible for anyone to read.

Ten days after Anjou's departure for Poland, Catherine rejoined Charles at Reims. There was little comfort for her in the meeting. The king was better, it was true, but the signs of death were clearly on him. Disease and the insupportable burdens of kingship had done their work, and Catherine's public optimism had a hollow ring. Despite his weakness, hunting was still Charles' passion—perhaps because it was the only thing in which he seemed able to succeed, perhaps because (as his enemies said) it was a channel for those strange lusts that could be quieted only by violence. In any case, he stayed in the saddle for hours at a time, riding at a pace that exhausted his attendants, never satisfied until he had killed his quarry, returning at nightfall, drenched in sweat and exhausted beyond speech.

France could not survive with such a king. Catherine knew it, yet she was powerless to change it. Anjou might have saved France, but Anjou, her warrior son, she had sent into Poland. It was difficult to believe as one looked at the emaciated body of the king, his skin like parchment, his eyes yellowed and heavy-lidded, that this was the "wonderful child" whom Michieli had described twelve years before. "Everything that can be hoped for in a king," the Venetian had written, "in his gifts, in his spirit, in affability, in generosity, in courage—one can hope for it all in him." Even then, however, Michieli had acknowledged, "He is not very strong; he eats and drinks very little and will have to be managed very carefully in bodily exercise. . . . He loves feats of arms and all the exercise which undoubtedly is worthy of a prince, but too violently. . . ." [17]

After Anjou's departure Charles threw himself tumultuously into the business of government. It was, undoubtedly, an effort to prove himself—to his Council; to his enemies; to the gossipmongers who were whispering that the king had gone mad following St. Bartholomew; most of all, perhaps, to his mother, who obviously preferred his brother. It must have seemed singularly unfair to Charles that he who had been burdened with kingship since the age of ten, who had accepted his mother's counsels without demur should never be first in her affection. Yet even while his resentment mounted, he continued to let her govern him, so that the Nuncio wrote in annoyance, "This is a king who lets himself be ruled by his mother." [18] It was a habit too deep-rooted to be broken now.

Shortly after Christmas, Charles and Catherine traveled to Chantilly to visit Montmorency to discuss the state of the kingdom. François de Montmorency had assumed the role formerly played by his father. He stood opposed to the ultra-Catholic position, sought to placate the Huguenots without joining them, and continued his family hostility to the Guises. The Parisians had no love for Montmorency, seeing him with the same dangerous influence over the king that Coligny had once exercised. The Florentine ambassador, who shared their feelings, wrote anxiously during Charles' sojourn at Chantilly, "If Montmorency continues as he has begun . . . there is no doubt that he will become more important than ever in this kingdom." [19]

Montmorency's influence was not sufficient, however, to restore peace to a kingdom charged with distrust. One of the most far-reaching results of the August massacre was the shift in the political attitude of the Huguenots towards the throne. Formerly, they had always maintained that they were the loyal subjects of the king, protesting that whatever activities they engaged in were to "free" the king from the "pernicious influence" of such men as the Guises. Following the massacre, however, their royalist sympathies were called into question. What happened on August 24 seemed to them a betrayal by their king. For the first time they began to dispute their allegiance to the crown. The spontaneous attacks on the king, the queen mother, the Guise family that had followed the massacre gave way to a more measured—and far more deadly—series of pamphlets proposing the question of "lawful revolt."

From the fall of 1573 to Charles' death, nine months later, pamphlets poured through France, questioning, suggesting, approving the right of a people to take arms against a king when that king had proved himself an irresponsible tyrant. A *Political Dialogue Treating of the Power, Authority, and Duties of Princes* asked, in effect, how far one should support tyranny and at what point the people of a kingdom have the obligation to "take arms" in order to "defend their life and liberty." "Is it lawful," queried the author, "for a people and the nobility to resist by arms the treachery and cruelty of a sovereign lord?" François Hotman in his *Franco-Gallia* posed the same basic questions, while Bèze in his *Du Droit des magistrats* argued that absolute power can be exercised by God alone, that although the king shares in that divine power, royal power is always contingent on the sovereign's responsible fulfillment of his duties. *Le Reveil-Matin*, more radical still, did not hesitate to argue in favor of tyrannicide.

In effect, the pamphlets maintained that royal power is not absolute, that it is accountable to the society which it governs, and that should it be used irresponsibly, the lawful delegates of that society have the right to oppose such tyranny. Such terms as "election," "right of the people," "popular sanction" occurred more and more frequently. Nothing could be more inimical to the Valois concept of kingship.[20]

Such literature indicated beyond question that the Huguenots were far from being simple "Gospellers," with their eyes turned solely towards a celestial kingdom. The possibility of absorbing them quietly into the kingdom by granting them full liberty of cult was no longer feasible. Although many of the simple people might have been content with such a measure, their leaders were obviously following another vision. The questions they proposed went far beyond any religious issue, even beyond their personal hostility to the king. They were bringing to the fore a new concept of kingship tinted darkly with the republicanism of Geneva.

The Huguenots were strengthened by a tenuous alliance with a group of moderate Catholics, the Politiques, under the leadership of Montmorency-Damville, the second of those powerful sons the constable had left behind him. The policy of the Politiques was very close to that which the queen mother had long championed: religious toleration as a means of domestic harmony, compromise rather than civil war. One of the bitter fruits of the massacre was, for Catherine, to find that her antagonists were men whose vision was so close to what her own had been and to recognise that in an irremediable way she was now alienated from the cause of harmony she had so long espoused. She had forfeited the trust even of those who had formerly defended her.

"Catherine de Medici is not only an Italian, but a Florentine," ran a contemporary attack. "And among all nations Italy takes the prize for shrewdness and subtlety; and in Italy the prize goes to Tuscany; and in Tuscany to Florence. . . . When this art of deception falls upon someone who has no conscience—as happens very often in people of this country—I leave it up to you to imagine the evils that might befall. And, after all, Catherine is of the House of Medici."[21] The massacre, it was felt, had revealed the full scope of her duplicity. While she had spoken so winningly of peace, she had been firing the forges for war. She had duped Coligny; she had duped Jeanne d'Albret. The marriage she had proposed as a symbol of peace had been consummated with the bloodiest kiss in history. Catherine would never be trusted again. The Politiques, in disgust, moved away from the throne and closer to the betrayed Huguenots.

They maintained that they meant no disservice to France, that they wished to serve their country by a policy of toleration which would heal old wounds, break down the barriers between opposing interests, and restore the kingdom to its former greatness. They were weary of the factions that reduced the court to chaos, of a corrupt and irresponsible system of taxation, of the continued refusal to call the Estates. Their prime concern was not religious but rather a question of *bien public*. The common good of the kingdom was the tie that bound them.

If there was any doubt of the power of such an alliance, the court had only to look south, where the political acumen of François La Noue and Montmorency-Damville had created in the Midi something akin to a rival government. Yet despite the fact that these were men of unquestioned leadership, the Politiques dreamed of another leader, someone whose position would immeasurably strengthen their cause. They set their sights on the Duc d'Alençon. History makes the choice seem a strange one, for as future events were to prove, Alençon was gifted with that dark power of counteralchemy which could turn even bright coin into failure. It was not, however, a dynamic leader the Politiques sought, but a man with royal blood who would be malleable to their desires. In this light, Alençon was a perfect choice.

The climate of the court had made Alençon responsive to such wooing. He was the youngest and the least of the royal children and had been treated accordingly. His disaffection was obvious. For a while his mother had busied herself with his proposed marriage to Elizabeth, but soon more pressing business had intervened: Charles must be assisted in ruling his kingdom; Anjou must be helped to the Polish throne. What happened to Alençon was always of less importance.

Even as a child he had won neither his mother's affection nor her approval. When he was only nine, Catherine had written of him in amusement to the Duc de Guise, "I have just returned from Amboise where I saw a little blackamoor whose brain is full of nothing but war and tempests."[22] Although that had been ten years earlier, *le petit moricaud* had changed very little. His head was still full of wars and tempests, and his heart was filled with great bitterness. It was a singularly dangerous combination.

For some time Charles had found his youngest brother troublesome. As early as the fall of 1572 he had been anxious over Alençon's Huguenot sympathies. Although he had served with the royal army at the siege of La Rochelle, his loyalty was already in question. "Watch him," the king had advised Anjou, warning him against giving any authority to his younger brother, who, he feared, might use it in favour of the Huguenots. Forced always to an inferior position under a brother he despised, Alençon longed for the day that Anjou would depart for Poland so that on him would fall the mantle of his brother's authority. It was a vain dream, however, for neither Charles nor Catherine was to trust him with the position of lieutenant general of the kingdom.

Perhaps had the "little blackamoor" been given a position of responsibility, they might have won his loyalty. It is a questionable hypothesis, for Alençon seems from the first to have been lacking in that vital string which resonates to such concepts as loyalty, love, integrity. It was a music he never learned—perhaps because he had never been taught it. While one is at first tempted to dismiss Alençon as the most contemptuous type of opportunist, made more despicable by his inability to succeed even in dishonour, perhaps he was not the basest of Catherine's children but the most sensitive to his environment. Reared in an atmosphere of plots and counterplots, in an atmosphere where truth saying was either a luxury or a folly, he was quick to learn that survival was his own responsibility, that what he wanted he must pluck with his own hands. To his destruction, he never realised that his ambition, his distrust of his mother, his envy of his brothers made him a fruit very ripe for other people's plucking. Preening himself on using others, he was ultimately the most exploited of all.

Although in the fall of 1573 he had been in touch with William of Orange and was reputedly considering an offer to lead the Flemish uprising, he now turned from that scheme to the leadership offered him by the Politiques. Despite the distrust of his own family, Alençon was not, at this point, universally mistrusted or disliked. Some thought highly of him. He seemed to be the only son who had not fallen under Catherine's ruling thumb. He had ostensibly been less engaged in the massacre than the other members of the royal family. He was admired for his independence of mind and his reckless daring. The scheme drafted by the Politiques offered Alençon a position of partisan leadership. They cherished the hope that with Charles' death—and there were few who did not believe this was imminent—Anjou might be excluded from the throne because of his present commitment in Poland. In that case, Alençon would be the rightful inheritor. Were he, then, bound to the Politique cause, the king would be theirs. Rival parties would be despoiled of their power, civil discord could be brought to an end, and France united once again.

The first step in such an enterprise was to secure the person of the duke. But, as Alençon warily explained, this was not to be easy. His growing friendship with Henri de Navarre had made him more suspect than ever, and both he and Navarre were closely watched. So began the Conspiracy of St. Germain, an enterprise to "rescue" these young gentlemen from the duress of the Valois court.

Towards the end of February the queen mother was advised that groups of horsemen were gathering close to St. Germain and that some of the servants had seen arms being carried to Navarre's quarters. Charles, who, since the massacre, had seen plots everywhere, was in terror. The gates were at once closed and manned, the Swiss Guard was alerted, and Alençon brought into the king's presence. His cringing responses to the angry denunciations of the king and his mother evoked only disdain. "Your Holiness should be aware that this is a man of no courage," wrote the Nuncio to Rome, after hearing the account of Alençon's behaviour. He confessed everything, grovelling on his knees, begging the king to believe that he meant him no harm, that he deserved every punishment, even death itself. "The duke remains disheartened and half-silly," wrote Cavalli, noting the marked contrast between Alençon's desperate efforts to win the king's pardon and Navarre's unflinching composure.[23]

Charles, however, was less concerned with the punishment of the wicked than with his own safety. His conduct now was sadly different from his youthful exhilaration at the danger he had faced during the Enterprise of Meaux. Six years before he had been peeved at the constable's refusal to let him be in the vanguard; now, despite the relative security of St. Germain, he gave orders for an immediate departure for Paris. The king's panic infected the court, and in a tumult of confusion, horses, wagons, carriages were loaded with whatever was at hand and took to the open road. "Some could be seen without their boots, others without their hose or shoes," recorded De Thou.[24] The terror was out of all proportion to the actual danger, for no more than 200 men had gathered about St. Germain.

It might have been a ludicrous scene had not the king's condition endowed it with the elements of tragedy. Charles was the last to leave. The excitement had made him ill, and he was forced to travel slowly by coach. Eight hundred Swiss rode with him, but neither they nor his mother could ease the discomforts of the journey. Although it was only a few leagues from St. Germain to Paris, they broke their cold, slow journey to rest overnight at the château of the Comte de Retz at St. Cloud. When Catherine suggested that they take up residence in the Louvre, Charles, despite the effort that travelling cost him, would have none of it. For Charles, the Louvre was safe from the living but not from the dead. Perhaps—as the Huguenot preachers affirmed—he did meet the ghosts of the dead in his dreams or hear their cries drifting up in the mists rising off the Seine. Perhaps he still smelled blood. In any case, he preferred to take up residence in the grey battlemented château of Vincennes. If anything, it was more sinister with its small windows, high towers, and thick walls, but at the moment it held fewer terrors for the king.

Vincennes, however, was to provide neither peace nor security. The preceding December Charles had written to his governors, warning them against "persons who go from house to house stirring the lords and other people to rebellion and disobedience under pretext of the public good."[25] What he had learned at St. Germain and was to learn again at Vincennes was that the persons he described were of his own household. It had been the policy of Charles and the queen mother to treat the events at St. Germain lightly. Both Alençon and Navarre had been commanded to submit statements affirming their loyalty to the king and their determination to oppose his enemies. With such avowals Catherine seemed content, although there were those like the Cardinal de Lorraine who warned that unless the king took more severe measures, his enemies would continue to revolt. Even Dr. Valentine Dale, the English ambassador who had replaced Walsingham, was surprised by the amity which prevailed, writing to Burghley, "The King is making merry with Navarre and the Duke . . . using them with better countenance than ever he did."[26]

It was neither love nor mercy, but the pragmatism of his mother, that dictated the king's attitude. Although Catherine never succeeded in controlling Alençon, she could read her youngest son very clearly. He had failed, he had been humiliated and publicly reprimanded, and now he was kept leashed. Unless the leash were long enough to give him a sense of liberty, he might try to destroy them all. By smiles and promises she thought to lull his passion for freedom, but something overwhelming had awakened in Alençon. Neither the luxury of the court nor the blandishments of his mother or his mistress could tame it. Ambition was in him like a cancer. He had his own fever, making his blood race as wildly as the king's and, ultimately, causing his destruction.

During March the tension throughout France grew. The Comte de Montgomery—the young lord who had been responsible for Henri II's death fifteen years earlier and who was now a Huguenot leader—had invaded Normandy with English arms and English soldiers. Provence, Dauphiné, Guyenne were all in arms "against tyranny." Incendiary pamphlets multiplied; placards denouncing the government or satirising the royal family were posted strategically, one even appearing on the queen mother's door, reading, "The King of Poland in Poland, Monsieur the Duke in England, the Queen Mother in the earth, and the King at peace."

Meanwhile, another plot, again involving Alençon and Navarre, was taking shape at Vincennes. On April 6 Alençon presided over a secret meeting in which

it was decided that another "escape" would be attempted on April 9. Both François de Montmorency and the Comte de Brissac attended the meeting, although
they later maintained their presence was an effort to dissuade Alençon from his
dangerous scheme. Once again, everything depended on secrecy, but there was
little hope for secrecy in a court where Catherine had her paid "ears" everywhere. Yves de Brinon reported all, and on the morning of April 7 Catherine revealed the plot to the king.

Furious, he knocked his breakfast tray to the floor, screaming, "This treason is
insufferable!" So violent was the king's initial anger that Cavalli wrote he
thought both princes would be condemned to death on the spot.[27] Again it was
Catherine who counselled moderation. Her fury against her ungrateful, misshap-
en son was as implacable as Charles', but as she watched the image of death become more visible in the king, she hesitated to leave the throne without an heir.
If Alençon and Navarre were executed and Charles were to die, what jeopardy
might France then face? She had twice been witness of how eagerly ambitious
men fish in the troubled waters that rise after a king's death. While she would
never willingly put power in Alençon's hands, his presence would provide a
symbol of lawful authority. When she advised Charles to reserve the "extreme
penalty" for some of the minor conspirators and place Alençon and Navarre under rigid guard, he agreed.

At once Vincennes became a fortress. The princes were apprehended and
forced to surrender their swords, while other members of the plot were rounded
up and arrested. The mood was very different from that of St. Germain, and Navarre later confessed he had feared for his life. Before the reign of terror ended,
more than 100 people allegedly involved had been imprisoned. Among them
were Montmorency and Brissac, Alençon's two questionable friends Boniface de
La Molle and Hannibal de Coconat, as well as the queen mother's little Italian
astrologer, Cosimo Ruggieri, who, it was said, had helped conjure evil spells
against the king.

In a meeting attended by Charles, Catherine, and the chancellor, the latter
strongly urged the king, "for the sake of the whole kingdom," to "make an ex-
ample and take severe measures," lest clemency appear "weakness and irresolution." This time justice, not clemency, was to prevail. "There will be no lack of
justice for these knaves; in order that the fire be extinguished at the beginning,
some heads must fall," Catherine reputedly told the Spanish ambassador Zúñiga. "Not only has an offence been committed against God and the king," she
continued, "but they have abused and deceived two young princes who still have
the taste of milk on their lips."[28] It was an amusing image for two young men
whose innocence could hardly have outlasted their infancy, but it was an image
typical of Catherine's policy. Although forced to acknowledge that a crime
against the state had been committed, she would not concede it had originated in

the bosom of the royal family. She would wreak her private fury on Alençon, but she was determined his public dignity as a Valois prince remain unassailed.

Alençon and Navarre spent a sombre Easter. They had dreamed of singing the paschal alleluias in the freedom of St. Maur; instead, they were kept locked in their separate rooms. Little information trickled through. Their personal servants had been replaced by the king's men; the gates were locked and guarded, and even those permitted to enter were thoroughly searched. From time to time, news of their fellow conspirators seeped in to them: Brissac and Montmorency, despite their protestations of innocence, were confined in the Bastille; La Molle had been arrested at Vincennes, and Coconat hiding at a covent in Paris. Both were to be put to the torture until they could be persuaded to tell the truth. For La Molle, the moment came almost at once; for Coconat, the torture had to be repeated, until he babbled out enough to convict him of treason. Although Alençon begged for their lives on his knees, both men (so handsome, it was said, that women swooned at the thought of their deaths) were publicly executed.

Their "confessions" were for Catherine the final proof that Alençon and Navarre had been the innocent victims of evil men. Even so, she continued to keep them under lock and key. When the English ambassador, having received a message from Navarre saying he feared for his life, questioned Catherine on the strict guard at the palace, she assured him it was only for the princes' own safety, adding confidingly, "We are all well guarded here."[29]

On April 13 commissioners from the Parlement of Paris were brought to listen to the cases of Alençon and Navarre. There was little original about Alençon's unctuous protestations of innocence and pleas for pardon. Navarre's statement, on the other hand, was less a confession than an apologia. As he rehearsed, by way of prologue, the facts of his life, he shifted the ground until it was not he who was on trial but rather a monarchy which had again and again betrayed his family, his followers, himself. The plot in which he had been engaged was no crime against the king, he declared, but a simple effort on his part to escape from a court where he lived in constant fear and suspicion.[30] It was the first public utterance of the man who, fifteen years later, would become the first Bourbon King of France. It is unfortunate that Catherine left no comment on Navarre's declaration. Both the rhetoric and the manner could not have failed to impress her. In the following years she was to discover that he was less his father's son than she had imagined; in fact, he was to become an adversary whose acumen matched her own.

The princes' statements did nothing to change their condition, however. Their confinement continued unabated. They saw no one; they had no access to the world outside Vincennes. When the English ambassador tried to get in touch with them, he was forced to the dubious recourse of a bribed servant. As the king's health grew more precarious, their chance of regaining their freedom diminished, for Catherine was at pains to follow Anjou's advice sent from Poland: "Everything must be done to keep the Duc d'Alençon from seizing power."[31]

During the last half of May the prisoners might as well have been condemned to an oubliette, for they seemed totally forgotten in the anxiety over King Charles' health. "The King is reduced to skin and bones," the English agent wrote; "his legs and thighs are so weak that he cannot hold himself up." For some time Charles had been haemorrhaging from the mouth; now he began to suffer from subcutaneous haemorrhages. On May 23 all audiences were cancelled, and the king's physicians assembled in his chamber to seek some remedy for the convulsive breathing and heavy sweats. Charles was past remedy, but he submitted once again to being bled and purged. "Useless remedies," commented Simon Goulart, "which only weakened him further."[32]

Catherine has left no record of her thoughts during the final days of Charles' illness. She, who had so often complained she had no one on whom she could depend, found that now literally true. Anjou was in Poland; Alençon was a traitor. L'Hôpital and the constable were dead. The constable's eldest son she had imprisoned, and his second son was doing all he could to set himself up as master in Dauphiné. Even the Guises were not at court. Of all those with whom she had matched wits, there was no one left: Condé, Antoine, Jeanne D'Albret, François de Guise—all dead. She was fifty-five, and she had outlived them all—even a husband and two royal sons. Her solitude was immense, and over it lay the shadow of a further loss.

It is impossible to believe she did not recognise how close Charles was to death. She had seen death too often to trust the bland reassurances of the physicians. Yet nowhere did she betray herself. Her letters are full of firm confidence in the king's recovery. In early May, in a letter to the Duke of Savoy, she expressed her joy in her son's response to the medicine prescribed. "Thanks be to God," she wrote, "there is nothing more than a very great weakness and the remains of a cough, which is nothing." And even as late as May 23 she wrote Fénelon in England: "My son is feeling better and better . . . and his fever is constantly dropping. He has had five attacks of fever, but the doctors are hoping that he will have only one or two more to make the number seven in all; for these attacks are now very slight, thanks be to God!" Four days later she wrote the magistrates of Paris that there was every reason to hope for an "entire cure." It was, no doubt, her way of countering the panic that might ensue if the people were aware of how close the king was to death. In fact, she deceived no one. Paris seethed with gossip and rumours, and those at court were already writing with simple futurity, "When the king dies. . . ."[33]

By the end of the month Charles himself had faced the truth, and on May 30 he wrote to Matignon in Normandy, "You have heard of my illness before this . . . today I have reached that state where I am waiting to know God's pleasure for me, for all human things are in His hand."[34] The preceding fall Charles had signed letters patent establishing that should he die without male issue, the throne would pass to his brothers. Now, in a letter written the day before his death, he affirmed that Catherine, who during his illness "had exercised greater care than ever of my affairs and those of my kingdom," would act as regent "until the King of Poland, who is my legitimate successor, will arrive." Both Alençon and Navarre, he concluded, have promised to obey the new regent "according to the love and affection which they bear her."[35]

Charles had reached the limit of his strength. He could retain no food—his only alleviation a little ice to cool his parched lips. When Catherine came to report a successful battle at Domfront in which Montgomery, the Huguenot leader, had been taken, he said nothing, and then, as from a long distance, "All human things are no longer anything to me."[36] On the morning of May 30, after a night of agonised breathing, the king died. Catherine was with him, and his last words were for her: "Ma mère," he said. Some thought it was an unfinished wish, but Catherine heard it as her son's last filial expression of affection and dependence.

Mother of the King

Henri, by the grace of his mother, uncertain King of
France.

—Anon.

Chapter XII

For the third time Catherine closed the eyes of a king in death and gave commands for the intricate ceremonial.

Death dignified Charles. Often labelled mad, sick, unnatural during his life, now, as Goulart cynically commented, he was spoken of "as though he had been the most accomplished and holiest person who had ever lived." Arnaud Sorbin stumbled in his efforts to praise the king adequately, and Blaise de Monluc foolishly affirmed, "I would dare say that had he lived he would have done great things."[1]

Hyperbole and reflection, however, were the work of the outer circles; within the court itself there was no time for backward glances. The king's body was embalmed and placed in a metal casket for the forty days preceding burial. About the casket gathered twelve members from the four major religious orders whose duty was to intone the endless prayers and sprinkle the casket repeatedly with blessed water from their silver asperges. In an adjoining room the king's effigy was seated, clothed in a satin tunic embroidered with fleurs-de-lys, a crimson cloak trimmed with ermine over its shoulders and wearing a crown resplendent with precious stones. Within those two rooms were represented the full cycle of life and death, of human glory and human limitation—what man might acquire and what, finally, he was forced to surrender. Within the ritual was a powerful truth, but Catherine had no time for it. On June 1 she moved the court to the Louvre, leaving only the religious and a few minor noblemen to keep Charles company at Vincennes.

At the Louvre she erected another fortress. All but the main gate was ordered locked, and this was strongly guarded by the royal archers and the Swiss Guard. This, she knew, was the strategic moment for an uprising, and this she intended to take every precaution against. Vincennes had been too far from Paris; from the Louvre she could keep the city under scrutiny, alert to the first signs of unrest. Well aware her regency was regarded with "great misliking" by many, she lost no time in strengthening it. By June 3 letters of confirmation had been registered at the Paris Parlement explaining that Catherine had assumed this responsibility "at the request" of Alençon, Navarre, the Cardinal de Bourbon, and others. A circular letter, under Navarre and Alençon's signature, had already gone out, enjoining the governors of the provinces that while they awaited the return of Anjou, they "help and obey" Catherine, who "with her prudence, wide experience, and singular devotion to this crown," would exercise the position of regent.[2]

Meanwhile, Catherine herself wrote at length to her ambassadors and other notables, expressing her great sense of loss at the death of her son and her reluctance in assuming the burden of regency. "I have accepted this charge, even though it had been my intention to put aside all such affairs and seek peace and tranquillity of life," she explained.[3] It was a protestation not even the naïve would believe. If anything, age had increased Catherine's energy. Despite her bouts of ill health, she had an extraordinary capacity for action: She outrode her courtiers, exhausted her servants, overworked her secretaries, so that one of them complained that his arm was lame with too much writing. Intrigue, too, had become a way of life for her. Awkward and inept at first, she had been drawn against her will into the dance; soon she discovered a hitherto-unplumbed ability, and before long she found herself where the music was fastest. Often she danced for her life, and the danger made her inventive. She set the measure with intricate steps of her own devising, often tripping with some unexpected movement those who tried to keep pace with her. The rhythm of the music had found its way to her pulse. Navarre touched that pulse when he commented shrewdly many years later, "Madame, you grow strong on this trouble; if you had peace you would not know how to live."[4]

Within hours of Charles' death she had directed a letter to Poland, addressing her son no longer as "Anjou" but by his Christian name: Henri of France. It was a letter of mingled regret and consolation that her favourite would soon govern France:

> I thought I would despair at seeing the love he showed me at the end, not being able to leave me, and begging me to send for you in all haste. . . . As for the rest, he is dead, having received the sacraments. . . . the last word he uttered was "*Ma mère.*" This has been an extreme grief for me and I find no other consolation . . . than to see you here soon, for your kingdom has great need of you.

And then with a clear cry of her heart, she wrote, "If ever I were to lose you, I would bury myself alive with you." There was, however, to be no need for such drama. Henri was the only son she was not to lose by death. Instead, she lost him year by year, in a thousand disillusionments and misplaced hopes. Before he left Poland, she wrote confidently, "I am sure that there has never been so wise a king." In fact, the "wise king" had already begun to play the fool.[5]

It is interesting to speculate what might have happened to Henri had he not been recalled so quickly to France. It is impossible to believe he would have long remained in a kingdom so alien to his taste. From the first, he had felt no affinity for Poland, and on his arrival at Cracow, his feeling of alienation grew. He hated the cold, the heavy snows, the dark massive architecture of the palace. His nobility, tall, robust men, dwarfed him by their size and silenced him by their language. He made no effort to adapt but withdrew with Valois reserve into the circle of his French attendants. He had come to reign according to the Valois tradition—a mingling of divine will and intrigue. Even before reaching Cracow, he had written Rambouillet to be sure that his apartments had sufficient private exits and entrances, adding, "You know my mother's inclinations on this subject."[6]

When news of his brother's death reached him on June 12, he received it with a joy only slightly alloyed with family sorrow. What he did then is a presage of that folly of which his life is full. Without taking counsel or advice, without even advising his ministers, he stole out the secret exit of his apartment and, accompanied by a few attendants, drove his horse like a thief or a madman to the Polish frontier. It was a ludicrous departure, and in amusement a contemporary versifier wrote an ode in which he had Henri sing:

> Farewell, Poland, Farewell. Farewell
> To your deserts, your waters, your waves covered by ice and snow.
> Farewell, O country, an eternal farewell.
> Your airs, your customs have so displeased me
> That all must be entirely changed
> If ever more I shall return to this place.[7]

At the beginning of July he arrived at the border of the Venetian states. Italy would have appealed to him at any time, but coming after the loneliness and chill of Poland, it lay before him as an earthly paradise. Like a prisoner condemned to live in darkness, he celebrated his deliverance, absorbing the sunlight of Italy, feeling grace and warmth flow back into him. None of Catherine's children was possessed of more natural charm and graciousness than Henri, and the people who now came to welcome him felt the full breath of it. Du Ferrier wrote to Catherine on July 6:

> I have found him as healthy and joyful as you could wish. . . . He is giving great pleasure to the princes and lords who have come to welcome him—and, indeed, to all the people and to the villages through which he passes. He is admired by everyone, not only for his pleasant disposition but also for that royal sweetness and humanity which lights up his face. . . . If the predictions that have been made about him come true, then he will be one of the greatest princes in the world.[8]

Although the letter was everything Catherine could desire, it would have pleased her even more had Henri himself written to her describing his impressions of her native country. Except for a short letter from Austria at the end of June, however, he had left her in silence. That letter had been a cause of great joy, for in it he had told her that he intended to depend on her advice in everything, concluding, "I am your son who has always obeyed you, and I am more determined and resolved than ever. I am overcome with happiness at the thought of seeing you."[9] All of Catherine's hopes converged on his return. Her hopes for her son and for France under his rule were limitless. Her warrior-king, the hero of Jarnac and Moncontour, was nonpareil.

On July 10, after the prescribed period of mourning, Charles' body had been taken, in solemn procession, to the Church of St. Antoine-des-Champs. Two days later the final funeral mass was celebrated at Notre Dame, and his body interred beside his brother and father at St. Denis. At the end of the service, in symbolic ritual, a herald had cried, "The king is dead," and broke Charles' staff in two. But as his voice echoed and died amidst the vaults of the basilica, a second herald proclaimed, "The king lives, long live Henri III!"[10] It was the first public utterance of the new king's name, and to Catholic Paris it had a very sweet ring.

Not all France shared this joy, however. The Huguenots and even the moderate Politiques—now championed by Montmorency-Damville—remembered with anxiety Henri's fervent espousals of Guise policies. Catherine, aware these were hazardous months, ruled with a heavy hand. François de Montmorency was kept in the Bastille; Alençon and Navarre, although they had been moved to the Louvre, had not regained their liberty. Their windows were barred, and their guard was increased. Twice they had tried to escape: once disguised in women's clothes and again through a postern gate left unlocked. Although both attempts had failed, Catherine was alarmed by evidence that England was offering them substantial aid. In June she had observed that Sir Thomas Leighton had attempted a whispered conversation with Alençon, and she had written in indignation to Fénelon that Elizabeth was misinformed if she thought these young princes were being unduly humiliated. "On the contrary," she observed, "they are very happy, and I am very pleased with them."[11]

Towards the end of July she became increasingly annoyed at England's continued interference, especially when she received word of renewed English activity around Calais. This time she wrote to Elizabeth herself, advising her that Alençon was being "seduced' by certain Englishmen who are telling him that "you will give him 50,000 écus as well as men to help him form an army . . . not only to stir up trouble in this kingdom but in all Christianity." Catherine was not usually so overt in her attacks and Fénelon, fearing Elizabeth's response, warned his queen "to moderate . . . the suspicion you have shown towards this princess . . . lest she enter openly into a league with the Protestants."[12] Catherine's stubborn response was to tighten the regulations around Navarre and Alençon, scarcely letting them out of her sight wherever she travelled, so that

Dale in amusement called them "her chickens," writing to Walsingham that Alençon "dares not speak to any man nor any man to him."[13]

In such humour the court arrived at Lyons in the savage heat of August to await the arrival of the new king. Mists rose from the sluggish rivers surrounding the city, and at midday Lyons drifted to sleep, half-invisible in the shimmering haze. Catherine had been advised to delay her trip until she had received further word from Henri, but the queen mother was more impatient than a bride. No matter the subject of her letters, they were all set to the same melody: the arrival of Henri. "When my son comes" became her leitmotiv.

The impatience was all on Catherine's side, however. The eager king, who had spurred his horse to death in his haste to leave Poland, was pressed by no urgency when he reached Italy. On July 15 he was met at Conegliano and, in the company of the French ambassadors Du Ferrier and De Foix was brought south to Venice. The "Jewel of the Adriatic" aroused the sybarite in him, and Henri responded to it like a lover. He was at once stimulated and lulled. Poland was forgotten—and so, indeed, was France. For once his Medici blood was in his favour, as was his fine, subtle Valois heritage with its exotic pleasure in the arts.

In Venice he was welcomed with "trumpets and cannon," while 100 handsome young gentlemen were put at his service. The dukes of Nevers and Ferrara and the Papal Legate Buoncompagni waited to conduct him to three gondolas draped in black velvet, violet, and cloth of gold. Even the oarsmen seemed mysterious and seductive in their yellow satin robes and Turkish turbans. After the solitude of Cracow, he was exhilarated by the crowds gathered in the square to see him as he entered San Marco's for solemn prayers of thanksgiving.

For nine ecstatic days he attended banquets and parties and dances. He glided beneath the *arcs de triomphes* Palladio had designed in his honour; he visited the boutiques on the Rialto and the artists' studios. He sat for a portrait by Tintoretto, who painted him with exaggerated royal bearing—graceful, handsome, the high ruff giving shape and character to his narrow Valois face. No portrait painter ever captured his regal charm so well. The grace was there, but so also were the high intelligence, the power to penetrate and to command. Something else, however, found its way into the portrait, something that betrayed itself in the subtle femininity of the hands and an impenetrable reserve in the eyes. It was not a face to win easy confidence, nor did it suggest easy contentment.[14]

For the moment, not a single wind ruffled his pleasure. Everything about Venice delighted Henri, most of all, perhaps, the responsiveness of the people to his own person. There was only one critic to dissent from the unanimous applause. The Papal Legate was not impressed. He found the French king cold and reserved, his colour poor, and his head more like a Spaniard's than a Frenchman's. The purple slippers and small purple cap struck him as affected and frivolous.[15] But Buoncompagni's criticisms were lost in the general adulation to which Henri responded by bestowing gifts with royal prodigality—perfume, jewels, enamels, a diamond of unusual beauty to the doge. When his treasury became empty, he borrowed from his hosts with the same beneficent gestures and the same winning grace. That he left debts behind him is evident in a letter written to Du Ferrier from Cremona. "I hope to send you from Turin," he promised, "all the gold, silver, and securities necessary for the pearls and other things that I bought at Venice."[16]

Although Henri's letter had been written on August 9, it took him more than three weeks to complete the journey across the mountains of northern Italy to Turin and almost another month for the final eastward journey to Lyons. Catherine, who had written to Fénelon on August 6, "He is now at Turin and will soon be at Lyons," was sadly deceived. Not only did Henri dally, but he acted as though he had forgotten that a country, sorely in need of the strong hand of leadership, was anxiously awaiting him. In August Dale wrote in some puzzlement to Burghley, "From July 17 through August 6 there has been no news from the King of France."[17]

While Catherine waited, she drew up a memorandum that she sent to Henri through the chancellor Cheverny. It was not only a summation of her hopes for her son, but a testament of her own political experience. "To enter his kingdom like a prince" was the goal she set for him, listing some of those elements that would make his rule secure: Let him not espouse favourites, nor "let one man hold all"; let him be diligent, dealing with matters personally, especially fiscal matters, which should be reviewed daily; let him be firm so that from the beginning he will be recognised as master, otherwise people will be inclined to say, "He is young, we can make him do whatever we please."[18] It was a masterful document, concise, cogent, practical, capable of changing the state of France. The tragedy was that the young man who arrived in France during the first week of September was already incapable of carrying it out.

When, at last, word was brought of the approach of the king, the royal family rode west across the plateau of *les terres-froides*—a singularly inappropriate name during the early September heat—to meet Henri at Le Pont-de-Beauvoisin. Of that initial meeting, only Margot, already at odds with her brother, recorded her impressions. "Although the season was very hot . . . there came upon me so great a chill that I shivered all over," she wrote ominously, noting this was "a secret intimation of what was to come."[19] Catherine left no account of her reactions, although Zúñiga observed in his despatches to Philip that the queen mother wept. If so, it may have been in mingled joy and disappointment.

The change in Henri was patent. His fresh colour had been replaced by a darker, sallow look. The cut of his hair and the toque he affected made his face seem thinner. Buoncompagni's comment that he looked more Spanish than French was not without justification. In dress, however, he mirrored nothing of the austere Spanish taste, but rather the flamboyance of Venetian fashion. In everything he indulged his passion for violet satin. His tunics and capes were ornamented with

buttons and ribbons of violet and red; his sleeves were slashed in the new fashion; bracelets of coral and silver tinkled on his wrists and pendants dangled from
his ears.

When he made his royal entrance into Lyons, late on the afternoon of September 6, the streets and windows teemed with people. Many remembered the handsome boy who had attended his elder brother Charles when the court had stopped
there ten years before. Then his vitality had been in marked contrast to the frail,
languid king. They had hoped that same vitality would restore France. Their initial enthusiasm, however, was replaced by what De Thou describes as
"distaste."[20] The king's manner, it was true, was impeccable. He rode through
the city in a large carriage, facing his mother to whom he showed "great rever-
ence"; he greeted the city elders attentively, accepting their promise of loyal
service and assuring them of his reciprocal devotion.

He was correct to a fault, but the warmth his subjects had anticipated was lacking. He had, it seemed, placed a limitless distance between himself and the people he had returned to govern. They noted his Italian bonnet, his affectations of
dress, his heavy-lidded, almond eyes, and they found him foreign. His courtiers,
used to a certain friendly ease with their master, were soon affronted by the regulations Henri set: he would eat alone with an elaborate ritual of etiquette; the
number of those having access to the royal presence was to be drastically cut, the
hours when he would be available limited. His Council would be reduced, and
important matters deliberated in secret.

The result was immediate and disastrous. "There is great confusion at court,"
Giovanni Morosini wrote to Venice, "for these changes . . . seem so unbearable to the courtiers that many of them have left for their homes, unable to bear
the thought of not seeing the king more often or of not being able to speak with
him with the same familiarity to which they were hitherto accustomed."[21] Nothing could compensate for the goodwill of his servants, and Catherine, who clearly recognised the need for a sovereign to be present, cordially and informally, to
his people, must have witnessed these sudden shifts with painful misgiving. Had
Henri been a Philip II—austere, silent, given to solitude and hours of meticulous
labour—such a course of action might have worked. As it was, the image of the
aloof monarch was immediately dissipated by the image of the fop, dancing all
night, giving jewels he could not pay for to the women who flattered him, pursuing frivolity as he had once pursued glory. "All his instincts for valour have disappeared," Michieli noted in his despatches, and even the loyal Monluc wrote
sadly, "I have found him completely changed."[22]

Catherine's loyalty kept her silent, although her disappointment must have
been proportioned to her dreams. When, in a moment of foolish prodigality, the
king ceded certain lands to the Duke of Savoy without the advice or consent of
his outraged Council, Catherine did what she could to palliate his folly. Some
follies, however, she could not palliate. Already he had lost Damville and the

Politiques by his autocratic refusal to discuss their terms in a conference held earlier at Turin. Now he made it clear he did not intend to grant concessions to the Huguenots, to reduce taxation, or to call the Estates. He would subject Dauphiné and Languedoc to his authority, he would clear France of her enemies, and— since no other course seemed possible—he would do it by force of arms. It was the reckless decision of a man who had not learned to take stock of his resources. The same impulse that had led him to buy beyond his means on the Rialto now led him to far more dangerous extravagances. His cruel order to burn the crops in Languedoc and his willingness to accept Spanish help in putting down his own subjects only diminished his authority further.

By November, 1574, France was again in open conflict, with four royal armies in the field, one of which was captained by the king himself. Although the military bearing that had once impressed his captains was clearly lacking, Henri still prided himself on his soldierly skill, boasting he would soon clear France of its enemies. Towards the end of November, however, the king received news that completely demoralised him: Marie de Clèves—the wife of Condé—with whom he had been passionately and fatuously in love for almost two years had died in childbirth. When he received the news, he fainted, and for the next few days he lay senseless with grief. When he reappeared, the extravagances of his dress had been replaced by something even more bizarre. His earrings and bracelets had been laid aside for a string of death's-heads exquisitely carved. His hose, his doublet, his cloak were of unrelieved black. The fact that no King of France wore black even for a death within the royal family marked even more the erratic nature of his behaviour.

Religion now replaced Eros, and for the first time Henri's morbid sensibility found relief in a passion for penance. As once he had used his own blood to write to the beautiful Princesse de Clèves, now he joined the Battus—a group of flagellants—to shed his blood in the pure cause of religion. It was the first public manifestation of the taint which was to poison all that was fine in him. The garden had produced its first *fleur du mal*. Augier de Busbecq with marvellous understatement wrote to Maximilian: "I am frightened that everything is not golden here."[23]

Catherine, however, determined to do what she could to *make* it golden, began the preparations for her son's coronation. With a kind of naïve superstition, she hoped to cure France of its ills by anointing her son with chrism and crowning him with gold. But no simple ritual could transform Henri into the leader France needed. The Papal Legate Frangipani had stated the case astutely when he had written in December to Cardinal Cuomo: "The true and proper remedy for the evil from which this kingdom suffers will be a king who has courage, who understands what it is to be a king, and who wishes to be one. . . ."[24] The will to rule was lacking in Henri, although there still remained a great desire to play the king—to dress the part, to dazzle the audience. His actions were reminiscent of the games the royal children had played years before—romping in makeshift bishops' robes or preachers' ruffs, mocking in their levity the roles they played. Even then there had been those at court who had frowned on such games, but Catherine, more permissive, had excused them, saying these were only the normal games of children. It was Henri's misfortune that he had never outgrown his love of make-believe.

In a country ruined by war and debt the player king was to no one's taste.

Catherine's disappointment must have been enormous. For almost ten years she had been directing her hopes to this favourite she called "My Eyes." He had been in France for five months, and during that time there had been scarcely a single action to justify her hopes. The Politiques had found him intransigent; his captains, indifferent; his nobles, arrogant. Even his health was a disappointment, for, as Salviati noted, after a night or two of pleasure he was so fatigued that he could not leave his bed for a week. That a coronation ceremony would be sufficient to change all this seemed unlikely, but Catherine held tenaciously to any hope for gilding the royal image.

In fact, the coronation accomplished the opposite. The long journey from Lyons to Reims had been cold and dangerous. The winds from the Alpilles blew unchecked across the plains of the Massif Central; gusts of snow formed drifts to slow the royal progress; the rivers ran high and deep. More stormy than the weather itself was the young king. Weary, ill-tempered, and still locked in melancholy over the death of Marie de Clèves, Henri III suffered his coronation.

The king who, it was rumoured, did not have money to buy new cloaks to replace the threadbare vesture of his pages was crowned without great luxury. It was too early for flowers to decorate his path, and the cathedral retained the winter's cold despite the throng of people and the vast number of smoking torches. Those near the king reported that when the crown was placed on his head, "he said aloud that it hurt him" and that twice it had started to slip.[25]

Shortly after the *sacre*, "so quick and secret as to be almost clandestine," Henri married Louise de Vaudémont. She was, it was said, a "handsome" girl, noted for her virtue. "A peaceful, devout spirit," the diarist Pierre de L'Estoile called her, but she was cousin to the Guises, a fact which displeased many who saw it as "the thin edge of the wedge" for increasing Guisard power. It was a further disappointment for Catherine, who not only recognised the danger of having the House of Lorraine so near the throne but had had far greater ambitions for her son than this. The preceding fall Busbecq had spoken of the possibility of the new king's marrying his brother's widow, Elizabeth of Austria, and in November, Philip II had written of a marriage between Henri and one of his daughters. There is no evidence of what happened to either of these negotiations or what now impelled the king to this unlooked-for alliance. Someone observed Louise resembled Marie de Clèves. This might have stimulated the king's morbid imagination, but Catherine, for whom marriage was always a political tool, could hardly have found it satisfying.[26]

In these months the son ran counter to his mother's wishes in everything. She had advised that he make himself cordially available to his nobility; instead, he had withdrawn from them, making of his room "a sanctuary" and of himself "a god." "We have never had so much bowing and scraping," wrote Louis Regnaut, a member of the court. "It would be far better for us to learn to live in peace rather than to have all these monkey tricks," was his forthright conclusion.[27] Catherine had also cautioned her son about surrounding himself with "favourites," who insinuated themselves into high places, not through merit but through flattery. A coterie of young men might be acceptable in a young prince, but in a king it could arouse only hostility and jealousy. Yet Henri had already gathered about him "those wild young men," the *mignons,* on whom he would lavish his attention and a fortune he did not possess. Money was such a daily problem at court that L'Estoile commented, "The common gossip is that the king doesn't have enough money for his dinner; he has to borrow the funds he lives on."[28]

The ritual pomp with which the impoverished king surrounded himself only dissipated the loyalty and respect of his people. In June Busbecq wrote ominously to Maximilian:

> I see that the respect for the Majesty of the King has been weakened in a strange manner and that the minds of men grow wild, having shaken off their respect for the name of King just as animals shake off a strong yoke. . . . If, finally, there be war in France and if Condé will come with great forces,* as it is thought, the struggle will not be concerning religion or place or whose opinion ought to prevail or whose popularity will be preferred before the King, or who will manage the kingdom, but clearly who will reign.[29]

There was no exaggeration in Busbecq's appraisal. Henri's brusque treatment of Damville, whom he had met in Turin the preceding August, and his later refusal to treat with the Huguenot delegates had had ruinous consequences. In January, 1575, formal articles of agreement between the Politiques and the Huguenot delegates had been adopted, and Damville placed at the head of their joint forces. He was a popular figure—a brave soldier and a decisive administrator— and Busbecq soon wrote, "Gentlemen are flocking under his standard." Despite his radical position, Damville consistently maintained that his purpose was to "give his life to save the kingdom for the King and against his evil councillors."[30]

---

*Condé had earlier escaped to Germany, where he was soliciting help for the Huguenots' cause.

In April delegates had been sent by the Huguenots to confer with the king. Mild and diplomatic in their approach, they seemed at first capable of achieving a peaceful settlement. Their manner, however, belied the tenacity with which they adhered to their principal demand: the restoration of the liberal legislation registered thirteen years earlier and known as the Edict of January. What disrupted the conferences is not clear. Some maintained that Henri, badgered by the delegates' persistence, lost his temper and threw their request into the fire. Others indicated that Catherine flatly refused their demands and that her son followed her lead. The image of Catherine as tyrant had become increasingly accepted as the king's weakness had become more obvious. "The king is entirely submissive and the regent has triumphed," Salviati wrote.[31]*

Throughout May and June Catherine engaged in a series of letters to Damville, assuring him her son was willing to do anything to bring peace and begging his help and influence in this cause. In August she was writing in the same vein to Condé, begging him to listen to the king and not be so likely to take the counsel of those men who had gained his ear too easily. "Take the true path," she begged him, assuring him he would live much more happily in fulfilling his obedience to the king. Her words had little impact, however, for since the massacre all her promises were suspect. Both Catholics and Protestants mistrusted her equally, interpreting all her actions as personal power plays. "Her aim is always to remain in power," Michieli wrote bluntly in his report to Venice. And in a letter to Cardinal Granvelle, an observer commented, "Those who have just come from Paris say that the people are very discontent at seeing the youth and laziness of their king who leaves himself entirely in his mother's hands, who rules him according to her fancy, which could cost him dear someday."[32]

Of other periods of her life, Catherine left some record of her emotions, admitting that she was alone, fearful, mistrustful, unable to confide in anyone, not sure what offers of help she could prudently trust. Of this period she has left nothing, yet it must have been a time of increasing loneliness. In early spring, shortly after her return to Paris, she learned of the death of her daughter Claude, wife of the Duc de Lorraine. Wearied from the long months of intermittent travel and even more by disappointment in her son, she was undone by this unexpected loss. She took to her bed, "weeping long." Of the seven children she had raised past infancy, Claude was the fourth to die: François, Elizabeth, Charles, and now Claude. Only three remained, and two of them—Margot and Alençon—had already forfeited her trust. Henri alone was left to bear the full and demanding weight of her love. To that love he responded with an apparent insouciance that baffled and wounded his mother. Far from sharing her grief at his sister's death, he remained unmoved, continuing his round of banquets, balls, hunting parties as though Claude had been nothing to him.

* Salviati's language is inexact; Catherine ceased to be regent on Henri's return from Poland.

Already Henri had begun that ruinous pattern of sidestepping the tragic and burdensome aspects of life, losing himself in pleasure, religion, abstract philosophy. It was clear to Catherine that he was forfeiting his royal power, yet even in his folly she loved him and would gladly have carried the burden he could not manage. Experience had taught her the value of power, and she could not bear to see it slip away so carelessly from her son. Yet with every effort to shore up the king's power, she was met with the accusation that she sought it for her own sinister advantage. It was the inevitable result of the massacre that Catherine be isolated in a prison of mistrust.

Chapter XIII

The court during the summer of 1575 was a nightmare of discord and suspicion. Shortly after Henri's return, he had pardoned his brother and his cousin Navarre, but it was no more than a paper pardon. In fact, they continued to be under humiliating surveillance, with men to "dog them wherever they go." Margot, whose childhood enmity for her brother Henri had increased with her marriage, now allied herself with the "thorny princes," less out of affection for her husband than out of dislike of her brother. Margot's stance only complicated the family web of hostility and mistrust. "It is a very hell among them," Dale wrote to Walsingham, "not one content or in quiet with another, nor mother with son, nor brother with brother, nor mother with daughter."[1]

In July the tension was heightened by evidence that Alençon was in continued communication with Condé.* The king upbraided him sharply, warning that if he did not change his way, he should be "chipped straighter." Catherine, convinced that Alençon's passion for liberty and power would only be swelled by such reprimands, sought to counter them by maternal indulgence and an effort to advance her youngest in small ways she hoped would content him. Even in this, however, she displeased the king, who, blaming Alençon's boldness on Catherine's lenience, commented, "It is you, Mother, who do hold him up by the chin."[2]

The fever consuming Alençon, however, would never be alleviated by the small favours Catherine could provide. That desire to rule which in Henri had been alloyed with so many baser metals in Alençon ran clean and pure. It had replaced the blood of human affection or prudence. The irony was that of all of Catherine's sons, the only one destined never to wear the crown of France pulsed with a desire to reign. Catherine's intuition about Alençon soon proved right. On September 15, unable to endure the constraint of the court any longer, he man-

---

*When Henri became King of France, his title, Duc d'Anjou, passed to Alençon. For reasons of clarity, however, I have retained the title of Alençon.

aged to escape, leaving behind him dismay, anger, and recrimination. The following day Morosini wrote to Venice: "Yesterday the event took place, which has constantly been dreaded, and which may be considered to be the total ruin of this unfortunate and ill-starred kingdom: namely, Monsieur, the Duke of Alençon escaped from the Court."[3]

The escape had been simple. Alençon, while on an "errand of love," had slipped quietly out of the lady's back door and, in a borrowed coach, headed due west for Dreux, where, it was reported, several hundred armed men awaited him. Henri, wild with fear and anger, immediately ordered all ports under surveillance and put the Duc de Nevers in charge of the pursuit. Meanwhile, he wrote an official account to his nobles, vigorously denying the rumours that Alençon had fled because there had been plans to put him in the Bastille or some other "safe" place. "God is my witness," the king wrote, "of the fraternal love I have always borne him." His avowal of brotherly love was somewhat vitiated, however, by his threatening injunction to "apprehend and arrest him wherever he is and bring him to me." Henri, always prone to exaggerated emotions, now showed himself totally unable to maintain his composure during the first real crisis of his reign. "He acted as if the kingdom were lost," wrote Goulart; "there were cries of alarm on all sides, and all of France was full of couriers and packets to the governors of the provinces, whom he begged and adjured to be faithful to him."[4]

Alençon showed himself far more self-possessed. Upon his escape, he had written directly to the king, protesting his loyalty but also protesting the king's injustice to him and his servants. He took the opportunity of regaining his liberty, he explained, "in order to avoid the danger to my life, having been advised . . . that a place in the Bastille had been prepared for me. . . . Nevertheless, such is the devotion I bear to your service and to the peace of this kingdom that I ask only the safety of my person and the right to spend my days in freedom."[5]

Catherine, meanwhile, had already undertaken negotiations with Alençon. Even more than the king, she recognised the danger of having him abroad in the kingdom, gathering a rebel army around him. Despite Alençon's declaration that he wanted nothing but the preservation of the kingdom and the reestablishment of its former laws and statutes, he showed little interest in the rapprochemont Catherine attempted to effect. In the two weeks following his flight she had travelled south from Mantes into Houdan, through the wooded hills around Dreux, past Châteaudun, and finally into the château region of Chambord. To her pleas to meet with her, he first answered that it would give him "great joy" to see her but a few days later protested he was in great haste to reach Beaugency and could not stop until he had crossed the Loire.

Catherine, indefatigable, continued her pursuit, and finally, on September 29, 1575, a meeting was arranged between Chambord and Blois. Later she wrote Henri that when Alençon saw her coach, he dismounted at once and ran to meet her. His apparent delight in seeing his mother, however, did not make him any more amenable, for he continued to accuse the king of preferring the Guises and of planning further imprisonment for him. When Catherine begged her son not to make "two kingdoms out of one," she received no answer. For two days they dickered without agreement.

By now she had given over blandishments, and shortly before one of her meetings with Alençon, she wrote to him bluntly, attempting to open his eyes to the fact that he risked everything he had set his heart on by openly opposing his brother. Once again it is a question of evil counsel:

> I am not concerned with who finds this good or bad, but I intend to bring this kingdom to peace and your own life to safety. I know very well that there are those who will tell you that this is not so; and why? . . . They dare not say that it is for their own interest that they want to endanger this kingdom and put your life in jeopardy. . . . I beg you to think this over. . . . Please forgive me for speaking to you like this, but my affection for you forces me to speak thus. . . . I shall conclude now, begging God to counsel you well.[6]

Throughout October Catherine remained at Blois, persuading, coercing, threatening. She tried to mask her panic at the news that Thoré, the third of the Montmorency brothers, had joined Alençon with more than 1,000 horse. The original group who had joined Alençon at Dreux had now swelled into a force with the dangerous title of the Army of Monsieur. Despite the men who flocked to him, however, Alençon made no overt effort to organise for war. In fact, he seemed entirely content to do nothing. He travelled about the countryside, talking of establishing a headquarters at Orléans, making demands that La Charité be given him, pricking the king by his hostile presence.

Throughout the fall he remained in the country around the Loire, always close at hand but never accessible. The "little blackamoor," as Catherine had described him in his childhood, was beginning to shape his role. He would never be a great warrior—it was not a role he aspired to—yet in his own way he would draw blood. He was quick and deft, and his sudden movements were hard to follow. Even when he did nothing, he was a source of anxiety, for his very inaction threatened like a lowering storm. Before his short life was over, he would drive his royal brother near madness. It was a meagre achievement, but in Alençon's jealous eyes it passed for a kind of success.

For Catherine, nothing was more difficult to bear than these anxious days of fruitless waiting and false hopes. In another mood she would have enjoyed the weeks away from Paris. Blois was very beautiful in the fall. The fields had been harvested; the foliage along the banks of the Loire had turned golden. Some of the leaves had already fallen, and the flat, fertile land was visible for miles. Other parts of France might have more exotic beauty, but nothing equalled the quiet grace of Touraine. On all sides rose the great châteaux François I had loved so well: Chambord with its great round towers and perfect symmetry; the jewelled elegance of Chenonceaux; Amboise with its mingled history of splendour and horror; the quaint medieval charm of Chaumont. Yet Catherine was aware that if war were to come, this tranquil land would suffer the fate of so many other regions of France. An autumn melancholy overcame her, and she wrote to Henri that she was "saddened" at the thought that "such a beautiful kingdom is in such danger."[7]

What she had anticipated as the work of days stretched into weeks without bringing her appreciably closer to her goal. In mid-October Busbecq wrote sceptically, "They think that tomorrow Alençon will return to his mother in the town of Blois to obtain peace. But to me the whole thing is an object of suspicion, and even if he should return, I think that nothing would be agreed upon."[8] Busbecq was right. It was the end of November before peace was concluded. The six-month truce that was ultimately signed at Champigny on November 21 solved little. On that same day Catherine wrote in anger to the king, complaining that the Huguenots maintained she was not empowered to make such a settlement and that, consequently, Alençon should never have signed it.[9] In any case, his signature meant little, for he made no effort to disband his army and continued his communication with Condé. The Huguenot leaders La Noue and Turenne had already brought reenforcements, and Condé was leading German reiters into France to join the Army of Monsieur.

In everything Alençon had the ascendancy. Catherine had never anticipated such a conclusion. She had hoped by conceding to some of his demands to win him back to the crown. Thus, she had persuaded the king to free Montmorency and Brissac from the Bastille, to send Alençon—as a beneficent gesture—his silver plate, horses, and personal servants, to give him the places of surety he demanded. In return, Alençon conceded nothing. By February, 1576, he had at least 30,000 men at his service, with the possibility of more.

Then on February 6 came an unforeseen danger: Henri de Navarre escaped from court to assume the leadership of the Huguenot cause.

Navarre, amiable and aimless, had lulled all suspicions. He had taken no part in Alençon's flight; indeed, it hardly seemed to have interested him. He was often seen in the company of the Duc de Guise and his brother Mayenne. Even more often he was in the company of the women of the court (especially in that of Catherine's Circe, the blond and beautiful Charlotte de Sauves), for although Navarre's sophisticated wife saw little in him to admire—he was neither handsome nor polished—he was beginning to acquire a reputation as a very satisfactory lover. Far from being politically dangerous, he was rather a subject for amusement. Even Cavalli, ordinarily so astute, had written to Venice that Navarre seemed very much like his father, rather light-headed and lighthearted, and, consequently, "considered of very little importance."[10]

His escape, so totally unlooked for, left the king in despair. A few days after

his departure Henri wrote to Michel Castelnau, Sieur de Mauvissière, his
newly appointed ambassador to England,

> I considered him so united to me that he would never be able to separate him-
> self . . . he told me that he intended to return to sleep here yesterday evening; but
> instead of returning he sent me word by Sieur de St. Martin that he had been told
> that I was going to have him arrested. As God is my witness, I have never had any
> thought or desire to do this. . . . I deeply regret this, for he leaves under such a
> false impression . . . that it will only hinder further the peace that I have done my
> best to procure. It is all very discouraging.[11]

It became more discouraging as news poured in of the Huguenots who flocked
around Navarre "to take their master home." Soon, it was said, he had at his dis-
posal some 3,000 horse and 9,000 foot. Should this force join the Army of Monsieur, France would be ruined.

Once again Catherine set herself to the task of drawing up a durable peace.
The crown had less than ever to bargain with; everything was on Monsieur's
side. There were even those who goaded Alençon to move to Paris itself, yet despite a more than reasonable hope of success, he hesitated. It was precisely this
element of vacillation that Catherine hoped to utilise, shaking his confidence in
his councillors and playing on his greed with promises of a great appanage
should he return to his family who loved him. Catherine had not been well that
winter—so crippled by sciatica that it was difficult for her to walk or even to
stand for any lengthy period. She was growing old, and her children's quarrels
exhausted her. The English ambassador noted in a letter to Walsingham that "her
eye was nothing like so quick as it was wont to be."[12] Her determination, however, was as keen as ever.

The winter and spring of 1576 were a nightmare. In addition to the combined
forces of Condé, Alençon, and Navarre, German reiters were brought into
France under the leadership of John Casimir of the Palatinate. They were, if one
can believe the chronicles, a terror. Brutal, undisciplined mercenaries, they
owed allegiance to no one. War was a matter of contract, and looting part of the
just rewards of a dangerous profession. As they crossed the Moselle and headed
towards the rich country around Dijon, the peasants fled in panic towards the for-
tified towns, loading their possessions into wheelbarrows or small carts, sweeping their cows and sheep before them. To protect themselves, they walked in
small bands, staves or pitchforks their only defence. Burgundy and the Bourbonnais were soon laid waste. At Langres, the promises of immunity were worthless: The town was pillaged, all moveables piled into wagons, and the houses of
the peasants fired. Not even John Casimir could control his mercenaries.

By March Catherine could listen to no more. She was tired of the councillors
who warned that in the king's weakened position he could procure only a shame-

ful peace. For her, there was no "shameful peace"; there was only the shame of war, the shame of France destroying itself. On March 13 the delegates from the Politiques and Huguenots met with the king's Council to present their articles. For a week the negotiations continued until the Council, declaring the demands of the Huguenots "exorbitant," stalked from the council chamber. Still, Catherine was undaunted. For the next six weeks she wrote letters, she conducted secret interviews, she cajoled, she made promises. During the first week of May she drew the opposing factions together again.

This time they met at Châtenay, near Sens, in an isolated house, set in an open field to allay the possibility of ambush. Alençon was a member of the meeting, and although there is every evidence to indicate that Catherine lost little love on her youngest cub, now she showed herself all mother. He was, as she described him, her *fils égaré*—her wandering son who had come back to the family fold. As a sign of happiness in this reunion and as a pledge of his royal brother's goodwill, Alençon was given the provinces of Berry, Touraine, and Anjou, along with an annual revenue of 100,000 gold crowns.[13]

It was an extraordinary settlement, one that drew bitter criticism on Catherine's head. The Catholics felt she had humiliated the king before his rebel brother. The Huguenots mistrusted this sudden largesse, claiming she was subtly weakening their power by leading Alençon back to the bosom of the royal family. The peace that was eventually signed at Beaulieu on May 4 was sharply criticised everywhere. The Guises were furious, the Pope wrote in protest, and the king, it was rumoured, wept with chagrin when he signed it. "Monsieur's Peace" it was called contemptuously.

Catherine was not proud of the peace, but she was realist enough to acknowledge she had had few options. The power had been solidly behind Alençon. He could have taken what he wanted by force or strategy, and then even the illusion of power would have passed from the king's hands. As it was, she had maintained that illusion. She had listened graciously, she had conferred, she had temporised, and ultimately she had conceded. Concession was a royal prerogative, and Catherine had attempted to handle it royally. It was a political principle with her never to manifest her desperation. Following the Conspiracy of St. Germain, following the escapes of both Alençon and Navarre, she had refused to acknowledge the extent of the trouble, so that the English ambassador noted in amazement, "The Queen still does not admit the great enmity in her family."[14] She was more than aware that the Peace of Beaulieu granted extraordinary privileges to those of the Religion—indeed, the Huguenots themselves seemed surprised at such liberties—but she had established peace, she had given them all a breathing space.

How the illusion of Henri's power would be preserved was an even more difficult problem than the peace itself. His indolence and frivolity had become a subject of public mockery. In mid-July, accompanied by his queen (whose grace and modesty had won the people's affection and sympathy), Henri returned from Normandy with cages of chattering, long-tailed monkeys, multicoloured parrakeets, and tiny dogs purchased at Dieppe. This abnormal desire for exotic little animals was but one more affectation in a personality already verging on the bizarre.

A noticeable change had come over the king in the course of 1576. The exaggerations in his dress had become more pronounced: More and more he affected black satin with heavily embroidered shirts and enormous collars; his graceful Valois hands flashed with jewels, and he was rarely without heavy pendants in his ears. His use of powder and rouge had grown more obvious, and his manner markedly feminine. Although it was gossiped that he was still a frequent visitor in the brothels of Paris, more and more of his time, his money, his energy were consumed by his *mignons*—those exotic young men with their long, curled hair, their little velvet bonnets, and their heavy, cloying scents. "There is beginning to be a lot of talk about the *mignons*," wrote L'Estoile, "who are hated and scorned by the people, as much for their haughty manners as for their effeminate and immodest appearance, but most of all for the excessive liberalities of the king towards them. Popular opinion holds that this is the cause of the people's ruin."[15]

Against the *mignons* Catherine was helpless. Aware of her son's tendency to surround himself with adulation, she had warned him early against cloistering himself with favourites to the envy of the rest of the court. But Henri could not hear her. Now she tried to impress him with the needs of the kingdom: Their treasury was empty, their credit diminished; the people laboured under a ruinous burden of taxation; the reiters had refused to leave France until they had been paid. Most of all, there was an increasing demand for the Estates that had been promised according to the peace terms of Beaulieu. Henri remained strangely unmoved by her recital. Like Charles, he vacillated between frenetic activity and withdrawal. Even the decision of the Polish Diet that he could not retain a claim on the Polish throne for himself or for his heirs seemed a matter of indifference to him.

King Henri was but twenty-five, yet the dynamism of youth was already wasted. His passion for honour and glory which had once sent his mother's hopes rocketing had been extinguished. The more urgent the problems of the kingdom, the more he withdrew into his disordered bower of bliss. For years she had cherished the belief that he was that *Chyren* of whom Nostradamus had prophesied. "At the head of the whole world will be the great *Chyren*," the seer had written, and she had interpreted *Chyren* as an anagram for *Henri*. But there was little greatness here; even the will to greatness had atrophied. Late that summer placards appeared all over Paris proclaiming derisively, "Henri by the grace of his mother, uncertain King of France, imaginary King of Poland, janitor of the Louvre, warden of St. Germain-l'Auxerrois.''[16] The son she had envisioned as France's Messiah had, instead, become its laughingstock.

On December 6, 1576, the meeting of the Estates General, in question since before the death of Charles IX, opened at Blois. Although the crown had no affection for such gatherings, nothing was omitted to make it an occasion of royal splendour. As Catherine had once relied on Henri's coronation to gild the crown, so now she relied on the Estates. If the king could be seen in his majesty, some of the scurrilous gossip might quiet. Even more, were Henri to see himself in full royal splendour, he might recapture his high concept of kingship.

Blois was an ideal stage. The best of the Middle Ages and the Renaissance converged there. The graceful blend of brick and stone, modulated into the finest of Gothic design, was juxtaposed to the ornate Renaissance patterns planned by the lavish taste of François I. Although Blois lacked the picturesque setting of Amboise and the elegance of Chenonceaux, it had something solidly royal about it. In its long history it had given birth to kings and celebrated their triumphs. More than 200 years of French royal history was in its walls. With the grandeur of its architecture, its wealth of sculpture, its elaborate furnishings, Blois was a perfect setting for displaying the King of France—benign, majestic, attentive to the needs of his people, with the full weight and glory of the fleur-de-lys behind him.

On the morning of December 6 the delegates, assembled in the courtyard, were summoned by name to take their places in the hall. They filed through the audience chamber with its black and white marble floor, patterned in the popular Italian design, and into the great hall, its columns decorated with violet velvet embroidered with fleurs-de-lys, its walls hung with tapestries recalling deeds of valour and royal might. On both sides of the hall the delegates took their places, episcopal purple, the flamboyant robes of the nobility, and the sober dress of the bourgeoisie distinguishing the three estates. At a signal from the herald, they rose as the members of the royal family entered to take their places on a dais decorated with purple and covered with rugs, for the hall was cold in December. Last came the king, tall, royal, self-possessed, set apart in his majesty by the satin canopy above him.

Nothing had been spared to make him royal, and despite the ludicrous image he had projected during the last year, Henri was still capable of playing the role of monarch. Now, as he turned to face the delegates, he was grave and commanding. With a gesture at once graceful and imperious, he bade them be seated as he took his place on the dais. On his left sat his queen, Louise, pale, quiet, unobtrusive. On his right, his mother, a portly woman of fifty-seven, who through the years had come increasingly to look the part of the Italian shopkeeper. Beyond her, stooped, dark, sullen, was Alençon, the "wandering son," who had divided a kingdom and who was now displayed by the victors like a proud trophy. All his promises to champion the Huguenots and Politiques had been insubstantial. The first wind had blown them away, and Alençon, his vanity temporarily satisfied, was back in the bosom of the royal family.

In front of the king, the four secretaries of state sat at their table; and, a little apart, sat the most important man of the realm, the chancellor, René de Birague, in his long black gown and square chancellor's cap. Despite his position and influence, to France at large Birague was simply "one of the brood of Italians," one of Catherine's leeches who swelled upon the blood of France. "No fleur-de-lys blossomed in his heart," wrote the Duc de Nevers, as he commented contemptuously on the cracked voice and imperfect diction that made the chancellor so difficult to understand during the Estates.[17]

As Henri rose to address the Estates, the nimbus of kingship was upon him. For the moment the bizarre affectations of dress were gone. He stood, as a king should, alone. He wore neither bracelets nor earrings. His white satin doublet and velvet cloak gave him a simple majesty, and from his dais he seemed even taller than he was. For a moment he recovered something of the commanding presence Tintoretto had captured in his portrait. When he rose to speak, there was silent attention in all three sections of his audience.

Henri was reputed to be one of Europe's most eloquent princes. He was, as well, something of an actor, with an actor's sense of timing and sensitivity to his audience. He had a voice that carried despite its softness. It modulated easily from petition to command, from fear to hope. He had dissipated many of his gifts, and he rarely had the psychic energy to bring together those qualities with which he had been natively endowed. He was aware, however, that the future of France and his own future lay in a successful issue of the Estates, and towards this he bent all his energies. He welcomed the delegates, assured them of his confidence, then recalled to them the glories of a former France, "the happy and glorious reigns" of his grandfather and his father. For himself, he continued, he would prefer death to a divided kingdom, preferring that "the tomb might close over me, rather than that I should witness the calamities which harassed the reigns of my deceased brothers."

What he said was temperate, designed to alienate no one, for he recognised the desperate need for unity. He expressed his desire for a good and stable peace, assured the delegates that "all the regulations and ordinances that may be made by me in this assembly will be kept inviolable," and reiterated his determination to return France to its former glory. France's destiny was his, he affirmed, and should it founder, he would have no desire to live: "Often have I been moved to pray to God that He would be pleased in His mercy to deliver my people speedily from their misfortune or in this flower of my age to put an end to my reign and to my life." At one point Catherine was moved almost to tears, for amidst his pleas for peace, her son turned to her, publicly acclaiming all she had done in piloting the kingdom "through the boisterous waves and fierce winds of faction and division that assailed it on every side. . . . All those who love France," he concluded, "must render eternal praise for her great vigilance, magnanimity, and prudence with which she has maintained her regency in order to save the kingdom."[18]

While he spoke, he held the majority of his audience captive; his promises were their dreams. No hour of eloquence, however, was sufficient to erase his months of misrule. Even as he swore that all his promises would be "inviolably kept," the Huguenots in the south were protesting vehemently that the Peace of Beaulieu had *never* been kept—and that the king's men had been among the first to violate it. Even closer to the nerve was the king's own conduct: the indolence which kept him from his cabinet and the serious affairs of state, the prodigality with which he spent a public fortune on private luxuries, the offices bought and sold, the merciless burden of taxation, the manipulation of the clergy—all that vast fortunes might be amassed to please his favourites and amuse the court.

The first show of royal splendour had been dazzling, the first hour of royal suasion had been moving—but it was not enough. His antagonists were too suspicious and too powerful to be placated by rhetoric. Even before the Estates had convened, the Huguenots had inveighed against them, maintaining that the manner of election (often held as part of Catholic Church ceremonies) precluded the possibility of just representation. Condé and Navarre had declared the assembly null and illegitimate and refused to participate in it.

The Huguenots, despite the liberal provisions of the Peace of Monsieur, were in a precarious position. Alençon, once he had discovered that the butter was sweeter on the king's bread, had found no difficulty in deserting his former allies, taking with him many of those moderate Catholics who had never been easy with an alliance against the king. Thus, the Huguenots found themselves a smaller remnant than ever, with no other resources than a paper peace and promises of royal benevolence. The Estates, which Condé had worked so tirelessly to bring about, had been transformed from a forum in which they could speak freely to an elitist group from which they had been excluded.

Condé was faced with the bitter truth that the riches of the peace he had brought so exultantly to his coreligionists were turning to ashes in his hands. When Navarre counselled patience, Condé shook his head: before the Estates had convened, he had, impetuously but realistically, renewed negotiations with John Casimir for cavalry and foot soldiers to help him in "resisting tyranny."

The greatest threat to the crown was to come, however, not from the overt opposition of the Huguenots but from the obdurate Catholics under the subtle leadership of the young Duc de Guise. For several years Catholics throughout France had banded together to keep France Catholic at all costs. Although originally small religious groups, swearing simple fidelity to the faith of their fathers and

llegiance to the Pope, united under the aegis of a powerful leader, they had become a political and military organisation capable of endangering not only the
Hugue- nots, but the throne itself. This was the basis of the Catholic League which
the Duc de Guise had already begun to manipulate with extraordinary skill.

Henri de Guise was an ambitious young man of twenty-six. From his father he
had inherited military genius, courage, and panache. With the ugly wound received at the Battle of Dormans, he had also fallen heir to his father's title: *Le
Balafré*. For zealous Catholics the title had long been a rallying point: As the old
duke had led them to victory in Italy, had defeated the English at Calais, and
stood firm against the impudent encroachments of the Huguenots, so this new
balafré—this new scar-faced one—would become their leader.

The king's first substantial evidence of how dangerous his handsome grand
master might be came with the publication of the *David Memorial*. The *David
Memorial* (taking its title from the name of the man in whose possession it had
been discovered and made public by the Huguenots) purported to be notes from a
secret council which had plotted the overthrow of the Valois dynasty. The rationale behind the plot affirmed that the House of Guise was the true descendant
of Charlemagne ("his green and flourishing shoots"). The Valois were simply
the reprobate descendants of the inferior branch of Capets. In order to bring
about the rightful shift in power, the Duc de Guise, backed by the military
strength of the Catholic League, would "free" France from its dissolute and illegitimate ruler. The Huguenots would be outlawed; Alençon, Navarre, and Condé
would be imprisoned; Catherine and her irresponsible son would be safely im-
mured in some remote monastery. Then, continued the *Memorial*, Guise would
be at liberty to ascend the throne and restore France to the glory of Charlemagne.[19]

The Guise faction naturally denied the validity of the *David Memorial*, affirming that it had clearly been manufactured by the Huguenots to discredit them.
Whatever the king believed of the *Memorial*, it made him see the Duc de Guise
in a new light and underscored the peril of his own position. He could neither oppose the league nor permit such a powerful machine to be captained by Guise. In
an effort to steer between two mortal dangers, he was to make a decision more
deadly than either: He resolved that when the appropriate moment came, he
would publicly assume command of the league. While secretly encouraging the
local associations of Catholics, he publicly espoused the discussions of religious
liberty taking place in the Estates. By the beginning of 1577, however, such duplicity was no longer useful, and the king announced his resolution to maintain
only one religion in the kingdom. *Un roi, une foi, une loi* had once again become
the law of the realm.

In an Estates composed largely of Catholics, the initial response to the king's
decision was unquestioned elation. As for Catherine, she immediately perceived
the tragedy of Henri's decision. To reestablish a single faith would end the possibility of compromise and inevitably plunge France back into civil war. In Cath-

erine's mind, nothing justified such conflict. It is ironic that the "Legend of St. Catherine" has presented Catherine in such cruel and brutal colours, for in many ways she was less barbarous than the age she lived in. The waste of war shattered her. To see the fields of France ravaged by battle angered her. She was not only a shopkeeper, but also something of a farmer, delighting in the rich yellow fields of rye and wheat. Useless destruction offended her unquenchable zest for living. She had inherited the Medici enthusiasm for art and architecture, for good food, for a fine horse. War destroyed not only life, but all that made life pleasurable. In her eyes, nothing could justify such wholesale desolation. Now when she heard the king lean on his coronation oath to explain his sudden shift in policy, affirming that at his *sacre* he had sworn to uphold the Catholic faith and defend France against heresy, she was seen to turn to the Cardinal de Bourbon, saying tartly, "Persuade the king not to be so devout."[20]

Catherine was not alone in her horror of civil conflict. Although the Estates had voted overwhelmingly in favour of maintaining a single faith, the delegates were divided on the issue of war. In the debates that followed, Catherine, despite her son's displeasure, rose to state her position before the assembly. It was a simple, forthright speech, more personal than one might expect from the woman who for so many years had dissembled her feelings:

> I am a Catholic, and I have as good a conscience as any. In the time of the former king my son, I have risked a great deal against the Huguenots and I am still not afraid of them. I am now fifty-eight years old and I am ready to die and I hope to go to heaven. But I will not authorise the Catholics to destroy this kingdom. If there are those who do not care about the loss of the state in order that they will be able to say that they have maintained the Catholic religion, or if there are those who hope to profit from its ruin, then I have nothing further to say—but I will not be one of them.[21]

The dissembling Italian could hardly have been more straightforward. She was openly for peace but considered herself no less a Catholic for that. As for those who wanted war, let them recognise the peril in which they placed their country. The king, who had retreated strategically behind the power of the Catholic group, was embarrassed and angered by his mother's blunt statement in favour of peace. "Madame," he was overheard to say, "this is the third time you have spoken to me about peace; I tell you quite plainly, do not speak to me about it again, for I do not wish to hear it."[22]

Perhaps it was after this rebuff that Catherine was seen crying, bitterly distressed at the path her son had taken. She was far from acknowledging defeat, however. During the first week of January, she wrote a lengthy memorandum to the king, praising his resolution to have but a single faith in the kingdom, assuring him that he could count on God's help in so holy a cause, but suggesting that since God did not "love vengeance or cruelty," perhaps some way other than war could be found to implement his resolution. Should it be possible to win over the Huguenot leaders, she reminded him, then the rest might take care of itself.[23]

Four days later delegates departed to meet with Navarre at Agen and Condé at St. Jean-d'Angély. Condé's initial distrust was vindicated by this latest reversal of the king, and in a burst of fury he refused to speak with the delegates. Navarre was more temperate. Yet although, as the Tuscan ambassador noted, he made "a modest enough reply," he did not capitulate a hair's breadth. He listened respectfully—some said even with tears in his eyes—but shook his head when his return to Catholicism was broached, reminding his listeners that faith could not be regulated by the sword. Someday, if his own religion were to be in error, he would consider this step. War, it seemed, was inevitable.[24]

If the Huguenots could not be wooed, they might still be weakened, however. Thus Catherine turned to the tactical steps for procuring the defection of the leader of the Politiques, Montmorency-Damville. Damville was the most gifted of the Montmorency family. By his mid-thirties he was not only governor of Languedoc but a marshal of France and lieutenant general in Guyenne, Provence, and Dauphiné. While remaining a staunch Catholic, he found the crown's attitude towards freedom of religion untenable. When at Turin, Henri III had brusquely repudiated his position, Damville, too proud to accept rebuff even by his king, had formally united the Politiques with the Huguenot cause. It was a tenuous alliance, for Huguenots and Catholics were mutually distrustful.

Damville did little to alleviate the problem. Independent and autocratic, he found it hard to accept the spirit of republicanism indigenous to the Huguenot spirit, nor had he any desire to lift a rebel standard against the king. Even so, he remained a popular leader, with a large following, especially among the soldiers who respected both his courage and his tactical skill. It was precisely the ambiguity of Damville's position that Catherine now hoped to exploit. In January Catherine wrote to her son: "As for Marshal Damville, it is he whom I fear most, for he has the ability, the experience, and the largest following. I urge you, therefore, to spare nothing to win him over. To my mind, success or failure rests upon his action. . . . Offer him anything and everything he wishes in order to overcome his mistrust and calm his suspicions."[25]

Catherine, meanwhile, turned her efforts to the conquest of Damville's wife. Charlotte de la Marck, young, pretty, ambitious, had already grown restless with life in the south. Montpellier, with its Huguenot synods and assemblies, its grave and sombre code of morals, its penchant for sober and frugal living, had never satisfied her dreams. When the queen mother's invitation to come to court arrived, she found it irresistible. After her departure, the atmosphere at Montpellier grew manifestly hostile, and the Huguenots, suspicious of Damville's Catholicism and annoyed by his autocratic rule, repudiated him as governor. Catherine's advances were perfectly timed. "Offer him anything and everything," she had advised her son with blunt cynicism. While the Huguenots levelled charges against Damville, the king dangled gifts. Solitary and defenceless, Damville had but little choice. By spring the "Fox" had taken the bait and returned to court.

That same month the Estates were formally closed. The brilliance in which they had begun had been short-lived. Henri had little patience with the slow, grinding machinery of government. In his eyes, to be king meant to dazzle, to command, to bestow; it had nothing to do with argument and debate, with the endless revision of documents and the questions and quibbles of parliamentarians. Countered in his efforts to play the beneficent sovereign, he took refuge in a role which always solaced him: the King of Splendour.

On the night when a group of Italian actors came to perform their "lewd play" before the company at Blois, the king outdid himself. He appeared powdered and rouged, with beauty spots on his cheeks, his wide collar open, his neck bent beneath ten strings of precious pearls, while his small black toque glittered with diamonds "heavy as pieces of ice." He dazzled more than he knew, for as he walked through the ballroom the little gold and silver chains ornamenting his dress jangled until the king seemed like some giant music box that someone had set playing—but that in a short time would wear itself out.[26]

It was not simply his frivolity but even more his response to the Catholic League that diminished Henri's role as sovereign. By assuming its leadership, he had, it was true, saved himself from Guise domination. He had made the very instrument shaped to unseat him an instrument of his own power. It was an extraordinary coup which not only saved him from a powerful enemy, but placed that enemy at his service. Henri had, as most cornered creatures will, caught the nearest way, but his act was to have consequences from which he never escaped.

By assuming the championship of the league, he had made himself a partisan. By allying himself with a faction within his kingdom, he had forfeited his position as universal mediator and become an enemy to a portion of his people. For Catherine who had edged her way through the deadly factions following the death of François II, using all her skill to free the monarchy from partisanship, Henri's action could be seen only as defeat, not simply for his person but for the concept of kingship as she valued it.

What had transpired at Blois had sadly disappointed her. In fact, no one left Blois satisfied. Those who had hoped for a permanent measure of religious toleration had seen the Articles of Beaulieu contravened and the Huguenots become an outlawed people. Those who had favoured war had been frustrated and angered by an empty treasury and a people worn so threadbare by taxation that war could not be satisfactorily waged. The Huguenots were, of course, bitter and despairing. The Guises, whose political genius had welded the league, found themselves despoiled of the machinery they had created. The young Duc de Guise

ho had dreamed of captaining an army and winning France for himself, rode
ut of Blois empty-handed. "Fickle Fortune," ran the rhyme, "Fortune whose
heel turns, casting one man up, another down. . . ." For the moment he had
een cast down, but he would be patient; he would wait. And when his moment
ame, he would be alert to seize it.

Persistent Mediator

There is not an hour of the day or night when I am not trying to find some peaceful means of remedying the situation.

—CATHERINE DE MEDICI

Chapter XIV

As Guise rode north to his estates, two armies took to the field: the Army of the West under his brother Charles de Mayenne—whom the king found to be of "more governable temper and inclination"—and the Army of the East led by the spidery figure of Alençon, recently appointed lieutenant general of the kingdom. Inflated by his position and eager to prove his valour, he descended along the Loire, passed through the fertile vineyards around Issoire and Ambert, and then besieged the town of La Charité. It was less a battle than a massacre. Alençon offered no quarter to the inhabitants, and when the killing was over, La Charité resembled a charnel house. It was his first taste of military victory, and it went to his head like vintage wine.

Arrogant with victory, Alençon turned west to Plessis-les-Tours, where the court sat, no longer fearful of the wit and mockery of the king's *mignons*. For once, the favourites were set aside as Henri made preparations to receive the warrior-hero. On May 15 the gardens of the old fortress were transformed into a Renaissance fairyland. "The king who played at everything" had for a moment assumed the role of benign brother. With lavish display he squandered 60,000 francs on the heavy green satin cloth the women in attendance wore. Green was the symbolic colour of growth, of hope, of luxury. In this case, it was the colour of folly, for no one could countenance the excess lavished on this ball.

The king's extravagance was superseded three weeks later, on June 9, when the queen mother gave a ball for her victorious son—a ball that would become proverbial. The scene was the sumptuous château at Chenonceaux. No expense had ever been spared at Chenonceaux. The impressive entrance with its great shade trees, the gardens of every kind, ritualistic in their colour and design, the quiet blue-green waters of the Cher visible from almost every room—Chenonceaux was in itself a spectacle of elegance and taste. But Catherine wished that for this night it become something more. Occasionally Catherine's Medici love of splendour—generally restrained by the practical banker in her nature—broke

229

forth, and when it did, what she planned was flamboyant, erotic, and frankly pagan. Such was the ball at Chenonceaux which, it was said, cost upwards of 100,000 pounds.

The king himself presided, dressed like a woman, in pink and silver damask, his throat covered with strings of pearls, the enormous sleeves of his gown embroidered with emeralds and pearls in trefoil design. His emerald and diamond earrings were so heavy that they distended his earlobes, falling almost to his shoulders. His hair had been powdered violet, and the precious stones ornamenting it winked and glistened, so that in the dusk it seemed as though great fireflies had been caught and imprisoned. Escorting him were the most beautiful of the queen mother's ladies-in-waiting, clothed only in transparent veils. Despite her flair for the bizarre, the queen mother herself was dressed in simple black, befitting her image as *Regina Madre*. Queen Louise and Margot were in sharp contrast—Margot with her "neck open to the wind" and her unquenchable vitality; Louise so quietly dressed, so quietly mannered that no one thought to describe her at all.[1]

What the queen mother had hoped to gain by such a spectacle is difficult to guess. Her maternal love for Alençon would never have impelled her to such largesse. Yet whatever her aim, she failed, for the complaint against the ball was loud.

The celebrations to honour the "wandering son" were out of all proportion to his triumphs. Actually, there were no decisive victories or defeats in the dreary war that dragged on through the summer of 1577. Very few had wanted this war, and now neither side had the money or energy to pursue it. By fall it was obvious to the Huguenot leaders that they would be wise to settle for peace. The port cities of Oléron and Brouage had been taken, and La Rochelle gravely inconvenienced; Issoire had been reduced to rubble, the countryside of Guyenne ravaged, and the western provinces of Anjou and Maine plundered and terrorised.

On September 17 the Peace of Bergerac—or the King's Peace, as it was called—was concluded. At best it was a *modus vivendi* that acknowledged the existence of another form of Christianity while continuing to curb it. Although it conceded the right of the Huguenots to dwell in peace throughout the kingdom, it restricted their right to worship to certain designated places. Such compromise pleased no one, nor did either side trust the king to see the peace enforced. There was a distinct note of scepticism in the report that Sir Amias Paulet, Elizabeth's ambassador, drew up for his sovereign. "God grant that it may be made with that sincerity that becomes the oath of an anointed king," he wrote.[2]

Henri had continued to lose prestige that summer. For while reports were brought to him of the threat of famine, of unnatural storms with wind strong enough to uproot trees and flatten harvests, and hail that killed small animals in the fields, he ignored it all, continuing to divert himself with the *mignons*, who

arrived at the royal retreat at Olinville, "florid and frizzled . . . their hair ornamented, their crests raised high." For them he engaged the Italian company I Ge-
losi, who, the righteous citizens of Paris maintained, "taught nothing but for-
nication and adultery." His time was given to his monkeys, his miniature dogs,
and his wild ass. He was especially intrigued by a dwarf, "no bigger than a child
of three," which had been sent him as a gift from Poland. By comparison with
these things, he found the affairs of his kingdom of desultory interest.[3]

Catherine blamed her son's childish preoccupations on the *mignons*. Her hatred of them was implacable, for she recognised that they were not simply frivolous but dangerous as well. The king's affection had made them reckless and arrogant. They braved those who were less favoured, provoked duels over trifles,
and, most dangerous of all, made Alençon the butt of their jokes. While once her
youngest might have been content to sulk and dream of vengeance, now he had
been emboldened by his few military victories. There was no need for the hero of
La Charité to be kept at court, leashed to a brother who despised him and under
the eye of a mother whose mistrust was patent. Power had stirred in Alençon,
and he was determined to wield it. His dreams of glory had become more imperious. His brothers had all ruled kingdoms, and he was determined to follow suit.

While Henri squandered his natural gifts, Alençon gathered his small talent
and put it hard to work. He was like a man who looked through a jeweller's loupe
and saw in magnified splendour the jewel he sought. Its brilliance fascinated him;
for such a gem as this he would, without regret, sell all that he possessed. Although by his treacherous desertion he had forfeited the leadership of the Huguenots and the Politiques, a much more precious jewel now hung tantalisingly
close: "Defender of the Netherlands."

The Netherlands had long been an issue in French politics. Even during the
reign of Henri II, the "rebels" had begged for help against what they condemned
as "Spanish tyranny." During the reign of Charles IX, his secret talks with William of Orange had given rise to rumours that the French king was becoming
Protestant in his sympathies. Intervention in the Netherlands had been one of the
major factors augmenting hostility against Coligny, who had been willing to engage France in war against Spain to assist the beleaguered provinces. No voice
had been so consistently and purposefully raised against such intervention as
Catherine's.

It was typical of the devious-minded Alençon that his thoughts of glory should
focus on the Netherlands, now grown increasingly turbulent under the newly
appointed governor, Don Juan of Austria, hero of Lepanto and bastard brother of
Philip II. Don Juan was no diplomat—he lacked the patience and skill for the
conference table. He was a soldier, brusque, imperious, and unaccustomed to de-

feat. His arrogance and uncertain temper aroused the Netherlands States General against him and led them to look with renewed interest towards France—and Alençon.

There was a cautious streak in Alençon, however, and he had no intention of espousing a cause about which he had so little firsthand information. He needed an agent to observe the terrain, judge the difficulties, and assess the support he could expect. Such an agent must be intelligent, cunning, and above suspicion. By the spring of 1577 Alençon had conceived an ingenious scheme. Margot would reconnoiter the Netherlands in his behalf. Her wit, her beauty, her daring made Margot perfect for the role of royal spy.

The friendship between the enchanting Margot and her ''blackamoor'' brother is one of the most interesting relationships in the royal family. There was, in their own time, the suggestion of incest; the accusation, however, seems insubstantial, although the term ''strange bedfellows'' may indeed be used of them. So diverse in character, they were brought together by mutual humiliation. They were Catherine's youngest children—her least important and her least loved. If we can trust Margot's memoirs, we see her reared in abject fear of her mother, not daring to speak freely to her, trembling if she was looked upon, while her brother Henri became her mother's ''single love.'' ''Her kindness to me diminished,'' she wrote; ''she made her son her idol, wanting always to please him.'' This manifest favouritism bred in Margot a petulant antagonism to both her mother and her brother.

Her marriage to Navarre only fuelled the fire. It was not her marriage, but her mother's marriage, a political union to bring peace to France. Her desires, even her religious scruples, went unheeded. ''I begged her,'' she wrote, ''to have pity on the fact that I was a Catholic and that it would grieve me very much to marry someone who was not of my religion.''[4] Despite her pleas, the negotiations had continued. It is safe to conjecture, in light of Margot's temperament, that it was less religion than the quality of her bridegroom that made her apprehensive. She who had been described as ''more beautiful than a goddess'' could hardly rejoice at being married to her country cousin. She soon discovered, though, that the country cousin was as disinclined to her as she was to him. It was a disturbing revellation to a bride who had considered herself her husband's superior in every way.

When in February, 1576, her husband fled from court, she was accused by her brother of complicity, despite her humiliating avowals that she knew nothing of Navarre's plots, that, indeed, she barely saw her husband. ''He never found time to come and see me,'' she explained. ''He came in late and rose early, being wholly taken up with Madame de Sauves.'' Despite her denials, the king had her confined to her apartments and placed under guard.[5] Her mother did nothing to sweeten her arrest. One need not invoke incest to explain the bond that grew up between Margot and Alençon. They were exiles from royal favour, they were schemers, and they took a vindictive delight in stirring up trouble.

Under pretence of visiting the spa at Liège, Margot received permission to journey into Flanders. On July 6 an elaborate retinue began its journey up the Picardy road to the border town of Le Catelet. Margot lacked none of the Valois love of display, and the procession was enough to leave the Picards gaping at the roadside. It might have been the olden days before France was constantly in arms, when François I and Marguerite d'Angoulême dazzled the countryside by their royal progresses. "I rode in a litter constructed of pillars," Margot wrote proudly, as she described the hangings of ruby velvet, embroidered with opal and gold, the glass windows glittering with various mottoes and devices wrought in the panes. "Every one of them was different," she continued, "some in Italian, others in Spanish."⁶ Behind her, and only scarcely less elaborate, came the litters of her ladies-in-waiting. Following them on horseback rode ten maids of honour, and last of all came the six coaches and carriages carrying the rest of her attendants and the ponderous chests of clothes and equipment.

Margot was a good traveller and a keen observer, and she missed little of the scene around her—the variations in architecture, the different patterns of the gardens, the public lighting that kept the streets of the cities as "bright as day," even after sundown. She noted with special delight the curious clocks at Valenciennes, intrigued with the moving figures and the melodies accompanying the striking of the hours. She never forgot her principal task, however, for it was the people far more than the clocks and gardens who merited her scrutiny. Margot had inherited a certain adroitness in pointing the conversation, and even in the midst of a ball or dinner she tested reactions to Spanish rule, to the new governor, Don Juan, to their hopes for independence. It was at Cambrai that she first began to employ her charm, a charm to which the governor of the citadel soon fell captive. He insisted on riding partway with her, promising her whatever help he could give. She was even more successful at Mons, where the Comte de Lalaing and his beautiful wife led the old Catholic party which still considered the King of France the "lawful suzerain of the Netherlands." In such an atmosphere, the suggestion that her brother Alençon might be able to help them gain their freedom from Spain was received gratefully.

At Namur, Margot met the man she wished to impress and to scrutinise: Don Juan. Bastard son of Charles V, Don Juan considered himself a figure of Continental importance. He was all that the rules demanded of a Renaissance hero: young, handsome, reckless. If his maternal blood was less than royal, then it simply enhanced the romantic aura of this gallant by-blow of the emperor and Barbara Blomberg. Like Alençon, he cherished victory above all, and Lepanto had gone intoxicatingly to his head. Again like Alençon, he was aggrieved not to have a kingdom to rule as his own. When Philip offered him the governorship of the Netherlands, he accepted with alacrity, for he saw his rule there as a stepping-stone to a far more magnificent position. The hero of Lepanto was a man of perilously high expectations. He had long dreamed of invading Scotland and with Scottish forces solidly behind him—and the beautiful Mary Stuart as his bride—subjugating England to his will.

The charming Margot who met Don Juan at Namur knew little of all this intrigue, however. She was there to impress and observe and—should it seem to her interest and that of her brother—to allure. The next few days were all she could have desired in gaiety and homage. Namur rose to the occasion, and Margot found herself in a whirl of banquets, balls, and fêtes. Don Juan, too, played his part, publicly accompanying Margot, paying her the honour of dining alone with her, escorting her on a gaily decorated boat along the cool waters of the Meuse. Musicians accompanied them everywhere, and Margot found it easy to become attuned to these new Spanish rhythms. A master of the dance, she now turned all heads as she and her host—one dark, the other fair, in the best romantic tradition—executed in perfect grace the stately and ceremonial pavanne of Spain. After four days of festivity, Don Juan led Margot to the boat that would take her to Liège, bidding her a ceremonious Spanish farewell.

Margot found Liège limitlessly pleasing, and for six weeks she indulged her taste for wit and gallantry, while discovering all she could of the temper of the people and their possible response to Alençon. Her visit came to an abrupt ending, however, when a letter from Alençon warned her of the king's suspicion over her prolonged absence. She must leave Liège at once, he warned her, for the Spanish, apprehensive of her presence, were already laying plots to capture her. Margot suddenly found herself in the ludicrous position of a spy who has let himself be lulled to sleep in hostile country. Her position was dangerous, as well as ludicrous, and one must admire the resourceful woman who started the long journey home with nothing to protect her but her wits. They were, however, the best wits Valois blood had produced in more than a generation; Margot was gifted with a rugged ingenuity she now used to her utmost.

Everywhere, she found, the people were suddenly in arms. At Huy, a little town on the Meuse, halfway between Namur and Liège, she lay all night in the public inn, listening to the shouted threats of the drunken villagers who had surrounded the building. At Dinan things were more turbulent still. In astonishment, Margot learned that the gallant Don Juan who had flattered and charmed her now had plans for her capture. With desperate haste she abandoned her litter and took to horse. Near Cateau-Cambrésis her party barely eluded pursuit by a group of armed Huguenots. They rode all night, reaching Le Catelet and safety in early morning, weary and shaken, but triumphantly free. She had fooled them all: Huguenots, Spanish, Dutch—even her perfidious brother. Back on the comfort of French soil, she was more determined than ever to give her support to Alençon. It was October before she joined her young brother at La Fère and

December before they rode into St. Denis, where they were greeted, noted Margot, "with great cordiality" by the king and the queen mother. There was no scene, no recriminations, no accusations of disloyalty, for the king could ill afford any action that might disturb the tenuous peace.

The year 1578 brought no relief to France in either foreign or domestic affairs. Rome was openly opposed to the conciliatory Peace of Bergerac, Spain was actively displeased over Alençon's possible interference in the Netherlands, and Elizabeth of England hedged and hesitated in the matter of the French marriage. Internal affairs were equally bad. Early in 1578 Catherine wrote to the king from Champagne, where she had gone to see conditions for herself: "Things are in a worse state than they are thought to be; I beg you to control your finances very carefully in order to raise money for your service without having to rob your people, for you are on the brink of a general revolt—and whoever tells you otherwise deceives you."[7]

Henri's answer to his mother's advice was simply to invent new ways to spend money. In the spring of 1578 he inaugurated a new religious "order," the Order of the Holy Spirit, which he defined as an organ for the defence of the Catholic faith, but which, in fact, was no more than an elaborate coterie of his *mignons*. The installation alone cost 200,000 crowns, which the king demanded be raised from church property—since it was for a religious cause. The Pope, infuriated, not only refused permission but ordered the Nuncio to absent himself from the ceremony. Paris, too, was enraged at this new display of luxury, as the people watched the chevaliers walking in solemn procession, their black velvet mantles symbolically embroidered with golden lilies and tongues of fire.

Where the money came from they could not imagine, for even the taxation under which they laboured would not have sufficed; but bribery had become an accepted procedure, and L'Estoile, with his keen lawyer's eye and sardonic pen, noted in his journal:

> All the offices in France are being sold to the highest bidder, but most of all those in the courts—against all law and reason. . . . The most abominable is the traffic in benefices, the great majority being held by women or married men . . . even to infants still at the breast, so that it would seem that they come into the world bearing a cross and mitre. . . . In short, it is not possible to imagine a crab more twisted and contradictory than the government of France.[8]

Catherine did what she could to make her son realise he was stirring up his people against him. But as she talked, noted Goulart, "He busied himself with his rosary or with devising the steps and measures of a new dance"—an exaggerated description but one which comes metaphorically close to the truth.[9]

While Henri continued in his role as King of Trifles, Alençon was moving steadily towards his dream of glory. Throughout the fall of 1577 and 1578 the correspondence continued between Alençon and his sister and the States General of the Low Countries. They wrote to Margot thanking her for her solicitude and begging her to "continue and persevere." In reply she assured them of the "singular desire I have to help you in so just a cause," repeating Alençon's concern for the "peace and conservation" of their country.[10] The closer Alençon came to his dream, the more intolerable his position at court became. The *mignons,* more powerful than ever, toyed with him beyond endurance, mocking his dress, his stature, his failures in love.

In an effort to avoid open conflict between her sons, Catherine encouraged Alençon to leave court temporarily on a hunting expedition. At the last moment, however, the king revoked his permission, further humiliating his brother by ransacking his rooms in search of incriminating papers. Although the king discovered nothing more than an indiscreet love letter, he confined Alençon to his apartments, deaf to Catherine's pleas for clemency.

The result of such arbitrary action was inevitable. Determined to brook no further tyranny, Alençon made plans to escape. On the night marked for his flight Margot—by far the coolest member of the family—supped with her mother, then retired to her room, dismissing all but her three most trusted women. Dragging out the heavy rope she had smuggled into her apartments inside a mattress, she tied it to her casement. "And thus," wrote an amused contemporary, "the First Prince of the Blood, heir presumptive to the throne, escapes through a window at the risk of breaking his neck." First went Alençon, dangling like a monkey, then came his secretary Simier, "pale with fear," and last of all his loyal valet Cange.[11]

Once out of Paris, they took the road running west to Angers, leaving Margot to face the royal anger. Despite the overwhelming evidence implicating her (in addition to everything else, the chimney in her room had caught fire when she tried to burn the telltale rope), Margot simply denied all. Her brother, unable to cow her, turned to the problem of getting Alençon back to court before he implicated France in a war.

Once again it was the queen mother who, despite her sixty years, took to the road to win back her wandering son. The English ambassador had once prophesied: "Someday they will cut each other's throats," and as the envy between her sons grew, the prophecy seemed close to fulfilment.

When, three years before, Alençon had fled from court, he had responded to his mother with a show of affection; this time he made no pretence. When she arrived at Angers, there was neither welcome nor provision for lodging. Amias Paulet, in surprise, informed his queen, "The Queen Mother was two days at Angers before she spoke with Monsieur who was lodged in the castle and his mother in the town."[12] The initiative was left to Catherine.

Even when she arrived at the château, she was not treated as queen mother but obliged to enter through the narrow wicket gate like any ordinary person. It was an inauspicious interview. Alençon could not be persuaded to return to a court where, he said, he had been mocked and baited. He did, however, assure her he had no intention of stirring up trouble in France. It was less than Catherine had hoped for, but she was grateful for even that much. On her return to Paris, she wrote to a lady of her court, "I have been away from court for a month, running after my son who often causes me great suffering, for I fear that he will do something foolish again. But thanks be to God, I have found him determined to do nothing which could displease the king, his brother, or change in any way the peace of this kingdom"[13]

Alençon, meanwhile, had written to the king, explaining that he had left court only because of the way he had been treated by the *mignons* and because of his impatience for his Flanders campaign. Such a campaign, though less dangerous than civil war, would put France in grave difficulty with its neighbours, for both Philip and Elizabeth had made it very clear they would tolerate no intervention in the Low Countries. In May Catherine again set out in search of Alençon. This time she was armed with some very handsome temptations: In exchange for Flanders, the king would give him a rich southern appanage, renew marriage negotiations with England, or—if he preferred—undertake them in any of a half dozen courts. Flanders was but dream and shadow; what Catherine offered was solid substance.

Alençon listened, he thanked her, he smiled, but he did not give an inch. He was weary of promises; he had outgrown his mother's arbitrary system of rewards and punishments. He wanted something for himself, something he could win by his own merits. He wanted a kingdom.

Nothing Catherine said could keep Alençon from levying troops for his Flanders expedition and assuming the title "Defender of the Netherlands." The troops gathered throughout the summer of 1578 were a source of fresh anxiety for a France already devastated by unruly soldiers. Alençon's recruits were, according to a contemporary, "men of any religion and every condition—even brigands and highway robbers." They terrorised the people, desecrated churches, and pillaged wherever they could. "Often one sees along the road," wrote Haton, "people bruised and torn, covered only with an old shirt—having fallen into the hands of one of these bands."[14]

Alençon might have been less zealous in massing an army had he been aware that the bright promises of the Netherlands States General were extremely provisional. They feared lest their alliance with Alençon displease Elizabeth, for it was obvious that only England had sufficient funds to help them effectively. Nor were they blind to Alençon's true quality. Beneath the swagger and exalted promises ran a vein of personal vanity which, they recognised, might well place his individual glory above their cause. He had already made his way to two dissimilar beds; there was no telling how many more he might be lured to. They were more than willing to use him for what he could accomplish, but they would need more proof of his constancy before they would entrust him with power to rule.

The same week that Alençon reached the border, leading 8,000 foot soldiers and 800 cavalry, his mother rode out of Olinville for a sixteen month journey. Her purpose: to confirm the shaky peace, to bring assurance of the king's good-will to the disaffected provinces in the south, to meet with Navarre and establish a rapprochement. It was a very different caravan from the one that, fourteen years before, had lumbered out of St. Maur. Then she had brought her young son Charles, just reaching his majority, to be presented to his people. Despite the difficulties, it had been a journey of great hope, for in 1564 the country had only begun to suffer the anguish of civil conflict. Now it had endured it for more than fifteen years. In that time the face of France had grown old. It had been ravaged by those who should have loved it, and the signs of that violation were clear.

In the summer of 1578 no rain had fallen for months, although the sky grew dark and ominous with lightning, and the low rumble of thunder teased the farm-ers' hopes. Streams dried up, rivers narrowed, and the meadowlands lay parched and racked. The Seine and the Marne were lower than anyone had ever seen them. Cattle died of thirst, and windmills stood motionless in the fields. In a landscape still as death, famine and plague moved perceptibly, leaving still more horror behind them. Religious processions wound slowly through the wasteland, their petitions for the mercy of rain rising in hypnotic chant.

Yet neither God nor their king heeded their prayers. In Normandy, Brittany, Burgundy the poor had risen in desperation, begging to be delivered from the im-possible burden of taxation the king continued to impose. But Henri had retired beyond the cries of his people. The English ambassador was astonished at this unnatural ability to withdraw from reality. "Many find it strange," he wrote, "that the King, not being ignorant of these dangerous drifts, remains at his house of Olinville as a prisoner without comfort or counsel, either careless or senseless of the ruin of himself and his realm like to ensue if good counsel do not prevent it."[15]

Henri's apathy was in marked contrast with the decisive energy with which his cousin Navarre was leading the Huguenots. In the three years since he had es-caped from court, Navarre had proved himself a dynamic leader. While failure paralysed the King of France, it stimulated the King of Navarre. "I will spare nothing, not even my own person," he wrote to Damville as the Huguenots' for-tunes grew more imperilled. Desperate for money, he authorised the sale of his own forests at Champrond, Châteauneuf, and Castelmoron, hoping that the money from the timber would sustain his army for a few months longer. Cath-erine, who had once dismissed her son-in-law too lightly, had come to recognise him as a formidable opponent. To win him to the king's side was the primary motive in her long journey south.

Catherine's progress was a source of unending speculation. The fact that she was bringing Margot back to her husband after a three-year separation increased that speculation. Did Margot wish to go? She had said that she would rather "be a queen at Pau or Nérac" than "a hostage at Paris," yet Paulet had written to England that he saw no evidence she was interested in leaving the fashionable French court for her rustic husband, concluding, "Most people think . . . that the Queen of Navarre has no devotion for going into Gascony." Was she then, once again, being coerced by her mother and her brother? And if so, to what end? Was her role, perhaps, to inveigle Navarre back to court and thus weaken Huguenot power? The questions were unanswerable, and even Paulet, with his genius for following devious motivations, admitted defeat: "I think no man can tell what will come of this second marriage between the King of Navarre and his wife."[16]

Catherine, for whom marriage was always a powerful political tool, had already suggested a union between Condé and Mademoiselle de Vaudémont, sister of the queen, and between Alençon and Navarre's sister, Catherine de Bourbon, in an effort to forge bonds between the court and the Huguenots. Navarre, however, was not to be caught so easily. The years spent at the Valois court had taught him much of nets and snares and the most effective ways of escaping them. Such marriages as Catherine suggested would inevitably weaken the Huguenot leadership. Navarre's own marriage had once brought that party to the cliff's edge, and he was determined that would not happen again. His refusal of the queen mother's suggestions only increased her determination to visit him personally.

The caravan that left Chenonceaux during the second week of August was not grandiose, but it was still "a travelling city," with its ostlers and wagon drivers, its tailors and goldsmiths, cooks and carpenters. Even more, it was a city of diplomats: cardinals and bishops to add colour and rank; Fénelon who for so long had been ambassador at the court of Elizabeth; Claude Pinart, Catherine's secretary of state; Guy du Pibrac, recently named president of the Paris Parlement; Louis de Lanssac, the chief of her secretaries. Along with these shrewd advisers, she had also brought her "flying squadron," those beautiful and sophisticated women of her court, who, she was frank in avowing, often had their own diplomatic value.

It was an impressive assembly whose courage and vitality were matched by Catherine's own. Near sixty now, stout almost to obesity, ridden with rheumatism, still she journeyed resolutely over the rough roads, in her litter or on muleback, with no personal complaint so long as what she was doing would make for the good of the king her son and his kingdom. During that summer she had written to her trusted adviser Pomponne de Bellièvre, who had remained at court to help the king: "I would infinitely regret the trouble I have taken to come here if I had to return like a disabled ship; if God does me the grace of doing as I wish, I hope that this realm may benefit by my work and that it may remain peaceful."[17]

She had set herself a very high endeavour and one that depended not only on her efforts, but on the goodwill of Navarre. From the beginning, hints made Catherine distrustful of that goodwill. Although he had written every encouragement to her, assuring her of his great desire to see her, once she approached the seat of his power Navarre's interest waned. Initially he had promised to meet her at Cognac, where his wife made her royal entrance on September 12. But as early as August 25 Paulet wrote Elizabeth that he had heard Navarre intended " to excuse himself."

A week later the royal party moved on to Bordeaux, where they were welcomed by Armand de Biron, governor of Guyenne. A house had been prepared for them overlooking the water, and here the city officials came to pay their homage. Soon after, Margot made her solemn entrance, royal in every detail. She rode a white palfrey "richly caparisoned." She herself was dressed in orange, glittering with silver and gold. People could not get their fill of her, wrote a contemporary who observed that they "kept looking at her, admiring her, and praising her to the skies."[18] For a week they remained, honoured and fêted—and still waiting for Navarre.

Towards the end of the month, anxious and irritable at Navarre's apparent indifference, Catherine wrote him: "[It] is not possible to reach any profitable decision unless I have a chance to speak to you. . . . Come to dine or stay the night, whichever you please, just so long as I have an hour to talk with you . . . and put an end to all these comings and goings." Navarre, however, was not ready to put an end to his "comings and goings."[19] He had discovered that postponement and delay were excellent weapons for gaining the upper hand. By the beginning of October Catherine, nervous and impatient, willingly conceded to whatever rendezvous Navarre indicated. Although she was glad to leave Bordeaux, she did not consider the time she had spent there wasted. On September 29 she wrote the king: "Tomorrow I hope to leave this city, leaving everything so well ordered that I believe—as do the lords of your council—that everything will continue in peace and union."[20]

Two days later, on an unseasonably hot October day, the meeting with Navarre took place in a house in Casteras. Here, for the first time in two and a half years, Margot saw her husband and Catherine had the opportunity to appraise her son-in-law. Navarre was now in his twenty-sixth year. Since his escape, he had become a general, a king, a leader of men. He wore his experience well. The effortless charm, the shrewd wit were still there, but they were coloured by a gravity and command. In general, Catherine was pleased with what she saw and that evening wrote at some length to her son: "He was escorted by a handsome troop of gentlemen, all in good order and well mounted. He found me and the Queen of Navarre, your sister, . . . awaiting him in an upper room of the house; with a very becoming manner and, apparently, with deep affection, he welcomed us very cordially."[21]

The initial conferences met with no obstacles. In principle, both sides wanted peace. Both found civil war deplorable; both agreed to a strict enforcement of the edict of peace. When they descended to particulars, however, the issues became prickly. Navarre maintained that despite the king's reiterations of goodwill, the edict was not kept. Catherine countered by reproaching him for the places the Huguenots had taken by force, to which Navarre answered simply that the Huguenots were destitute and "hunger may explain many things."[22] It was a subtle rebuke on the government of her son, but Catherine ignored it. She could not afford the luxury of a quarrel.

Navarre's greatest complaint, however, was against Governor Biron. Although Biron was a loyal and unquestioning servant of the king, Catherine bore him little love. She found him proud and intransigent. Without doubt he was a good soldier, but good soldiers were sometimes an embarrassment in peacetime. Unless Biron and Navarre could be brought to harmony, there seemed little chance for peace in Guyenne. It was Margot, with a new gift for influencing her husband, who persuaded him to meet with Biron.

Instead of leading to a rapprochement, however, the meeting ended in a near duel. Catherine, vividly remembering the two adversaries facing each other with swords drawn, wrote her son that night:

> Biron found the King of Navarre in my room, who spoke to him more roughly than your sister and I had expected. . . . The marshal was very angry. I assure you I did not know what to do to straighten matters out, but the good offices of your sister and the Cardinal de Bourbon and the great pains I myself took with both of them succeeded in restoring their relations after a fashion.[23]

Despite this setback, Catherine felt generally encouraged. The letter she wrote the king from Agen on October 11 was, despite its realistic appraisal of difficulties, frankly optimistic. Navarre had been to see her that morning, and she had been pleased by his attitude. The series of conferences they had decided on were to be held on October 15 at L'Isle-Jourdain. They might run into some difficulties with this, she acknowledged, but then added shrewdly, "If we have to postpone the day, I want this to come from him . . so that he cannot say afterwards that there was any change in the agreement which we have signed together."[24] Having already suffered through something of Navarre's system of postponements, she was determined that nothing on her part would delay their meetings further.

This letter, close to 3,000 words in length, is one of the first of those astonishingly detailed accounts she sent her son almost daily during her travels in the south. Nowhere is her determined energy more in evidence than during these months.

With much of the day spent in travelling, in public functions or private interviews, much of the night must have been spent writing to her son. The fact that the actual penmanship was done by secretaries does not seriously detract from her labours. She missed nothing: a word, a look, the tone of an argument, the shifting ground of a conference—all were stored in that receptive memory until she had time to record them in full detail. Despite the arthritic pains in her hands, her attacks of gout, the lingering bouts of colic, her body still obeyed her indefatigable will.

By Renaissance standards Catherine was an old woman—and, indeed, she looked it with her sallow skin and "rheumy eyes" and the abnormal corpulence that made it laborious to assist her off her donkey or into her litter. But she had disciplined her body to the demands of her ambition—an ambition that would not be satisfied until France was at peace and her son secure on his throne. "My son," she concluded her letter, "I tell myself that you will want to hear all the details of what is happening here in what concerns your service and that is why I do not want to omit anything. . . . There is not an hour of the day or night that I am not thinking of some means to remedy the situation peacefully."[25] She did nothing without informing the king: the letters sent to the leaders of Guyenne and Languedoc; her private talks with Montpensier, with Bourbon and Biron; her appraisal of Navarre and the best means to confirm him in loyalty to the crown; her distribution of money to win the vacillating to her side.

In reply, she heard nothing. Her son neither acknowledged her letters nor provided the materials she sometimes asked for. She asked him to advise her ("let me know at once what your wishes are"), to indicate how he wished her to treat certain problems ("please send me all the papers and memos dealing with this subject"), to reenforce her promises by his own word. "My son," she wrote in desperation towards the end of October, "send me at once a letter written in your own hand for the King of Navarre." Even such demands as this seemed unable to arouse the indolent Henri.[26] On October 31 she was again pleading with him, begging him to put into effect at least some of the practical machinery for the operation of the edict, for, she informed him, although the Huguenots said they would obey it, they wanted more than her word that the king intended to take the edict seriously.

From time to time, inserted between the layers of political conniving, she provided an admission of what her task was costing her. "Knowing your holy and upright intention," she wrote, "I have accepted this charge, although at my age and in this season it is very heavy and very difficult to sustain—especially to be so long without seeing you; but for so worthwhile a task and one which you have so much at heart, I wish to spare nothing."[27]

Her situation was made more uncertain by a renewal of Navarre's delaying tactics. She herself had never favoured L'Isle-Jourdain as a meeting place. "We shall not find much by way of food or lodging," she had written Henri. Yet any effort to change this rendezvous met only with further delay. Throughout October and into November Catherine and Margot dallied in Toulouse. It was not an unpleasant sojourn, for Toulouse was a proudly Catholic city, and the homage it paid the queen mother was gratifying. On November 1 she celebrated the Feast of All Saints in the cathedral. It was the last of the autumn feasts, the herald of winter.

What she had thought would be weeks had already lengthened into months. The crops were harvested; the grapes were in; already the vines drooped under the first winter frost. Still she could not move Navarre. Never for a moment did she believe his excuses. She knew that he continued to mistrust her, that he remained unaffected by the terms of endearment larded into her letters. One could hardly blame Navarre. For four years he had danced to Valois music; he had been permitted no steps not dictated by the Dancing Master. He was his own master now, and he intended to make certain Catherine realised that he would devise the measure.

During the first week of November he promised he would meet her at L'Isle-Jourdain. In relief, she wrote Henri, assuring him that the conferences which would bring peace to France were soon to begin. On her way to their rendezvous she stopped at Pibrac and, in a sudden surge of high spirits, wrote to her old friend the Duchesse d'Uzès, "It is so beautiful here that I wish the King of Navarre would have no more fear of me and that he could hold our conferences here."[28] Her high spirits were short-lived, however, for the next twelve days were spent in waiting. Her dancing partner had left her to her own devices.

L'Isle-Jourdain, green and fertile in summer, shaded by giant trees and close to the cool waters of the Vienne, was intolerable in winter. Barren, damp, wind-wracked, it had few comforts to ease the queen mother's long days of waiting. By November 8 her patience had worn thin, and she wrote her son: "I am furious and annoyed as well at having been here for three days without hearing any news from the King of Navarre, nor from Fénelon, whom I sent to hurry him up. I have just sent another messenger. . . . I understand that he is staying overnight at Mauvezin in order to be here for dinner tomorrow. If that is so, I hope that in a few days we shall know his real intentions." Three days later he had still not arrived. "If he had any consideration for my person, he would act very differently," she wrote indignantly, recalling the "suffering" endured in making "such a long journey in such a bad season." Two days later she wrote again: "If he does not wish to come, then I am determined to go to find him. . . . I beg you," she continued, "write to him yourself and tell him very firmly how harmful these long delays are to your service and to the good of the kingdom."[29]

Her annoyance was further aroused when, on November 13, Navarre sent a messenger explaining he did not feel safe in coming to L'Isle-Jourdain and suggesting the conferences be held instead at Pamiers, a little mountain town in the foothills of the Pyrenees. "I was angry," Catherine stated, "for I know very well what kind of town this is and what kind of people live there; for the most part they are brigands and people of evil life, without any respect for any prince. In addition, it is a city situated in the mountains with such a bad climate that there is still snow there in the month of June—and, even worse, the roads between here and there are so terrible that it would not be possible to go there now."[30]

That Navarre would seriously suggest such a rendezvous was in itself an insult. But if she were obdurate about Pamiers, Navarre was equally so about L'Isle-Jourdain. Finally, on November 19, Catherine left for Auch with no satisfaction beyond a shadowy promise for a meeting at the Huguenot citadel of Nérac the following month.

Fearful lest the king think she dozed in his service, she wrote placatingly: "I have missed no opportunity. . . . Hour by hour we hasten things. . . . We do not lose any time." Her son had none of Catherine's sense of urgency, however. He had his *mignons,* his prayers, his Platonic discussions. Beyond that, he seemed incapable of responding—even to Catherine's undiminished affection. "There is nothing in this world which would give me greater happiness than to be with you," she wrote, yet avowing she was more than willing to sacrifice even this joy if by her absence she could increase his security.[31]

Catherine, meanwhile, had journeyed from Auch to Nérac, where, on December 15, Margot made her formal entrance. For the past five months Margot, for the first time in her life, had found herself in amity with her mother. Not only had she been able to influence Navarre, but she had proved the substance of her promise to help her royal brother. Catherine, surprised and delighted, had already written favourably of her to Henri: "I don't want to forget to tell you, my son, that my daughter, the Queen of Navarre, is doing everything possible in all these matters for the good of your service." Margot sparkled beneath this unaccustomed approval. Navarre, too, seemed genuinely happy to have her with him, and the Florentine ambassador Sinolfo Saracini commented favourably on their "true and reciprocal love," speculating on Margot's probable pregnancy. Her entrance into Nérac was royal in every way. As Queen of Navarre she rode in the place of honour between her husband and his sister Catherine. Guillaume de Salluste Du Bartas who had been commissioned to compose some verses for the occasion apostrophised her as a "nightingale," "blackbird," and, best of all, "the most beautiful creature in the world."[32] Moved by such romantic flattery, Margot won the affection of the crowd by spontaneously offering the young speaker representing the Gascon muse the rich embroidered scarf she wore. It was Margot at her best: lavish, spontaneous, generous to imprudence. They were characteristics that she shared with her brother and that won them both friends and enemies galore.

The next week Navarre spent proving to his wife that Nérac, despite its reputation for gravity, could be as gay and lavish as Paris. Margot loved it all, but Catherine grew restless; and, a few days before Christmas she left, with her daughter, for Port-Ste.-Marie, a little town situated on the Garonne, equidistant from Nérac and Agen. For six weeks she remained in the abbey of Paravis, doing all she could to effectuate the abortive conferences for peace. She wrote almost daily to the king, describing her discussions with Navarre and the other Huguenot leaders and explaining her efforts to dispel the general suspicion with which she was treated. Finally, her perseverance triumphed, and on February 4, four months after her first interview with Navarre, the conferences opened at Nérac.

Chapter XV

The opening session of the conference went well. Navarre was a gracious host, and Jean de Scorbiac, the Protestant orator, spoke eloquently in the king's interests, indicating "the great hope" they had in Henri's goodness and reminding the delegates of their duties to their sovereign. Although Catherine intended to leave most of the oratory in Pibrac's hands, she did reply to Scorbiac, praising their goodwill and pointing out the "affection the king has for all his subjects," and his great desire to see the edict of peace truly enforced.

For the next twenty-four days Catherine was to work the delegates as she worked her secretaries. She gave them no respite. They were up before dawn and sometimes remained at the council table until midnight. Before it was over, Vaence was ill from fatigue and Pibrac had had to retire to his bed. Catherine, too, had begun to stumble under the weight of her own demands. Shortly before her departure for Port-Ste.-Marie, Navarre had found her in bed. Although she had been deathly sick all night, she was determined she would be well enough to leave for Nérac in a few days. She arrived on time and missed none of the sessions, but the strain was obvious.

The conferences at Nérac established a precedent in Huguenot affairs. Previously, any efforts to bring Catholics and Protestants together had been concerned with religious issues. At Nérac there was not even the hint of theological discussion: the concerns were purely political. Catherine was convinced that, without immediate peace, France would come to its ruin. Therefore, she was willing to make concessions, but she was also aware that too great liberality to the Huguenots would only involve the crown in new imbroglios with the Catholics. Since both sides had agreed to the Peace of Bergerac, she would devote herself to practical steps towards its implementation.

The Huguenots' most clamorous demand was for sufficient "towns of surety" they could count on as places of refuge. On February 12, she wrote her son that after lengthy deliberation they had agreed on all the articles "except for the towns they hold, which they do not wish to give up, saying that this provides them with security, alleging . . . that were it not for the retreat they had at La Rochelle at the time of St. Bartholomew, they would all have been lost.'' Interestingly enough, this bloodless and parenthetical comment is Catherine's single written allusion to the massacre. The following day she was presented with a document demanding fifty-nine towns, an impossible condition, to which she replied, ''I told them that I saw that they were making fun of me.''[1] Six days later, in a sudden capitulation, Navarre announced he was willing to agree to six towns for a period of six months. Ultimately, the deputies agreed to fourteen. And with that agreement, the articles were ready for signing.

On February 25 Catherine wrote triumphantly in her own hand: ''The conference has been concluded, thanks be to God, and we have determined on the complete enforcement of the edict.''[2]

It had not been an easy month. Never before had she engaged in such persistent bargaining. Only once had she come close to losing her temper when, as she sat down to supper one evening, the delegates had come, asking her permission to depart on the grounds that no agreement could be reached. She raised her voice, noted Damville's secretary, and ''spoke to them royally,'' warning that unless they cooperated she would have them all ''hanged as rebels.'' The threat was sufficient to bring them back to the council table.[3]

It was not until after the articles were finally signed on February 28 that she felt a great burden of fatigue descend upon her. In a short letter to the Duchesse d'Uzès she acknowledged, ''I am still so exhausted from this conference and from having to write so much that I am not going to send you a long letter at this time.''[4] Although she wrote again on March 8 that she expected to be in Avignon by the end of Lent, in fact, she was to spend the remainder of March in Agen. If anything, she had underestimated her exhaustion, which made her a prey to various illnesses. Towards the end of the month she admitted to the king that the doctors had insisted on renewed purging to rid her of a terrible cold that had seriously affected her eye. She was, she acknowledged, unable to travel.

To remain in Agen was a worse suffering than sickness itself, for now the peace was confirmed she was fanatically anxious to return to Paris, doubtless because she was concerned about the state of the government, but even more, it seems, because of her passionate longing to see her son. When, in February, he had thanked her for what she was doing, she responded that there was no need to thank her; it was *she* who should thank him for the privilege of working in his interest. ''I thank you with all my heart,'' she wrote, ''for those sincere letters that you have been good enough to write to me . . . having seen by them how pleased you have been with what I have been able to do for your service, for which I busy myself heart and soul and will continue to do so, for there is nothing in the world I want so much as to see your kingdom in peace and tranquillity.''

The thought of returning to that ''dear son'' now became her single preoccupation. During the first week of March she wrote the Duchesse de Nemours, reiterating her hope of being in Avignon within a few weeks, continuing, "and if it please God, soon after settling affairs in Provence, to go to the king my son, whom I have a great yearning to see, for I have never been so long without this privilege since he was born. When he was in Poland it was only for eight months, and now it is already seven and a half."[5]

There is something both touching and awesome in the thought of this woman who had undertaken for so many years to guide the destiny of one of Europe's greatest powers, a woman sometimes ruthless, often tyrannical, now old and sick, lying in her bed, ticking off on her fingers the weeks since she had seen her son and the weeks before she would see him again. Learning he had just recovered from a serious fever, she wrote in a frenzy of maternal love, "He is my life and without him I wish neither to live nor to die. I believe that God has had pity on me, since I have had so much sorrow through the loss of my husband and my children, and that he will not crush me by taking him also. . . . I bless God for restoring him to me, and I pray that it may be for longer than my own life, so that as long as I live I may see no harm come to him."[6] When one considers her gratitude for a single crumb of his affection, it is impossible to imagine her joy had Henri been able to respond fully to her love. Her humility before this unresponsive and ungrateful son is one of the greatest paradoxes of Catherine's life.

By the beginning of April she was well enough to be on the road again, spending a week at Toulouse and then going on to Castelnaudary for her final parting with Navarre and Margot. Just as at the beginning Navarre had deceived her about his intentions, now at the end he continued to cloak them, leading her to believe he would return to court with her. To bring Navarre back to court would be her supreme triumph. It would remove him from Guyenne, where it seemed inevitable his clashes with Biron would continue, it would weaken his leadership with the Huguenots, and it would be the palpable and incontrovertible sign of harmony in the kingdom.

On April 12 she had written elatedly, "My son, since writing my other letter, Pibrac (who has just this morning returned from L'Isle-Jourdain) has reported to me from my daughter . . . that the King of Navarre will come with me when I return to you. . . . My son, this is the greatest good that could come to you. . . . Without doubt peace will be established here if it turns out that he will come with me—as I'm sure he will." For the next two weeks Navarre continued to hold out limitless hope while promising nothing, so that, on April 26, Catherine was forced to concede, "I still do not really know if my son the King of Navarre will come with me."[7] By the end of the month it was clear Navarre would not move from the south.

Despite this disappointment, their final meeting was not unpleasant. On the day of her departure Catherine was surprised and touched to learn that Margot, alone in her room, was weeping bitterly at the thought of their separation. It is one of the few tender references Catherine ever made to her daughter. This time she was genuinely pleased with Margot: She had promised loyalty to her brother, and she had agreed to stay dutifully in the south, presiding over the small, rustic court of Nérac. The following day Navarre met his mother-in-law at Fanjeaux. He expressed deep sorrow over her departure, speaking—as Catherine wrote later—"with an open heart and all sincerity, or else I am the most mistaken woman in the world."[8] He rode by her coach for a while, then watched as she continued on the road to Carcassonne.

Catherine still had six months of travelling ahead of her. She was very weary and would much preferred to have turned north to Paris. Yet she would never reveal to her son how painful this journey had been. It was in her letters to the Duchesse d'Uzès that she admitted the difficulties of the last months. Riding through the plague-infested towns of the south, she wrote:

> Were it not for the plague, I would bring you news of your estates, but Uzès and all its neighbourhood is so very much infected that the birds flying past the place fall dead. This has forced me to take the other road, between the lakes and the sea. There we had to spend two nights in tents, camping thus in the service of my king, whom I long to see again in good health. As for me, my health is good, except that Port-Ste.-Marie brought on an irritating catarrh which has turned into sciatica. However, this does not prevent my walking, not so well, though, but that I am forced to have a little mule to ride when I need it. I think that the king would laugh if he saw me on it.[9]

"In the service of the king" had become her leitmotiv. It cooled the weather, softened the makeshift camp beds, speeded the laggard days. Some explain this single-mindedness in terms of that *affetto di signoreggiare* of which she had been accused many years before. Perhaps that dominant desire to rule had taken a strange turning, so that she no longer wished to rule in her own person but in the person of her son. Still the mystery remains: the mystery of her unfeigned love for a son who grew year by year more faithless.

It was November, 1579, before Catherine reached Paris. Provence, Dauphiné, Languedoc, all "tormented with quarrels," had detained her for six months. Physically and psychologically at the end of her strength, she bristled before everything: the distrust and quarrelsomeness of the people, the dangerous roads, the uncertain weather. Most of all, she was angered at the continued insurrections by such powerful southern leaders as the Marshal de Bellegarde.

Were it simply a matter of another paltry noble working out his envy in a local revolt, Catherine would not have been so disturbed. Bellegarde, however, had widened his circle of sedition to include both Spain and Savoy. Having felt he had been unjustly deprived of the governorship of Languedoc and egged on by

Philip and the Duke of Savoy, who saw this as one more opportunity for weakening French royal power, in the spring of 1579 he took over the territory of Saluzzo. Throughout the heat of July and August, Catherine attempted to bring Bellegarde to terms. She wrote repeatedly to Navarre and Margot, begging them to influence him towards peace, and to Bellegarde himself, asking that he meet with her, assuring him he would be "completely satisfied" by her proposals.

In mid-October Bellegarde and Catherine finally met in Montluel, a little town in the government of the Duke of Savoy. Savoy had insisted on honouring the queen mother with a royal entrance, and Catherine, accompanied by her court, walked through Montluel beneath a canopy of crimson velvet, along a street highly perfumed against a recent outbreak of plague. Small recompense for the trouble Savoy had caused her, but if graciousness would gain her ends, Catherine was willing to be gracious. She accepted the extravagant welcome of Savoy and the gifts Montluel offered her.

A week later she had achieved her end and wrote triumphantly to the king, "After all my arduous labours . . . there has been a happy conclusion." She described in detail the conference held in her rooms at which Bellegarde, on his knees, had paid her appropriate homage, assuring her "of the strong desire and great affection he has always had for your service." That evening, after supper, he returned and "stood at the foot of my bed," continued Catherine with her unique mixture of political acumen and maternal naïveté. "I showed the Marshal your picture . . . and said to him, 'There is the king your master to whom I have led you and who has loved you so much and done so much for you.' At which, looking at you with tears in his eyes, he told me that you were very handsome and just as he had wished you to be."[10]

In actual fact, Bellegarde's final repentance cost him nothing, for Catherine had had to confirm him as governor of Saluzzo under the king's power. Although she continued to refer to her negotiations as a victory for the crown, it was obvious the shopkeeper, whatever face she might put on the transaction, had not been able to drive her usual hard bargain.

Catherine had lost something of her resilience and keenness during her months in the south. An English agent reported he had "never seen her so upset" as during the Bellegarde affair, and although the Venetian Girolamo Lippomano continued to praise her unquenchable energy, Paulet noticed a subtle change in her. In his last audience before being replaced by Sir Henry Cobham in November, 1579, he wrote: "She doth somewhat decay and by her physicians doubted to decline towards apoplexia. It seemed to me that in her conferences with me her voice and strength was not altogether in as good order as I looked for and I have since found the opinion of others to be the same."[11]

Although she had lulled the south to rest, there was no end to the queen mother's anxieties. Alençon was by now deeply engaged in the Netherlands. Even before her departure south, he had begun to raise troops for his enterprise. She had tried every tack to dissuade him. She had invoked his love for France and his fraternal duty to the king, but Alençon heard nothing but the martial music beyond the border. It promised glory, and the word pulsed with the power of an incantation. Against such a spell, Catherine was helpless. Fearful of the repercussions in Spain and England, she wrote hesitantly to Philip, explaining Alençon's actions as the high spirits of "youth." She wrote Elizabeth, too—for England had made it very clear it would brook no French meddling in the Netherlands—acknowledging, "Up to this very moment we have done everything possible to divert or dissuade our son the Duc d'Alençon from this enterprise, wanting nothing so much as to live in peace, friendship, and neighbourliness with you." [12]

In fact, one of Catherine's main "diversions" offered to Alençon had been an English marriage. In the spring of 1578 Sir William Stafford had been sent to France expressly to determine the king's attitude towards Alençon's involvement in the Low Countries and, if feasible, to renew the marriage negotiations. Elizabeth, like Catherine, undoubtedly hoped the lure of marriage might turn Alençon from the Netherlands. But no mere marriage, not even one to the fabled Gloriana, could deflect Alençon from his goal. By the fall of 1578 he had unequivocally declared himself the "Saviour of the Netherlands." The news came to Catherine as she waited in the south for her first conference with Navarre, and she wrote the king in both sadness and anger: "As for what you have written to me concerning the present affairs of my son, your brother . . . you know how deeply this has wounded my heart with regret to see him so badly counselled." [13]

Alençon, meanwhile, was discovering to his sorrow that the Netherlands was a country of ambivalent loyalties. Many of the towns he had come to "save," passively repudiated him, preferring to accept the concessions of their new governor, Alessandro Farnese, Duke of Parma, to open warfare with Spain. Bewildered and betrayed, Alençon took refuge in France, where, towards the middle of February, he received a letter from Queen Elizabeth, a letter so warm, so affectionate and understanding of his humiliation that it succeeded in rekindling his interest in an English marriage.

Alençon's inability to cope with the Netherlands was precisely what Elizabeth had hoped for, yet the letter she wrote to him during those bleak February days was, on the surface, one of tender regret. On closer scrutiny, however, the tone is exactly the one she maintained throughout their relationship—patronising, blandishing, very close to ridicule. There is something profoundly tragic in this little spindly prince, so quick to take offence where none was meant, who let himself be dandled unawares on the brink of mockery. "I assure you," Elizabeth had written on February 14, "I am much displeased that that ungrateful multitude, a true mob, should so misuse such a Prince; and I think that God, if not men, will be revenged on them for it, and am glad that you have safely escaped their iniquitous hands." [14]

Meanwhile, both Catherine and Mauvissière were busily encouraging Alençon to visit England. The time was ripe at last, and in mid-March Alençon slipped quietly into Paris to be reconciled with his brother and ask his approval of his English voyage. Henri rose unexpectedly to the occasion, greeting Alençon with "joy and cordiality."

It was Catherine's dearest wish come true, and with her unquenchable optimism she determined to believe that Alençon's madcap schemes were at end. On March 24 she wrote to him from Agen: "My son, I have been infinitely happy to have news of you at last and to hear of your good and sincere intention to hold back nothing which could sustain the friendship which should exist (both by reason and nature) between your brother and you. . . . Believe me, my son, you have more reason for happiness now than you ever had through those other extravagant counsels that were given you. You must believe that we want to preserve all your rights and your splendour." As for his marriage to Elizabeth, she approved of it in every way and felt he should hesitate no longer in making the journey to England. "I assure you," she continued, "that the king will help you in every way he can, although one must recognise that he does not have all the means he would wish in order that you go as you would like." But, she added practically, it might be better in the long run to take a small retinue of well-chosen people rather than to attract too much attention by his grandeur.[15]

The possibility of Alençon's doing what had been so long under discussion caused a flurry of activity. Jean Simier had already been despatched to England to prepare Elizabeth for his master's coming. Catherine now wrote in haste to the king, begging him not to dally and advising that he help his brother "with a sizeable sum, such as your own affairs will permit." The Florentine ambassador reported that the English queen was "wholly taken up in these marriage negotiations" and that he sees this as "a very solid chain" for uniting these two kingdoms. Elizabeth alone hung back, withdrawing modestly and questioning whether it might not cause embarrassment for Alençon to come all that distance before a firm commitment had been made. Elizabeth's quiet demur was overlooked in the general gaiety, and in early July Alençon, with a small retinue, left Paris for Boulogne-sur-Mer, whence he embarked for England.[16]

For eight joyful days Alençon basked in Elizabeth's warmth. If his appearance shocked her, she did not show it; if his meagre suite disappointed her, that, too, she kept hidden. Her subjects were less tactful, however, and there were some amusing verses circulated about "Our French Ulysses." Alençon was jubilant, confident the marriage was all but made. Two months after his return to France that confidence was reaffirmed when he received two gifts from Elizabeth: a jewelled cap band (reputedly worth 4,000 crowns) and a watch, with an accompanying letter:

> I send you this little letter written with my own hand to your Highness, to assure
> you of my good health. . . . I send you two little gifts. I would that in wearing
> the one around your neck you should so wear your memory of me the whole day
> long. And in the other, I would have you see an image of the crown of this king-
> dom, which quickly I would set upon your head with my own hand were I capable
> to do as much.[17]

With protestations such as this, there seemed little doubt the marriage between
France and England, so long in planning, would soon take place.

Only Simier, Alençon's handsome emissary, who—it was gossiped—had
wielded his own fascination for Elizabeth, maintained his scepticism. "I will
wait until the curtains are drawn," he wrote, "until the candle is extinguished
and my lord in bed—and then I shall speak with more assurance."[18]

The first months of 1580 confirmed Simier's cynicism. Winter somewhat
cooled Elizabeth's ardour—if, indeed, the days at Greenwich had been motivated by anything beyond political advantage. Soon Alençon received a letter that,
though it began tenderly, ended with an impenetrable question. "For my part,"
Elizabeth wrote, "I confess that there is no prince in the world to whom I would
more willingly give myself than to yourself, nor to whom I think myself more
bound, nor with whom I would pass the years of my life." But, she continued,
how was she to reconcile the delicate question of conscience involved in marriage with a professed Catholic? And even if she were able to cope personally
with this problem of religion, how could she demand the consent of her subjects?
"I would not deceive you," she concluded, "by not laying before your eyes
openly how I find the case."[19]

There is no record of Alençon's reaction to this unlooked-for hindrance, but
Catherine was adamant. "There is nothing in the world I have desired and still do
so much as this marriage," she wrote to Mauvissière, determined no question
of conscience should stand in its way.[20] Catherine understood Elizabeth too well
to put such credence in her religious scruples; if she hesitated, her motive was
elsewhere.

Just as Alençon's fortunes began to totter in England, they were, by a strange
accident of compensation, strengthened in the Netherlands. No sooner had
Alençon withdrawn in chagrin to France at the end of 1578 than it had become
obvious to the Protestants, now banded together in the Union of Utrecht, that the
concessions offered by Parma were inadequate. If they were to wrest from Spain
the liberty they felt to be their due, they would need power beyond their own.
Their hasty repudiation of Alençon, they now realised, could well spell their own
destruction. Thus, in March, 1579, one of their leaders wrote, "I feel a deep regret . . . at seeing the affairs of my lord our defender proceed so badly . . . as though we had never received any benefits from His Highness
. . . which makes me fearfully afraid that our ingratitude may provoke the divine vengeance."[21]

By the following August the Protestant party had published a manifesto declaring Philip a tyrant with no right to their allegiance. The sovereignty they refused to Spain they offered to Alençon. It was more than he had ever been offered before, and he leapt for the prize. He answered their letters at once, assuring them of "the very great happiness" he felt and the hope he had for "a profitable conclusion of your affairs," which, he foolishly avowed, "have been and will continue to be for me as dear as those of [France]."[22]

For Catherine—still weakened and depressed by one of the most serious bouts of illness she had suffered in years—the affair was disastrous. For the heir presumptive to the throne of France to assert in a public letter that the concerns of a set of quarrelling Protestants in a tributary province were as dear to him as the interests of France was beyond her imagination. That Alençon had now accepted formally the leadership of a country in open revolt against the King of Spain simply augmented the horror.

The news had come to her in Paris, a city mute beneath a pall of sickness and death. The *coqueluche*, a virulent form of whooping cough, had swept through Paris in June. There was no remedy. The victims simply suffered through the convulsive pains, the vomiting, the sweats, and—if they were strong—they recovered. The *coqueluche*, however, was but the prelude to the plague itself, which, a witness maintained, claimed 30,000 lives in Paris that year. Tents were raised in a section of the city in a vain effort to localise the contagion. Those who could fled to the country. Homes were abandoned, shops were closed, and as l'Estoile noted, the merchants, deprived of a livelihood, spent their time, like common idlers, "throwing dice on street corners." The poor people, noted the Tuscan ambassador, "can find no way to make their living."[23] At night, thieves plundered the deserted houses and looted the empty shops.

Paris, however, was suffering from something more squalid and shameful than poverty or sickness. Moral decay had become its most deadly affliction. Offices of the highest rank continued to be bought and sold; taxes were raised to pay for a court that wenched and fought like a common street gang. It was all clearly beyond the king, who, though not yet thirty, was already old.

Henri's pallor was marked, his hearing seriously impaired, and he was often so exhausted by a game of tennis that he had to take to his bed. Sir Henry Cobham at an audience that August was shocked at the king's condition. Arriving in the company of Sir William Stafford to present letters from Queen Elizabeth, he found Henri totally unable to cope with affairs of state. He was like a man already senile. Even the effort to read the documents seemed too much for him, and Cobham terminated the audience quickly. That evening he wrote to England: "So perceiving that His Majesty did sweat and the humour of his watery eyes somewhat drop which troubled him in the beginning to read the Queen's letter. . . . Mr. Stafford took his leave and I also departed."[24]

The king's illness was even more disturbing since there was not as yet an heir

to the throne. Louise, like the queen mother before her, had been subjected to ev
ery known remedy for sterility: diet, baths, potions, prayers, pilgrimages—all to
no avail. It was becoming the popular position, however, to ascribe the failure
not to Louise, whose patient fidelity had impressed the people, but to the vices o
the king. It seems strange that Catherine did not express more apprehension con
cerning the king's childlessness until one recalls that she had waited for ten years
to bear a son; doubtless, she assured herself, Louise would in time give birth to
an heir.

In the summer of 1580 there were more urgent concerns to absorb Catherine
The preceding May the sporadic skirmishing in the south had risen to full-scale
war. The Lovers' War, as it was mistakenly called, had nothing to do with love
Its trigger points had been the arrogant posturing of Biron and the refusal of the
Huguenots to return their "towns of surety" in accord with the Articles of Nérac
In April Navarre had written the king protesting his loyalty but justifying hi
declaration of war because of the "misery with which we have been reduced
through the faults of your ministers and officers."[25] Catherine replied at once, re
minding Navarre of the promises he had made, warning him against evil council
lors, assuring him that she advised him as a true mother, and concluding, "I can
not believe that you want to ruin this kingdom as well as your own—and this i
what it will mean if war breaks out again."[26]

This time her coercion was powerless to stop the conflict, and from Apr
through November France was again in open civil strife.

Neither age nor ill health had entirely undermined Catherine's ability to see a
advantage. Now, unable to avert war, she did what she could to make it serve he
ends. She cajoled the king into appointing Alençon his mediator in the south.
was a risky and complex gambit with a triple goal: She hoped Alençon would
indeed, conclude a peace; she hoped, too, that this service would reduce th
king's enmity towards his brother; most of all, she relied on its keeping Alenço
too busy to pursue his dangerous goals in the Netherlands.

The tactic was partially successful. By the end of November the Peace of L
Fleix had been satisfactorily concluded and Bellièvre had written in hig
praise of Alençon:

> Had your son, Monseigneur, not been here to maintain affairs and to put an end
> to the infinite problems which arose from hour to hour . . . it would have been
> impossible to continue; but he had taken so much to heart the service of the king
> and shown himself so eager for all his actions to be satisfactory to His Majesty's
> will that, finally, through his efforts, peace was concluded.

There was every reason to believe that, as Catherine expressed it, she would se
"a complete reconciliation of all my children."[27]

Her final goal—to deflect Alençon from the Netherlands—was not, howeve
to be so easily achieved. If anything, Alençon was more deeply embroiled the

Musée Condé, Chantilly

Catherine de Medici

Philip II of Spain

Elizabeth de Valois, daughter of Catherine, wife of Philip II of Spain

Henri de Navarre, husband of Marguerite
de Valois, son-in-law of Catherine
Bibliothèque Nationale, Paris

Jeanne d'Albret, Queen of Navarre, wife
of Antoine de Navarre, mother of Henri
de Navarre
Musée Condé, Chantilly

Antoine de Navarre, husband of Jeanne d'Albret, father of Henri de Navarre
Bibliothèque Nationale, Paris

Gaspard de Coligny,
Huguenot leader
*Bibliothèque du Protestantisme
Français, Paris*

Henri de Guise,
son of François de Guise
Musée du Louvre, Paris

Michel de L'Hôpital,
Chancellor of France
Musée Condé, Chantilly

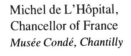

an ever as 1580 drew to a close. While he had been negotiating in the south, a delegation from the States General of the Low Countries had drawn up a treaty, affirming Alençon's formal obligation to the Netherlands. Not altogether trustful that Alençon could accomplish all he so cavalierly promised, William of Orange demanded a clause indicating that Alençon could count on the alliance and support of the King of France. Henri's initial reaction was wholesale rejection. Yet, as Catherine pointed out, this was hardly the time to alienate Alençon, who, at that very moment, was being trusted with soothing tempers in the south. Should the king refuse to honour the clause, Alençon was more than capable of wheedling a promise from the Huguenots to join him in the Netherlands. Convinced by his mother's counsel, Henri promised that "moved by the desire for the good and greatness of his brother," he would "help and assist him with all his power."

Intoxicated with his own good fortune, Alençon wrote at once to the States General accepting their offer of sovereignty: "Considering the zeal and commendable affection which you have so freely shown me, I will with greater earness accept the election and choice you have wished to make of me for your prince and lord . . . promising you that at the peril of my life, I will undertake the restitution and restoration of your former liberties."[28] It was, he thought, at last the beginning of renown. The courts of Europe would see where true Valois glory lay—not in the Italian shopkeeper with her bourgeois tendency to conciliate and temporise; certainly not in the erratic and irresponsible King of France. The true seed of Valois greatness lay in Alençon. The Netherlands had recognised his destiny, and soon England would follow suit. Elizabeth, although she pretended to stumble over the matter of religion, would ultimately be seduced by his person and his triumphs. Sovereign of the Netherlands, consort to the Queen of England. The stuff of dreams was taking substantial form.

Chapter XVI

Catherine heard the music to which Alençon marched, but to her, it was a dirge for France.

She recognised now that in her efforts to buy him off, she had simply empowered him to act against her. Accustomed to governing her children, she had not seriously doubted she could bring this runt of her litter to her bidding. By the end of 1580, however, Alençon had resolved to move out of the south to go to the relief of Cambrai, then under siege by Parma. Two days before Christmas Catherine wrote him from Blois. It was a long, desperate letter beseeching him to desist from his enterprise in the Low Countries. It was now winter, she reminded him, a time when no one can wage war satisfactorily. She warned him he was under the sway of evil councillors. She reminded him that France was not yet truly at peace, that he was needed to continue his wonderful work of reconciliation with the Huguenots, that his enterprise would incur the anger of Philip against France, that Elizabeth, who so dearly loved him, was opposed to this invasion. Not Flanders but his help in establishing peace and strength in France would be his glory. "My son," she concluded, "I beg and adjure you for your own honour . . . to postpone your enterprise."[1]

Although Alençon paid no attention to his mother's plea, neither did he go to the immediate assistance of Cambrai as he had promised. Throughout the winter he remained in the south enlarging his forces. At the beginning of May he wrote to the States General, apologising for his long delay, but assuring them he had already levied forces and hoped to persuade his mother to provide him with additional subsidies.

In fact, he had ignored Catherine's summons to visit her at Blois, and during the second week of May she followed him to the town of Alençon. The three days she spent with him simply widened the breach. He would agree to nothing. He boasted he had the full confidence of Navarre, who had promised to assist him, then mocked his brother, saying, "I am every bit as good a Catholic as the

king, although I don't visit as many churches.'' Catherine, goaded by this ridicule of her ''beloved son,'' lost her temper and, turning on Alençon's companions, accused them of ruining the kingdom: ''These are your schemers and councillors who have brought all these disturbances upon us and whom I would like to
see punished and brought to the gallows.'' Alençon would brook no such criticism, and calling his followers to him, he left.[2]

This warfare within her own house taxed Catherine to the limit. ''I have only
you two,'' she had written earlier to the king, ''and I would like you to be lords
of all the world.'' Instead, it seemed her two remaining sons would pull down the
pillars of the very house they had been born to defend.

Throughout March the king had been so sick that Cobham reported it was rumoured he ''did not have long to live.'' At the end of the month his weakness
was extreme, and Catherine, in her double worry over her two sons, was seen to
''weep.'' In April Henri was forced to retire from court, leaving Catherine to
manage the affairs of state. ''He has withdrawn to St. Germain-en-Laye,'' Hator
noted disapprovingly in his journal, ''according to some, for the cure of the
shameful disease which afflicts him.''[3]

When he returned in May, instead of gratitude for the double burden his mother had carried, Henri was annoyed at her continued conciliation in the face of
Alençon's obduracy. His criticism depressed her disproportionately, and the English ambassador noted in his despatch: ''Bitterly and with many tears [she]
complained to the King that she perceived her counsels were not acceptable to
him,'' and begged his permission to retire ''if she were no longer to be
heeded.''[4] It was a hollow request, for Catherine knew that the king, despite his
pretensions to power, could not do without her.

In addition to the constant worry over Alençon's plans, there was the redoubled interest in the English marriage. After so many delays, negotiations now accelerated, and in March, 1581, thirteen commissioners left for England. They
found Elizabeth at her most charming. She herself greeted them in the great hall
of Westminster. She conducted them to bull- and bearbaiting, to private musical
gatherings, even demonstrating her own skill by playing the spinet for them.

As for the terms of a treaty or a marriage, they could pin her to nothing. She
slipped free from their determinations while treating them with such largesse that
argument was impossible. They returned to France, ''laden with honours and silver plate,'' but with few conclusions concerning their original mission. Although
the queen had agreed to drawing up a document for the ''celebration and solem-
nisation of marriage,'' such a paper, misleading in its details, adroitly skirted the
major issues of religion and an Anglo-French alliance.

Elizabeth, meanwhile, continued her affectionate communication with Alençon. In early spring he had apparently sent her flowers, which she acknowledged
by a letter whose coquetry is almost embarrassing in a woman near fifty:

My dearest, I humbly thank you for those sweet flowers gathered by that hand whose little fingers I would bless a thousand times . . . they are as fresh as though they had been gathered this very minute, and so remind me very deeply of your own verdant affection toward me. . . . I have been careful not to lose a single leaf or flower despite all the other jewels I have.[5]

In July Elizabeth, to affirm her seriousness of purpose, sent Sir Francis Walsingham to the French court to treat exclusively of her marriage. Walsingham stands out as one of the few people who were favourably impressed by Alençon. At their first meeting he wrote back to England that he found him to speak "with as singular a grace as any person that ever I knew." And later that summer he advised the queen mother he considered her youngest son was "such a one as was like to yield as great honour as ever did childe to mother."[6]

Catherine must have found the opinion ludicrous as she engaged in her last despairing efforts to keep Alençon out of the Netherlands. His actions terrified her, and fear was Catherine's nemesis. It made her precipitate and irrational, leading her to abandon a carefully charted course for phantom security. Eight years earlier fear had propelled her into the massacre; now it led her into one of her most devious and unsuccessful paths of diplomacy.

Apprehensive that Alençon's involvement in the Netherlands should cost him his marriage, as well as a war with Spain, she now suggested that he relinquish his English marriage in favour of an alliance with one of the infantas of Spain who would bring him the Netherlands as part of her dowry. To Catherine the solution was ideal: It would dissipate the hostility between France and Spain, it would win Alençon the kingdom he wanted, and—best of all for the peace-loving Catherine—it would all be accomplished without violence. The fact that she had just given Walsingham every assurance of a marriage between France and England seemed of little consequence. Perils were to be faced in the order of their importance, and for the moment the English lion was the least dangerous.

Surprisingly, Alençon, though he raised difficulties, did not entirely demur. Like his mother, he had a short memory, and the thought of a marriage with Spain dimmed the remembrance of those fresh flowers sent to Gloriana. At once Bellièvre was despatched to Parma's camp to negotiate for a truce, while Catherine, with her unremitting caution, continued her conferences with the unsuspecting Walsingham. Parma, however, was intractable, observing that talk of neutrality came rather late when Alençon's troops were already on the border.[7]

Alençon, irritated at this rebuff and despairing of a truce, refused to wait any longer and on August 18 entered Cambrai. Two weeks later he pushed east to take Cateau-Cambrésis. Jubilantly, he sent out dozens of letters, describing the ease with which he had accomplished this "singular victory" and the overwhelming happiness of the people he delivered. For a brief moment the praise, the gratitude, the honour he had dreamt of all his life were his.

Yet despite his success and the pleas for help coming from the besieged city of Tournai, Alençon began to talk of disbanding his army temporarily, pointing out that it would be very difficult to keep it together during the winter months. Such inconstancy gave proof that Navarre's evaluation of him some months earlier had hit the mark: "I cannot persuade myself that he will ever perform anything that is great, nor preserve those honours which are now heaped upon him."[8] In effect, Alençon had turned his interests once again to England, completing his plans for a visit to Elizabeth that was to last for three months.

If Elizabeth had been cordial to the French commissioners, she now demonstrated an affection and ardour for Monsieur which surprised even those who knew her best. Gloriana fulfilled even Alençon's golden dreams. Her "little Frog" was cherished, fondled, flattered. The queen herself played Aurora to his waking, bringing him bouillon in bed, cancelling meetings of her Council so she might not be separated from him. The Spanish ambassador Bernardino Mendoza, contemptuous and frightened at the pace of the courtship, wrote in annoyance: "The Queen doth not attend unto other matters but only to be together with the Duke in one chamber from morning to noon and afterwards til two or three hours after sunset. I cannot tell what a devil they do."[9]

On November 22 Mendoza's fears were realised, and he had the unpleasant task of writing Philip that there was public evidence of a marriage between the French heir apparent and the Queen of England.

According to Mendoza, the conclusive moment had come one morning as Alençon and Elizabeth walked together in the gallery, where they were approached by the French ambassador, who asked what he might write to his master. "She replied," wrote Mendoza, " 'You may write this to the King: that the Duke of Alençon shall be my husband,' and at the same moment she turned to Alençon and kissed him on the mouth, drawing a ring from her own hand and giving it to him as a pledge. Alençon gave her a ring of his in return, and shortly afterwards the Queen summoned the ladies and gentlemen from the presence chamber in the gallery, repeating to them in a loud voice in Alençon's presence what she had previously said."[10]

Such news had wings. Enea Renieri wrote at once to Florence, "Monsieur has just changed kingdoms by having espoused the queen." In France Henri III plumed himself, saying, "I am King of France and my brother is King of England." Catherine at once gave orders to her jewellers to design a bracelet for Elizabeth, to be worn "between the elbow and the shoulder," decorated with astrological signs symbolizing happiness, fortune, and fertility. The whole was to be cast in gold, diamonds, and other precious stones, and when it was finished, it was reputed to cost 30,000 crowns.

In England the news was variously received—with elation, with dejection, with suspicion.[11] To many it was beyond imagination that Elizabeth, whose person and office gave her so wide a choice, should have settled her affections on this pockmarked little Ulysses from across the Channel. One anonymous observer wrote the Count of Nassau: "Nothing is more true nor more exact than the verse of Ovid on Ulysses: 'He was not handsome but he possessed the art of words and all the goddesses of the sea were enflamed with love for him.' "[12]

The "goddess of the sea," however, seemed almost immediately to have regretted her decision. Elizabeth realised she had gone too far. What had been done on November 22 was beyond public generalities or private promises: She had announced in the presence of many her intention to marry and had sealed her words with an exchange of rings. The next two months were spent attempting to extricate herself.

Alençon, however, was blind to all her subtle efforts to withdraw. He had come to woo Elizabeth with that same singleness of purpose with which he had ridden into the Netherlands. In both cases his easy success had suprised and elated him. He would not let victory slip from his hands. When Elizabeth suggested their exchange of rings had been premature, that there were many weighty matters still to be considered, Mendoza reported that Alençon had cried, "If I cannot get you for my wife by fair means and affection, I must do so by force, for I will not leave this country without you."[13]

Elizabeth, however, had no intention of becoming his wife, for Alençon in his present state was of maximum use to her. She could dangle him as a threat before Philip, as a promise of help before the Netherlands, as a bargaining point for a profitable alliance before Henri and Catherine. Once she was married to him, many of these advantages would dwindle. During the remaining weeks of his visit she continued her delicate game. She hinted at the difficulties in their union but never attempted to end the negotiations. When Alençon left England on February 8, the Tuscan ambassador noted that Elizabeth accompanied him as far as Canterbury, "with the greatest show of love for him . . . and with promises of assistance."[14]

For Alençon, it was sufficient proof he had conquered Britannia.

Two days later, disconsolate at what he had left, but exhilarated by the increasing pleas for help from the Netherlands, he arrived at Flushing and proceeded at once by water to Antwerp. His expectations were more than justified, for he was welcomed, as one witness reported, "not otherwise than the Hebrews awaited the coming of the Messiah." Here he was formally crowned Duke of Brabant and invested with the cloak of his office by William of Orange. Twenty thousand citizens were on hand to welcome him, and for four days triumphal processions, bonfires, feasts, speeches, and flattering verses celebrated the arrival of this "Clarissime Princeps."

There were those, however, not so easily seduced by lavish spectacle. They had already marked a lack of constancy in this young man, who, despite their manifest need, had dallied for three months in the chamber of the English queen. He might still have dallied had they not sent him an ultimatum warning him that if he did not come at once, he would lose his chance forever. In addition, there had been rumours he had been secretly treating with Spain. While there was no substantial evidence to support the charge, they watched narrowly while he resumed his Catholic practices in a country which for some time had prohibited them. They disliked his autocratic stance. Although they wanted a saviour, they did not, by that fact, want a ruler. They did not intend that his title should carry sovereignty, for they were weary of rulers who, as they put it, "nibbled their liberties."

Towards the end of March, oblivious of the temper of the people, he addressed the assembled States, managing in his narcissism to use every term they found objectionable. He swore to observe faithfully all the treaties and to act "as a good and lawful *prince* should in order to *rule* his *vassals* and *subjects*."[15] This was Valois language, and they did not care for it.

In fact, it was daily more obvious that Alençon lacked the resources to carry out his promises. He had no money; his troops, a mere rabble, ravaged the countryside. The Earl of Leicester who, at Elizabeth's bidding, had accompanied him from Dover, wrote contemptuously, "The Duke of Alençon is already like an old boat gone aground on the sand and waiting for the wind and tide to release it."[16] Only Alençon sustained the illusion of greatness.

Throughout the summer and fall his reputation waned. Despite the fact that in France he was called king, he had little power in the Netherlands. Knowing he could not maintain his army without additional funds, he multiplied his letters to his brother, his mother, and even Elizabeth, pointing out to Gloriana that she would hardly want her future husband to be humiliated by insufficient funds. But the relationship Alençon took for granted was increasingly doubtful on the other side of the Channel. While Alençon wrote glibly that no preparations remained for the marriage but to "order his clothes," Elizabeth evaded the issue. Catherine, far keener than her son, had already noticed a certain "coldness" in Elizabeth's manner, pointing out drily, "They are fine words, but there is always some hitch which makes me fear."[17]

By the summer of 1582 Catherine's attitude towards Alençon had begun to shift. Should both the English marriage and his involvement in the Netherlands founder, he would be forced to return to France, and that, for everyone concerned, would be intolerable. Referring to Alençon's shaky position, she wrote in August to Bellièvre, "I am in great pain. . . . Because of what I am to him, it could not be otherwise." And, as usual, she ended by ranting against those "evil councillors," who were responsible for his ruin.

It was her inevitable excuse for all her sons. They were but children—gullible, easily influenced, led down paths they would not otherwise have chosen. The consequences of their actions were never wilful deeds, but "accidents." They were betrayed, misinformed, badly counselled, but rarely culpable. Although she wrote, "I see no remedy except to commend him to God and to pray for him," her pragmatism could not be satisfied by such a mystic course. Soon she was wheedling the king to help his imperilled brother.[18]

Henri's enmity towards this "blackamoor" who would endanger France to win a dukedom for himself was, however, deep and bitter. That same August he wrote angrily to one of his secretaries of state, Nicolas de Villeroy, of the demands that he risk war to save Alençon's "snout." "It's wonderful what this little monkey would make us lose," he concluded. "May God have pity on this kingdom, for without Him I think we are no better than a weathercock; but I am saying too much. . . ."[19]

The king was hardly in a position to help the "little monkey" even had he wished to do so. No matter where he looked he saw the signs of ruin. Queen Louise, long subjected to popular remedies for sterility, had grown thinner and more withdrawn than ever. The king himself, after a severe bout of toothache, had agreed to have several teeth "plucked forth" and at the same time fell prey to a series of painful boils covering his head. Small wonder the English agent could report, "He waxes much subject to melancholy humours."[20] Unable to find support in human remedies, he took refuge during the summer of 1582 in his religious mania, visiting shrine after shrine, donating gifts, leaving money for vigil lights to be kept burning day and night, always with the explicit desire that God would provide him with an heir. Catherine, meanwhile, had managed to borrow money for Alençon, and on October 29 she wrote the Duc de Montpensier, assuring him of 50,000 crowns for the army he had agreed to command. "Get into Flanders with them as quickly as you can," she urged him, for "all my son's hope lies with you."[21]

Had Catherine been aware of the bloody end to which these troops were destined, she might have hesitated. Alençon's prestige had palpably diminished. It was now clear to the Netherlanders that their royal duke was capable of fulfilling few of his lavish promises. In addition, there were rumours that he would not hesitate at treachery in seizing certain cities for his own aggrandisement and, even worse, that he had been covertly involved in an attempt on William of Orange's life.

Realising he was losing ground, Alençon determined to take by force what he could not win by diplomacy. Strengthened by the soldiers brought by Montpensier and Biron, he planned a series of attacks on Bruges, Dunkirk, Ostend, and Antwerp. On January 16, under pretence of reviewing the troops, he ordered the gates of Antwerp opened, and he, with his French troops, marched into the city. What followed was assuredly not part of his plan. His soldiers, unpaid and badly disciplined, went mad in their lust for plunder. But the people of Antwerp, after the first moments of surprise and horror, battled the foreigners with every available weapon. At once the drawbridges were raised, and the French troops were pinned in the city they had hoped to capture. When the carnage was over, some 12,000 soldiers were dead, it was reported, and many more taken prisoner.

It was treachery of the most blatant kind. Alençon was, of course, forced to withdraw at once, moving the remnant of his army west to disband them at Dunkirk. The event was to become known as the Fury of Antwerp or, by some, the Folly of Antwerp. It was, in fact, the Folly of Alençon—one from which he never fully recovered.

Catherine was stunned. She did her best to brazen the event out by writing at once to William of Orange of her "deep regret" concerning the "accident that has befallen my son." But no effort to make this seem an unprovoked act of violence on the part of the citizens of Antwerp was credible.[22] Alençon himself had tried that path in a declaration sent to the city magistrates in which he recalled how he had risked all for the good of this people, how they had never fully trusted him or placed true power in his hands. Now he had suffered the final insult. "This extraordinary indignity," the "little respect" and "scorn" with which he had been treated had embittered him beyond words. But his declaration lacked substance; it was a transparent effort to avoid his own culpability.

Whatever trust or hope the people of the Netherlands had still retained in him had been forfeited. No effort to regain his lost dignity was to be of any avail. "Since France was France," wrote Roger Williams to Walsingham, "France has never received so great a disgrace."[23]

Even then Alençon did not recognise the signs of his own fall. Ambition had become a disease. It distorted his senses so that where others heard the slow cadence of defeat, Alençon still heard the trumpet call to triumph. Throughout the spring, it was obvious he intended to retain his title of Duke of Brabant and to save what he could of "his lands" from the encroachments of Parma's forces. After an ambiguous accord made with the States General of the Netherlands, he journeyed in early April to Dunkirk. Never robust, his health was now seriously undermined, and he arrived by litter, "not much better than dead," as one observer commented. The Tuscan ambassador Giulio Busini summed up in a terse phrase Alençon's condition at this time: "completely stripped."[24]

During his weeks at Dunkirk he suffered his first haemorrhage, and towards the end of the month Catherine learned he had been close to death. A few days later the doctors reported he had partially recovered from this bout of what was labelled tertiary fever. Catherine, always foolishly optimistic where her children's health was concerned, wrote gratefully to Bellièvre, "God has had mercy on us, not giving us more trouble than we are able to bear. . . . God has helped him this time and I beg Him with all my heart that He will continue to do so in the future."[25]

By the beginning of July Alençon had recovered sufficiently to go to Abbeville, where he continued his efforts to muster an army to save Dunkirk from Parma's advancing troops. Few recruits responded, however, for, as one old soldier put it, "Who the devil would want to go into Flanders when no one ever comes back?"[26] Still undaunted, Alençon turned again to the king, reminding him it was in the French interest to keep Dunkirk and Cambrai out of Spanish control. But Henri refused to be drawn into Alençon's schemes.

During the second week of July Catherine, in another effort at domestic peace, travelled to Chaulnes to see Alençon. Age and persistent attacks of rheumatism and gout had made travel increasingly difficult for her, and when she arrived, she wrote the Duc de Nevers that it was so hot she could not move from her room. She mustered up the energy to talk to Alençon, however, promising him in the king's name to give him the lieutenant generalcy of the kingdom, as well as an income of 200,000 francs, if he would give up his enterprise in the Low Countries and return to court. Although Alençon made some vague promise to comply, it was clear he had no intention of keeping it. Even when Dunkirk fell to Parma's troops, he still talked about a new army to return to Flanders—this time to "help" Cambrai.[27]

By some remarkable feat of strength, Alençon did, in fact, enter Cambrai on September 2. Despite the continued opposition of his mother, his brother, even his military councillors, he pulled together a sizeable army and again took the road to glory. His victory was as ephemeral as all his dreams. Funds he had anticipated from France did not arrive; the reiters never appeared. There was neither money to pay his troops nor provisions to feed them. "We will all die miserably of famine," wrote one of the despondent captains.[28] By October the soldiers had begun to disband despite Alençon's pleas to hold on for just a few more days. The citizens of Cambrai, vexed by his continued failure, indicated they would prefer to open their gates to Parma rather than continue as they were.

On October 13 Alençon, denouncing the ingratitude of those he had given his life to help, led the ragged remnant of his army out of Cambrai. He had reached the nadir of his military fortunes, but a humiliation of another kind awaited him. After eleven years of sporadic negotiations, the English marriage foundered at last.

For some time, Elizabeth had watched Alençon's fortunes with apprehension. When Sir William Stafford had arrived in Boulogne that September, what he saw made him feel that such a marriage would demean England's queen, and he wrote forthrightly to Elizabeth:

> For Monsieur, I am sorry, being a prince that for her Majesty's sake I have honoured, that my duty to her binds me to write what I find. All the way from the seaside hither where at other times I have found him honoured and loved by the people, I now find him ten times more detested than the King. Here I find men's opinions little amended, he being generally taken for a man that moveth nothing, is grounded upon nothing but inconstancy and is only thought to have some cunning and deceitful wit because, being inconstancy itself, no man can tell when to take hold of him.[29]

Stafford's reports confirmed Elizabeth's own judgements, and when Alençon, now bereft of hope, wrote seeking her aid, he received in reply not the affectionate letter of his Gloriana, but that of an offended monarch who had her own house to tend and who felt no obligation to assist a sovereign too weak to tend his own. "Whoever has given you this advice has thought to make a blemish on our friendship or to break it altogether," she wrote. "Do you not remember, Monsieur, against how many friends I have to prepare? . . . Is the King, your brother, a prince so weak that he cannot defend you, without another neighbour who has enough on her back. . . . I hope, among other things, that you will remember that he is very worthy of tripping who enters the net."[30]

Alençon had, indeed, entered the net, and throughout the cold rains of November he lay dazed by his own fall. He had withdrawn to Château-Thierry, where Catherine came early in the month. What she saw shocked her. Never robust, Alençon was now reduced to skin and bones, weakened by haemorrhages and fever. For hours he would lie bathed in sweat, gasping for breath. Frequent purgings weakened him further, although Catherine continued to believe the doctors when they assured her of his recovery. Like Alençon himself, she refused to recognise that his illness was mortal and continued to talk of his military future, of means for reconciliation with his brother, of other possible marriages—now that Elizabeth no longer seemed interested.

Catherine herself had suffered a serious illness earlier that fall. Although she called it simply colic, it attacked her everywhere. She could eat nothing. Her face was badly swollen and very painful; her arms and leg, too, were severely enflamed. She herself was inclined to underplay its severity, but her doctor wrote the king in harrowing detail of the case and its treatment. Although by the end of October she could write that she was much recovered, the bout had left her weak and despondent.

She could hardly be blamed for depression, for 1583 had been a year of defeats and disappointments. In July of that year Catherine's persistent claim to the throne of Portugal was brought to an end by the final defeat of French forces in the Azores. Her title, a vague and shadowy affair going back to the thirteenth century, was first brought to the fore in 1578 after the death of the bizarre Prince Sebastian, once Margot's suitor. His immediate successor, his uncle, Cardinal Henry, died in January, 1580, after a brief period of power. These shifts were carefully watched by Sebastian's other uncle, Philip II. He recognised Portugal as a lucrative, if not an influential, kingdom and was greedy for the trade with the East Indies, the wealth of Brazil, and the possessions in Africa the control of Portugal would bring. Even before Cardinal Henry's death, Philip had engaged an army to move towards Portugal. Six months later the dubious claimant to the throne, Don Antonio, had been forced into hiding, and Philip's army, under Alba and Santa Cruz, had marched successfully into Lisbon. The following spring

Philip received the allegiance of the Cortes—the Portuguese Parliament—and his coup was complete.

Catherine, however, continued in her stubborn refusal to acknowledge Philip's authority. From 1579 to 1583 a good portion of the queen mother's correspondence focussed on her claim to Portugal. Long after Philip had been clearly accepted and the union of the two crowns had become a fait accompli, she continued writing her various ambassadors directing them to urge her claim to Portugal. When the Spanish ambassador Juan Batista de Tassis pointed out that all her activity was useless, since Philip had already successfully won Portugal, she replied indignantly that it was not her fault, that she had certainly tried to dissuade him. Again, when he cautioned her that she invalidated her talk of peace by continuing to prepare warships, she countered by pointing out that it was, after all, Philip who had "forced his way into Portugal to the prejudice of the kingdom and of justice." Throughout everything, she remained adamant in maintaining her right to Portugal.[31] When the exiled Don Antonio arrived in France begging help, Catherine assured him of their assistance, being very careful, however, not to acknowledge him as king lest this jeopardise her own title.

By June, 1582, a French fleet was on its way to Terceira in the Azores under the command of Filippo Strozzi, Catherine's beloved cousin. The fleet consisted of some fifty-five ships carrying approximately 5,000 men. Outwardly, it was a navy to reckon with, but many engaged in the enterprise were sceptical of its success. Although Strozzi himself, aboard the lead ship, *St. Jean Baptiste,* wrote that it was a "large beautiful ship," well equipped and carrying "a fine troop," some of the contemporary accounts are less favourable. They spoke of the incapacity of the commanders, the inexperience of the soldiers in coping with problems of the sea, the lack of freshwater and palatable food because of the long delay in getting under way.[32] Those who saw the enterprise as ill-omened were soon proved right.

The Marquis de Santa Cruz, who had already helped Alba so successfully in the Portuguese coup, now met Strozzi with forty ships and 7,000 men. The battle was a disaster for France. Strozzi was killed. Even more humiliating, many of his officers and sailors were executed, not according to the code of naval warfare, but brutally, as pirates, since Santa Cruz maintained no state of open war had ever been declared between France and Spain.

A few weeks after Catherine received the news, she wrote Du Ferrier in Venice, "You can imagine what sadness and chagrin I feel over the loss of my cousin, M. de Strozzi, as well as of the treatment accorded to the subjects of the king my son."[33] It is extraordinary that Catherine, despite this enormous loss and personal humiliation, should still refuse to capitulate to Spanish power. Instead, she began plans for another fleet to sail for the Azores the following summer. Once again, Santa Cruz was victorious, writing in jubilation to Philip, "I have granted my soldiers three days of looting. The trials of the rebels have already been held; as for the French, they will get their turn since they have insisted on returning despite the punishment we inflicted on them last year.''[34] This second failure was definitive; Catherine abandoned her claim to Portugal. Although many of her biographers have claimed that she had never intended to win Portugal, that she had maintained her claim simply as a handle by which she might bargain with Philip for a peaceful settlement in the Netherlands and a marriage between France and Spain, it was a costly—and foolish—price to pay. One is inclined to agree with the Florentine ambassador who referred to the episode slightingly as *suo capricio de Portogallo*— her Portuguese caprice.[35]

"The Leaden Echo"

I do not see what there is to be hoped for here. God must be very angry and we very wicked people that we must suffer such great evils.

—CATHERINE DE MEDICI

Chapter XVII

The year 1583 was tragic for Catherine. In addition to her own defeat, all three of her children during the space of that year had, to use Elizabeth's metaphor, fallen into the net. They had tripped badly, not only ruining their own fortunes, but precipitating France into greater crisis.

For some years, it had been apparent to most of France that they could hope for little from their king. Throughout the winter and spring his actions had grown increasingly erratic. In January he had, without consultation, levied an enormous tax which the people insisted they could not pay. The following months he took refuge in religion, startling his court by returning from a pilgrimage on foot, walking in mud up to his knees, while his royal carriage lumbered beside him. When he reached Paris, he was forced to his bed.

Not long after, his religious mania found expression in instituting a new order of penitents. Led by the king, the members of his newly formed congregation walked through the Paris streets singing the *Salve Regina*, while the dull spring skies unleashed a torrent of rain. To the people, it was a sheer farce. A Paris monk was imprisoned for calling it a "procession of atheists and hypocrites," and at the Louvre, 100 pages were flogged for insolently mimicking the royal procession. The Venetian ambassador Lorenzo Priuli noted with regret, "The condition of this kingdom is very bad . . . I lament that the King should take so little care for the dignity and the interests of the crown."[1]

As the year progressed, the king's health deteriorated, and he was often in a "fainting condition." Evil dreams kept pace with his illness, and he was soon beset by delusions of persecution. The queen mother could no longer conceal his incapacity, and after an audience, Stafford wrote cynically to Walsingham, "His disposition is not to answer anything of importance upon the sudden; whether from discreetness or inability I leave to your honour's judgement."[2] It was more and more obvious that royal power was wielded not by the king but by his two favorite *mignons*, Anne, Duc de Joyeuse and La Valette, Duc d' Épernon, on whom he squandered not only money, but power and position.

Even the queen mother's remonstrances were brushed aside, for, as the English agent wrote, "Her credit is very small." The court had become a vipers' tangle, and Stafford, always quick to rejoice at French misfortune, wrote Walsingham:

> "Thanks be to God they are all divided, the two brothers and the Queen Mother all in several factions, the King for his own minions, caring for nothing else; the Queen Mother to maintain her credit and to seek still to rule and govern which is almost gone with her; Monsieur to keep himself abroad with some reputation to the world and to show that he hath great credit to do much good and mind to do more, and in truth, neither dealing well with brother, mother, Protestant, Papist, nor friend."[3]

It was not only Alençon and the king who were at loggerheads. By the summer of 1583 Margot had become the focus of discord.

Catherine, who had never abandoned hope of getting Navarre back to court, continued to urge him during the winter of 1582 to come to Paris with his wife. As usual, he seemed pleased at the prospect, but as the time grew near, he pleaded business at home. During the spring of that year, Margot arrived at court alone. Her first months were deliriously happy, for although she had written of the charm of the court at Nérac, she was too much a Valois to be satisfied for long with the small pleasures of the south. She longed for the breadth of Paris, of St. Germain, of Chenonceaux.

Despite the continued crisis in French economy, the court continued to live in splendour. The queen's gowns were still cut from the most exquisite cloth, stiff with gold and silver embroidery. The banquet tables were sumptuously furnished with every variety of food. The service itself was such that the English ambassador's wife described it in wonder: "crystal glasses set in gold as of many different fashions as I have never seen."[4] By comparison, Nérac seemed a pale interim whose pleasures were as stiff as the Huguenots' coifs. At Paris Margot no longer had to accommodate her dress—or her manner—to the exigencies of Protestant morality. She could dance again—and she did, whirling through the court with the grace and charm that had made her the most desirable princess in France. The Duc de Guise, once her reputed lover, no longer interested her. He had grown lean and serious, she noted. Nor did she seem to miss her husband, though at her mother's request she continued to write him in an effort to wheedle him into returning to court.

From the beginning of Margot's visit, Catherine had been shocked and bewildered by the relations between her daughter and her husband. When she learned that Fosseuse, the youngest and prettiest of Margot's ladies-in-waiting, had been

Navarre's mistress, she remonstrated with her daughter to dismiss her, pointing out that she should not be subjected to such indignity. When this news reached Navarre, he was furious and subjected Margot to a tongue-lashing, delivered by one of his men at court. Humiliated and angered, his wife replied, "If my birth placed me in some condition where I would be unworthy to be your wife, this answer would be bad enough, but being what I am, it is entirely unsuitable."

Catherine, too, wrote furiously to Navarre. Although usually the diplomat, she was a lioness where the honour of her children was concerned, and the letter reveals a side of Catherine seldom seen:

> I was astonished at the language which Frontenac used. You are not the first young husband who has been imprudent in affairs of this kind, but I think you must be the first and indeed the only one, who has afterwards used such language to his wife. This is not the way to treat women of her house, to upbraid them publicly at the whim of a little courtesan. . . . I will not believe that such a message came from you, for you are too well born not to know how to treat the daughter of your king and the sister of him who commands this entire kingdom as well as you yourself.[5]

The letter ended with another plea to come to court, where all these misunderstandings could be resolved. "Trust my advice which I give you as a mother who loves you and wants your happiness." Catherine's reproach, however, elicited no apology from her son-in-law, and Renieri soon noted, "The Queen of Navarre has declared that she no longer wishes to live with her husband who is a liar and a Huguenot."[6] To even the score, Margot had resumed her romantic involvement with Jacques de Harlay, Sieur de Champvallon, master of horse for Alençon, whom she had last seen some eighteen months earlier when her brother had visited Nérac. Whether or not he was, as some claimed, openly her lover, it is true Margot was foolish in her infatuation. Her extravagant apostrophes knew no measure: he was her "beautiful sun," her "lovely angel," her "Narcissus."[7] His recent marriage only heightened his attraction for her.

Such conduct confounded Catherine, who counted on Margot's influence to keep her husband at peace with the crown. As for the king, everything his sister did plagued him. By the summer of 1583 there was thunder in the air, and when the storm broke, it turned a domestic squabble into an international scandal. The episode in which the king insulted his sister has been overlaid with flamboyant details, but Busbecq, a generally reliable witness, described it as a public scene, reporting that the king had spoken "in front of many," upbraiding Margot with all the lovers she had had since her marriage, citing evidence of times and places—even the existence of an illegitimate child—and ordering her to leave Paris. Margot, according to Busbecq, "appeared to have nothing to answer by way of justification."[8] If she had hoped for a champion, she was bitterly disappointed, for Champvallon had fled—presumably to the safety of Germany.

Catherine was distraught. Not only did such an episode present an image of a France torn and weakened at its very core, but even more painfully, it distorted her own image as the *Regina Madre,* guarding her children in the circle of her protective love. At once she sent for Margot, seeing her in her favourite garden of the Tuileries. But even in that idyllic atmosphere of green lawns and playing fountains, she could not cool the air. She assured Margot the king would be willing to reach some amicable solution, provided that Margot, on her part, did not speak "sharply or sourly" to him. Margot, however, would make no promises. She saw no reason why the accused should respond with humility while the terms for peace remained in the hands of the unjust accuser. She replied simply that her brother was all too ready to believe ill of her and that the accusation that she had borne a child was the grossest lie. Catherine, desperate, reminded her that since it was the king himself who had commanded her to leave Paris, she had no other course.

Catherine had failed to arouse either fear or compunction in her daughter, and the English agent, missing no detail, wrote in his report, "Thus the daughter departed from the Queen Mother without weeping or changing of countenance, passing forth into the next chamber where with a cheerful countenance she took her leave of the princesses and all the other ladies."[9]

On August 8 Margot left Paris, journeying south "with a small confused train." They made their way slowly, for Margot—though loath to admit it—was not sure what her destination was to be. Navarre had already made it clear that he had no intention of taking back a wife who was "publicly besmirched" without some "suitable satisfaction."[10] The king by his public accusation had overreached himself. A domestic quarrel had become a problem of foreign relations. Stafford, who observed his confusion, wrote: "The King would have all the matter die. . . . But the examinations have gone so far . . . that I think in the end is like to breed some broil, for the King of Navarre hath plainly sent to the King that he will not receive her, and demands justice of his wife if she have offended; if she have not, of those that falsely accuse her."[11]

Catherine, seeing the result of her son's irresponsible anger, took to her bed sick in body and spirit, too weary to undo the tangled skeins, yet knowing that ultimately the responsibility would lie with her. At once Bellièvre, her most trusted diplomat, was sent to Navarre, but even he found the path to reconciliation a difficult one. "I do not think that it will be easy to persuade the King of Navarre to take back his wife without some suitable satisfaction," he wrote.[12] Catherine had none of her son's psychic need to appear guiltless; if public satisfaction were demanded, she would willingly provide it. When negotiations grew more tense, she sent the most pacifying instructions possible to Bellièvre, assuming a false share of the responsibility for Margot's disgrace. She assured Navarre that things had been overstated in the reports. The scandalous rumours he had heard were, she avowed, only lies to stir up bitter feeling against the royal family. Navarre knew Catherine too well not to sense she was assuming a responsibility not rightfully hers, but he admired her determination to swallow reproach and insult to keep France at peace.

Navarre, however, was not to be content with the bread of humility; he intended to use this affair as a weapon to win territorial gains for the Huguenots. Margot would be received at the court of Nérac only when her brother had made over certain specified towns to the Huguenots. The negotiations took months, and Margot for the first time in her life was left totally without resources. Neither beauty nor charm availed: She was a wife "besmirched," and there was no place for her.

For a while she took up residence at Châteaudun, looking down from the castle into the valley of the Loire. It was a beautiful and romantic spot, but Margot's thoughts were too dark to see beyond the deep precipice, an image of what her life had become. In her wretchedness she was driven to write humbly to her brother: "Sire, your judgement must be my true judge. . . . Put aside your anger and consider what I have had to endure in order to obey you. . . . I am still your servant and your sister and you are my only comfort." To the queen mother she wrote, speaking darkly of suicide, asking that after her death someone would testify to the true state of her life so that finally "it will be made known to everyone the wrong that has been done me."[13]

If she hoped to win mercy and compassion, she failed. Her brother knew of no way of righting the situation without compromising his own position, and her husband had no intention of sacrificing his unexpected advantage. It was the spring of 1584 before Navarre permitted her to join him at Nérac. Some said it was an affectionate reunion; others that Navarre scarcely looked at his wife and that throughout dinner her eyes were filled with tears. Catherine, however, rejoiced in the reconciliation, thanked Bellièvre for all he had done, and wrote him a last letter of advice to be conveyed to Margot: "I pray God," she wrote, "that she may live like a woman of good character and honour and like a princess of her position ought." She should, the queen mother continued, be surrounded only by good and virtuous people.

> Should she say that I am not, tell her . . . being what I am, known by everybody, having lived as I have up to my present age, in time she will be able to do the same without offence to God or scandal to the world. . . . But now . . . I think she should reject everyone who is not worthy to be near a wise and virtuous princess, who is still young and who, perhaps, thinks herself to be prettier than she is. I don't know who will say this kind of thing after you have left, for, of course, now that she is with her husband I won't write to her any more, for he'll see the letters. Tell her not to let him make love to the women of her household.[14]

While Margot had been vowing suicide from Châteaudun, Alençon had been fighting his battle against death at Château-Thierry. His illness had made him only more tenacious of power, and he continued to try to hold onto Cambrai, accusing his brother of betraying the promises of help he had made him. "I am so upset by all this that I don't know what to say," wrote Catherine to Bellièvre.[15] Alençon's hopes were bolstered by William of Orange, who hoped, through Alençon, to hold Henri III to his vague promises of help against Spain.

This, undoubtedly, was at the bottom of Alençon's sudden appearance in Paris. Without warning, at two o'clock in the morning of February 11, he appeared in the queen mother's bedchamber, still booted and cloaked from his journey. Catherine, roused from sleep, at once embraced her "little blackamoor" and sent for the king. The Tuscan ambassador at once reported this unanticipated reunion:

> They say that as soon as the king entered the room, Monsignor threw himself at his feet, begging him to pardon him and to excuse his youth, admitting that His Majesty was indeed his master and king and that in the future he would obey him. So manifold were his words of love and submission that the king lifted him up, embraced him, and told him that his love was all for him, that he was now convinced that his servants had made false reports about him, that he loved him as a brother and son, and since he had no heir, he would give him the succession of his kingdom.

This flamboyant reconciliation, so sudden and unexpected, undid Catherine, who, continued Busini, "began to cry, saying, 'I thank God that after so much trouble He has given me the grace of seeing both of you here in front of me, united and at peace. Believe me, I am going to die very happy.' "[16]

Catherine could hardly have failed to recognise that Alençon's sudden overture was simply another artifice to get the promised men and money from the king; so desperate had she become, however, that even the semblance of peace satisfied her. Whatever Alençon had hoped to gain through this reconciliation was never realised, for less than a month later he was again mortally ill at Château-Thierry. On March 14 L'Estoile noted that Catherine had left to see her son, "who lies very ill, bleeding at both nose and mouth."[17]

For the next four weeks, despite short periods of relief, his condition deteriorated. On April 16 an alarming swelling appeared in his throat, and Stafford reported to Walsingham that Alençon was "given over of the physicians as no man of this world." Even so, Catherine, buoyed by false hope, wrote to Bellièvre towards the end of April that her son was better and that the doctors hoped for a recovery.[18] "But," wrote Stafford, "they say this for outward show," for no one who had seen Alençon could believe it. Ghastly pale, thin to emaciation, he was now so weak that he "swoons as soon as he tries to rise." Yet during the periods of relief from the sweats and suffocation, he began to speak of a new army for the Netherlands, sending for pen and paper in order to write to his brother, pleading for help for "the poor Flemings."

At the end of May there was little change in his condition, and Catherine left to return to Paris. Still she deluded herself, writing Bellièvre, "I saw him yesterday and found him in fair condition, considering the sickness he is suffering from; . . . it made me hope . . . that he will be cured and that God will have mercy on me, who have already lost so much, and will not ask me to see anyone else die."[19]

On the afternoon of June 10 Alençon died at Château-Thierry. Catherine was not with him. She had stayed on in Paris. One wonders if she had purposely avoided his deathbed for reasons too subtle for even her to penetrate. Her relations with all her children, but especially with Alençon, were unusually complex. She could not love a son who rebelled against her guidance; neither could she entirely cast him off, for the fate of France depended to some degree on his loyalty. She needed him even if she did not love him. And, one suspects, she would have liked to have loved him, even felt a strong maternal duty to do so. Perhaps guilt rather than indifference kept her from Château-Thierry.

The retinue that surrounded Alençon could not have been very large—or, indeed—deeply moved by their loss. Alençon lacked the ability to inspire loyalty. Preening himself on using men to his own advantage, he himself was ultimately the most used. The Flemings had exploited him; his soldiers had deserted him; Elizabeth had abandoned him. In him the vices of the Valois had become a caricature. False, foolish, narcissistic—even his good points had become distorted. Ambition might have strengthened him; instead, it had swelled in him like a cancer, feeding on his vitality, blinding him to the world of reality.

Although Catherine looked upon her last-born with disdain, there were some qualities they had in common. They were opportunists, often tempted foolishly to seize the immediate advantage rather than wait for enduring victory. They were devious and manipulative—Catherine with far greater skill than her son. Most of all, they were almost fatuously optimistic. They could not believe in failure. Such optimism kept Catherine going beyond the limit of human endurance; in Alençon, however, it simply propelled him from one scapegrace adventure to another and, finally, to his ruin.

As so often the case, where there was little personal grief, there was a great outward show of mourning. For three days Alençon's funeral cortège travelled west to Paris, while people who had often been frightened and contemptuous of the impetuous little prince now lined the roadside, wondering what France would do with the heir apparent dead.

Those he had betrayed and who, in turn, had betrayed him wrote of their grief. William of Orange expressed his "great sadness" at this "tragic news," extolling the "great courage" with which Alençon had "undertaken the cares of this country."[20] From England Walsingham wrote, "Monsieur is dead. Melancholy doth so possess us as both public and private causes are at a stay for a season." And the French ambassador, speaking of Elizabeth's reaction, wrote: "As for the queen she is still, in appearance, full of tears and regrets, telling me that she is as a widow woman who has lost her husband and how I know that the late Monsieur was as much to her and how she ever held him hers, although they had not lived together, and many other speeches.'' He then added perceptively: "She is a princess who knows how to compose and how to transform herself as suits her best.'' To Catherine, Elizabeth wrote in eloquent grief, "But for myself, I find no consolation if it be not death, which I hope will make us soon to meet. Madam, if you could see the image of my heart you would see there the picture of a body without a soul; but I will not trouble you more with my plaints, having too many of your own."[21]

In fact, Catherine did seem bowed with anguish. News of Alençon's death had reached Paris during the night, but Henri had waited until morning to tell his mother. Twice, noted Busini, she raised her hands—those delicate, tapering hands her sons had inherited—to her face to brush away the tears. Perhaps they were less tears of loss than of regret—regret for all Alençon might have been and for her own maternal failure. That same day she wrote to Bellièvre, "You can imagine what my grief is like; consequently, I am not going to write you a long letter. You can imagine what it is like to live so long that I see everyone die before me, yet I know that one must conform one's self to the will of God and that all belongs to Him."[22]

As for the king, he was determined to give his brother so royal a funeral that it would quiet for good the gossip of jealousy and rivalry between them. Alençon's body, accompanied by his captain Biron and 400 horsemen, was brought first to the monastery of St. Magloire in the suburb of St. Jacques. Here, just at sundown, the royal family came to pay homage to the youngest Prince of the Blood. They were preceded by the Swiss Guard, their muffled drums rolling like thunder in the hot summer air. Then came King Henri, dressed in violet mourning, his Spanish horse also caparisoned in violet cloth. He was attended by the cardinals, their scarlet robes muted into purple, and the members of the court robed heavily in black. Catherine, ponderous in her heavy funeral robes of tawny, accompanied the procession in a litter. The following day the body was brought to Notre-Dame-des-Champs, and on Tuesday to the Cathedral of Notre Dame. On Wednesday the final obsequies took place at St. Denis. Here Alençon was laid to rest beside his two kingly brothers, François and Charles, achieving at last his lifelong goal: to sit in equality beside the kings his brothers.

Alençon was not yet thirty when he died, but for more than ten years he had worried the kingdom and tormented the king. He had enjoyed baiting his brother, enjoyed setting up insoluble conundrums for the royal family. If he could not have what he wanted, he found a perverse satisfaction in keeping it from others. In this sense, his death was his masterpiece, for with it the last possible Valois successor to the throne vanished, confronting France with a dilemma that would plunge it into war for ten years to come.

With the death of Alençon, the sword that had dangled for so long over the royal family fell at last. The Valois line was coming to an end. None of Catherine's sons had provided male children, and the Salic Law prohibited the throne from passing to the distaff side. Consequently, by the law of blood, Henri de Navarre, great-nephew of François I, was now the lawful successor to the French throne. To most of France the prospect was intolerable. That a Huguenot should ever wear the crown of France was unimaginable. Even those who leant towards religious toleration baulked at the prospect, for in a period where church and state were indissolubly linked, the religion of the monarch inevitably became the religion of the state. *Cujus regio, ejus religio* still obtained.

The immediate solution was for Navarre to abjure his heresy and return to Roman Catholicism.

For years Catherine, aware that one day they might be faced with this crisis, had done all she could to wheedle Navarre back to the bosom of Rome. She had always failed, yet Navarre had never categorically denied the possibility of such a move. His answers were always tolerant, amiable, leaving the door open for future negotiations. Even before Alençon's death, she had encouraged the king to send someone to treat with Navarre. In mid-May, Épernon, the most powerful of the *mignons,* set out for Gascony. Although his ostensible purpose was to visit his sick mother, most of the foreign diplomats narrowed the point of the journey to something political. L'Estoile noted in his journal that Épernon's commission was to Navarre and that he carried letters from the king begging his cousin to 'come to court and hear mass.''[23]

In the days between Alençon's death and his funeral, Catherine busied herself with ensuring the success of Épernon's journey. She needed Margot's help in dissipating the inherent distrust between Navarre and the king's *mignon.* Yet Margot herself loathed the *mignons,* Épernon in particular, blaming them in part for the calumnies she had endured at court. It took all of Catherine's maternal force and all of Bellièvre's diplomacy to win Margot to their side. Margot's experience had not yet taught her the art of submission. "Stiff-necked," her brother Charles had once called her, and she was still stiff-necked. She refused flatly to see Épernon or to do anything to make his interview with her husband more successful.

Catherine was furious, and throughout June and into July she bombarded Bellièvre with instructions for Margot. "Tell my daughter that she is simply increasing my anguish," she wrote the day after Alençon's death, and a month later she was still writing, "If she keeps acting like this, she must realise that the king will never wish to hear her spoken of again." Such a threat could hardly have perturbed Margot, who was convinced her royal brother would happily see her dead. Bellièvre's diplomacy was pushed to the extreme as he tried to

phrase Catherine's increasingly acerbic messages into something Margot migh
find acceptable: "Although you have lost your brother for whom you bore an ex
traordinary love, yet God has spared the queen your mother, who is more con
cerned about you than about her own life. . . . I write to you on the expres
command of your mother, begging you to accept her instructions."

Worn down at last, Margot agreed to receive Épernon. Her letter to Bel
lièvre histrionically portrays herself as a poor defenceless woman, exploite
by her family. "I see clearly that I can neither flee nor avoid this interview," she
wrote. "My life is reduced to the condition of a slave, for I must obey tha
strength and power which I am incapable of resisting."[24] Having agreed to enter
tain Épernon, she intended to do so with royal splendour. Dissatisfied with he
own household, she borrowed dishes, tablecloths, napkins, silver plate. Whe
Épernon arrived at Nérac on the evening of August 4, he found a gracious hostes
and an impressive banquet.

The three days spent at Nérac was his third interview with Navarre. Initially
they had met at Pamiers, where he had explained the real purpose of his visit
Since the king had abandoned the hope of children, he wished to settle on Na
varre the legitimate succession of the throne. The French nobility would, he ex
plained, acclaim him on the single condition that he become a Catholic. Na
varre's answer was gracious but unequivocal: Such a course was impossible
Aware of the gravity of his mission, Épernon was not to be so easily defeated and
cajoled Navarre into a second meeting to be held at Pau during the first days of
July.

A man of extraordinary ambition, Épernon found it inconceivable that Navarre
would reject a crown on the simple grounds of religious loyalty. He took Na
varre's refusal at Pamiers as no more than an initial gambit, the first move in a
complex and devious game. His initial letter to Bellièvre was cheerful and op
timistic. In this he was not alone. One of Margot's ladies-in-waiting later wrote
of how well things were going, and Busini noted in his report that the "cordial
ity" and "signs of friendship" between the two men left little to be desired.[25] As
it turned out, it was a false optimism on all sides, for Navarre never wavered.
When he bade farewell to Épernon, it was with great good wishes for the king,
but with a steady rejection of his proposal.

To anyone who knew Navarre, it was clear his refusal to return to the Church
of Rome was not wholly a religious one. Navarre was no zealot. Catherine and
her son-in-law shared something of the same attitude in their approach to reli
gion. It was a necessary element of life, but neither creed nor cult was so impor
tant that a country and a people should be ruined on its account. As a matter of
fact, Navarre often found himself out of favour with his own ministers, who
found his life-style too broad for a Huguenot leader. He, in turn, was often impa
tient with the intransigent attitudes of his "grave ministers" and the republican
ism of his most religious followers. The real issue for Navarre was not theology

) much as political pragmatism. Where would the decision to recant carry him? he king's promises were handsome, generous—and unreal. Had the king been ther than he was, it might have been possible to grapple realistically with the ifficulties involved. But Navarre knew better than to trust either the judgement r goodwill of the king.

Henri was a subject of scorn everywhere. Catherine wept, reported Stafford, at what she saw him becoming, "saying that her son was ravished out of her hands y them that possess him." The winter preceding Alençon's death, he had start- d a new confraternity, the Jeronomists, centred in the Bois de Vincennes. It was) be a confraternity of penance, the members dressed in muted grey, their silver late engraved with a cross, their days filled with hours of penitential prayer. 'His companions do it only for his sake and all mock it," wrote Stafford con- emptuously. The Tuscan ambassador had already begun to refer to him in dis- lain as *Il Vescovo*—the bishop—rather than the king.[26]

Even Alençon's death, with its consequent dilemma over the right of succes- ion, did not arouse Henri from his fantasies. By July Stafford noted that every worthwhile prince or nobleman had left court, fed up with a king who did noth- ng. He was a man beyond himself, unable to grapple with the terrifying realities urrounding him. "If it stood upon the loss of his state," commented Stafford, 'if he had a foolish toy in his head, or a monk's weed to make or an *Ave Marie* o say, he would let his State go to wrack." He had become the very inverse of a uler, for, as Stafford noted perceptively, "He is without value to seek to do him- elf good, and without courage to seek to do others harm."[27]

Catherine was beside herself. Alençon's death was easy to bear compared to Henri's daily deterioration. He was too weak to act and too stubborn to let her act n his place. "Poor Queen Mother," wrote Stafford in a burst of compassion, 'to maintain a show that she hath some credit is fain to have all things come rom her and bear the burden of all, to please her white son that careth no more or her . . . than I care for her I never saw." That, of course, was the point which pierced her most deeply. Her son had wandered away from her into some dark land where she could not reach him. One day, desperately, she begged him o come to see her, but although he was less than a kilometre away, he wrote beg- ging her to excuse him "and neither came to her nor suffered her to come to him; so that she went back again weeping and marvellously discontent."[28]

Into this desperate atmosphere Navarre's refusal to abjure his heresy came like he drums of death. The king, lost in his fantasies, began to talk of divorcing the queen so that he might have heirs, boasting to one of his noblemen that his chil- dren would live to "piss in the graves" of those now plotting against him.[29] This alk of paternity was, however, but one more illusion, for it was clear that it was the king, not the queen, who had failed to provide an heir.

Only a fool would put faith in the promises of such a king—and Navarre was no fool. Henri had promised him that once he had abjured, the Catholics would

accept him. Perhaps. But the odds were against it. It was not the custom to make
kings of repentant heretics. Despite Navarre's reputation for lightning-quick
strokes in battle, in politics he was a cautious man. There was no proof that a return to Catholicism would gain him a Catholic following, but there was incon-
testable proof it would lose him the Huguenots. It was not a step he could risk
for, as a friend said later, "He did not wish in changing his religion to lose
friends of whom he was sure, in order to acquire others about whom he was
doubtful." In addition, such a rapid change would argue "hypocrisy, inconstancy, infidelity"—all of which would make him unworthy to be a king. "As this
matter is from God," he concluded, "it is from Him that I await clear and certain
inspiration."[30]

Although to many at court Navarre's decision was a tragedy, to one family it
was a feast following years of famine.

Navarre's steadfast refusal to abjure placed the Duc de Guise in a pivotal position. With the succession to the throne so dubious and the Catholicism of France
so threatened, it was the perfect moment to reanimate that Catholic League he
had headed some eight years before. At that time, in an unexpected coup, the
king had deflected the power of the league by assuming its leadership. Guise had
been forced to acquiesce, to step aside and play the patient courtier. Although he
had made no overt moves in the meantime, he had not lost sight of the goal, doing what he could to keep the league alive. "From the ashes of the Duc d'Alençon," wrote the Italian historian Davila in his poetic vein, "the half-extinguished
sparks of the league began to revive and burn afresh."[31] There was solemn truth
behind the metaphor, for it was the question of succession that provided fresh im-
pulsion for the league.

The rekindled league was far more influential than those which had sprung up
in the provinces prior to the Estates of 1576. Although the general goal was the
same (to preserve the Catholic faith in France), the specific objective (to keep the
crown from the Huguenot King of Navarre) had an immediacy that appealed to
people of many different classes. Popular support was increased by stirring up
fear of what France might become under a heretic ruler. They had but to look
across the Channel to see what happened in a country where a Protestant ruled:
Catholics imprisoned, Catholics tortured to betray their associates—racked,
burned, disembowelled. Catholics forced into a bitter life of lonely exile. And all
for no greater crime than their loyalty to the Church of Rome.

Such propaganda was a powerful weapon, and soon merchants, farmers, students, professional men flocked to join the league, which alone could save them
from such horrors. In addition, the league of 1584 was far better organised than
its predecessors. Based in conservative Paris, under Guise's resolute leadership,
it fanned out into the provinces, its goal and structure clearly controlled.

By mid-July of 1584 Busbecq noted that the Guises' influence was "very great" and that they dreamt of "seizing power."[32] Those who thought the duke might try to gain the throne for himself underestimated his cunning, however. Aware of the weakness of his claim, he endorsed, instead, the sixty-three-year-old Charles, Cardinal de Bourbon.

The choice was perfect for Guise's purposes. Not only was Bourbon's claim far more valid than his own, but equally important, Bourbon was a man the Guises could easily dominate. Like his brother Antoine before him, he was overwhelmed by Guise flattery and the golden promises dangled before him. A contemporary described him sadly as "that good man, doting with age, permitting himself to be flattered with these vain hopes, [making] himself the bauble of the Duke's ambition." The Huguenots were less flattering, calling him the Red Ass and mocking the speed with which he abandoned his cardinal's robes for a royal dress.[33]

Throughout the summer the power of the league grew. Every major city had its association conducted with military precision. Guise, meanwhile, was gathering friends around him, travelling into Burgundy and Champagne, promising arms and horses to those who would follow him in his exalted cause and speaking "big and very contemptuously of the king." Yet even when Henri received word of this activity, he did not stir. "He does nothing to bring them down," wrote Stafford in amazement, making no effort to stop the "open assemblies. . .in which everyone knows that the subject is how to get the Cardinal of Bourbon in first place."

By November Henri was at last frightened into action by rumours the league had entered into a pact with Spain. On November 11 he issued letters patent accusing of treason all those "making leagues, associations, intrigues and practices against the estate of the realm."[34] His words lacked the resonance of authority. Scarcely heard, they drifted away, with no effect other than to show Guise that in some ways he was already the king's master. Bolstered by their popular success, the heads of the league met in secret council at Joinville, the ancestral home of the House of Guise, during the days between Christmas and the New Year.

There is a sinister cast to the events that took place in the château of Joinville, for here Guise entered definitively into a pact with a foreign power. For years Spain had attempted to seduce French noblemen. In 1562 Philip of Spain had worked to cajole Antoine de Bourbon to his side; ten years later he made unsuccessful overtures to his son. Throughout the years he had drawn imperceptibly closer to the House of Guise. Neither side, however, would admit the personal ambition that drew them towards this marriage; both continued to avow that their accord stemmed from a mutual desire to preserve France Catholic in order to maintain the unity of Christendom.

At Joinville Henri de Guise and his younger brother Charles de Mayenne were the chief delegates representing the league. François de Mainville represented the

Cardinal de Bourbon. Juan de Moreo and Juan Batista de Tassis, one of Spain's most trusted diplomats, represented Philip. By the Treaty of Joinville, "an offensive and defensive union for the conservation of the Catholic religion and the extirpation of all sects and heresies in France and the Low Countries" was formed, and the Cardinal de Bourbon became the acknowledged heir of France. There was more than that to it, however; it was also a secret treaty with Spain in which Guise promised to help Philip regain certain lands lost to France at Cateau-Cambrésis in return for a yearly subsidy to assist Guise in his war against the heretics. The treaty was to remain secret until March, when Philip would begin his payments and the league would make an open declaration of its purpose.[35]

The secrecy vowed at Joinville was poorly kept. Early in March the king was warned that a "great and powerful army" was being levied, composed not only of Frenchmen but also of "foreigners." On March 10 it was learned the Cardinal de Guise had sent a boat up the Marne filled with armour and weapons. A week later the duke was said to have taken Châlons and then Langres, Chartres, Dijon, and various towns in Dauphiné. Sometime during that month, anxious that their plans were being prematurely uncovered, the Cardinal de Guise arrived at court to assure the king that what he heard were simply "jealous rumours." There was, he assured Henri, no substance to the gossip that troops from Spain and Savoy had crossed the borders into France. The cardinal's explanation was unconvincing, and the king turned away from him coldly.[36]

The threat to the throne was obvious, yet the more the power of the league increased, the more paralysed the king became. Danger had unhinged him. He stayed nowhere for more than a few days, constantly changing his dwelling, his plans, his resolutions. "He is so strange a man of disposition and so unknown in his proceedings that no man can settle any judgement upon his actions," Stafford noted. Elizabeth of England, reading her ambassador's reports and bewildered by such apathy, wrote in contempt, "Jesus, was there ever a prince so smitten by the snares of traitors without the courage or counsel to reply to it!"[37] Stafford's persistent efforts to have audience were unsuccessful, and during the Lenten carnival he noted in disgust, "Impossible it is this day to have the King for he is even at this hour running up and down the streets like a madman."[38]

Only the most trivial detail seemed able to engage him. While Guise had been at Joinville resolving the fate of France with the Spanish delegates, the king had closeted himself to draw up a new plan for the reform of the dress and etiquette of the court. Peers of his Council were to be in violet velvet from October to May; satin was to be substituted during the summer months. Members of his household were to be distinguished by a specially designed silver fleur-de-lys. Even the ritual for offering the king a glass of water was described in detail. The contrast with Guise was ludicrous. The pulpits of Paris—all manned by sympathetic Guisards—inveighed against this *roi fainéant,* this do-nothing king, while the secret presses poured out an endless stream of lampoons—described by Busini as "scurrilous pasquinades." Henri was now totally without authority, and the people's answer to his denunciation of the league was to flock to it in increasing numbers.

By the time he was aroused to the magnitude of his betrayal it was too late. Guise was seizing French cities with Spanish arms and Spanish money while the Holy See was bestowing special indulgences on those who worked for the league's interests. By some sleight of hand, Henri found he had become the enemy of his country and the betrayer of his faith. "A prince such as I . . . should not be blamed and accused of lack of piety and zeal for religion," he responded helplessly to the Nuncio.[39] But despite his protests of fidelity to the faith, the Catholics continued to treat him as an enemy.

The only offer of help came from his cousin Navarre, whose refusal to become a Catholic had been the proximate cause of league power. Now he offered men and arms for the king's service—24,000 foot and 3,000 horse by the end of May—if Henri would accept them. Desperate as he was, the king hesitated. While he did not want to alienate the Huguenots, realising they were his only bulwark against the league, yet he could not afford an open liaison with them. Such action would merely bolster the league. It would be sufficient evidence for saying the King of France was delivering the country into the hands of heretics. He thanked Navarre for his offer but begged him to remain quiet, taking no overt action against the league.

The king's plight seemed hopeless, and Stafford commented sombrely, "If he were my king, I would pray God to help him."[40]

Henri's declining power and the heightened arrogance of the league had brought the queen mother to a paroxysm of grief and anxiety. All her efforts to warn her son had been wasted. "We are here marvellously troubled," wrote the English ambassador, "the Queen Mother weepeth and taketh on and cryeth out upon the King who having listened to none of the warnings now cannot put three men together. . . . The poor old woman is in her bed, sick for very melancholy."[41]

But the son who for so long had dismissed his mother's solid advice now turned to her with naïve confidence that somehow she could deliver him. Without an army he could count on, without money or popular support, he leant on the only one who had not deserted him. Like a frightened child, he begged his mother to go to the Guises and make whatever compromise she could. The "Old Lady," so long out of favour, was now pushed onto center stage and given a role no one else would undertake.

Chapter XVIII

On March 19, 1585, just a month before her sixty-sixth birthday, Catherine, still not recovered from her last bout of colic and catarrh, crawled into her litter to be taken to Épernay, where she hoped to meet with the Guises. It was gossiped that she was suffering severely from gout, but she denied it fiercely, admitting only to a "little pain" in her knee.

Although not a difficult journey, it taxed her resources. The days when she could laugh about riding her little mule through the narrow roads of the Pyrenees were over.

On March 28 she took up residence in the celebrated abbey at Épernay and waited there with her ministers. Her entourage was considerable, including her seasoned diplomats Lanssac and Pinart and a newcomer to the diplomatic scene, Pierre d'Espinac, Bishop of Paris, a glib, ambitious man who was to act as liaison between the league and the court. While she waited, the league issued the overt declaration planned at Joinville.

Although Guise continued to call it "the declaration made by the Cardinal de Bourbon," it was common rumour not only that the Cardinal had nothing to do with writing it but that he had not even seen it until it was publicly circulated. The Declaration of Péronne (as it was called) was a closely reasoned argument, written, as a contemporary noted, in a "strong and noble style." In it the cardinal explained the purpose of the league (to guard the faith menaced by a heretical prince) and declared himself heir apparent to the throne. The declaration pointed out that the faith of France was endangered by bad government, accusing those who had "slipped into the king's friendship and weakened his authority." The nobility was enslaved, it continued, the clergy bowed beneath the weight of tithes, and the people straitened by taxes of every kind. "The Church must be made integral, the nobility restored to their dignity, and the people helped." This was to be the task of the league.[1]

Although the Declaration of Péronne did not hesitate to level oblique insults at the king, it ironically flattered and besought the queen mother. "We very humbly beg the queen, mother of the king, our honoured lady, without whose wisdom and providence we would have been scattered and lost, for the faithful testimony she can give of our faithful service." What they hoped to gain by such praise is difficult to guess. Not even Guise ("a man puffed up with vain hopes") could have expected Catherine to sanction their activity.[2]

In the next few weeks it became evident how empty their flattery was, for instead of cooperating with the queen mother's request for a conference, they remained annoyingly absent. Tired of waiting, Catherine spent a few days at Château-Thierry, returning to Épernay on Easter Day. Her health had taken a turn for the worse, and Lanssac wrote the king that she had suffered heavy chills and fever during the night. Yet indefatigable as ever, she wrote to Guise, "I am asking you to come here tomorrow so that we can begin to negotiate, hoping that God will give us the grace to reach some good conclusion for the service of the king my son." To her surprise, Guise arrived the following day. Despite his victories, she had never seen him less assured. "I found him very melancholy," she wrote to the king, "and when he had entered, he began to weep." He was, throughout the interview, more secret than ever, evading her questions, silent before her accusations. "I could get nothing out of him," she wrote in exasperation.[3]

For the next four weeks she pressed in vain for a series of conferences. Her letters have little to report beyond the daily exasperations of useless waiting. One evening the Duc de Lorraine arrived, vowing his fervent desire to serve the king, but then riding off before she could get him to commit himself to anything. Later the Cardinal de Bourbon (the *Petit Homme,* as Guise condescendingly called him) came to Épernay. "He wept and sighed, showing regret in being involved in these things but impelled by our religion." The Cardinal de Guise, too, whom she met on her way to mass, was bowed and sad, weighed down with sorrow over the course of events. Yet whatever melancholy they displayed to Catherine, the Duc de Guise was writing confidently to his friends, "Evidently God favours our plans. . . . All is going well."[4]

They were like characters in a play, acting out roles they thought Catherine would find acceptable. They were playing with her; she knew it, yet she could not put an end to it. It was like a fever dream, in which remembered faces drift in and out, smiling, disappearing, making reassuring promises that are never remembered. Meanwhile, her side and shoulder were badly inflamed, causing her agonising pain. Her physician Miron ordered her bled, a precaution against congestion of the lungs. "Yet," wrote Miron to the king in admiration, "this does not stop her from busying herself in the affairs of Your Majesty as always."[5]

By the time the conferences were seriously under way towards the end of May Catherine's natural optimism was eroded by her poor health, the enforced delays, and the falsity of the Guises. In the past, there had always been something exhilarating about the bargaining table. She understood the nuances of trade, the subtle flow of give-and-take, ensuring that both parties would ultimately be satisfied. She knew that a good bargain demanded good merchandise. Always in the past she had had something valuable to trade with. Now it was excruciatingly clear to her that she had nothing. The overt goals of the league had won popular support, and its military success insured its superiority. Backed by Spanish troops and at least a halfhearted approval from the Holy See, it was already victorious.

Guise made his demands clear from the outset: The Roman religion alone would be practised in France; the Cardinal de Bourbon would be recognised as their apparent to the throne; Guise would be given command of royal troops. The next four weeks were a comedy of the bitterest sort. The Duc de Guise first dallied, then intimidated her with a show of strength. "Troops are marching and arriving from everywhere around here," she wrote apprehensively to the king. The Cardinal de Bourbon declared boastfully, "Our fight is for the honour of God. . . . I tell you that you will see, God willing, the most magnificent army that has been seen in five hundred years in this kingdom."[6]

Sometimes too sick to be on her feet, Catherine had to negotiate from her bed. "I am so sick to my stomach that I cannot write to you," she apologised to the king. A few days earlier she had begged him to excuse her for not writing in her own hand, explaining that her jaw was so swollen with toothache that bending her head increased the pain intolerably. "The cardinal and the duke have arrived," she concluded, "I have tried to tell them the great mistake they are making."[7] The scene is painfully ludicrous: the old queen, grotesquely awkward in her movements, peering from her bed, her face enflamed with toothache, warning the "Master of the World" that he was in error.

Throughout June he continued to play with her, although the outcome was clear. "It is not so much that it hurts me to be ridiculed," she wrote with a strange humility to her son, "as that it is so lacking in respect to you."[8] By the first week of July the bargaining was over and the queen mother journeyed south to Nemours, where the treaty between the crown and the Guises was to be signed. Her sense of failure weighed on her like death. Often in the past she had been forced to compromise more than she had wished, but never before had she been so stripped of everything.

Yet it was not, as she had said to her son, her own humiliation that chiefly concerned her; it was the fate of France. What the league proposed was terrifying. It had become clear as she bargained with Guise that despite his triumphs, Guise was no longer his own master. The Spanish subsidies keeping his troops

together had already subjected him to Philip's authority. "The Spanish pensioner," he was later called. Catherine could see no end. Her son had trusted her to
avert the calamity, and she had failed.

On July 9 she signed the Edict of Nemours, knowing her signature strengthened not only Guise but France's implacable enemy, Philip of Spain. So often
prodigal of words, despair now made her silent. "I have this morning sent the
articles of peace to you," she wrote briefly to her son.[9]

By placing military authority in the hands of Guise, the Treaty of Nemours
effectively disarmed the king. "The king is on foot and the league on horseback," commented L'Estoile caustically.[10] It also nullified whatever small religious freedom existed. Heretics were barred from public office; ministers were
given one month to leave the country; all subjects must make profession of the
Catholic faith within six months or suffer exile. The treaty was tantamount to a
declaration of war. The king's brave words of defiance of the league—"I would
rather be split in two than engage in such cowardice"—were now a mockery.

Defiance had given way to resignation. When, the following week, the king
met the Guises at St. Maur, it was with a great show of cordiality. He offered
them his hand to kiss and then embraced them "with a smiling and joyful countenance." But Cavriana, who observed the scene sharply, was not taken in:
"There will never be any friendship between them, for there is a mutual mistrust
which grows day by day." He later commented: "Poultice is added to poultice;
it alleviates the pain, but it will not cure it."[11]

No one in France was more stunned by the agreement at Nemours than Navarre. Throughout the spring the king had given him every reason to believe he
was drawing closer to him as his only hope against the league. Navarre had
advised him, encouraged him, offered his troops and finest military leaders. That
the king, knowing so well the designs of the league, should have capitulated was
unthinkable. Later Navarre told one of his captains that when he heard the news,
he buried his head in his hands. "And," he continued, "I felt such fear for the
evils falling upon my country that half of my beard turned white."

Anger replaced despair, and three days later he wrote the king:

> I understand that a peace has been concluded without me and, indeed, against
> me. You have joined your enemies to ruin your servants, your most faithful sub-
> jects and those who have the honour of being your nearest relatives. Even more,
> you have divided your forces, your authority, your resources to make them the
> strongest who are armed against you. I find this very difficult and almost
> unendurable.[12]

It was the first in a series of letters designed to force the king to realise how
deeply this new treaty imperilled the throne and thus to cut him free from his
bond with the league. Navarre continued to remonstrate with Henri, reminding
him that the king himself had admitted these were his enemies, that their religion

was only a pretence, that they would ruin the country. At the same time he wrote Catherine, recalling that he had the king's own word promising that nothing prejudicial to his interests would be done without notifying him. "Yet now," he continued, "I understand that suddenly there is a treaty of peace against both his subjects and me. . . . He is arming those rebels against himself," he warned, while reiterating his "devotion for both Your Majesty and the state." A month later his letters were still unanswered, and in urgency he wrote, "Please let me know what you intend."[13]

While Navarre waited, the league, heady with success, pushed its advantage. For some time, it had been influencing the Holy See to take a stronger stand against the French heretics. In July the Duc de Nevers and Cardinal de Vaudémont had been sent to Rome expressly for that purpose. They found the new Pontiff, Sixtus V, less accommodating than they had hoped. He praised their zeal but cautioned them against disloyalty to their king. He would neither issue a bull in approbation of the league nor excommunicate Henri de Navarre. During the course of the summer, however, the pressure brought to bear by the Spanish ambassador Enrique, Count of Olivares, as well as the course of events in France, led Sixtus V to a change of heart. On September 9 the bull *Ab immensa*, announcing the excommunication of those two "sons of wrath," Henri de Navarre and Henri de Condé, was officially promulgated.[14]

Navarre was outraged and in his first fury instructed his agents in Rome to set up placards on the street corners, addressed to "Monsieur Sixtus, the self-styled pope"—a retaliation for the Pope's reference to him as the "so-called king." Then began the serious task of countering the excommunication and questioning the Pope's right to meddle in such matters. He wrote to the Parlement, to the bishops, to the nobles, to the third estate. Navarre was a master rhetorician, not with the high rhetoric of the schools, but with a rhetoric shaped by wit, a strong political intelligence, and an extraordinary gift for dealing with men. The conclusion of his document addressed to the third estate was bound to move the common man: "It is not myself I pity, but you," he wrote. "I pity myself only because I do not have the power to defend myself without causing innocent people to suffer. . . . I sympathise with all your evils. I have tried every means of saving you from civil war and I will not spare even my life."[15]

To the king and queen mother he was implacable, warning them with desperate urgency where their course would lead them. "I can foresee the day, Madame," he concluded his letter to Catherine, "when both you and the king will see perhaps too late whose hands you have armed." Catherine immediately sensed the far-reaching effects of Navarre's excommunication and wrote to Villeroy:

> In all this, I see harm only for the king, for if I saw that he had the means to be strong as I wish he were, I would not give a button for all these practices and deal-

ings; for there would be neither pope nor king, and even less his subjects who would not consider themselves very happy, the former to please him and the latter to obey him. . . . I would be sweet to all of them, popes and kings, to gain the means to possess such forces as would enable me to command and not to obey them.[16]

The league's exultation over the bull was necessarily short-lived. It was soon clear that instead of reducing Navarre's power, it had enormously increased his popularity. France as a whole disliked Roman interference in French affairs. That had been palpably clear during the Council of Trent. Even the threats to excommunicate Jeanne d'Albret, two decades earlier, had won many people to her side, and Henri de Navarre was a far more popular figure than his mother had been. Even the king responded indignantly at this overextension of papal power. When Sixtus wrote, asking Henri to promulgate the bull, a courtier overheard the king rasp, "It seems that the Pope would like me to act as his provost marshal in France."[17]

The strong Gallican spirit that had always made France mulish in the face of papal interference was now displayed in favour of Navarre. Montmorency-Damville, who for years had vacillated between the cause of the Politiques and his loyalty to the crown, now definitely declared for the Huguenots. Other important captains, too, despite their Catholicity, were edging away from the league and towards Navarre. At the end of the year Guise wrote in contempt (but also no doubt in fear) of those "cold Catholics" who were veering towards the "heretics." In fact, these were men who had small patience with heresy but who were determined to oppose the foreign influence the league was now overtly bringing into France. Although Guise had told Parma he wished his Spanish troops to display the arms of Lorraine rather than the red cross of Spain, no one doubted where these troops had come from or who, ultimately, commanded them.

Following the Treaty of Nemours, Navarre had issued a declaration opposing the league and stating his position. What was done at Nemours must be condemned, he declared, for it was "a peace made with strangers at the expense of the Princes of the Blood; with the House of Lorraine at the expense of the House of France; with rebels at the expense of obedient subjects; with agitators at the expense of those who have bought peace by every means in their power. . . . I intend to oppose it with all my heart," he continued, "and to this end rally around me, according to my position in the kingdom, all true Frenchmen without regard to religion, since at this time it is a question of the defence of the state against the usurpation of foreigners."[18] The declaration touched the spirit of French nationalism and strengthened that image of Navarre as the true flower of France, willing to oppose, even with his life, the infiltration of "foreigners" into the homeland.

What Navarre carefully evaded, however, was the fact that he himself was simultaneously writing to "foreign powers," in an effort to engage support. The kings of Sweden and Denmark and the German princes had been contacted, but it was chiefly the Queen of England on whom Navarre relied. Playing on her fear of Spain, he warned her Philip's involvement in French affairs was but the first step to "regaining his full authority," reminding her that Spain was determined, even at the expense of her neighbours, to reach "the summit of her grandeur." For her own interests, if not for the cause of religion, it would be to her advantage to counter Spanish power.

Elizabeth was receiving the same advice from many of her diplomats, who warned that her own house might very well be "set on fire" if the conflagration in France were not speedily extinguished.[19] As usual, she hesitated, unwilling to incur the enmity with the French crown that overt help to Navarre would inevitably entail. Instead, she engaged in her usual circuitous assistance, sending money to a European agent, who in turn delivered it to Duke John Casimir in payment for troops to be sent to Navarre.

The more news Catherine received during the summer of 1586, the more she was terrified by the extension of the conflict. It took little imagination to envision France destroyed by foreign powers. The conflict was heightened by further betrayal in the royal family: Margot, despite all her avowals of loyalty to her brother, her mother, her husband, had fled from Navarre to join the league.

Margot's conduct, always erratic, had now become unfathomable. Was she motivated by simple hatred of her husband? By a desire to even the score with her brother? Had she been seduced by one of Guise's hollow promises? Her own explanation—that she feared Navarre's mistress, Madame de Guiche, and had fled for her life—is totally out of character. Margot's actions remain inexplicable.[20] In March, 1585, she had gone, with her husband's permission, to spend Easter at Agen, a southern town included in her appanage. Here she had stayed, playing the role of a charming guest, insinuating to the chief men of the city that she was in "great danger" from her Huguenot husband. They responded with sympathy, assuring her of protection and fortifying the city as she had recommended.

Soon after the league had openly declared itself, however, the "hapless lady" showed herself a tyrannous mistress. She turned Agen into a fortress, increased the heavy burden of taxation, billeted her soldiers in private households, and refused permission for the citizens to leave when the city was endangered by plague. By October Agen had had more than enough of Margot. Warned that the irate townspeople would not hesitate to seize her, the imperious Margot fled in haste, riding postillion, like a farm girl.

At Carlat, an impregnable fortress in Auvergne, she found a precarious refuge. Whatever promises Guise had made to her, they had not included the destitution she experienced at Carlat. The château had been ravaged by the wars. Many of its buildings had been used as barracks and stables; the windows were shattered, the doors swinging on broken hinges, the furniture hacked to pieces or stolen. Here Margot spent the winter, ill from the perishing cold and gusty winds that buffeted the unprotected basalt hill where the château stood. Although some of her valuables were later sent to her from Agen, they did not protect her from the cold or from a penetrating sense of desolation.

In mid-September Guise had written Philip, boasting that the "Queen of Navarre has allied herself to us." He assured Philip that Margot would be of great use in impeding Navarre's plans and asked for a subsidy for her since she was badly in need of money. No money came, however, for it was part of Philip's policy to keep Guise on a short tether, providing him with only enough funds to ensure his continued dependence. Although at some point there was talk of a marriage between the Spanish king and Margot, once she was safely allied to the league, such talk was never continued.[21]

Margot's defection was an extraordinarily bitter blow for Catherine, who wrote when she learned of it: "There is not a single day that does not bring some new trouble. . . . I have never suffered so much. . . . I realise that God has given me this creature for the punishment of my sins."[22] Later, however, she wrote Margot at Carlat, offering her own more comfortable château at Ibois. Margot, typically, refused, unwilling to admit the humiliation she was suffering. "I thank Your Majesty very humbly for the château you have offered," she wrote her mother. "I have no need of it, thank God, being in a very pleasant place, in the company of many people of honour, and living in both respect and safety." As for waging war, she denied it, assuring her mother that whatever she did, she did it only to save herself from "falling into the power of those who have wished to deprive me of my possessions, my life, and my honour."[23]

Margot's subterfuges had always been transparent. It was obvious to anyone who knew Carlat that life there could hardly be the gracious existence she pictured. Catherine's kindness was also transparent. She had acted less out of compassion for her daughter than from a determination to withdraw her from league influence. Having failed, she let her son have his way. The king soon had soldiers on his sister's trail, and the following year she was taken into custody.

Some said the king would have ordered Margot's death were it not for the restraining hand of his mother. At the beginning, her fate seemed little better than death, for she was imprisoned in the fortress of Usson, where Louis XI had kept his most important prisoners, boasting that they were safer there than at any other prison in France. "Only the sun can force an entrance here," a contemporary had noted. In time, Margot's natural buoyance replaced her despair, and for eighteen years she continued to live her strange, secluded life at Usson. Here she established a bizarre little court, preening herself as a patron of the arts—in reality growing fat and eccentric, painting herself grotesquely, growing out of touch not only with politics, but even with fashion. Half-forgotten, the "dangerous queen" imperilled no one.

In 1586, however, it could not have been foreseen that Margot's betrayal would ultimately be so useless. She seemed then like another dangerous force strengthening the power of the league, a power the king could find no way of deflecting. In February the king sent for Guise. What he hoped for from the confrontation it is hard to say. From the beginning it was an unequal contest. Guise was in the full flow of his power: tall, lean, resolute, the scar of Dormans giving him a military distinction. By contrast, the king looked twice his age. His hair had turned entirely white. Pallid and stooped, his face and neck scarred with boils, he was no match for his adversary. For three months Guise stayed on at Paris, despite rumours that the king was secretly plotting his death, that, in fact, he had already hired an Italian to assassinate him. To outward appearance, he seemed to be enjoying Henri's favour, though Cavriana, always suspicious, warned, "They can never be friends." When, finally, Guise left for Châlons in mid-May, he had succeeded in insinuating himself still further into popular favour, thus, L'Estoile noted, "undermining the foundation of the king's support."[24]

While Guise was engaged in "secretly undermining" the power of the king, the king was doing all he could to cut himself loose from his treaty with the league. Far more inclined to trust Navarre than Guise, he now engaged in new negotiations with his Huguenot cousin. Always secretive, the king had now become furtive. Although the Spanish ambassador was aware that a secret plot was in the offing, he could not find out what Henri planned. Some of those he questioned allayed his fears, telling him that the king had nothing in mind, that all his stealthy activity was simply the symptom of an unhinged mind. "Although he sits up nearly every night writing memoranda in his own hand, until two in the morning, he burns them all the next day. They say that all he writes is about the religious orders." Many assured him, concluded the ambassador, that "the king's reason is unhinged and it is feared he will shortly lose it altogether."[25]

Despite his bizarre conduct, the king was still lucid enough to know where his advantage lay. Aware of the liaison between Guise and Spain, he hastened his plans to bring about a truce with Navarre, making it clear that if Navarre became a Catholic, there would be no further objection to his inheriting the throne.

Nothing would so effectively contain Guise's schemes as Navarre's conversion. It would be the dissolution of the league and the ruin of his own ambitions. Navarre had shot a perfect bull's-eye when he had indicated that the leaguers were not, as they claimed, a Christian people who wanted the conversion of heretics but ambitious men who wanted their destruction. Philip, who had as much to lose as Guise, was willing to take every measure to block Navarre's claim to the throne. Informed of the king's hopes for his cousin's conversion, he wrote at once to Olivares in Rome:

I am told from France that steps are being taken with His Holiness to obtain his

permission for the Béarnais [Navarre] to recant. . . . This would simply be setting
fire to France. . . . Let His Holiness be undeceived with regard to the supposed
sincerity of the Béarnais. We might believe in it if he only asked to retire into a
monastery to do penance, but as it is the means for him to succeed to the throne, it
is clear it is only a pretence. The Church and the Inquisition declare relapse into
heresy to be deserving of capital punishment.[26]

Despite Guise's reaction, plans moved forward for a meeting between Catherine and Navarre. It was their only hope. France that summer was riddled with
misfortune. The crops had been blighted, and the threat of famine was added to
the threat of war. Stafford wrote in June to Walsingham: "no word of peace, nor
no regard to the great misery that is already and likely more and more to fall upon
this country. Yesterday I had it assured of one that came out of 'Avernia' that
there is many thousands there already dead for hunger, and in that extrem-
ity . . . they feed upon grass . . . like horses and die with the grass in their
mouths." Not only Auvergne had felt the bite of famine. Close to Paris, desperate gangs of people were cutting the half-ripe grain in the fields and stuffing it raw
into their mouths.[27]

Although most people had completely lost faith in the king, from time to time
his nobles wrote remonstrating with him. "The state in which I see France today
is both dangerous and tragic," wrote one in the summer of 1586. "It seems to
every man with good sense and judgement that the ruin of this beautiful kingdom
is already at the door. Yet, you, Sire . . . instead of trying to avoid this obvious danger, seem to run towards your own ruin and destruction." Such letters,
although they increased his terrors, did not give Henri the enabling power to act.
Again, he took refuge in religion, so that L'Estoile commented contemptuously,
"One can hardly get the king out of a monk's cell."[28]

That summer Navarre sent the Comte de Rosny (later to become famous as the
Duc de Sully) to court to see if some compromise could be reached. Sully, although not the most accurate of diarists, paints a picture of the king which, if not
entirely true in detail, catches the decadent spirit of the court. After noting that he
spent the night with Villeroy, he continued:

> On the day following, he presented me to the king, and I shall never forget the
> absurd attitude and paraphernalia in which I found this prince in his cabinet. He had
> a sword by his side, a hood upon his shoulders, a little bonnet upon his head, a bas-
> ket full of small dogs hung around his neck by a large riband; and he held himself
> so still that in speaking to us he neither moved head nor feet nor hands. [29]

Little wonder that there were increasing rumours of uprising and that the Paris
streets were full of "seditious verses." From across the Channel Elizabeth
watched in amazement while her fellow sovereign, twenty years her junior,

slipped into a lethargy like death. "Pardon me," she wrote him that June, "but it is my affection which dares me to speak so freely. Before God, I have no other motive but my love for you. I am amazed to see you betrayed by your own council, by those closest to you in the world and for you not to have wind of it. . . . For the love of God, do not sleep too long a sleep."[30]

The warning came too late. Henri did little that summer except encourage his mother to find Navarre and come to some agreement with him.

In July Catherine began active preparations for her journey. She attempted to forestall the league's criticism by writing to the Holy See, assuring the Pope she was acting only out of love for the Catholic religion, "begging His Holiness to believe . . . that all this . . . is because of my zeal to spread the glory of God." Guise, angered and anxious at the rumour that a secret truce had already been negotiated between Navarre and the king, wrote a thinly veiled warning to Catherine, who was resting at Chenonceaux. He reminded her that it was forbidden by the Church "to treat with excommunicated heretics," that it would be foolish for her to become involved in such an impossible task. "For," he concluded, "it would be very upsetting for us to be forced to disobey." At the same time he wrote to Sixtus V, assuring him they would "remain firm and constant in our resolution to follow the way of the Catholic religion for which we risk our lives."[31]

Despite his poise, there was a note of fear in Guise's communications that fall. Things were not going well with the league. Its military victories were far less impressive than he had hoped; the Pope was becoming sceptical of its true purpose; and most upsetting of all, Philip had become increasingly negligent in sending the subsidies promised by the Treaty of Joinville.

Catherine was less disturbed by Guise's discreet threat than by what she saw as she travelled through Touraine. Flood had been added to famine and plague. The Loire, usually a quiet, spacious river, had overflown its banks. Houses and bridges had been carried off, and from Roanne to Nantes the land lay submerged. When the waters receded, the smell of decay was everywhere. The crops were gone. The fertile fields were black and thick with mud. Everywhere lay carcasses of cattle and, close to them, the bodies of farmers who had tried to save their herds. As she passed through Tours, the queen mother was met by the mayor and the elders, begging her for assistance.

Helplessly, she wrote Bellièvre in her own hand: "It is the most pitiable spectacle in the memory of man. . . . Besides pestilence, famine, and war, there has come a flood which has drowned many people and an enormous number of cattle, so that all this poor people are crying out for mercy." With every fresh calamity, she was increasingly convinced that only peace could bring salvation to France. "May [God] have pity on this poor afflicted realm," she concluded.

"We will give Him the greatest thanks if it may please Him to give us a good and lasting peace, for that is the only way to restore this realm; otherwise, I see no way in which it can be saved."[32]

She was still at Chenonceaux in October, chafing under the delays imposed by Navarre. Although her faith in her mission had been affirmed when Navarre published a declaration in which he asserted he would be willing to agree to the judgement of a "free, national council," yet he still hedged in concluding arrangements for a meeting. Catherine's experience made her the most practised negotiator in France, but now her very experience militated against her.

She was, in a sense, too much the professional to win easy confidence. She had engaged in too many worthless treaties and signed her name to too many ineffective truces. She had hedged too much and promised too glibly. An anonymous Frenchman, writing to a friend living in Rome, commented perceptively: "I recall that when the queen began this trip, you found nothing impossible that she would put her hand to; you considered peace a certainty because she was willing to treat for it. As for me . . . I have always believed that she was very adroitly chosen, yet I have found in this very advantage many disadvantages, and in that which seemed most perfect, many limitations."[33] The point was well made.

In addition, Catherine's failure at Nemours had further blemished her record. Many, infuriated by the power this treaty had given the league, accused her of selling her own son to the Guises. Busini's bland confidence was misplaced when he wrote, "Peace will be made because Catherine de Medici has never turned her attention to anything in this kingdom without bringing it to the end she desires."[34] With the development of the league, she had entered on her days of failure.

In mid-October Catherine left Chenonceaux, journeying along the Loire to Tours, then turning south, past the white elegance of Azay-le-Rideau, and west into the Huguenot country of Aunis. She had agreed to meet Navarre at La Mothe-St.-Héraye, despite her complaints that this was a very bad location "for my health, my age, and all the illnesses I suffer from."[35]

A few days later, she moved to the town of St. Maixent. It was a courageous move, for here she was on the very edge of enemy territory. Undoubtedly her move was meant to demonstrate to Navarre how much she trusted him, putting herself freely in his hands. Navarre, however, remained aloof, using those delaying tactics he had perfected in the months preceding the conferences of Nérac six years earlier. It was a technique that immediately strengthened his position by reducing the queen mother to the role of suppliant. "My son," she pleaded, "do not play with me any longer," arguing that peace could only be achieved if he were willing to see her. In reply, however, she received "only sweet words and excuses."[36]

Throughout November she remained at St. Maixent. She had brought with her
a brilliant suite, including the Duc de Montpensier, snatched from the influence
of the league; the Duc de Nevers, whose conscience kept him oscillating from
side to side; her Italian compatriots Gondi and Birague, as well as her "flying
squadron." Yet despite the efforts at gaiety, her nervous anxiety became daily
more apparent. Her proximity to the Huguenot stronghold in the west could not
but have influenced her. She became increasingly preoccupied with the possible
interception of her letters, writing Villeroy that she had had no news from Paris
for ten days and questioning him about the number of letters from her that had
reached the king. "It is a great suffering to be always fearful," she concluded.[37]

The conferences, which eventually opened on December 13, took her even
farther south and into more dangerous territory. Navarre had finally agreed to
meet her in the small town of St. Brice, equidistant from Jarnac and Cognac. The
house made available was sufficiently surrounded by open country to protect
them against ambush. It was, as Catherine described it, situated in a pretty park
on the banks of the Charente. Here she and Navarre were to have their separate
apartments, gathering in a "beautiful, large room" for their conferences. Those
conferences, in which Catherine had put all her trust, continued for five days and
accomplished nothing. Navarre had never believed in them, convinced they were
but one more spur to prick him to conversion. "I used every subterfuge to avoid
it," he wrote later, "for I could see that no good would come of it for us."[38]

From the beginning the meeting took place in an atmosphere of fear and hostility. The gates were manned with two opposing guards: fifty Catholics and fifty
Huguenots facing each other, fully armed. Even the "beautiful room," which
had so pleased Catherine, could not counter the atmosphere of recrimination.
Legend has it that when they met, Catherine, fearing that Navarre might be
armed, was seen to "cover him with infinite caresses," embracing him, running
her hands over his sides, until, finally, with a laugh he unbuttoned his doublet,
declaring, "You see, Madame, I keep nothing hidden."[39]

It had been six years since the queen mother and her son-in-law had met. For
Navarre, they had been years of hardship and often of disappointment, but they
had matured him. He was small, wiry, hard—a resolute and decisive leader. His
shrewd eyes with their veiled lids gave little away. Betrayal and suspicion had
bred in him an ironic style, a detached amusement for the charlatanism he was so
adept at discerning. At Nérac he had been pleased to find himself his mother-in-
law's match in diplomacy. At St. Brice he discovered he was her superior. Although she had written him often, complaining that she could no longer travel as
she had when she was younger, that his constant shift in plans was more than she
could cope with, he was not quite ready for the change in Catherine. The queen
who embraced him at St. Brice was an old woman. She moved heavily from her
chair, balancing herself awkwardly on her swollen legs. Her colour, never good,

was now unhealthily sallow. It was obvious that with this trip she had pushed herself to the very frontiers of endurance.

Throughout the day, as the winter light sifted through the tall arched windows the thrust and parry continued unabated, with neither side able to gain a signifi cant advantage. That same night, in a long letter to Henri, Catherine described in detail the substance of the day's conference. While she had complained of th bad treatment she had received by all the delays Navarre had imposed on her, he complained of having been judged without having been heard. He had said there was no point in their talking since several armies were already banded together to ruin him. She had reiterated that she had done everything he had wanted ''with out regard for my time, my age, and the difficulty of the season,'' that she had truly believed he would open up the ways of peace, warning him that if he re fused to do so, ''he will regret it all his life.''[40]

The pattern of recrimination established in their first interview continued to the end. Navarre had been right—there was nothing to be gained. But Catherine knowing her son was doomed unless some truce could be made with the Hugue nots, pushed for a continuation. Despite Navarre's open avowals that he could not, at this time, turn Catholic, still she hoped some agreement could be reached What she failed to realise was that Navarre, not the king, was profiting from thi delay, for Navarre was impatiently awaiting the arrival of German reiters. The king, meanwhile, wrote desperately to his mother, instructing her to offer Na varre anything—pensions, land, position at court. Experience had taught him ev ery man has his price. ''I am convinced,'' he wrote Catherine, ''that there is a chord that can be touched.''[41] But Navarre was proving himself a man beyond the king's experience. He would not be bought—partially, no doubt, because of loyalty to a cause; partially, too, because it was very clear the king lacked the power to keep his promises.

Catherine and Navarre met for the last time on December 17. Although some sporadic bargaining continued through the first weeks of the New Year, it was clear, even to Catherine, that nothing was to come of this. ''Here we are in the rain and the wind,'' she wrote bleakly to Villeroy after Navarre's departure.[42] Overwhelmed with melancholy, she made preparations for an escort which would enable her to withdraw in safety. For six months she had trained all her energy and all her hope on what she might be able to accomplish with Navarre In fact, she had achieved nothing. He had toyed with her and, ultimately, out manoeuvred her.

Twice in eighteen months she had been worsted in the very game on which she had always prided herself. First the Guises and now Navarre. The Florentine shopkeeper no longer controlled the merchandise. Now others determined the price, and she had no course but to accept it. ''Heaven, earth, and the abyss are all against this poor kingdom,'' she wrote, ''and I do not see what there is to be hoped for here. God must be very angry and we very wicked people that we must suffer such great evils with no hope of escaping them unless He himself turn His hand to our help."[43]

Several years before she had written to her confidante, the Duchesse d'Uzès, that no cost was too dear for her to pay in the service of the king. She had not known then that failure was to be included in the price.

Chapter XIX

Before Catherine began her return to Paris, she learned of an event that would have serious implications for French affairs: Mary Stuart had been executed for treason at Fotheringhay on February 18.

The news was not entirely unexpected, for the verdict had been handed down by the English judges the preceding fall, yet the execution of one queen by another was sufficient to shock Europe. Catherine had not seen her daughter-in-law since, twenty-six years before, she had sailed from France to assume the rule of her "own country." Then, scarcely nineteen, she had embarked for Scotland with the arrogance of youth, buoyed by her beauty and her charm, the tragedy of her husband's untimely death lightened by the thought of future glory.

It was a glory that was constantly to elude her, however. From the beginning, her manner was out of style with her rugged Scottish courtiers. They considered her haughty, vain, imperious; she was half-French—and she was Catholic. In a country dominated by the theology of John Knox, these were heavy liabilities. She was also (although her admirers would never admit it) a little foolish. She was determined to be a queen in the French manner, and her autocratic stance often made her defy those who would tell her the truth and slip unawares into the nets of those who would flatter her. Her mistakes were enormous. Ambivalent and ill-advised, she fell from folly to folly. She was probably neither wicked nor impeccable. Had she not been a queen, it might have been enough, in those days, for her husband to speak roughly to her from time to time, keeping her indoors when her emotions seemed likely to get the better of her.

Queens, unhappily, are not so easily managed. Held responsible for the murder of one husband and forcibly separated from the second, she had fled to England, trusting her cousin Elizabeth to save her from her rebellious subjects. Instead, she suffered nineteen years of arrest, during which time she was ceaselessly involved in plots to regain her liberty—plots that inevitably threatened Elizabeth's position. With the Babington Plot in 1586, Mary was finally convicted of treason, and despite the concerted opposition of Catholic Christendom, she was executed.

The reactions to her death were as ambiguous as her life had been. When news of her condemnation had reached France the preceding fall, Bellièvre had at once been sent to England to plead for clemency. But Henri's avowal that he would "impeach with his whole power" the intended execution of Mary Stuart was not taken seriously.[1] Caught as he was in the power of the league, Henri could ill afford to weaken his relations with England.

Mary Stuart had long been a "cause" for the House of Guise, always a clannish family. The ties of blood were also strengthened by family ambition. There had been talk for years among the Catholics in Spain and even in France that Mary, not Elizabeth, was the lawful Queen of England. This was the thesis around which Don Juan had spun his giddy plans for English "intervention" in 1576. It was a thesis Philip of Spain was still considering with meticulous attention. It would extend the scope of Spain and the league—and this the French crown could not risk. England and France needed each other as a bulwark against increasing Spanish power. Neither could afford to let the divisive figure of Mary Stuart estrange them.

Yet the issue was even more complex. So firmly had the Queen of Scots become identified with the "Catholic cause" that not to uphold her was to put one's orthodoxy in question. Consequently, when Stafford sought an audience to explain to the king the "true events" surrounding Mary's death (Elizabeth's course now was to maintain that she had not intended that the death warrant—which she had signed—be used), he was greeted coldly by the secretaries of state, who, according to the Venetian ambassador, replied that "the deed was an impious and inhuman one; and that the king and all France will be obliged to show their displeasure."[2]

Catherine echoed her son's position. Her letters are full of sympathetic references to the "poor queen," her "beloved daughter-in-law," to the "pain and sorrow" she felt over these tragic events.[3] Neither she nor her son could have acted otherwise. Not to have interceded vigorously for Mary Stuart would have been used as incontrovertible proof they were secretly on the side of the Protestants—proof the league would use to great advantage. In fact, some months before, the Spanish ambassador Olivares had attempted to persuade the Pope that if Mary Stuart went to her death, "it would be by the very knowledge and consent of the King of France," since the Queen of England would never "venture to offend him in so important a matter."[4] Scylla or Charybdis. England or the league. There seemed no way the king could avoid them both.

The Guises, with intrepid skill in turning everything to their own advantage, now exploited their cousin's death. This, they pointed out to the French people, was precisely what they had been warning them of. This was how Protestant monarchs dealt with the innocent—respecting not even royalty itself. What could the ordinary citizen hope for should a Protestant accede to the throne of France? Soon the beautiful, but often foolish, Queen of Scots was enshrined with the nimbus of sanctity. The Church had another martyr. The pulpits of Paris lauded her, wept over her, and fulminated against those who had brought her down. In death Mary Stuart had her French court around her again. Acclaimed at her arrival in France as "the most perfect child" and later, at her marriage to François II, as "the most beautiful woman in the world," in death she had caught the light again, winning homage as "the martyred queen."

Nowhere did the news of her death receive a more penetrating response than at the Escorial. The preceding July Mary, unwilling that the throne should pass to her Protestant son, informed Philip, through Mendoza, that if he would agree to "sustain" her, she would "cede and grant by will my right to the succession of this crown to the king, your master."[5] It was an extravagant promise, more extravagant still when one realises that the crown she alluded to was not merely that of Scotland but also of England. Consequently, with Mary's death, Philip considered himself the rightful inheritor of the English throne. With a sudden burst of activity, he began to put in motion the complex machinery he referred to as the Enterprise of England, and what history has called more symbolically the Armada.

Catherine, meanwhile, unaware of Philip's plans and of the part France was to be forced to play in them, travelled west towards Paris. She was faced with desolation everywhere. "If only the king would become resolute," she wrote wearily to Bellièvre. "If only they saw him strong enough to take the defensive and the offensive, I think we would hear a very different language spoken here," she continued, alluding to the haughty rhetoric of the league.[6] There seemed little chance of the king's becoming resolute, for with each fresh reversal he slipped deeper into his world of fantasy. At the same time that Catherine was hoping for a change, Mendoza was writing contemptuously, "The King has done nothing but dance and masquerade during this carnival without cessation. The last night he danced until broad daylight, and after he had heard Mass went to bed until night. He then went to his Capuchin Monastery where he is, refusing to speak or to see anyone."[7]

By March 24 Catherine was back in Paris, staying at the convent of Les Filles Repenties, which she had founded. So riddled with gout she could barely get in and out of bed, she was already acceding to her son's pleas that she go to Reims and attempt to make some compromise with the league. It was not a boast but a simple statement of fact that she wrote to Bellièvre: "God strengthens me and increases my ability far more than my sex is accustomed to in all these matters in which I am engaged."[8]

On May 24, exactly two months after her return to Paris, Catherine was in Reims, where she was met by the Duc de Guise and his brother Mayenne. They were courteous and deferential—and maddeningly vague. When she told Guise that her principal task was to find out what was displeasing him, assuring him that "the king was in a very good disposition to advance him more and more," he evaded the issue, assuring her, in turn, that he always felt in the good grace of the king. When she led the discussion to the king's desire that the league relinquish the towns it had seized in Picardy, again he evaded the issue. "When I saw that they did not reply," she wrote to the king, "I answered that you would be very much displeased."[9]

She continued to speak as though the king were still king, when it was clear to the leaders of the league that he was not. Her extravagant statements amused the Guises. They no longer had to humiliate her, as they had felt compelled to do at Épernay: at Reims Catherine humiliated herself, promising wildly, prodigally, and unrealistically. It was, commented Guise drily, a little like the scene in the Gospel where Satan promises the world to Christ. All very nice, but not his to give.[10]

Nothing came of Catherine's intervention, and on July 4 Guise and the king met face to face. The result was disastrous. Guise, "speaking very plainly" and "pushing aside all talk of peace and other harmful schemes," forced the king to "embark openly in this war."[11]

The king was a man torn in two. So long spitted on the horns of a dilemma, he scarcely knew who he was or what he thought. Gian Francesco Morosini, who that spring had been sent as Papal Legate into France, wrote of him with rare perception: "He fills the role of two people: a king of hope and a king of tears. He wants the defeat of the Huguenots and yet he dreads it; he dreads the defeat of the Catholics and yet he wants it. These diverse but powerful emotions fill him with anguish and make him distrustful even of his own thoughts."[12]

Henri's decision actively to join the league left Navarre stricken. Once more the Huguenots issued a formal declaration, affirming they had not taken up arms against the king but "for his cause and service" and to succour France, "overwhelmed and groaning beneath the heel of the tyranny of the league."[13] They doubled their recourse to Elizabeth, who ultimately followed the advice of her minister, who saw aid to the Huguenots as the most practical means of keeping Spanish power in check.

By September, 1587, the "War of the Three Henris" was fully mounted. Guise had a powerful army in the north, the king's army was in position in Touraine, and the king's *mignon* Joyeuse was ready for a flamboyant battle in the south. By comparison, the army of the third Henri, Henri de Navarre, looked small, rustic, and very tired. In fact, his army was just that. It was not an army to win battles but to engage in small skirmishes and forays. But what it lacked in polish, it compensated for in energy and speed. In October it was ready to travel northeast to meet the Swiss and German mercenaries due to enter France through Lorraine. But for once, Navarre had cut his precision timing too close: He did not realise that Joyeuse's army, glorious with polished armour, velvet cloaks, and flying pennants, was on top of him until it was too late. Penned into the small town of Coutras, backed by rivers too deep and swift to ford, there was no alternative to battle.

Coutras is a battle that has been embroidered into every Navarre legend: the Huguenots quietly taking their places in the predawn mists; the moments of prayer as the pastors led them in the French translation of David's psalm of victory ("This is the day that the Lord has made"); the contempt of the enemy, who took their bowed knees as a sign of cowardice; Navarre himself, his white plume distinguishing him wherever the battle was fiercest. And then the first signs of unexpected opposition—the first signs that the psalm singers were also swordsmen; the tough, unanticipated resistance to the royalist cavalry charge. So unexpected was the Huguenot defence that Joyeuse's forces broke and scattered. They never regained their first power. Before the day was over, Joyeuse, in his gaudy plumage, lay dead on the field and the Huguenots had won an overwhelming victory. It was a bewildering and unanticipated conclusion. For the first time, the league took the Huguenot forces seriously.

The Huguenot triumph was short-lived, however. Within two weeks Guise had righted the balance by inflicting deadly losses on the German mercenaries in the fertile fields of the Beauce. "Saul killed his thousands, but David his ten thousands," the league sang exultantly.

While the Huguenots and the league divided their triumphs, the king lived in defeat. Since both parties were, in effect, his enemies, every victory imperilled him. Earlier that fall Catherine had written him, "My son, I am so upset to see you so close to this terrible storm that I scarcely know what to write to you." She worried for the state of France but, most of all, "for your own person which is so very dear to me."[14] Like her son, Catherine scarcely knew what she wished for. She feared the victories of the Huguenots, yet confided secretly to the king that she was terrified at the rumours that Guise was on his way to Paris.

"A king of hope and a king of tears," Morosini had written of Henri. It was also a portrait of his mother.

Shortly before Christmas the king returned from his few months in the field. He was welcomed unenthusiastically. As far as the people were concerned, he had done nothing but lead an army out and lead it back again. The victories belonged to Guise. Christmas was bleak, but it would have been far bleaker had the king known that forty members of the Sorbonne had taken a secret decision that one had the right "to remove the power of government from the hands of incapable princes."[15]

"Now began the year 1588 which all judicial astrologers had called the wonderful year, because they foresaw so great a number of strange accidents, and such confusion in natural causes that they were assured that if the end of the world came not, there would happen at least an Universal Change."[16] Thus a contemporary historian ushered in the twelve months that began so hopelessly.

At once the astrologers were justified. Cold, famine, flood struck France with renewed force. And on January 24 Paris was overspread by a fog so dense it turned the city into night. In midafternoon torches smoked in the heavy air, while bewildered citizens stumbled against one another in the shadowy streets. "It was so dense and the atmosphere so dark," noted L'Estoile, "that two people walking in the street together couldn't see each other."[17] The fog was, of course, interpreted as a "sign."

Northwest of Paris, in the town of Nancy in the province of Lorraine, another kind of darkness was gathering. Here at the end of January a Guise family conclave was held to reaffirm the Articles of Nemours and bring more rigorous pressure to bear on the Huguenots. The king must declare himself more openly in support of the league and in condemnation of heresy. He must remove from his Council certain people suspected of Huguenot sympathies. He must see that the decrees of the Council of Trent were carried out and the Inquisition established. The clauses dealing with the lives and property of the Huguenots were detailed and severe. When the articles were presented to the king in February, he hesitated, attempted to evade, and ultimately capitulated. He had no alternative. The league was, as never before, in the saddle.

Even had Henri been able to call on Navarre for help, Navarre was now too straitened to give it. The victory of Coutras had been but a flash. It had had no lasting effects except to stir up strenuous dissension in the Huguenot ranks, for many felt that Navarre had dallied, failing to take advantage of his own gains. Meanwhile, the Swiss and German mercenaries accomplished nothing. They had travelled south of Lorraine, inflicting no injury on Guise lands, but sweeping through the fertile country of Burgundy. They terrorised the inhabitants along the Loire, firing their houses and crops and heaping their unwieldy waggons with plunder. Their leaders could not discipline them. Aimlessly they wandered through the countryside, refusing to engage the king's army, maintaining they were paid to fight the Duc de Guise, not the king.

Soon, however, France began to take its revenge on their destruction. Dysentery broke out in their ranks with such virulence that their army could be traced by the trail of bodies in its wake. "I would never have believed their terrible death rate," wrote Guise, who followed them. "I swear to you on my honour that I have seen more than eight hundred fallen bodies."[18] The reiters abandoned the thought of fighting, but unwilling to relinquish their rich plunder, they used up their remaining strength in trying to push their heavy waggons through the muddy land. The weight of their loads had caused the wheels to sink up to their axles in the mire. They creaked and groaned before the feeble efforts of the soldiers, but they did not move. The waggons, hopelessly stuck, were left to rot beside the corpses of their comrades.

The failure of the reiters was also a failure for the Huguenots and, consequently, a victory for the league. Following the Articles of Nancy, an anti-Guisard pamphlet commented trenchantly:

> The king, being thus bound to the league, is consequently bound to his own ruin, is bound to leave his arms in their hands. From his ruin will be built the House of Guise: from the weakening and death of his authority, the advance and crown of theirs. . . . The king stripped of authority and despoiled of strength; the king under their thumb, to reign at their discretion, and only insofar as they wish.[19]

Despite the anti-Guisard hyperbole, this was a statement as simple as truth. The king knew it and was momentarily moved to exert his authority. For the first time in months he spoke, said one of his secretaries, as though he expected to be obeyed. It was a transitory pause in the headlong plunge to destruction. Guise was more master than ever, writing the queen mother with impenetrable deference, assuring her he wanted nothing but to please the king.

That March, in one final effort to halt the league, the king sent Bellièvre into Lorraine to see what terms could be reached. From the beginning it was clear his mission would founder. The Masters of the World had no need for compromise. Catherine, confident in her old friend's ability, wrote him several times, assuring him she knew the difficulties of the task and reiterating her confidence that he was doing his best.[20] It was the first mission of such a nature for which she had not been chosen. Although she knew that physically she was no longer capable of arduous journeying, Catherine undoubtedly felt the prick of hurt pride.

In the past her son had often pushed her aside, yet desperation had always impelled him to call her back. Now, desperate as he was, he had looked elsewhere for help. She had failed him twice in the last three years: He had sent her to Épernay to trip the Guises, and instead, she had helped them into the saddle; he had sent her south to intercept Navarre, and she had brought home a specious truce that had afforded Navarre time to strengthen his army. He would not send her out again. With her crippling gout and her teeth that ached so badly that one could hardly understand what she said, Madame Catherine was becoming useless.

The events of that spring were sufficient to justify all the astrologers had predicted of unnatural occurrences and of a "Universal Changement." The *deus ex machina* who was to bring about the "Changement" was the King of Spain. Slight, stooped, so sedulously devoted to his desk that he was sometimes called the Clerk of the Escorial, Philip had dreams that were immense. He dreamed now of shifting the world ever so slightly on its axis and of establishing a new and invincible seat of power. The lever he intended to use was the Armada. With the death of Mary Stuart, plans for the Armada forged forward. Philip was filled with a "holy impatience" to conquer England and restore the unity of Christendom.

Spain was filled with a ferment of shipbuilding, yet so carefully was the secret guarded that not even Elizabeth's practised agents could probe the mystery. Determined that his enterprise be flawless, Philip took steps to ensure that the Armada would have a straight course to England without interference. To this end, he employed the help of his pensioner Henri de Guise, now so deeply in his debt he could refuse him nothing. To keep France from intervening on the side of England, a "broil" must erupt in France that would leave time for nothing else. Paris was already in a mood for sedition; the league was king in all but name. During the first week of May Guise was to enter Paris, obtain possession of the king's person, and make himself master. Meanwhile, the king's *mignon* Épernon was to be drawn out of Picardy to assist his royal patron, thus leaving the northern shores free for the passage of the Armada.

So secretive were the plotters that not even all those engaged in the enterprise knew the chain of command. "The man who arranged the dance" (as Cavriana put it) was Bernardino de Mendoza. Recently expelled from England as a source of discord and sedition, he was ideal as a secret agent. Secret, subtle, with a penchant for intrigue, he was eminently successful in the job with which Philip entrusted him. Early in the spring of 1588 he had written enthusiastically of the plans for the Paris uprising: "If this project is carried out, the king's hands will be so completely tied that it will be impossible for him even by his words and much more so by his acts to come to the help of the Queen of England."[21]

Despite the secrecy, there was evidence of something afoot. The preceding November Catherine, nervous about rumours from Spain, had written Longlée, her ambassador at Madrid, questioning him about the Spanish fleet: Was it really intended for the Low Countries or was France threatened?[22] One of those who had specific knowledge of what was planned was Nicolas Poulain, a respected Paris official, a member of the Sixteen, as the league's Parisian organisation was called, and an agent of the king. At great personal risk, Poulain uncovered what he knew of the plot to Henri, but either because he did not believe him or because he saw no way of escaping the noose, the king failed again to act.

Easter was late that year, but Easter had taken second place in the king's thoughts. His devotions were swallowed up in turmoil. He needed no secret information to tell him Paris was on the brink of revolt. The signs were everywhere. The pulpits fulminated against the king, warning the people he planned a bloody massacre to purge Paris of its Catholic leaders, as his mad brother had once purged it of the Huguenots. In fear and anger the people sent message after message to Guise, begging him to come save them. Guise, however, remained at Soissons—not hesitating, but awaiting the perfect moment. To support his resolution, Philip had sent Juan de Moreo, Philip's representative at the Treaty of Joinville, assuring Guise of Philip's continued support and dangling golden promises of what Spain would do for him when the Enterprise of England was complete.

Still the perfect diplomat, Guise continued to send respectful letters to Paris, writing the queen mother as late as May 3, "I beg God for the grace to have my actions recognised and judged only for what they are."[23] Despite his avowals of loyalty, however, the rumours that he was on his way to take Paris were so strong that on May 8 Bellièvre was despatched to Soissons to warn Guise that any effort to come to Paris would be interpreted as deliberate disobedience to the crown and that he would be held responsible for whatever turmoil ensued.

It was an angry Bellièvre who returned almost at once to Paris. While Guise had not openly defied the order, he had been arrogant and intransigent. Bellièvre warned the king that only the most resolute action could now keep things in control. "He told the King," wrote Stafford in his despatch, "that either he must give them what they wanted—which was not fit for a King to grant—or else he must show himself a King to them." Bellièvre had hoped, no doubt, to put the alternatives so starkly that Henri would be forced to a decision. Even this could not jolt the king into action. Instead, he parried his own sense of guilt by turning to Catherine "in great anger," enjoining her to see "what all her tactics came to." A momentary despair had vanquished the queen mother. She made no explanation or excuse but, noted Stafford, said simply that she had "done it all for the best," assuring the king she would comply with whatever he decided.[24]

The hour for decisions was running out. Shortly after Bellièvre had left Soissons, Guise, accompanied by less than a dozen men (he needed no more), also took the road for Paris. Riding all night, they arrived at St. Denis, just outside Paris, the following morning. Here they stopped to break their fast and then entered Paris unobtrusively through the Porte St. Martin. The duke had not gone far before he was recognised. The reaction of the crowd was pure elation. It was later conjectured that by the time he had reached the heart of Paris 30,000 people were at his service.

The events of the next five days are shrouded in secrecy and legend. As with the St. Bartholomew's Day Massacre, facts are confused and sometimes contradictory, for those who watched and recorded had very different angles of vision. As for motive, one can only conjecture, attempting to read in the larger context of their lives the mysterious and complex intentions of the three main characters.

Guise's first act on reaching the centre of Paris diverged from the plan so carefully outlined by Mendoza. Instead of turning down the rue St. Antoine to his own hotel, he turned in the direction of Les Filles Repenties, where Catherine was often in residence. She was there that morning, but despite Bellièvre's report, she did not believe Guise would dare enter Paris. His arrival was so unexpected that she turned white when she was advised of it. Why he had come to her she did not know; perhaps, as he had said so often in the past, in order that she might use her good offices to influence the king. But influence him towards what? Surely he could not expect her to counsel the king to abdicate

in favour of the man who had already humiliated them both so deeply
Composing herself, Catherine welcomed him drily, saying, according to som
accounts, that his welcome would have been more cordial had he come at anothe
time. Part of their conversation was public to anyone in the room. She asked hin
why he had come. He declared it was to clear his name of the slanderous report
being spread about him and to ask Catherine's intercession with the king. Wha
followed no one was able to hear, for she pulled him towards a window and thei
voices became inaudible. Not long after, she gave orders for her litter and
accompanied by Guise, travelled the short distance to the Louvre. They made a
extraordinary pair: Catherine, short and heavy, her unhealthy pallor accentuate
by her inevitable black dress; Guise, taller than she by a foot, handsome in whit
satin with a black velvet cloak thrown over his shoulders. For the first tim
Catherine heard at close range the cry that was to be the martial music of the nex
five days: *Long live Henri, Duc de Guise!*

Guise mounted the great staircase of the Louvre alone, for Catherine was to
short of breath to keep pace with him. Alone, he passed the king's guard, draw
at attention. The king, advised of his presence by Catherine's messenger, awai
ed him at the far end of the room, attended by several of his secretaries. In th
brief time Henri had had to prepare for Guise's entrance, he had turned to Al
phonse d'Ornano, his Corsican commander, asking if he, in his place, woul
have Guise killed. Ornano, a man of action, untroubled by the king's vacillation
made it clear that the king had simply to give the order. Even as Guise ap
proached, Ornano waited. For a moment, the prick of death had made Guise fee
faint, forcing him, according to one witness, to lean for support against a heav
chest. But the moment passed—as had so many moments of decision in Henri'
life—and Guise, who knew he had taken his life in his hands in coming to th
Louvre, must have felt the exhilaration of success. He had gambled on the king'
vacillation. And he had won.[25]
When in reply to the king's question, he began to explain that he had com
only to end the calumnies about himself, the king cut him off abruptly. If, as
contemporary recorded, Catherine, at that dramatic moment, entered the hal
saying, as she advanced towards her son, "I asked Monsieur de Guise to come t
Paris," we are faced with an insoluble mystery.[26] Had she so quickly gone ove
to Guise? Is this what he had had in mind when he had said he wanted her ir
tercession with her son? And had it taken so little to win her? It is impossible t
believe it, for in order to reach such a position, she would have had to erase he
whole political and personal history. While it is true that Catherine often prom
ised too glibly, swearing a fidelity she had no intention of maintaining, yet neve
had she been unfaithful to her son. Devious she undoubtedly was, but there i

othing devious about the years of loyalty, about the hardships endured and the miles travelled "in the service of the king."

Only if she had despaired utterly of her son could Catherine have capitulated thus to Guise. And the events of the next few days show that this was not true. Perhaps, and this seems the most plausible explanation, she had caught the temper of the room, surprised the speculative look in Ornano's eyes, and feared what her son might do. After listening to those wild, passionate voices acclaiming Guise as she was carried to the Louvre, she knew the king would not have a chance if Guise were killed. She might allay his anger if she herself assumed the responsibility for Guise's presence.

Whatever her motive, violence was averted. The nervous, uneasy conference continued for three hours. At the end Guise, having sacrificed nothing, left the Louvre through a secret door, making his way through the adoring crowds to the Hôtel de Guise. Catherine, too, was brought back through the streets to Les Filles Repenties, passing the deserted astrological tower she had built for her favourite Ruggieri. She no longer needed an astrologer. The events of the day and the cries of the crowds were sufficient indication of the future. "Yet will the whole world suffer upheavals, empires will dwindle, and from everywhere will be great lamentation," an astrologer had written of the year 1588. This was prophecy enough.

For the next two days conferences continued between duke and king. On May 10 Guise returned to the Louvre, this time accompanied by some 400 armed men—he had no intention of hazarding his life twice. They discussed the Articles of Nancy, the position of the Huguenots, Épernon's activities in the north. But throughout, they were men who evaded each other, their words like hollow balls, rolling aimlessly, touching from time to time but winning no advantage for either one. Guise played for time; Henri scarcely knew what he played for.

It was outside the conference room that the real activity was taking place. Small bands of league soldiers were moving steadily into Paris—perhaps as many as 1,500 by Wednesday morning. The king, too, gave orders for increasing his military strength. On the morning of May 12, in the hour just before dawn, 3,000 of the king's Swiss troops moved into Paris. With perfect timing and military efficiency, they were deployed throughout the city, neatly cutting off the league strongholds from each other. It was a masterful plan—more masterful because so unexpected. Even Guise was, apparently, wholly unprepared for this initiative by the king.

By early morning Paris was under the king's command. The do-nothing king had acted at last. Paris huddled silently during the early hours of Thursday. The markets were closed; the shops remained shuttered. The streets were empty and silent except for the occasional clatter of boots on the pavement or the intermittent jangling of arms. The Swiss, armed for heavy duty, found they had nothing

to do. With no enemy in sight, they broke ranks, casually strolling the street
they had been sent to patrol. The citizens, watching through half-opened blinds
found them not so terrifying after all. The more adventurous soon sifted into th
streets; others, more cautious, seeing that nothing had happened to their neigh
bours, followed them. Paris was soon alive again. There was no fighting, only
wary curiosity on the part of both soldiers and burghers.

The initial resistance to the king's soldiers came, as one might expect, fron
the Latin Quarter. From the streets around the Sorbonne, clerics and student
poured out, gathering momentum as they came, determined to show their defi
ance to the king's commands. In the Place Maubert they began to throw up ar
obstruction. They built it roughly, with their hands, from any material available
rocks, cobblestones, barrels, discarded pieces of wood. It was neither strong no
durable, but it was the first barricade in what was to be known as the Day of Bar
ricades.

With this action in the Place Maubert, the temper of Paris began to shift. A
short intervals throughout the city other barricades were thrown up, quick ane
effective ways of penning the king's soldiers where they were. At the beginnin₃
it would have been the work of a moment for the Swiss to push aside these rude
obstructions, but their commanders had been told no weapons were to be drawn
And the Swiss themselves had understood that their task was to protect the citizens of Paris from invading "foreigners." Unaware of what was happening, they
did nothing to stop the Parisians, even, in some places, helping them construc
their barricades.

As the king received reports of this unexpected resistance, his morning confi
dence waned, but despite the pleas of his captains, he continued to refuse permis
sion for any offensive action. Early that morning the Papal Legate Morosini hae
come to the Louvre, begging the king "not to ruin the most beautiful city in the
world." It seemed apparent he intended to do everything possible to comply with
the legate's request. His steady refusal for combat makes it impossible to believe
the Huguenot account that maintained the king had ordered that if there was trou
ble, he would not hesitate to put Paris to fire and sword. As continued reports
reached him, he finally ordered the withdrawal of the Swiss. The order came toc
late. By this time it was impossible for the soldiers to withdraw without blood
shed, for by now there were barricades almost every hundred feet.

What was happening throughout Paris in those late morning hours was a
strange mixture of spontaneity and premeditation. Sometime before Mendoza,
meticulous in every detail, had explained to the Sixteen how easily the city migh
be controlled by the simple expedient of barricades. It needed no special talent or
special weapons to construct them. Everyone could be employed, and yet, explained Mendoza, by such a simple measure an entire city could be bloodlessly
controlled. As for the citizens themselves, they danced effectively to Mendoza's
music, although they were undoubtedly ignorant of who piped the tune and why.

The Swiss, to their mortal surprise, now discovered they were the enemy. Still with no orders to fight, they tried to push through the barricades and withdraw in the direction of the Louvre. Clawing their way through the rubble, they were ripped and beaten, while stones were flung from windows into the narrow streets. Bewildered at the sight of their own blood, they sought desperately to explain that they were not enemies but friends, sent to protect the citizens from hostile forces. Knowing little or no French, they grasped awkwardly at phrases that would allay the citizens' fury. *"Bon Catholique,"* they cried, crossing themselves and begging for mercy. By this time they were fighting back, but even so, it was barely possible to make their way through the tide of Parisians closing inexorably around them.

At the Louvre Henri was in a torment of fear. Within a few hours the city he had controlled with such masterful strategy had turned against him. Fear was stronger than pride, and he sent a messenger to Guise, begging him to quell the riot.

His petition was an overt acknowledgement that Guise was master. Long acknowledged by the Parisians as their saviour, now he was acknowledged by the king.

Guise played the role with exquisite finesse. All Thursday morning he had remained apart, waiting quietly in the rue St. Antoine. While the streets were still passable, Catherine had come to him, begging, no doubt, that he use his influence to calm the people. There is no record of that conversation, but it had not moved Guise to action. He had waited until the turmoil had reached a crisis, until the king himself implored him, and then, careful to exonerate himself from any part in the storm, he set out to calm the waters.

Many contemporary accounts are careful to note that he went dressed in white satin, without a military escort, and armed only with a riding crop. His dress was symbolic of his limitless confidence—a confidence immediately justified. "The stupid populace," wrote L'Estoile in disgust, "[were] instantly calmed at the mere sound of Guise's voice."[27] When they began to cry, "On to Reims," Guise was quick to quiet them, however. He was far too much the aristocrat to be moved by the mood of the crowd. He wanted something more stable than kingship by popular acclaim. If Mendoza's power over the people was to play the music to which they danced, Guise's power was far greater. In Guise's hands, they became the very instrument he played.

By late afternoon the king's troops, carrying their dead and wounded, returned to the Louvre under Guise's safe-conduct. Again, Catherine made her way from the Louvre to the Hôtel de Guise to discuss what terms a defeated king might bargain for with his victor. The terms he offered were hard as adamant: Guise was to be made lieutenant general of the kingdom, his appointment to be confirmed in a meeting of the Estates; Navarre was to be excluded from the succession; Épernon and other "enemies of the league" were to be deprived of office; principal gov-

ernment posts were to be given to "faithful Catholics"; the king's private guard
the Taillagambi, was to be disbanded. In effect, all power would repose in Guise,
while the king would be left only with his title.

Assured of his success, Guise wrote that night to a friend, "I have defeated the
Swiss and a part of the royal guard, and am holding the Louvre so closely besieged that I expect to give a good account of all within it. This victory is so grea
that it will be remembered forever."[28]

Within the Louvre the discussion of Guise's terms continued far into the night
some of his ministers realistically counselling the king to accede to the duke's de
mands, others, headed by the queen mother, advising continued negotiation. A
they talked, they could hear the murmur of the crowd outside the walls, where
several hundred students from the Sorbonne headed a mob determined to rid Par
is of its king. Their intentions were dramatically clear.

Throughout the night the king, it was said, sat motionless in his audience
chamber, caught between the persuasive rhetoric of his ministers and the terrify
ing rumble of the mob. Having let so many moments of decision slip away, he
had now lost everything. Hindsight was a tormenting companion, admonishing
him that he should have paid more attention to Poulain, who had advised him o
an uprising; used force to keep Guise out of Paris; or—failing that—given Or
nano the signal he had awaited. In every case he had waited too long. Now there
was nothing left to do. One witness said he wept and, certainly, he had cause fo
tears—tears of rage, perhaps, at this great betrayal by his people; tears of impo
tence that being king, he had less power than his subjects; tears of remorse, the
bitterest of all tears, and the most useless.

There is little record of Catherine's reactions during those five days of tumult
We are told, however, that she, too, cried all during luncheon on Friday morning
yet despite her tears, she cherished a small hope that something might still be
won by negotiation. That afternoon, at her son's request, she again ordered he
sedan chair to take her to the Hôtel de Guise. Pushed aside after her failure t
deal successfully with Navarre and Guise, she was now again brought to the fore
That the "Eternal Negotiator" should be chosen for this final bargaining seem
totally appropriate.

Catherine's hope of success must have been very strong to sustain her throug
the next few hours. Although there was no actual fighting in the streets, the sens
of anticipated violence was palpable. The barricades were still in place. Incend
ary members of the league still moved among the people, exhorting them to fu
ther action. The blood spilt the day before had been just enough to waken the
taste.

No one in France (perhaps not even the king himself) was so hated by the Par
sians as Catherine. Although she had lived among them for fifty-five years, sh
was still a "foreigner," one of "that brood of Italians" that preyed on the cou
try's wealth. Despite her continued avowals that she was "a good Catholic," he

thodoxy was forever in question. The accusations against her were manifold:
e had poisoned the minds of her sons; she had compromised too much with the
guenots; she had let her Italian compatriots batten on France. They called her
zebel, that cruel Biblical figure who had slain the prophets of God, yet Jezebel,
ey recalled, had come to a brutal end, her body cast into the streets to be man-
d by dogs.

Well aware of how they hated her, Catherine set out in her chair (scarcely a
lwark against an angry crowd) to seek Guise. Age had made her vulnerable.
ow and ponderous, her keen gaze dulled, she was carried by her servants out
gate of the Louvre and into the waiting streets. One can only conjecture the
sponse of the crowd. A cry of anger? Of glee that their prey should be deliv-
d into their hands? A hush because, whatever else she was, she was queen
ther, and the Parisians had not yet lost their sense of royalty? It was a journey
extraordinary courage for a woman who had never become enured to fear. As
crowd shoved and jostled at her side, she may have remembered that child-
od journey down the Via San Gallo where, her little donkey pressed close
ainst Aldobrandini, she had been led from the security of the Murate to the
stile atmosphere of the Annunziata. That journey had been her first close brush
th violence and death. She had never grown accustomed to them. Throughout
r life they had both terrified and angered her. Yet now she stepped into their
idst in one final endeavour to save the king.

How she went is not clear. Possibly through the little streets north of the
uvre, past the Jeu de Paume, and finally into the wider rue St. Antoine. Not a
ig walk, yet it must have seemed interminable, for her bearers were forced to
p every hundred feet or so to be questioned and intimidated before they were
mitted to pass beyond the barricades. That her life was in danger there is no
ubt. She did not reach the Hôtel de Guise until afternoon.

For the next few hours, despite her fatigue and anxiety, Catherine engaged in
exhausting work of finding a move that might manipulate Guise into a more
nciliatory position. She begged him, as her son had directed her, to come with
r to the Louvre, assuring him the king would give him "everything that he
uld." Guise was unimpressed, "replying coldly," as L'Estoile recorded,
hat he did not trust the Louvre." When she pleaded with him to use his power
disperse the mobs, he shrugged, saying, "The people are like a bull which is
rd to hold back when it becomes excited."[29] Even her final cry—that she could
t believe he wanted to destroy the crown rather than serve it—won no conces-
ns.

The afternoon was waning when a messenger broke into their conversation:
e king had fled.

Both Guise and Catherine seemed genuinely shocked. Guise immediately ac-
sed the queen mother of "gulling" him, of deliberately holding him at the con-
ence table, to divert his attention from what was happening at the Louvre.

Catherine denied it emphatically, looking more bewildered and shattered tha
Guise himself. It is impossible to know whether this was consummate playactin
by one or both the characters or whether Henri's escape had been effected witl
out their knowledge. In any case, the fact was that as Henri waited throughou
the interminable hours of the afternoon, his fear undid him. He had no guarante
that his mother could bend Guise's inflexible demands; he had not even a guara
tee his mother would return to the Louvre alive.

When, towards evening, he learnt that the Porte Nueve had been left unguard
ed, he made the one immediate decision of his life. Taking a few companio
and ordering horses from the stable of the Tuileries, he walked from the Louvr
as though he were going to take some exercise. The plan was so bold, so une
pected that it worked. He rode unnoticed through the unguarded Porte Neuve ar
up through the steep streets leading to Montmartre. That night he slept near S
Germain-en-Laye and the following day was on the road to Chartres.

"And so," wrote a Huguenot commentator, "escaped the daintiest morsel
them all."[30]

"The Day of the Dagger"

I have been crushed in the ruins of the house.
—CATHERINE DE MEDICI

Chapter XX

O nce more, Catherine navigated the chafing crowds and returned to the Louvre. Whether she felt victorious or defeated depends on whether or not she had helped effect the king's escape. In any case, some of the tension had drained from the atmosphere. The hours of waiting were over. Something had happened: The king had acted at last. To many, of course, his action would be interpreted as a confession of defeat. "Fled!" the Pope was said to have cried in astonishment when he heard the news. "But why? For fear of being killed? But if he were to die thus, he would at least die as a king."[1] But Henri was not interested in martyrdom. Nor was his mother. A dead king was of no use. One must be alive to rule, and both Catherine and her son had an unyielding conviction of their divine right to rule.

That night, for the first time in almost a week, the Louvre slept. Little by little, the barricades were removed and the people went home. The following day Catherine received word from her son saying he was safe and ordering her not to follow him but to stay in Paris and continue her negotiations with Guise. As always, the king left the impossible tasks to his mother.

There were few people in Paris whom Catherine could rely on. Henri had taken both Villeroy and Bellièvre with him, leaving his mother only Pinart. Achille de Harlay, president of the Paris Parlement, would be on her side. Harlay was a solid royalist who, when hearing of the king's escape, had commented caustically, "It is a great pity when the valet ousts the master."[2] The city itself, except for the Parlement, was clearly in Guise's hands. Catherine at once leant on the Parlement's loyalty, explaining that the king had left, not because he intended to abandon his servants and the good people of Paris, but because of the inexcusable conduct within the city. He had gone to Chartres to maintain his authority and take up residence where he could continue to carry out the tasks of government. She, following her son's instructions, would remain in Paris, where she was sure she could count on the Parlement's goodwill. It was Catherine's first step in finding "some remedy which will cure this mortal wound."[3]

The king had left Paris on Friday night. By Monday the House of Lorraine was in Paris in full force. On Tuesday Guise drafted letters to all the major cities, as well as to the king himself, explaining the "troubles" that had rocked the city. The general unrest and misunderstanding had been caused by the king's "evil counsellors," he informed them. The actual violence had been triggered by the presence of "foreign troops" (the king's Swiss Guard), who frightened the people, who, understandably, had reacted to protect themselves. As for Guise's own entry, it was his last desperate show of fidelity, a living proof to the king that all the rumours about him were false. Surely, he pointed out, the way in which he had "saved" the king's guard (who would all be dead except for him) was sufficient proof of this.[4] It was a shrewd move on Guise's part to assume the initiative, to offer an explanation before one had been demanded. The explanation itself was smooth, coherent, and, in its way, correct. When, six days later, the king wrote his account of the same events, it was too late. To talk of his love of the Parisians, to assure them he would "forgive them" for what had happened was to employ meaningless phrases. The substance was all on Guise's side.[5]

One of Guise's ablest advisers during those uncertain days was Pierre d'Espinac, Archbishop of Lyons, who had played a minor role in the conferences at Épernay. Well spoken, subtle, excessively ambitious, he had taken his time in choosing sides. Despite his clerical status, it was not the cause of religion that had drawn him to Guise, but the chance for advancement. He was a cautious man, well qualified to balance Guise's natural arrogance. Now, in drawing up a strategy for maintaining their power, he advised Guise to stay on at court, winning everyone he could and at the same time quietly inserting his own men. He must keep the king from acting against him by a blend of friendship and power. He must also keep in the good graces of Villeroy and the other ministers, as well as in those of the queen mother, whose "only interest is her son's greatness."[6]

Guise had already been to see Catherine several times. The very night of her son's escape he had come to the Louvre, complaining of the "inopportune" departure of the king, who, he said, had no "reasonable motive" for mistrust. On May 20, just a week after the king's flight, Guise, the Marquis d'Elbeuf, and d'Espinac came to the Tuileries gardens at the hour for vespers to show Catherine the document he had drawn up as a provisional agreement between the king and the league. She read it over and shook her head. "I told them quite frankly," she wrote her son that night, "that I saw nothing in it that paid the proper honour to you." But Guise was "amazingly firm," refusing to admit there had been anything reprehensible in his actions. Three days later they met again, Guise reiterating that he wanted nothing for himself except to ensure what everyone wanted: "the security of the Catholic religion."[7]

Although Catherine was gaining no positive advantage, she was, at least, hindering the league's immediate success—so much so that the Cardinal de Guise, in annoyance, told the Nuncio she should be made to leave Paris so they could get on more quickly with their business. By the end of May two articles had been agreed on: Épernon was to be deprived of his power and the Estates were to be called for that fall. Knowing her son's affection for Épernon and fearful lest his anger and vanity impede the negotiations, she advised him, "You must forget and let drop everything that has happened and never speak of it again."[8] It is the tough and pragmatic counsel of a seasoned political opportunist. Had her son been capable of following it, the course of French history would have taken another direction.

Although Guise reigned as the undisputed King of Paris, the events of the Day of Barricades were not universally applauded. Morosini had, from the beginning, found the league's activities suspect, and now he wrote the Pope: "They are bad people . . . and of questionable goodwill."[9] Sixtus V found himself in a dilemma, wishing to approve the Catholic party, yet not willing to countenance rebellion against a lawful monarch. Morosini continued to report in the king's favour, assuring the Holy See that many in France were opposed to what had been done and that the inevitable result of this conflict would be the ruin of France. When Guise, nervous over Morosini's royal sympathies, assured him he wanted only "the defence of the Catholic religion and the extirpation of heresy," the Nuncio insisted that reconciliation with the king would have to be the first step. When Guise protested that the king would not agree to his demands, Morosini replied, "Moderate your demands."[10]

Catherine, seeing the chance of papal support, wrote at once to Villeroy, explaining that she had spoken with Morosini, "who has told me that the king has never had a better chance to win the Pope to his side than at present."[11] Morosini probably did not exaggerate a great deal in saying that many people repented that they had gone so far, yet having done so, they found it hard to retract. "We are all playing at malcontent," Pasquier wrote, as he reflected on those "grave mistakes" leading to the Day of Barricades: "the mistake of M. de Guise when he came on Monday with only seven companions, or the mistake of the king, who on Tuesday or Wednesday did not seize him as he could have done."[12]

England, of course, had every reason to be dismayed by the "commotion in Paris." A France in the grip of the league, would, inevitably, be a France against England. Elizabeth at once sent instructions to Sir Thomas Leighton, bidding him tell the king that "she cannot but marvel that a prince of his greatness and quality should take so weak and strange a course." She suggested he make use of the Huguenot forces for quelling this rebellion, for, she assured him, "No one who has the interests of France at heart will quibble because these are not Catholics." She exhorted him to "take courage, call Guise the traitor he is and much strength will come to him." Elizabeth's virile encouragement was lost on the King of Shadows.[13]

Only in Spain was there no complaint. "The misfortunes of the poor King of France, though truly pitiable, are not displeasing here," wrote the Venetian ambassador in Madrid.[14] At first Philip had been concerned over the king's escape, but Mendoza had assured him nothing could now happen in France to impede the progress of the Armada. Although by the end of the month Longlée, the French ambassador at Madrid, wrote in cipher to Henri, "It seems . . . that all the forces we see here and in Flanders will be used against the Queen of England," Mendoza countered the alarm by assuring Catherine the Spanish fleet had as its aim to clear the waters of English pirates who continually preyed on Spanish ships.[15]

Mendoza, however, had little credit left at the French court. For some time his conduct had been suspect and now it was obvious he had acted as a provocateur during the troubles in Paris. His role made the uprising still more frightening, for it indicated that the league was itself subject to a higher power and that Guise was, as a contemporary put it, simply the "valet of the King of Spain." "Indeed, there is no doubt," wrote Lippomano to Venice, "that the action of the Duke of Guise is taken in concert with the Ministers of the King of Spain and supported by them."[16] Such revelations made the fate of France more precarious still.

Throughout June negotiations continued. With every delay the league grew stronger, and Catherine wrote impatiently to her son, "The way this drags on is much to our disadvantage, but we cannot hasten it any more." It seemed that day by day more initiative slipped from her. She had tried to hold firm to a policy that would not humiliate the king, but she was realistic enough to know that they were all very vulnerable to the league's demands.

Aware that her son would interpret the terms she had to offer him as a betrayal of his royal position, she wrote in discouragement to Bellièvre:

> I would prefer to give away half of my kingdom and to give the lieutenant generalship to Guise, and to be recognised by him and by the whole kingdom, than still to tremble as we do now, lest worse befall the king. I know that this is a hard medicine for him to swallow; but it is harder yet to lose all authority and all obedience. It would be much to his credit if he were to come to terms in whatever way he could for the present, for time often brings many things which one cannot foresee, and we admire those who know how to yield to time in order to preserve themselves. I am preaching a sermon; excuse me, for I have never been in such trouble before, nor with less light to see my way out of it. Unless God put His hand to it, I do not know what will happen.[17]

By the middle of July the Articles of the Edict of Union had been agreed to, and the document was signed in Paris on July 15 by Catherine, Guise, and the Cardinal de Bourbon. In effect, it reaffirmed the Treaty of Nemours: The Catholic faith alone was to be practised in France; Protestants were excluded from the uccession; Guise was to be both lieutenant general of the kingdom and commander of the army; Épernon was to be excluded from the government, and the eague lords (Aumale, Nemours, Montpensier) were given command over his ormer provinces. It was no more, no less than Guise had demanded two months before; but the procedure, if not the conclusion, had preserved to the king some semblance of authority, and, in Catherine's eyes, this was of great importance. Following the registration of the edict by the Paris Parlement, there were the usual ceremonies—a solemn procession, a hymn of thanksgiving in the Cathedral of Notre Dame, bonfires in the streets. But, commented L'Estoile, there was "no real joy on the part of the people."[18] The storm, they sensed, had not yet passed.

The very ease with which the king had capitulated made the people uneasy. Stafford, sensing this continued unrest, wrote to Walsingham, "He hath granted them so much as they grow suspicious of the willingness of it." The people, he continued, feared that the king was planning some secret revenge, and Guise was constantly warned that he was being "cozened and deceived." When it was learned that he was going to Chartres to meet the king face to face, the people begged him to remain in Paris. But Guise, limitlessly confident, assured them he would rather trust himself to face such dangers than back off through weakness.[19]

When, however, on August 3, accompanied by Catherine and Bourbon, he met the king, he was greeted by neither anger nor recrimination. Instead, the king raised him to his feet and embraced him cordially, as though he had, as his mother had advised, "forgotten all that had happened." In fact, the king was never to forget those days of fear and humiliation. For the next six months they were to be his lodestar. For the most part he dissembled well, but from time to time, a flash of anger revealed the wound still festering. On the day of Guise's arrival he offered a toast at dinner. "To our good friends the Huguenots," he proposed, and then, almost as an afterthought, "and to our good barricaders of Paris." He smiled as he raised his glass, and Guise smiled back; but the hatred was very thinly veiled.

Stafford caught the mood when he wrote to Walsingham: "What will come of these meetings at Chartres, which nobody looketh any good of . . . I will send you word very speedily. . . . In the meantime I can assure you that though there be an union made in protestation and writing, I never saw minds more disunited."[20]

When the Estates opened in October, there had been a subtle and unexpected shift in power. Although Guise had successfully manipulated the elections so that nearly four-fifths of the delegates were solid leaguers, yet his popularity was not so unanimously assured as it had been a few months earlier. "I know the best sort be not in perfect love and charity with him," Stafford commented in late August. When, shortly after the opening of the Estates, the Duke of Savoy seized the French territory of Saluzzo, with the transparent excuse of "keeping it safe

from the Huguenots,'' his popularity was brought into serious question. Man
Frenchmen immediately conjectured that Guise was behind this act of aggres
sion, since it was well known that Savoy was in alliance with the league. In fac
Guise was innocent and, far from approving Savoy's action, wrote in anxiety t
Mendoza that ''this accident'' will ''upset all my intentions and plans.''[21]
might, he feared, drive the king into an alliance with the Huguenots.

The king, however, was playing a far more subtle game. He was determined t
regain his lost power—and he was determined to regain it alone. On September
he shocked the court by dismissing without warning all his ministers. His secre
taries of state Villeroy, Pinart, Brulart, his chancellor Cheverny, and even Pom
ponne de Bellièvre all were replaced by relatively unknown and inex
perienced men. The notes of dismissal were written in the king's own hand, pe
remptory notes, without explanation or excuse. ''Villeroy,'' he had written, ''
am very well pleased with your services; but please return to your house and re
main there until I send for you; do not seek the reason for my letter, but obe
me.'' The decision had been reached without consultation. It was an action en
tirely his own—as, in the future, he intended all his actions to be.[22]

The events of the last six months had driven Henri to the edge of destruction
Always inclined to suspicion, now wherever he leaned his weight, he imagine
the quicksand shifting beneath him; determined not to be sucked down, he re
solved to distance himself from all those he could not trust—most of all, from hi
mother. His dismissal of his ministers was, in fact, the dismissal of the quee
mother, whose men they ultimately were. They had served her before he ha
come to the throne. They were accustomed to ask Catherine's advice, defer t
her decisions, and to invoke his authority only when everything was settled.

Humiliation had distorted Henri's memory. He had forgotten the years whe
affairs of state were last on his list of priorities, when his mother—and the me
he now dismissed—had assumed the responsibilities he had found too burden
some. In his distrust he could recall only those areas where others had failed him
never those where he had been saved at enormous expense.

Catherine had diagnosed her son correctly when she had written to Bel
lièvre, ''I know that this is a hard medicine for him to swallow.'' Henr
lacked the inner resiliency which always permitted Catherine to endure humilia
tion without losing either self-respect or hope. ''We admire those,'' she had writ
ten to Bellièvre, ''who know how to yield to time in order to preserve them
selves.'' It was a philosophy she could not teach her son. To Henri, it seemed she
had yielded too much: He blamed her for her failure with Navarre at St. Bric
and with Guise at Nancy; he blamed her for continuing her negotiations during
the Day of Barricades when, now, it seemed, it would have been better to have
triggered Ornano. And later, after months of anxiety, she had presented for hi
signature the mortifying Edict of Union. From now on, surrounded by men who
would obey him, he would make his own decisions. With the news of the de

.truction of the Armada, he took fresh hope, knowing that Guise and the league would inevitably be affected by this Spanish reversal.

The Estates which convened at Blois the second week of October hardly re-. sembled those of a country bankrupt and in revolt. They were every bit as elaborate in pageantry and ritual as those Henri had presided over twelve years before. A solemn religious procession preceded their opening. The blessed sacrament was carried in full pomp, followed by the delegates in their ceremonial robes, marching four abreast, singing the familiar Latin hymns. For a few hours, at least, the king had succeeded in creating an impression of union and solidarity.

On the morning of October 16 the first plenary session began. Entering through the courtyard and up the wide marble staircase, the delegates took their places in the banquet hall. It was a sombre, impressive room, its heavy timbered roof and oak carvings unrelieved by the narrow embrasures that admitted little light. In his role as grand master, Guise led the king through the lines of delegates to his throne. Against the dark panelling, Guise stood resplendent. Dressed entirely in white satin, the jewelled orders of chivalry about his neck, his sword hilt studded with jewels, and in his hand a baton embroidered with golden fleurs-de-lys, he was the brightest thing in the room. "His eyes seemed to pierce through the assembly," wrote one of his admirers, "as if he would discover who were his friends and who his opponents; . . . his look seemed to say, 'I see you all, I know your thoughts.' "[23]

The king's opening speech was not without eloquence. He assured the delegates that with the goodwill of the people and his own unshaken resolution, the Estates could be the means of curing the nation's ills. He reiterated his intention "to make shine more and more the glory of God and our holy Catholic, apostolic, and Roman religion," to keep France from "falling under the domination of a heretic king," avowing he had no desire to be anything but their "faithful king." So far his speech was a collage of conventional phrases. But, he continued with a sudden change of tone, he alone was not responsible for the ills of the country; he had often been circumvented from doing the good he intended by ambitious and disobedient subjects. "By my Edict of Union," he continued, "I have expressly forbidden every association, formed without my authority; all raising of troops and money . . . and I affirm that those who continue in such criminal activity, despite my command, shall be held guilty of high treason." The arrow flew straight at Guise. He could not hide his anger and, noted L'Estoile, the duke "changed colour and lost his composure."[24]

The king's first overt act of independence was to be a very brief victory. Guise and the cardinal made it very clear that such a statement could not be written into the permanent record of the Estates. Deleting the king's indictment, they presented him with a modified version. Henri, still burning with the desire for mastery,

refused to sign. His resolution, however, was short-lived. Unequal to the alter
nate cajoling and bullying of the Guises, he eventually put his signature on a doc
ument appreciably different from the one he had drawn up. Some said he wept a
he signed it, recognising it as the greatest humiliation of all. L'Estoile, usually s
matter-of-fact, surrounds this act with emblematic darkness. "It was noted tha
during the retractions a great dark cloud and fog appeared," he wrote, "whic
made lights necessary in the middle of the day. Someone said that it was the la
testament of the king and of France that was being written and that a candle ha
been lighted to witness the last breath."[25]

Two days later the Edict of Union was unanimously signed by the Estates–
just as Guise had wished. "And so," wrote De Thou, "the league could no
afford to mock the king, who by each act really lost power and put them in grea
er arrogance."[26]

The episode made it evident the king could not outface Guise. If Henri were t
triumph over the King of Paris, he would have to find another way. As leagu
power triumphed in the Estates, rumours sifted through of new plots that woul
unthrone the king entirely and imprison him in some obscure monastery. Hardl
farfetched, for even in open daylight in his own château, Henri was subjected t
gibes and insults. Those closest to Guise cautioned the duke against pushing th
king too far, but he merely shrugged, saying, "This is a king who needs to b
frightened." Warned that even a weak man can be dangerous when at bay, h
pointed out that he had many friends at Blois, threatening that if anything wer
started against him, he would finish it "far more roughly" than he had at Paris.[2]

By December the delegates' enthusiasm had waned. They had accomplishe
what they had wanted and would have liked to return to their homes. The sple
dour of Blois provided little comfort for winter living. High above the Loire,
was open to the full sweep of damp river winds, while its thick stone walls an
narrow windows accentuated the cold. Even more chilling than the impenetrabl
gloom, however, was the pervading atmosphere of disaster.

During the months of the Estates, little had been seen of the queen mothe
With the king's dismissal of his ministers, her influence had diminished and sh
had disappeared from view. Except for a few enigmatic words in a letter to Be
lièvre, there is no record of her reaction to the king's radical and unanticipa
ed action. No record is needed, however, to reveal how deeply wounded sh
must have been. It was a public repudiation of the most brutal kind, comin
when there was nothing to cushion the blow.

Now in her seventieth year, stooped beneath the weight of her infirmitie
Catherine must have known, despite her unflagging optimism, that she was nea
ing the end of her life. It had been a life lived, as she had so often put it, in th
service of the king. That such service was not entirely sacrificial is obvious. Sh
had manifestly enjoyed her political role, with its exhilarating interplay of pov

er, and she had manifestly loved the son in whose name she had acted. She had, one might say, done what she wanted, yet this did not soften the final rejection.

She had appeared momentarily at her son's right hand at the opening of the Estates; she had acknowledged his public praise and gratitude for her work, knowing it was only a conventional gesture. As the days grew colder, the pain of her rheumatism crippled her, and she kept more and more to her apartments. She knew the king was being mocked and baited. She knew Morosini, terrified of Henri's reaction, had warned him that if anything "happened" to Guise, it would further contravene his authority. She heard the king had assured him he would "guard Guise's life as his own." But with no one to kerb his passion, she was not sure he would keep his promise.[28]

In the weeks before Christmas warnings to Guise increased. On December 10 he had written to Juan de Moreo, "You would not believe all the warnings I have received. . . . I am well taken care of by the help of God and the assistance of my friends, of which I still have a good number with me, so that my enemies do not know how to undertake anything." Later an anonymous note, folded into his napkin, cautioned him to beware. His only answer was a contemptuous "They wouldn't dare!"[29]

His fatal mistake was to underestimate not the courage, but the desperation of the king. For at some point during those short winter days Henri had decided Guise must die. When his ministers suggested less drastic steps (imprisonment, trial for treason), he rejected them. He had felt the tether twitch once too often around his own neck. Facing, at last, the fact that Guise would be master as long as he lived, almost single-handed he planned his assassination.

Shortly before Christmas the king announced that on December 23 he would leave for a little hermitage not far from Blois, where he would celebrate the feast. He called, consequently, for an early morning meeting of his Council. Shortly before eight o'clock Guise entered the council chamber, unaware the king's archers had closed ranks on the staircase behind him, barring any possible escape. He found the other members of the Council, including his brother the Cardinal de Guise, already assembled.

It was still dusk outside, and a chill, sleeting rain blew against the windows. Guise, with only a light cloak over his doublet, ordered a fire and nibbled at some sweetmeats while waiting for the Council to begin. As he sat, Louis Révol, one of Henri's new secretaries of state, brought word the king would like to see him. He arose, walking through the narrow doorway into the antechamber of the king's cabinet. No sooner had he stepped over the threshold than the door closed behind him. He turned, but the trap had sprung. A dozen of the king's personal guard, concealed behind the curtains, were on him.

Despite his wounds, Guise did not fall, but with superhuman strength dragged his assassins the length of the chamber. Not until he fell at the very foot of the king's bed did Henri emerge from hiding. Like a man half-dazed with dreaming, he murmured, "I did not know he was so tall," as he looked at the bloody figure stretched along the floor.

It had all turned out exactly as Mendoza had predicted four months before. "An open attack against him need not be feared, for he goes too well attended," he had written Philip; "the real danger is in the king's cabinet where one is only admitted alone and where one could be set upon by a dozen men."[30]

For several hours the long body lay where it had fallen, covered only with a grey cloak. When it was searched, a note was discovered with the incriminating sentence "700,000 pounds a month are necessary to maintain the war in France." The Cardinal de Guise and the Archbishop of Lyons had been arrested immediately, and within a few hours other members of the household were taken into custody, including the duke's young son, the Prince de Joinville, and the Cardinal de Bourbon. "The Day of the Dagger," which Cavriana had predicted months before, had come at last.

It is difficult to believe that Catherine had not heard something of the scuffle since the apartments where she was confined to bed were immediately under the king's, yet it was the following morning before her son came to tell her the news. Cavriana, her physician, was with her as Henri proclaimed triumphantly, "I am king now!"[31]

It was everything she had feared, and Catherine watched in bewilderment her son's exultation. She could share in none of his sense of victory, for her mind at once ranged ahead to the inevitable consequences. "Strike the shepherd and the sheep will be scattered." Perhaps. But she did not think so in this case. The league was too strong and Guise too much its idol for his death to go unavenged. Where her son saw victory, she saw only defeat.

Though still weak and feverish from an attack of pneumonia, she began at once to concentrate on those practical steps that might temporarily ensure the king's safety: What had he done to protect himself from Guise's followers? What orders had been sent to the cities to guard against uprisings? What explanation had he given the Papal Legate? But Catherine's anxiety scarcely touched her son. In his fantasy, he saw himself king at last, independent of them all—even of his mother. He would not let the "Old Lady's" distress darken his joy. He left, noted Cavriana, "seeming not in any way disturbed . . . which appeared to me really marvellous."[32] That afternoon he ordered the execution of the Cardinal de Guise—an act effectively negating whatever sympathy or support the Holy See might have given him.

Paris received news of the events at Blois just as the first celebrations for Christmas had begun. The city went wild with grief and fury. The king's arms were torn down and thrown into the Seine, statues and pictures of him were ripped and smashed, the royal apartments of the Louvre were looted, known royalists were led bound to the Bastille—and everywhere went up the cry of revenge for the murder of the King of Paris.

At Blois Christmas was sombre and silent, the king attempting to rally some support from the ambassadors, the queen mother still confined to her apartments. The news that her son had ordered the execution of the cardinal had staggered her. Although she had no love for him, she recognised at once how much Catholic support this would cost her son; in addition, she was superstitious enough to feel fear at shedding the blood of a prince of the church. "Ah, this poor creature," she was reputed to have said, "what has he done. . . . He has put his hand on a man who has often consecrated the body and blood of Our Lord. How will God ever pardon him? And what [and this was the crux of the matter for Catherine] will the other sovereigns say?"[33]

The events in the week between Christmas and New Year's remain obscure. Catherine had regained a little of her strength, but she still kept to her apartments with Cavriana in constant attendance. There is no record of conferences between Catherine and her son, although it seems probable that Henri must have come to her from time to time. Sickness had made her listless and depressed. She had no resources to meet such a crisis as this. Her natural resilience had deserted her, and Cavriana noted on the last day of the year, "Although . . . very experienced in matters of this world, nevertheless, she does not know what remedy to apply to so many present ills, nor to the ills to come."[34]

On January 1 Cavriana found her well enough to leave her chambers, and she at once ordered that she be taken to the Cardinal de Bourbon, who was still a prisoner. She left no record of why she went. It was, no doubt, for something more than a visit of consolation. Perhaps she hoped that she might work out some kind of compromise with the sixty-three-year-old prelate, who, according to the Act of Union, was now the successor to the crown.

For more than a week Bourbon had lived in fear of his life. All the dreams of greatness Guise had spun for him had not included such a fate as this. Bourbon was a man of neither courage nor initiative. His imprisonment terrified him. He knew Guise was dead; he knew the king's conscience had not stuck at the death of a cardinal. He must have recognised his own death would be the next logical step. Catherine's unanticipated presence did nothing to allay his fears. According to L'Estoile, he blamed her for everything—promises betrayed, treaties broken—and now—unable to believe that the ineffectual king could have acted so suddenly and so efficiently—he laid upon her the death of the Guises. "You will be the death of us all!" he swore at her.[35]

It was the final effort of the Eternal Negotiator. Chilled by her journey through the cold narrow halls, she returned, weeping, to her chambers. She could do no more. Failure had sapped her remaining energies, and for the next three days she lay in bed, shaken with chills and fever, her breathing increasingly laboured. On January 4 Morosini wrote to Rome, "She has a very high fever, and although the doctors say that it is merely a feverish cold and there is no great danger, the advanced age of the patient and her relapse are causing great anxiety."[36]

If she spoke during those final days, no one, not even the meticulous Cavriana has recorded it. D'Aubigne later noted that someone had heard a murmur, " have been crushed in the ruins of the house."[37] It was an ornate metaphor for the plain-spoken queen. Yet, surely, it was true. Finally, even the ability to mourn left her, and she slipped in and out of consciousness, all her strength consumed by that heavy, laboured breathing. On the morning of January 5 she was sufficiently conscious to dictate some final orders. At midday she died, surrounded by the king and a few members of the court. There were few familiar faces left, for she was the last of a generation, having outlived all but two of her children. Even the ministers who had served her faithfully throughout the years—Bellièvre Pinart, Villeroy—were not present.

Her body was embalmed and laid in state in the great audience chamber where so many of her diplomatic struggles had taken place. Although Henri, "the king who loved sad ceremonies," turned everything into black, there was little sign of deep mourning. Even the king—her "Eyes," as she had so lovingly called him—seemed more preoccupied than grief-stricken. His letter to the Holy See informing the Pope of that "personal affliction" with which God had visited him and describing his mother's last days, was dutiful—and perfunctory.[38]

The Huguenot Goulart noted in his memoirs: "Having dragged on for a few days, she died at the beginning of the year 1589, without anyone trying to prevent her or concerning themselves with her either in her sickness or death, any more than if she were the most worthless person in the kingdom. After her death . . . she was not spoken of any more than a dead goat."[39]

In Paris the news of the death of Madame Catherine was received with elation The citizens marched through the streets, waving lighted torches and crying, "So perish the race of Valois," as they extinguished their lights. At La Rochelle the Huguenots were equally triumphant, lighting bonfires and "adoring the judge ments of God" against the wicked. While the leaguers in Paris were crying for her body to be thrown into the common sewers, Pasquier, with more far-reaching vision, settled himself to writing a sonnet in her honour: "Here lies the flower of Florence," he began, apostrophising the queen who had taken such care to preserve her children (and the state) from violence.[40]

Although she had left a will ordering that she be interred in the resplendent tomb she had built at St. Denis, the tumult in Paris made this impossible. Instead, she was buried temporarily in the Church of St. Sauveur at Blois. The task of preaching the funeral sermon was entrusted to the Archbishop of Bourges. With exquisite subtlety, he evaded judgement, placing that difficult task in the hands of the Saviour to whom he entrusted her soul. While he praised Catherine's deeds—her courage, her energy, her diplomacy—and sorrowed with the son who was now deprived of such a mother, he ultimately lifted his eyes from Catherine to that eternal hope in which she had believed.[41]

It was Cavriana, whose steady devotion had kept him with her during those last comfortless months, who wept, without shame, at her passing. "We all remain without light, or counsel, or consolation," he wrote, "and to tell the truth, with her died what kept us alive. From now on, we must turn our thoughts elsewhere and find some other support."[42]

 *Epilogue*

Epilogue

Catherine de Medici's death barely stirred a ripple in the courts of Europe.

There had been a time when she had hoped to people those courts with her children: François, her first born, would rule France and, married to Mary Stuart, dominate Scotland; Charles would win the title of Holy Roman Emperor; Henri would have Poland; and Alençon would share with Elizabeth the throne of England. Her daughters, too, would find their places: Elizabeth in Spain, guiding the policies of Philip II; Claude affirming the loyalty of the Duc de Lorraine; Margot, by her marriage to Henri de Navarre, ending civil war and ultimately seducing her husband back to the Roman church.

They were dreams worthy of an empress. But the tortuous scheming, the conniving and intrigues that would bring them about were the work of the Italian Shopkeeper. It is the essential enigma of Catherine that she combined both roles in her person. She looked on thrones and crowns as though they were merchandise to be bargained for. In a sense she was right, but in staying so long in the marketplace, she lost that regal presence essential to kingship. The golden magic of such presence was, she felt, less important than the commonplace realism of the bargaining table. She was willing to sacrifice her own gilded image to win crowns for her children.

Yet in the end she lost, and having staked everything, she lost everything. No Valois ruled Europe. François, Charles, Alençon, Elizabeth, Claude were all dead. Margot was walled up, by her brother's orders, in the fortress of Usson. Henri alone wore a crown, yet Henri could hardly be said to rule. In fact, he had not ruled for years and now, with the murder of the Cardinal de Guise, the mortal threat of papal excommunication hung over him.

What, she had often asked, as she travelled on her little mule through a countryside ruined by civil war, what would happen to France? Death was merciful in sparing her the vision of the next few years. For less than eight months later her only remaining son was dead. Henri, last of the Valois line, was stabbed to death

339

in his own chambers by a religious fanatic. With his death, Henri de Navarre, who for so long had been the centre of contradiction, assumed the throne, plunging France into more bitter civil conflict than before.

All Catherine had hoped for was lost, and she with it. For it was more than her mortal life that was extinguished at Blois; it was the final remembrance of what she was. The cultivated Florentine, the faithful wife, the persistent negotiator disappeared behind the legend of the Sinister Queen. "She is spoken of no more than if she were a dead goat," a contemporary had written. It was a bitter fact, and history, which sometimes softens the harsh outlines of persons and events, has hardly been more kind, attributing to her more evils than any single person could have caused.

Her errors, it is true, were enormous, her policies sometimes dangerously erratic. Undoubtedly she was moved by that *affetto di signoreggiare* of which she was constantly accused. It would be difficult to find a Renaissance ruler who was not.

Yet behind the legend lay the portrait, and it was the portrait I had hoped to uncover. But a portrait, I discovered, has its own mystery. And that mystery must remain.

Notes

Notes

The following abbreviations have been used:

Arch. Cur.: Archives Curieuses de l'histoire de France.
BHPF: Bulletin de la société historique du protestantisme français.
CSP For.: Calendar of State Papers, Foreign Series, Elizabeth.
CSP Span.: Calendar of State Papers, Spanish.
CSP Ven.: Calendar of State Papers, Venetian.
EHR: English Historical Review.
LP Henry VIII: Calendar of State Papers, Letters and Papers, Foreign and Domestic, of Henry VIII.
Lettres: Lettres de Catherine de Médicis.
MP: Michaud et Poujoulat, eds. Nouvelle collection des mémoires sur l'histoire de France.
Petitot: Collection complète des mémoires relatifs à l'histoire de France.
RH: Revue historique
RHD: Revue d'histoire diplomatique RQH: Revue des questions historiques
RR: Revue rétrospective.

CHAPTER 1

1. Alfred von Reumont's *Die Jugend Caterina's de Medici* is the most complete source for the early portion of Catherine's life. All references are to the edition translated and annotated by Armand Baschet (*La Jeunesse de Catherine de Médicis*).

2. Fleurange, *Mémoires*. Petitot, ser. 1, vol. XVI, p. 325 *et seq.*

3. *Ibid.*
4. Reumont, p. 30.
5. Mariéjol, *Catherine de Médicis*, pp. 6–7.
6. Reumont, p. 42, n. 1.
7. Ariosto: *Opere minori*, p. 216.
8. Baschet, *La Diplomatie vénitienne*, pp. 176–78.
9. Varchi, *Storia Fiorentino*, *passim.*
10. Desjardins, *Négociations diplomatiques de la France avec la Toscane*, vol. II, p. 1113.

11. LP Henry VIII, vol. IV, pt. 2, p. 583.

12. *Cronica di Suor Giustina Niccolini*, in Reumont, p. 102.

13. Desjardins, *Négociations diplomatiques*, vol. II, pp. 1111, 1113.

14. Nicolas Raince in *Lettres de Catherine de Médicis*, vol. I, p. xi.

15. LP Henry VIII, vol. IV, pt. 3, p. 278; vol. VI, pp. 312–13, 564.

16. Alberi, *Relazioni degli ambasciatori veneti al senato*, ser. 2, vol. II, p. 282.

17. LP Henry VIII, vol. VI, *passim;* Granvelle, *Papiers d'état*, vol. I, pp. 472–550; Desjardins, *Négociations diplomatiques*, vol. II, p. 1068 *et seq.*

18. Reumont, p. 172.

19. Du Bellay, *Mémoires*. Petitot, ser. 1, vol. XVIII, pp. 205–09.

20. Louise de Savoie, *Journal*, Petitot, ser. 1, vol. XVI, p. 243.

21. Baschet, *La Diplomatie vénitienne*, pp. 407–08; Brantôme, *Oeuvres complètes*, vol. III, p. 243.

22. Bouchot, *Catherine de Médicis*, pp. 28–29.

23. LP Henry VIII, vol. V, p. 15; Monluc, *Commentaires et lettres*, vol. III, p. 137.

24. Ronsard, in Mariéjol, *Catherine de Médicis*, p. 35.

25. Freer, *The Life of Marguerite d'Angoulême*, vol. II, p. 185–88.

26. Baschet, *La Diplomatie vénitienne*, p. 430.

27. Alberi, *Relazioni*, ser. 1, vol. IV, p. 47.

28. Baschet, *La Diplomatie vénitienne*, p. 477.

29. Freer, *Marguerite d'Angoulême*, vol. II, p. 228.

30. Tommaseo, *Relations des ambassadeurs vénitiens sur les affaires de France au xvi siècle*, vol. I, p. 279.

31. Freer, *Marguerite d'Angoulême*, vol. II, p. 318.

32. Paillard, "La Mort de François I et les premiers temps du règne de Henri II, d'après les dépêches de Jean de Saint-Mauris," *RH*, vol. V (1877), pp. 84–120.

CHAPTER II

1. Baschet, *La Diplomatie vénitienne*, pp. 432–33; Tommaseo, *Relations des ambassadeurs vénitiens*, vol. I, p. 287.

2. Paillard, "La Mort de François I," p. 101; Freer, *Marguerite d'Angoulême*, vol. II, p. 340.

3. Paillard, "La Mort de François I," pp. 112–13.

4. La Planche, *Histoire de l'Estat de France . . . sous le règne de François II*, p. 114.

5. *Lettres*, vol. I, p. 6.

6. Ronsard, *Oeuvres complètes*, vol. III, p. 177.

7. CSP Span., 1517–1549, p. 327.

8. Tommaseo, *Relations des ambassadeurs vénitiens*, vol. I, p. 287.

9. CSP For., 1547–1553, #638.

10. Dianne de Poytiers, *Lettres inédites*, pp 219–222, 228.

11. *Ibid.*, pp. 78–79.

12. *Ibid.* Desjardins, *Négociations diplomatiques* vol. III, p. 253.

13. Baschet, *La Diplomatie vénitienne*, p. 479.

14. *Ibid.*

15. *Ibid.*, pp. 434–35.

16. Romier, *Les Origines politiques des guerres d religion*, vol. I, p. 20.

17. Emile Picot, "Les Italiens en France au XVI siè cle," *Bulletin Italien*, vols. I, II, III, IV.

18. *Lettres*, vol. I, p. 56.

19. Ribier, *Lettres et mémoires d'Etat . . . sou les règnes de François I, Henri II, François II*, vol. I 431.

20. *Lettres*, vol. I, pp. 80, 66; Dianne de Poytiers *Lettres inédites*, p. 102, n. 1.

21. *Lettres*, vol. I, p. 105.

22. Labanoff, *Lettres, instructions, et mémoires d Marie Stuart*, vol. I, p. 9; CSP For., 1547–53, #295.

23. CSP Ven., vol. VI, #95.

24. Kervyn de Lettenhove, *Les Huguenots et le Guex*, vol. I, p. 86.

25. CSP Ven., vol. V, #1005.

26. *Ibid.*, #993.

27. Ruble, "Le Traité de Cateau-Cambrésis," p 85.

28. Romier, *Les Origines politiques*, vol. II, p. 224

29. Baschet, *La Diplomatie vénitienne*, p. 44 *Lettres*, vol. I, p. liii; Alberi, *Relazioni*, ser. 1, vo IV, p. 72.

30. Bèze, *Histoire ecclésiastique des églises re formées au royaume de France*, vol. I, p. 121.

31. Brantôme, *Oeuvres complètes*, vol. VIII, p. 4.

32. D'Aubigné, *Histoire universelle*, vol. I, p 237–38.

33. CSP For., 1558–1559, #898.

34. Vieilleville, *Mémoires,MP*, ser. 1, vol. IX, 284.

35. Brantôme, *Oeuvres complètes*, vol. IX, p 448–49.

36. Vieilleville, *Mémoires*, p. 284.

CHAPTER III

1. Tavannes, *Mémoires*, Petitot, ser. 1, vo XXIV, p. 256.

2. CSP For., 1558–1559, #972.

3. Nabonne, *Jeanne d'Albret*, p. 103.

4. Davila, *The Historie of the Civill Warres France*, p. 35.

5. L'Aubespine, *Négociations, lettres, et pièce diverses relatives au règne de François II*, p. 115, n. 2 Bouillé, *Histoire des ducs de Guise*, vol. II, p. 19.

6. Desjardins, *Négociations diplomatiques*, vo III, p. 403.

7. Brantôme, *Oeuvres complètes*, vol. VII, p. 405.
8. Baschet, *La Diplomatie vénitienne*, p. 493.
9. *Lettres*, vol. I, p. 122; CSP For., 1558–1559, #1306.
10. Pasquier, *Lettres historiques*, p. 35; Desjardins, *Négociations diplomatiques*, vol. III, p. 404.
11. De Thou, *Histoire universelle*, vol. III, p. 381.
12. Mignet, "Lettres de Jean Calvin recueillés," *Journal des Savants* (1857), p. 411.
13. Bouillé, *Histoire des ducs de Guise*, vol. I, p. 2, n. 2; CSP For., 1559–1560, #552.
14. Delaborde, *Gaspard de Coligny*, vol. I, p. 397; la Planche, *Histoire de l'état de France*, p. 180.
15. CSP For., 1559–1560, #266.
16. Labanoff, *Lettres de Marie Stuart*, vol. I, p. 72.
17. L'Aubespine, *Négociations, lettres* . . . p. 7.
18. CSP For., 1559–1560, #685.
19. Mignet, "Lettres de Jean Calvin recueillés," *Journal des Savants* (1857), p. 384.
20. *Ibid.*
21. "Papiers de Noailles," *Le Cabinet Historique*, vol. XIX (1873), p. 25.
22. Castelnau, *Memoirs of the Reigns of Francis II and Charles IX*, p. 40.
23. CSP For., 1559–1560, #881.
24. Paillard, "Additions critiques à l'histoire de la conjuration d'Amboise," *RH*, vol. XIV (1880), p. 03.
25. *Ibid.*, p. 90.
26. D'Aubigné, *Mémoires*, p. 5.
27. Vieilleville, *Mémoires*, MP, ser. 1, vol. IX, P. 88.
28. Mignet, "Lettres de Jean Calvin recueillés," *Journal des Savants* (1857), p. 479.
29. *Ibid.*, pp. 480–81.
30. CSP For., 1559–1560, #952; Mignet, *Journal des Savants*, (1859), pp. 22–23.
31. CSP For., 1559–1560, #337; 1560–61, #32.
32. *Ibid.*, #777, 779.
33. Tavannes, *Mémoires*, Petitot, ser. 1, vol. XIV, p. 283.
34. CSP For., 1560–1561, #931.
35. Paillard, "Additions critiques. . . ." p. 345.
36. *Lettres*, vol. I, p. 142.
37. *Ibid.*, 140.
38. *Ibid.*, vol. I, pp. lxxix, 147; Croze, *Les Guises, es Valois, et Philippe II*, vol. I, p. 75.
39. Castelnau, *Memoirs*, p. 86.
40. Mignet, *Journal des Savants* (1859), p. 31; Croze, *Les Guises, Les Valois, et Philippe II*, vol. I, p. 0.
41. *Lettres*, vol. I, p. lxxxi.
42. Mignet, *Journal des Savants* (1859), p. 34.
43. Bordenave, *Histoire de Béarn et Navarre*, p. 06; Vieilleville, *Mémoires*, MP, ser. 1, vol. IX, p. 97.

44. Baschet, *La Diplomatie vénitienne*, pp. 503–04.
45. Layard (ed.), *Despatches of Michele Suriano and Marc-Antonio Barbaro*, p. 1.
46. Castelnau, *Memoirs*, p. 96.
47. CSP For., 1560–1561, #716.

CHAPTER IV
1. Layard, *Despatches of Suriano and Barbaro*, pp. 3–5.
2. CSP For., 1560–1561, #744.
3. Brantôme, *Oeuvres complètes*, vol. VIII, p. 408; CSP Ven., vol. VII, #278.
4. *Lettres*, vol. I, pp. 154, 155, 568.
5. Tommaseo, *Relations des ambassadeurs vénitiens*, vol. I, pp. 419, 421, 423, 543.
6. *Ibid.*, vol. I, pp. 437, 527, 557.
7. Romier, *Catholiques et Huguenots à la cour de Charles IX*, p. 3.
8. *Lettres*, vol. I, p. 568.
9. Romier, *Catholiques et Huguenots*, p. 8.
10. CSP For., 1560–1561, #789.
11. Mignet, *Journal des Savants* (1859), pp. 148–149.
12. Baschet, *La Diplomatie vénitienne*, p. 511.
13. Pasquier, *Lettres historiques*, p. 60.
14. *Lettres*, vol. I, p. 163, n. 1.
15. *Ibid.*, p. 577.
16. Romier, *Catholiques et Huguenots*, p. 43.
17. Tommaseo, *Relations des ambassadeurs vénitiens*, vol. I, pp. 521, 525; Layard, *Despatches of Suriano and Barbaro*, p. 12.
18. Tommaseo, *Relations des Ambassadeurs vénitiens*, vol. I, p. 521.
19. *Ibid.*, p. 425.
20. *Ibid.*, p. 555.
21. *Lettres*, vol. I, pp. 581, 584.
22. CSP For., 1561–1562, #28.
23. *Lettres*, vol. I, pp. xciii–iv.
24. Romier, *Catholiques et Huguenots*, p. 96.
25. *Lettres*, vol. I, pp. 174, 178, 179.
26. Romier, *Catholiques et Huguenots*, pp. 98, 105.
27. *Lettres*, vol. I, p. 592.
28. Dareste, "Hotman d'après de nouvelles lettres des années 1561–1563," *RH*, vol. XCVII (1908), pp. 298–99.
29. Haton, *Mémoires*, vol. I, p. 156.

CHAPTER V
1. Romier, *Catholiques et Huguenots*, p. 133.
2. Tommaseo, *Relations des ambassadeurs vénitiens*, vol. II, p. 119.
3. Aumale, *History of the princes of Condé in the XVIth and XVIIth centuries*, vol. I, pp. 340–41.
4. D'Aubigné, *Histoire universelle*, vol. I, p. 314.
5. CSP For., 1561–1562, #507.
6. *Ibid.*, #612.

7. Romier, *Catholiques et Huguenots*, p. 269; *Lettres*, vol. I, p. 238, no. 1.

8. *Lettres*, vol. I, pp. cxi, cxii, 242.

9. CSP For., 1561–1562, 713.

10. *Lettres*, vol. I, pp. 244, 247; Layard, *Despatches of Suriano and Barbaro*, p. 49.

11. CSP For., 1661–1662, #730.

12. Haton, *Mémoires*, vol. I, p. 187.

13. CSP For., 1561–1562, #921.

14. Romier, *Catholiques et Huguenots*, p. 311.

15. Pasquier, *Lettres historiques*, p. 98; Guise, *Mémoires*, MP, ser. 1, vol. VI, p. 490.

16. La Noue, *Mémoires*, MP, ser. 1, vol. IX, p. 594.

17. D'Aubigné, *Histoire universelle*, vol. II, p. 10.

18. *Lettres*, vol. I, pp. 283–84, 285, n. 2.

19. CSP For., 1561–1562, #587; Romier, *Catholiques et Huguenots*, p. 344.

20. Santa Croce, "Lettres," *Arch. Cur.*, ser. 1, vol. VI, p. 89.

21. Haton, *Mémoires*, vol. I, p. 235.

22. *Lettres*, vol. I, pp. 290–93.

23. CSP For., 1562, #238, 246.

24. Kervyn de Lettenhove, *Les Huguenots et les Gueux*, vol. I, p. 79; CSP For., 1562, #174, 188; "Journal de ce qui s'est passé en France durant l'année 1562," *RR*, ser. 1, vol. V, p. 169.

25. *Lettres*, vol. I, pp. 337–38, 346, 353.

26. Haton, *Mémoires*, vol. I, p. 305; Dareste, "Hotman d'après de nouvelles lettres," *RH*, vol. XCVII (1908), p. 305.

27. CSP For., 1562, #179.

28. Kervyn de Lettenhove, *Les Huguenots et les Gueux*, vol. I, p. 94.

29. CSP For., 1562, #914.

30. Layard, *Despatches of Suriano and Barbaro*, p. 58.

31. *Lettres*, vol. I, p. 436, n. 1; Nabonne, *Jeanne d'Albret*, pp. 176–81; Baschet, *La Diplomatie vénitienne*, p. 518.

32. CSP For., 1563, #12.

33. Castelnau, *Memoirs*, pp. 216–17.

34. CSP For., 1563, #354, 361; "Lettre . . . sur la mort du duc de Guise," *Arch. Cur.*, ser. 1, vol. V, pp. 171–97.

35. *Lettres*, vol. I, p. 516; Layard, *Despatches of Suriano and Barbaro*, p. 80.

36. CSP For., 1563, #354.

CHAPTER VI

1. Ronsard, *Oeuvres complètes*, vol. VI, p. 256.

2. *Lettres*, vol. I, p. 529.

3. *Ibid.*, vol. II, pp. 1, 4, xvi, v.

4. *Ibid.*, p. vii.

5. CSP For., 1563, #613, 636.

6. *Lettres*, vol. II, p. xv.

7. *Ibid.*, p. xvii.

8. CSP For., 1563, #930.

9. Castelnau, *Memoirs*, p. 260.

10. *Lettres*, vol. II, p. 76.

11. *Ibid.*, p. 98; Desjardins, *Négociations diplomatiques*, vol. III, p. 506.

12. "Avis donné par Catherine de Médicis à Charles IX," *Arch. Cur.*, ser. 1, vol. V, pp. 245–54.

13. *Lettres*, vol. II, pp. 102–03.

14. *Ibid.*, p. 157, n. 1.

15. *Ibid.*, pp. 119, xlvii: Bordenave, *Histoire de Béarn et Navarre*, pp. 124–26.

16. CSP For., 1564–1566, #487.

17. *Ibid.*, #524, 592.

18. *Ibid.*, #357.

19. Lettres, vol. II, pp. 218, n. 1, 217–18, 230, n. 3.

20. Champion, *Catherine de Médicis présente à Charles IX son royaume*, pp. 134–40; CSP For., 1564–1566, #754.

21. Tommaseo, *Relations des ambassadeurs vénitiens*, vol. II, p. 67.

22. *Lettres*, vol. II, p. xli.

23. *Ibid.*, pp. 258, 259 n. 2.

24. Baschet, *La Diplomatie vénitienne*, p. 245.

25. Champion, *Catherine . . . présente à Charles IX*, p. 285.

26. *Lettres*, vol. II, p. lxxvi.

27. *Ibid.*, pp. lxxvi–ix; Champion, *Catherine . . . présente à Charles IX*, pp. 279–93.

28. Granvelle, *Papiers d'état*, vol. IX, pp. 288–91.

29. Castelnau, *Memoirs*, p. 304.

30. *Lettres*, vol. II, pp. 297, lxxx–vi.

31. *Ibid.*, pp. 297–98.

CHAPTER VII

1. *Lettres*, vol. II, p, cii; Champion, *Catherine . . . présente à Charles IX*, p. 365.

2. *Ibid.*, p. 395.

3. CSP For., 1564–1566, #1100, 1685.

4. Lettres, vol. II, pp. 35–55, lxvii.

5. *Ibid.*, pp. 407–8.

6. CSP For., 1566–1568, #406.

7. Champion, *Charles IX, la France et le contrôle de l'Espagne*, vol. I, p. 68.

8. Baschet, *La Diplomatie vénitienne*, p. 520.

9. *Ibid.*, p. 525.

10. CSP For., 1566–1568, #1683; *Lettres*, vol. III, p. 58.

11. Turenne, *Mémoires*, p. 10.

12. Desjardins, *Négociations diplomatiques*, vol III, p. 528, n. 2.

13. Kervyn de Lettenhove, *Les Huguenots et le Gueux*, vol. II, p. 76, n. 3, 77; Champion, *Charles IX* vol. I, p. 88.

14. CSP For., 1566–1568, #1789.

15. Charles IX, *Lettres à M. de Fourquevaux*, p 125; De Crue, *Anne, duc de Montmorency*, p. 476.

16. *Lettres,* vol. III, p. 75.

17. *Ibid.,* 79.

18. Castelnau, *Memoires,* p. 329.

19. Granvelle, *Correspondance du cardinal de* *anvelle,* vol. III, p. 140.

20. Champion, *Charles IX,* vol. I, p. 123.

21. CSP For., 1566–1568, #1914.

22. Desjardins, *Négociations diplomatiques,* vol. , p. 569.

23. Haton, *Mémoires,* vol. I, pp. 426–27.

24. CSP For., 1566–1568, #2177, 2178.

25. *Lettres,* vol. III, pp. xxvii–iii.

26. Charles IX, *Lettres à M. de Fourquevaux,* p. 5; Granvelle, *Correspondance,* vol. III, p. 234; CSP or., 1566–1568, #2191.

27. "Lettres de l'amiral de Coligny," *BHPF,* vol. XI (1872), p. 455; Henri IV, *Recueil des lettres mis-*es, vol. I, p. 5; *Lettres,* vol. III, p. 143, n. 2, 159.

28. *Calendar of the Marquess of Salisbury at Ha-*eld *House,* vol. I, p. 1185; Lettres, vol. III, p. xxx; astelnau, Memoirs, p. 363.

29. Desjardins, *Négociations diplomatiques,* vol. , p. 576; *Lettres,* vol. III, p. 173.

30. Champion, *Charles IX,* vol. I, p. 138.

31. CSP For., 1566–1568, #2550; Haton, émoires, vol. II, p. 541.

32. De Thou, *Histoire universelle,* vol. V, p. 521.

33. *Lettres,* vol. III, p. 193; Forneron, *Histoire de* hilippe II, vol. II, p. 147.

34. *Lettres,* vol. III, p. xxxiii.

35. *Ibid.,* pp. 206, 210.

36. CSP For., 1566–1568, #2688.

37. *Lettres,* vol. III, p. 218, n. 1; Croze, *Les* uises, les Valois et Philippe II, Appendix IV, p. 336, ppendix V, p. 340.

38. *Lettres,* vol. III, p. 219; Croze, *les Guises, les* alois et Philippe II, Appendix VI, p. 377.

39. Haton, *Mémoires,* vol. I, p. 576; Champion, harles IX, vol. I, p. 185; CSP For., 1569–1571, #1, 2.

40. Desjardins, *Négociations diplomatiques,* vol. , p. 556.

41. *Lettres,* vol. III, p. 231, n. 2.

42. *Ibid.,* p. xlv.

HAPTER VIII

1. "Arrest de la court de Parlement contre Gaspart e Coligny . . . " *Arch. Cur.,* ser. 1, vol. VI, pp. 75–81; Haton, *Mémoires,* vol. II, p. 565; Kervyn de ettenhove, *Les Huguenots et les Gueux,* vol. II, p. 88.

2. *Ibid.,* vol. II, p. 207.

3. Catherine, *Memoirs,* p. 425; Monluc, *Commen-*aires et lettres, vol. III, pp. 456–57.

4. CSP For., 1569–1571, #1216.

5. Ferrière, *Le xvi siècle et les Valois,* pp. 184–85.

6. Ferrière, *Les Projets de mariage de la reine* *Elisabeth,* pp. 60–61; *Lettres,* vol. II, p. 307.

7. *Lettres,* vol. III, pp. 128–29.

8. Brantôme, *Oeuvres complètes,* vol. IX, p. 594.

9. Godefroy, *Le Ceremonial français,* vol. II, pp. 35–37.

10. Kervyn de Lettenhove, *Les Huguenots et les Gueux,* vol. II, p. 261; *Lettres,* vol. IV, pp. 25–26.

11. CSP For., 1569–1571, #1477, 1478.

12. *Lettres,* vol. IV, p. 26.

13. *Ibid.,* p. viii; CSP For., 1569–1571, #1521, 1571.

14. CSP For., 1569–1571, #1886.

15. Fénelon, *Correspondance diplomatique,* vol. IV, p. 186.

16. Digges, *The Compleat Ambassador,* pp. 133–34.

17. *Lettres,* vol. IV, pp. 74–75.

18. Tavannes, *Mémoires,* Petitot, ser. 1, vol. XXV, p. 192.

19. Charles IX, *Lettres à M. de Fourquevaux,* p. 362.

20. "Lettres de l'amiral de Coligny," *BHPF,* vol. XXI (1872), p. 457; "Papiers de Noailles," *Le Cabi-*net *Historique,* XX (1874), pp. 40–41; Desjardins, *Négociations diplomatiques,* vol. III, p. 643.

21. Haton, *Mémoires,* vol. II, p. 627; Desjardins, *Négociations diplomatiques,* vol. III,, p. 643; D'Aubigné, *Historie universelle,* vol. III, pp. 282–83.

22. La Huguerye, *Mémoires inédits,* vol. I, p. 95.

23. Digges, *The Compleat Ambassador,* pp. 125–26; CSP For., 1569–1571, #1920.

24. CSP For., 1569–1571, #1921.

25. *Lettres,* vol. III, p. 327; CSP For., 1569–1571, #1189.

26. *Lettres,* vol. IV, p. v.

27. *Ibid.,* vol. III, p. lxiv.

28. Roelker, *Queen of Navarre: Jeanne d'Albret,* p. 365.

29. Desjardins, *Négociations diplomatiques,* vol. III, p. 733.

30. Haton, *Mémoires,* vol. II, pp. 656–57.

31. *Lettres,* vol. IV, p. 76; Desjardins, *Négocia-*tions diplomatiques, vol. III, p. 724.

32. Jeanne d'Albret, *Mémoires et poésies,* p. 30.

33. Roelker, *Queen of Navarre,* pp. 372–74.

34. *Ibid.*

35. *Lettres,* vol. IV, p. li.

36. "Bref discours sur la mort de la royne de Na-*varre,"* BHPF, vol. XXXI, p. 29; Marguerite de Va-lois, *Mémoires et lettres,* p. 25.

37. Roelker, *Queen of Navarre,* p. 394.

CHAPTER IX

1. *Lettres,* vol. IV, pp. liv, 106, n. 2.

2. Desjardins, *Négociations diplomatiques,* vol. III, pp. 740–41.

3. Tommaseo, *Relations des ambassadeurs vénitiens*, vol. II, p. 155.

4. Marguerite de Valois, *Mémoires et lettres*, p. 26.

5. Kervyn de Lettenhove, *Les Huguenots et les Gueux*, vol. II, p. 439: Tavannes, *Mémoires*. Petitot, vol. XXVV, p. 256.

6. *Lettres*, vol. IV, p. lvii.

7. *Ibid.*, p. lvi.

8. *Ibid.*, p. lix.

9. Digges, *The Compleat Ambassador*, p. 233.

10. *Lettres*, vol. IV, p. lxxi.

11. Alberi, *Relazioni*, ser. 1, vol. IV, p. 281.

12. Tavannes, *Mémoires*. Petitot, vol. XXV, p. 291; *Lettres*, vol. IV, p. lxiii.

13. Alberi, *Relazioni*, ser. 1, vol. IV, p. 285.

14. *Lettres*, vol. IV, p. lxxi.

15. For contemporary accounts of the attack on Coligny and the massacre, see especially *Arch. Cur.*, ser 1, vols. VII, VIII, IX.

16. *Lettres*, vol. IV, p. lxxviii.

17. "Extrait des registres et croniques du bureau de la ville de Paris," *Arch. Cur.*, ser. 1, vol. VII, p. 213.

18. "Relation du massacre de la Saint-Barthéelemy," *Arch Cur.*, ser. 1, vol. VII, pp. 80–81.

19. Haton, *Mémoires*, vol. II, p. 1110, Appendix II.

CHAPTER X

1. "Deux lettres de Théodore de Bèze," *BHPF*, vol. VII (1858), pp. 16–17.

2. Champion, *Charles IX*, vol. II, p. 130.

3. *Ibid.*, p. 183.

4. Desjardins, *Négociations diplomatiques*, vol. III, p. 824.

5. Tommaseo, *Relations des ambassadeurs vénitiens*, vol. II, p. 155. déportements de la reyne Catherine de Médicis, *Arch. Cur.*, ser. 1, vol. IX, p. 3 *et seq.*

6. *Lettres*, vol. IV, p. 122.

7. *Ibid.*, p. cxviii.

8. Ferrière, *Le XVI siècle et les Valois*, p. 326.

9. Champion, *Charles IX*, vol. II, p. 109.

10. Ferrière, *Le XVI siècle et les Valois*, p. 326; Cenival, "La politique du Saint-Siège et l'élection de Pologne," *École française de Rome: Mélanges d'archéologiques et d'histoire*, vol. XXXVI (1916–1917), p. 146.

11. Forneron, *Histoire de Philippe II*, vol. II, pp. 331, 330.

12. Champion, *Charles IX*, vol. II, pp. 118–19.

13. *Ibid.*, p. 154.

14. *Ibid.*, p. 119.

15. *Ibid.*, p. 154.

16. Forneron, *Histoire de Philippe II*, vol. II, p. 333; Champion, *Charles IX*, vol. II, p. 157.

17. Pitteurs, "Un Ambassadeur d'Angleterre en

France sous Elisabeth," *RHD*, vol. XXIII (1909), 295; Digges, *The Compleat Ambassador*, p. 240.

18. Fénelon, *Correspondance diplomatique*, vol. pp. 113, 115, 122.

19. *Ibid.*, pp. 122, 128; Ferrière, *Le XVI siècle les Valois*, p. 331.

20. Digges, *The Compleat Ambassador*, p. 249.

21. *Ibid.*, p. 242; Fénelon, *Correspondance di lomatique*, vol. V, p. 135.

22. CSP For., 1572–1574, #84, 28.

23. Digges, *The Compleat Ambassador*, pp. 2 269.

24. "Mémoires de l'état de France," *Arch. Cu* ser. 1, vol. VIII, p. 14.

25. *Lettres*, vol. IV, pp. 117, 123.

26. Champion, *Charles IX*, vol. II, p. 299.

27. CSP For., 1572–1574, #1206.

28. Robinson, "Queen Elizabeth and the Va Princes, *EHR*, vol. II (1887), p. 63.

29. *Ibid.*

30. *Ibid.*

31. *Ibid.*, p. 65.

32. *Lettres*, vol. IV, p. 169.

33. *Ibid.*, p. 157.

34. *Ibid.*, p. 160.

35. *Ibid.*, p. 189; CSP For., 1572–1574, #769.

36. *Lettres*, vol. IV, p. 208.

37. Desjardins, *Négociations diplomatiques*, v III, p. 722; Cenival, "La politique du Sa Siége . . . ," p. 141.

38. *Lettres*, vol. IV, p. 156, n. 2.

39. Cenival, "La politique du Saint-Sièg . . . ," p. 151.

40. Champion, *La Jeunesse de Henri III*, vol. II, 198.

41. *Ibid.*, p. 202; *Lettres*, vol. IV, p. clvi.

42. Champion, *La Jeunesse de Henri III*, vol. III 199.

43. Goulart, *Mémoires de l'état de France s Charles IX*, vol. II, p. 16.

44. *Lettres*, vol. IV, pp. 172–73.

45. Barbot, "Histoire de La Rochelle," *Archi historiques de la Saintonge et de l'Aunis*, vol. III, 141.

46. Pasquier, *Lettres historiques*, p. 219.

47. Lettres, vol. IV, p. 195.

CHAPTER XI

1. Champion, *La Jeunesse de Henri III*, vol. II, 202; Choisnin, *Mémoires*, MP, ser. 1, vol. XI, p. 43

2. *Lettres*, vol. IV, pp. 225–27.

3. "Election et règne de Henri d'Anjou en P logne," *RR*, ser. 1, vol. IV (1885), p. 48.

4. Champion, *La Jeunesse de Henri III*, vol. II 128; *Charles IX*, vol. II, p. 119.

5. Desjardins, *Négociations diplomatiques*, v

p. 879; Champion, *La Jeunesse de Henri III*, vol.
. 143.

6. Champion, *La Jeunesse de Henri III*, vol. II, p.

7. *Ibid.*, p. 246.

8. *Ibid.*, p. 254.

9. CSP Ven., vol. VII, #560.

0. "Élection et règne," p. 73.

1. Champion, *La Jeunesse de Henri III*, vol. II, p.

; "Élection et règne," p. 68.

2. Champion, *La Jeunesse de Henri III*, vol. II, pp.
-62; Goulart, *Mémoires de l'état*, vol. III, p. 2; De
u, *Histoire universelle*, vol. VII, p. 12.

3. Champion, *La Jeunesse de Henri III*, vol. II, p.

4. Champion, *Charles IX*, vol. II, p. 281.

5. *Lettres*, vol. IV, p. clxxi.

6. Frémy, *Un Ambassadeur liberal sous Charles
et Henri III*, p. 208.

7. Tommaseo, *Relations des ambassadeurs
tiens*, vol. I, pp. 419–21.

8. Champion, *Charles IX*, vol. II, p. 317.

9. Desjardins, *Négociations diplomatiques*, vol.
p. 894.

0. Goulart, *Mémoires de l'état*, vol. III, *passim*;
sen, *Diplomacy and Dogmatism*, pp. 31–34;
res, vol. IV, p. clxxiv.

1. Goulart, *Mémoires de l'état*, vol. III, p. 423.

2. *Lettres*, vol. I, p. 618.

3. Champion, *Charles IX*, vol. II, p. 331; CSP
n., vol. VII, #573.

4. De Thou, *Histoire universelle*, vol. VII, p. 44.

5. Rocquain, *La France et Rome pendant les
rres de religion*, p. 165.

6. CSP For., 1572–1574, #1331.

7. Champion, *Charles IX*, vol. II, pp. 359, 362.

8. *Lettres*, vol. IV, p. cxcvii; CSP Ven., vol. VII,
1; Champion, *Charles IX*, vol. II, p. 368.

9. CSP For., 1572–1574, #1372.

0. Henri IV, *Lettres missives*, vol. I, pp. 60–70.

1. Champion, *Charles IX*, vol. II, p. 386 n. 3;
P For., 1572–1574, #1403.

2. *Recueil des choses mémorables avenues en
nce sous le règne de Henri II, François II, Charles
Henri III*, p. 230.

3. *Lettres*, vol. IV, pp. 297, 303.

4. *Ibid.*, p. 309, n. 1.

APTER XII

1. Goulart, *Mémoires de l'état*, vol. III, p. 370;
nluc, *Commentaires et lettres*, vol. III, p. 530; Sor-
, "Histoire véritable des choses mémorables ave-
s tant durant le règne que le jour du tréspas du
Charles IX," *Arch. Cur.*, ser. 1, vol. VIII, pp.
–331.

2. *Recueil des choses mémorables*, p. 233: Henri
IV, *Lettres missives*, vol. I, pp. 70–71.

3. *Lettres*, vol. IV, p. 308.

4. Henri IV, *Lettres missives*, vol. II, p. 252.

5. *Lettres*, vol. IV, pp. 310–11, 312.

6. "Election et règne," pp. 99–104.

7. Haton, *Mémoires*, vol. II, p. 1150, Appendix
X.

8. *Lettres*, vol. V, p. 59, n. 1.

9. Henri III, *Lettres*, vol. I, p. 357.

10. Jean de la Fosse, *Journal d'un curé ligueur de
Paris*, p. 170; "Le Trèspas et obsèques de
. . . Charles IX," *Arch. Cur.*, ser. 1, vol. VIII, pp.
257–70.

11. *Lettres*, vol. V, pp. 13, 24.

12. *Ibid.*, p. 53; Fénelon, *Correspondance diplomatique*, vol. V, p. 167.

13. CSP For., 1572–1574, #1509, 1462.

14. De Thou, *Histoire universelle*, vol. VII, p. 79.

15. Nolhac, *Il Viaggio in Italia di Enrico III di
Francia*, chaps. 6, 7, 8 *passim*.

16. *Lettres*, vol. V, p. 71, n. 1.

17. CSP For., 1572–1574, #1509.

18. *Lettres*, vol. V, pp. 73–75.

19. Marguerite de Valois, *Mémoires et lettres*, p.
84; Champion, *Henri III, roi de Pologne*, vol. II, p.
176.

20. De Thou, *Histoire universelle*, vol. VII, p. 81;
Champion, *Henri III, roi de Pologne*, vol. II, pp.
162–63.

21. Champion, *Henri III, roi de Pologne*, vol. II, p.
174.

22. *Lettres*, vol. V, p. xvi; Monluc, *Commentaires
et lettres*, vol. III, p. 531.

23. Busbecq, *Letters . . . to the Holy Roman
Emperor*, p. 39.

24. Champion, *Henri III, roi de Pologne*, vol. II, p.
274.

25. L'Estoile, *Mémoires-Journaux*, vol. I, p. 51; *Le
Sacre et le coronnement du roy de France* (1575).

26. Busbecq, *Letters*, pp. 40–41, 80; *Recueil des
choses mémorables*, p. 248; Bouillé, *Histoire des ducs
de Guise*, vol. II, p. 563; L'Estoile, *Mémoires-
Journaux*, vol. I, p. 50.

27. Ferrière, "Catherine de Médicis et les Politiques," *RQH*, vol. LVI (1894), p. 428.

28. L'Estoile, *Mémoires-Journaux*, vol. I, p. 53.

29. Busbecq, *Letters*, pp. 108–9.

30. CSP For., 1575–1577, #106.

31. Champion, *Henri III, roi de Pologne*, vol. II, p.
153; *Lettres*, vol. V, pp. 120, 131.

32. Granvelle, *Papiers d'état*, vol. V, p. 395.

CHAPTER XIII

1. CSP For., 1575–1577, #168, 176.

2. *Ibid.*, #58.

3. CSP Ven., Vol. VII, #636.

4. Henri IV, *Lettres missives*, vol. II, pp. 240, 243–44; *Recueil des choses mémorables*, p. 255.

5. "Documents originaux relatifs au rôle du duc d'Alençon . . . et à l'histoire du Tiers-Parti," *RR*, ser. 2, vol. V, pp. 274–75.

6. *Ibid.*, p. 260.

7. *Lettres*, vol. V, p. 142.

8. Busbecq, *Letters*, p. 140.

9. "Documents . . . relatifs . . . du duc d'Alençon," pp. 274–75; *Lettres*, vol. V, pp. 161–65.

10. Alberi, *Relazioni*, ser. 1, vol. IV, p. 320.

11. Henri IV, *Lettres missives*, vol. III, pp. 366–67; *Lettres*, vol. V, p. 185.

12. CSP For., 1575–1577, #583.

13. *Lettres*, vol. V, pp. 286–95.

14. CSP For., 1575–1577, #583.

15. L'Estoile, *Mémoires-Journaux*, vol. I, pp. 142–43.

16. *Ibid.*, p. 153.

17. Baird, *The Huguenots and Henry of Navarre*, vol. I, p. 130.

18. *Ibid.*, pp. 130–31; Boullée, *Histoire complète des états-généraux*, vol. I, p. 279.

19. *Mémoires de la Ligue*, vol. I, pp. 2–7.

20. *Lettres*, vol. V, p. lxxv.

21. *Ibid.*, p. lxxvi.

22. Desjardins, *Négociations diplomatiques*, vol. IV, p. 110.

23. *Lettres*, vol. V, pp. 231–32.

24. Nevers, *Mémoires*, vol. I, p. 470; Henri IV, *Lettres missives*, vol. I, p. 113.

25. Lettres, vol. V, pp. 233–34, 247; Palm, *Politics and Religion in Sixteenth Century France: A Study of the Career of Montmorency-Damville*, pp. 104–20.

26. Guillaume de Taix, in Freer, *Henry III, King of France and Poland*, vol. II, pp. 131–32.

CHAPTER XIV

1. Freer, *Henry III, King of France and Poland*, vol. II, pp. 138–39; Van Dyke, *Catherine de Médicis*, vol. II, pp. 227–28.

2. CSP For., 1577–1578, #225.

3. L'Estoile, *Mémoires-Journaux*, vol. II, pp. 159, 219–220; Haton, *Mémoires*, vol. II, p. 907.

4. Marguerite de Valois, *Mémoires et lettres*, pp. 12, 15, 24.

5. *Ibid.*, p. 33.

6. *Ibid.*, p. 90.

7. *Lettres*, vol. VII, p. 202.

8. L'Estoile, *Mémoires-Journaux*, vol. II, pp. 240–41.

9. *Recueil des choses mémorables*, p. 274.

10. Muller et Digerick, *Documents concernant les relations entre le duc d'Anjou et Les Pays-Bas*, vol. I, pp. 50, 73.

11. L'Estoile, *Mémoires-Journaux*, Vol. II, p 235–36.

12. CSP For., 1577–1578, #691.

13. *Lettres*, vol. VI, pp. 9–10.

14. Haton, *Mémoires*, vol. II, p. 965.

15. CSP For., 1578–1579, #393.

16. *Ibid.*, #21; 1577–1578, #607.

17. *Lettres*, vol. VI, p. 38.

18. Lauzun, *Itinéraire de Marguerite de Valois Gascogne*, p. 35.

19. *Lettres*, vol. VI, p. 46.

20. *Ibid.*, p. 43.

21. *Ibid.*, p. 47.

22. *Ibid.*, p. 48.

23. *Ibid.*, p. 64.

24. *Ibid.*, p. 68.

25. *Ibid.*, p. 73.

26. *Ibid.*, p. 83, 97–104.

27. *Ibid.*, p. 100.

28. *Ibid.*, p. 108.

29. *Ibid.*, p. 110, 113, 116–17.

30. *Ibid.*, 119.

31. *Ibid.*, pp. 119–34.

32. *Ibid.*, p. 134; Vaissière, *Henri IV*, p. 181.

CHAPTER XV

1. *Lettres*, vol. VI, pp. 260, 261.

2. *Ibid.*, p. 280.

3. *Ibid.*, p. 292.

4. *Ibid.*, p. 325.

5. *Ibid.*, p. 296.

6. *Ibid.*, vol. VII, p. 134.

7. *Ibid.*, vol. VII, pp. 335, 347.

8. *Ibid.*, p. 357.

9. *Ibid.*, p. 360.

10. *Ibid.*, vol. VII, pp. 171, 179.

11. CSP For., 1579–1580, #85; Tommaseo, *Relations des ambassadeurs vénitiens*, vol. II, p. 449.

12. *Lettres*, vol. VII, pp. 12, 33, 30.

13. *Ibid*, p. 53.

14. Harrison, *Letters of Elizabeth*, p. 129.

15. *Lettres*, vol. VI, pp. 315–16.

16. *Ibid.*, pp. 332, 316, n. 1; Desjardins, *Négociations diplomatiques*, vol. IV, p. 253.

17. Robinson, "Queen Elizabeth and the Valois Princes," p. 74.

18. *Lettres*, vol. VI, p. 374.

19. Harrison, *Letters of Elizabeth*, p. 136.

20. *Lettres*, vol. VII, p. 225.

21. Muller et Digerick, *Documents concernant . . . le duc d'Anjou et Les Pays-Bas*, vol. III, p. 12

22. *Ibid.*, p. 345.

23. Desjardins, *Négociations diplomatiques*, vol. IV, p. 336; L'Estoile, *Mémoires-Journaux*, vol. II, 365.

24. CSP For., 1578–1580, #387.

25. Henri IV, *Lettre missives*, vol. I, pp. 296–97.
26. *Lettres*, vol. VII, p. 252.
27. *Ibid*, pp. 452, 310.
28. Muller et Digerick, *Douments concernant . . . duc d'Anjou et les Pays-Bas*, vol. III, p. 508; Kervyn Lettenhove, *Les Huguenots et les Gueux*, vol. V, p. 39.

HAPTER XVI
1. *Lettres*, vol. VII, pp. 304–9.
2. Kervyn de Lettenhove, *Les Huguenots et les ueux*, vol. VI, pp. 137–38, 139, n. 1.
3. Haton, *Mémoires*, vol. II, p. 1047.
4. CSP For., 1581–1582, #200.
5. Calendar, Hatfield House, vol. II, p. 280.
6. Digges, *The Compleat Ambassador*, p. 433; urdin, *A Collection of State Papers Relating to the ffairs in the Reign of Elizabeth*, p. 353.
7. Read, *Mr. Secretary Walsingham*, vol. II, pp. –79.
8. Sully, *Memoirs*, vol. I, p. 92.
9. CSP Span., 1580–1586, #211–212.
10. *Ibid.*, #336.
11. Desjardins, *Négociations diplomatiques*, vol. ', pp. 413–14.
12. Kervyn de Lettenhove, *Les Huguenots et les ueux*, vol. VI, p. 231.
13. CSP Span., 1580–1586, #243.
14. Desjardins, *Négociations diplomatiques*, vol. √, p. 418.
15. Rocquain, *La France et Rome pendant les uerres de religion*, pp. 247–48.
16. Kervyn de Lettenhove, *Les Huguenots et les ueux*, vol. VI, p. 290.
17. *Lettres*, vol. VIII, p. 48.
18. *Ibid.*, p. 50.
19. *Ibid.*, p. 51, n. 5.
20. CSP For., May–Dec. 1582, #87.
21. *Lettres*, vol. VIII, pp. 68–69.
22. *Ibid.*, pp. 86–87; Prinsterer, *Correspondance de maison d'Orange-Nassau*, ser. 1, vol. VIII, p. 142; luller et Digerick, *Documents concernant . . . le c d'Anjou et les Pays-Bas*, vol. IV, pp. 299–300.
23. Black, *The Reign of Elizabeth*, p. 357.
24. Muller et Digerick, *Documents concernant . . . le duc d'Anjou et les Pays-Bas*, vol. IV, p. 406; esjardins, *Négociations diplomatiques*, vol. IV, p. 36, n. 2.
25. *Lettres*, vol. VIII, p. 183.
26. Kervyn de Lettenhove, *Les Huguenots et les ueux*, vol. VI, p. 466.
27. *Lettres*, vol. VIII, p. 111.
28. Kervyn de Lettenhove, *Les Huguenots et les ueux*, vol. VI, p. 478.
29. CSP For., July, 1583–July, 1584, #138.
30. Harrison, *Letters of Elizabeth*, p. 161.

31. *Lettres*, vol. VII, pp. 330, 399, 401.
32. *Ibid.*, pp. 384, 389–96, 394–405.
33. *Ibid.*, vol. VIII, p. 61.
34. Forneron, *Histoire de Philippe II*, vol. III, p. 155.
35. Desjardins, *Négociations diplomatiques*, vol. IV, p. 458.

CHAPTER XVII
1. L'Estoile, *Mémoires-Journaux*, vol. II, p. 112; CSP Ven., vol. VII, #795.
2. CSP For., May–Dec., 1582, #167.
3. *Ibid.*, #69.
4. *Ibid.*, 1579–1580, #189.
5. Marguerite de Navarre, *Mémoires et lettres*, p. 289; *Lettres*, vol. VIII, pp. 36–37.
6. Desjardins, *Négociations diplomatiques*, vol. IV, p. 421.
7. Lauzun, *Itinéraire de Marguerite de Valois*, p. 234.
8. Busbecq, "Lettres . . . 1582–1583," *Arch. Cur.*, ser. 1, vol. X, p. 94.
9. CSP For., July, 1583–July, 1584, #183.
10. Lauzun, *Itinéraire de Marguerite de Valois*, p. 240.
11. CSP For., July 1583–July, 1584, #183.
12. *Lettres*, vol. VIII, pp. 428–29.
13. Marguerite de Valois, *Mémoires et lettres*, p. 297; "Lettres inédites," *Archives historiques de Gascogne*, ser. 1, vol. XI, pp. 32–33.
14. *Lettres*, vol. VIII, pp. 180–81.
15. *Ibid.*, 132.
16. Desjardins, *Négociations diplomatiques*, vol. IV, pp. 487–88.
17. L'Estoile, *Mémoires-Journaux*, vol. II, p. 150.
18. CSP For., July, 1583–July, 1584, #539, 611.
19. *Lettres*, vol. VIII, p. 188.
20. Prinsterer, *Correspondance*, ser. 1, vol. VIII, pp. 406, 407.
21. Robinson, "Queen Elizabeth and the Valois Princes," *EHR*, vol. II (1887), p. 77.
22. Desjardins, *Négociations diplomatiques*, vol. IV, p. 514; *Lettres*, vol. VIII, p. 190.
23. L'Estoile, *Mémoires-Journaux*, vol. II, p. 153.
24. *Lettres*, vol. VIII, pp. 190, 194; Lauzun, *Itinéraire de Marguerite de Valois*, p. 289.
25. Desjardins, *Négociations diplomatiques*, vol. IV, p. 519; Lauzun, *Itinéraire de Marguerite de Valois*, p. 295.
26. CSP For., July, 1583–July, 1584, #566, 376.
27. *Ibid.*, #752.
28. *Ibid.*, #752, 756.
29. Desjardins, *Négociations diplomatiques*, vol. IV, p. 544.
30. Rocquain, *La France et Rome pendant les guerres de religion*, p. 266, n. 1.

31. Davila, *The Historie of the Civill Warres of France*, p. 499.

32. Busbecq, "Lettres 1582–1583," *Arch. Cur.*, ser. I, vol. X, p. 117.

33. Péréfixe, *The History of Henry IV*, p. 52.

34. CSP For., 1584–1585, pp. 31–33 (beginning with this volume dispatches are no longer numbered); Baird, *The Huguenots and Henry of Navarre*, vol. I, p. 294; Rocquain, *La France et Rome pendant les guerres de religion*, p. 270.

35. Jensen, *Diplomacy and Dogmatism*, p. 55.

36. *Lettres*, vol. VIII, p. 244, n. 1.

37. Black, *The Reign of Elizabeth*, pp. 364–65.

38. CSP For., 1584–1585, p. 301.

39. L'Épinois, *La Ligue et les Papes*, p. 20.

40. CSP For., 1584–1585, p. 354.

41. *Ibid.*, p. 343.

CHAPTER XVIII

1. "Déclaration des causes . . . " *Arch. Cur.*, ser. I, vol. XI, pp. 7–21.

2. *Recueil des choses mémorables*, p. 282.

3. *Lettres*, vol. VIII, pp. 454, 245–48.

4. *Ibid.*, pp. 269, 286; L'Épinois, *La Ligue et les Papes*, p. 10.

5. *Lettres*, vol. VIII, pp. 455, 457.

6. *Ibid.*, pp. 290, 292.

7. *Ibid.*, p. 265, 323–24.

8. *Ibid.*, 303.

9. *Ibid.*, p. 339.

10. L'Éstoile, *Mémoires-Journaux*, vol. II., p. 199.

11. Forneron, *Histoire de Philippe II*, vol. III, p. 232; Desjardins, *Négociations diplomatiques*, vol. IV, p. 620.

12. Henri IV, *Lettres missives*, vol. II, pp. 87–88.

13. *Ibid.*, pp. 98, 125–26.

14. "Déclaration de notre Saint-Père," *Arch. Cur.*, ser. I, vol. XI, pp. 49–58; Pastor, *The History of the Popes*, vol. XXI, pp. 278–84.

15. Henri IV, *Lettres missives*, vol. II, pp. 172–74.

16. *Ibid.*, p. 152; *Lettres*, vol. VIII, p. 350.

17. Baird, *The Huguenots and Henry of Navarre*, vol. I, p. 366.

18. Henri IV, *Lettres missives*, vol. II, pp. 129–30.

19. *Ibid.*, pp. 54–56.

20. Lauzun, *Itinéraire de Marguerite de Valois*, p. 268 *et seq.*; Merki, *La Reine Margot et la fin des Valois*, p. 318 *et seq.*; *Lettres*, vol. VIII, Appendix V.

21. CSP For., 1584–1585, p. 462.

22. Croze, *Les Guises, les Valois, et Philippe II*, vol. I, p. 352. Appendix 13; vol. II, p. 277, appendix 1.

23. *Lettres*, vol. IX, p. 38.

24. Desjardins, *Négociations diplomatiques*, vol.

IV, p. 621; L'Estoile, *Mémoires-Journaux*, vol. II, p. 119.

25. Croze, *Les Guises, les Valois, et Philippe II*, vol. I, p. 315.

26. Henri IV, *Lettres missives*, vol. II. pp. 141–42; L'Épinois, *La Ligue et les Papes*, p. 49.

27. CSP For., 1586–1588, p. 8; L'Estoile, *Mémoires-Journaux*, vol. II, p. 120.

28. *Mémoires de la Ligue*, vol. II, p. 100.

29. Sully, *Mémoires*, vol. I, p. 135.

30. Henri IV, *Lettres missives*, vol. II, p. 227.

31. *Lettres*, vol. IX, p. 22; Croze, *Les Guises, les Valois, et Philippe II*, vol. I, p. 380, Appendix 29.

32. *Lettres*, vol. IX, p. 53.

33. *Mémoires de la Ligue*, vol. II, pp. 76–77.

34. Desjardins, *Négociations diplomatiques*, vol. IV, p. 668.

35. *Lettres*, vol. IX, p. 68.

36. *Ibid.*, pp. 78, 97.

37. *Ibid*, pp. 87, 88.

38. Henri IV, *Lettres missives*, vol. II, pp. 263–64.

39. Vaissière, *Henri IV*, p. 278.

40. *Lettres*, vol. IX, pp. 111–13.

41. Brémond d'Ars, "Les Conférences de Saint Brice," *RQH*, Vol. XXXVI (1884), p. 515.

42. *Lettres*, vol. IX, p. 123.

43. *Ibid.*, p. 166.

CHAPTER XIX

1. Calendar, Hatfield House, vol. III, p. 206.

2. CSP Ven., vol. VIII, #477.

3. *Lettres*, vol. IX, pp. 155, 166, 191, 194.

4. CSP Span., vol. IV, #11.

5. *Ibid.*, vol. III, #581.

6. *Lettres*, vol. IX, p. 196.

7. CSP Span., vol. IV, #24.

8. *Lettres*, vol. IX, p. 196.

9. *Ibid.*, pp. 205–17.

10. Croze, *Les Guises, les Valois, et Philippe II*, vol. II, Appendix 6.

11. *Ibid.*, Appendix 10.

12. L'Épinois, *La Ligue et les Papes*, p. 81.

13. Henri IV, *Lettres missives*, vol. II, pp. 294–97.

14. *Lettres*, vol. IX, pp. 230, 241.

15. L'Estoile, *Mémoires-Journaux*, vol. III, p. 136.

16. Péréfixe, *The History of Henry IV*, pp. 71–72.

17. L'Estoile, *Mémoires-Journaux*, vol. III, p. 138.

18. Croze, *Les Guises, les Valois, et Philippe II*, vol. II, p. 28, n. 2.

19. *Mémoires de la Ligue*, vol. II, p. 270

20. *Lettres*, vol. IX, pp. 331–32.

21. L'Épinois, *La Ligue et les Papes*, p. 125.

22. *Lettres*, vol. IX, p. 300.

23. *Ibid.*, p. 486.

24. CSP For., 1586–1588, vol. XXI, pt. 1, p. 605.

25. L'Estoile, *Mémoires-Journaux*, vol. III, p. 145.
26. "Histoire de la journée des barricades de Pa-," *Arch. Cur.*, ser. 1, vol. XI, pp. 365–410; Mat-gly, *The Armada*, p. 229.
27. L'Estoile, *Mémoires-Journaux*, vol. III, p. 146.
28. Mattingly, *The Armada*, p. 242.
29. L'Estoile, *Mémoires-Journaux* vol. III, p. 149.
30. *Recueil des choses mémorables*, p. 304.

CHAPTER XX

1. L'Épinois, *La Ligue et les Papes*, p. 149.
2. *Ibid.*, p. 155.
3. *Lettres*, vol. IX, pp. 337–39; L'Épinois, "La conciliation de Henri III et du duc de Guise," *RQH*, 1. XXXIX (1886), p. 58, n. 2.
4. "Lettre du Roy sur l'esmotion advenue à Pa-," *Arch. Cur.*, ser. 1, vol. XI, vol. XI, pp. 444–48; Lettre escrite au Roy par Monseigneur le duc de Guise," *Arch. Cur.*, ser. 1, vol. XI, pp. 449–57.
5. L'Estoile, *Mémoires-Journaux*, vol. III, p. 153.
6. "Instruction à Monsieur de Guise . . . par Archeverque de Lyon," *Arch. Cur.*, ser. 1, vol. III, . 15–22 *passim*.
7. *Lettres*, vol. IX, pp. 339, 342–43.
8. *Ibid.*, p. 353.
9. Hübner, *Sixte-Quint*, vol. II, p. 200.
10. L'Épinois, "La Réconciliation de Henri III et du c de Guise," p. 55.
11. *Lettres*, vol. IX, p. 355.
12. Pasquier, *Lettres historiques*, pp. 286, 300.
13. CSP For., 1586–1588, pp. 633–36.
14. CSP Ven., vol. III, #675.
15. Longlée, *Dépêches diplomatiques*, p. 377; *Lettres*, vol. IX, p. 348.
16. CSP Ven., vol. VIII, #675.
17. *Lettres*. vol. IX, pp. 372, 368.
18. L'Estoile, *Mémoires-Journaux*, vol. III, p. 156.

19. CSP For., June–Dec., 1588, p. 5.
20. L'Estoile, *Mémoires-Journaux*, vol. III, p. 156; CSP For., June–Dec., 1588, p. 62.
21. CSP For., June–December, 1588, p. 99.
22. Villeroy, *Mémoires d'état*. Petitot, ser. 1, vol. XLIV, p. 44; Desjardins, *Négociations diplomatiques*, vol. IV, p. 822.
23. Matthieu, *Histoire des derniers troubles de France*, vol. I, p. 119.
24. *Mémoires de la Ligue*, vol. II, pp. 481–500; Matthieu, *Histoire des derniers troubles*, pp. 119a–124b; L'Estoile, *Mémoires-Journaux*, vol. III, pp. 158–59.
25. L'Estoile, *Mémoires-Journaux*, vol. III, p. 158.
26. *Mémoires de la Ligue*, vol. II, p. 507.
27. L'Épinois, *La Ligue et les Papes*, p. 219.
28. *Ibid.*, p. 221.
29. Valois, *Histoire de la Ligue*, p. 287, Appendix II. L'Estoile, *Mémoires-Journaux*, vol. III, p. 163 *et seq.*
30. L'Épinois, *La Ligue et les Papes*, p. 199.
31. Desjardins, *Négociations diplomatiques*, vol. IV, p. 843.
32. *Ibid.*
33. Valois, *Histoire de la Ligue*, p. 300, Appendix IV.
34. Desjardins, *Négociations diplomatiques*, vol. IV, p. 852.
35. L'Estoile, *Mémoires-Journaux*, vol. III, p. 167.
36. L'Épinois, *La Ligue et les Papes*, p. 273.
37. "Le Martyre des deux freres," *Arch. Cur.*, ser. 1, vol. XII, p. 89.
38. *Lettres*, vol. X, p. 395, n. 1.
39. *Recueil des choses mémorables*, p. 315.
40. Pasquier, *Lettres historiques*, p. 386.
41. *Lettres*, vol. IX, pp. 498–510.
42. Desjardins, *Négociations diplomatiques*, vol. IV, p. 853.

 *Bibliography*

Bibliography

The vast body of material available precludes an exhaustive bibliography. This is a selective list, limited to those items directly helpful in preparing the manuscript. The bibliographical form has been simplified to provide only essential data. Whenever suitable, the abbreviations listed for the reference notes have been used.

ALBERI, EUGENIO, ed. *Relazioni degli ambasciatori veneti al senato.* Florence, 1839–1862.

ANQUETIL, LOUIS PIERRE. *L'Esprit de la Ligue.* Paris, 1771.

ARMSTRONG, EDWARD. "Constable Lesdiguières," *EHR,* Vol. X (1895), pp. 445–70.

AUMALE, HENRI D'ORLÉANS, DUC D'. *History of the Princes of Condé.* London, 1872.

BAGUENAULT DE PUCHESSE, "Catherine de Médicis et les conférences de Nérac," *RQH,* Vol. LXI (1897), pp. 337–63.

_____. "Dix années de la vie de Marguerite de Navarre," *RQH,* Vol. LXXIV (1903), pp. 158–62.

_____. "Les Négociations de Catherine de Médicis à Paris après la journée des barricades," *L'Académie des sciences morales et politiques,* n.s., Vol. I (1903), pp. 697–709.

_____. "La Politique de Philippe II dans les affaires de France," *RQH,* Vol. XXV (1879), pp. 1–66.

_____. "Le Renvoi par Henri III de Marguerite de Valois et sa réconciliation avec le roi de Navarre," *RQH,* Vol. LXX (1901), pp. 389–409.

BAIRD, HENRY MARTYN. *History of the Rise of the Huguenots of France.* New York, 1907.

————. *The Huguenots and Henry of Navarre*. New York, 1886.

BARBOT, AMOS. "Histoire de La Rochelle," *Archives historiques de la Saintonge et de l'Aunis*, Vols. XVII, XVIII.

BARTHÉLEMY, EDOUARD, "Catherine de Médicis, le duc de Guise et le traité de Nemours," *RQH*, Vol. XXVII (1880), pp. 464–95.

BASCHET, ARMAND. *Les Archives de Venise*. Paris, 1870.

————. *La Diplomatie vénitienne*. Paris, 1862.

BEAUVAIS-NANGIS, MARQUIS DE. *Mémoires*. Paris, 1862.

BÈZE, THÉODORÉ. "Deux lettres de Théodore de Bèze," *BHPF*, Vol. VII (1858), pp. 16–17.

————. *Histoire ecclésiastique des églises réformées au royaume de France*. Paris, 1833.

BILLON, FRANÇOIS DE. *Le Fort inexpvgnable de l'honnevr dv sexe feminin*. Paris, 1555.

BLACK, JOHN BENNETT. *The Reign of Elizabeth*, Vol. VIII, of the *Oxford History of England*. Oxford, 1959.

BLAIR, EDWARD TYLER. *Henry of Navarre and the Religious Wars*. Philadelphia, 1895.

BORDENAVE, NICOLAS. *Histoire de Béarn et Navarre*. Paris, 1873.

BOUCHOT, HENRI. *Catherine de Médicis*. Paris, 1899.

BOUILLÉ, RENÉ. *Histoire des ducs de Guise*. Paris, 1850.

BOULLEÉ, M. A. *Histoire complète des Etats-Généraux*. Paris, 1845.

BRANTÔME, PIERRE DE BOURDEILLES, SEIGNEUR DE. *Oeuvres complètes*, ed. L. Lalanne. Paris, 1864–82.

"Bref Discours sur la mort de la Royne de Navarre," *BHPF*, Vol. XXXI, (1882), pp. 12–30.

BRÉMOND D'ARS, GUY. "La Saint-Barthélemy et l'Espagne," *RQH*, Vol. XXXV (1840), pp. 386–412.

————. "Les Conférences de Saint-Brice," *RQH*, Vol. XXXVI (1884), pp 496–523.

BROWN, HORATIO. "The Assassination of the Guises," *EHR*, Vol. X (1895) pp. 304–32.

————. "The Death of Catherine de Medici," *EHR*, Vol. XI (1896), pp 748–50.

BUISSON, ALBERT. *Michel de l'Hospital*. Paris, 1950.

BUSBECQ, *Letters of Ogier Ghislain de Busbecq*. Tr. R. E. Jones and B. C. Weber. New York, 1961.

————. "Lettres: 1582–83," *Arch. Cur.*, ser. 1, Vol. X, pp. 53–138.

CABIÉ, EDMOND. *Ambassade en Espagne de Jean Errard, seigneur de St. Sulpice*. Paris, 1902.

Calendar of Letters, Dispatches . . . Between England and Spain, Preserve at Simancas.

Calendar of Letters and Papers, Foreign and Domestic, of Henry VIII.

Calendar of the Manuscripts of the Marquess of Salisbury Preserved at Hatfield House.

Calendar of State Papers, Foreign Series, Elizabeth.

Calendar of State Papers, Foreign Series, Mary Tudor.

Calendar of State Papers and Manuscripts in the Archives of Venice.

Calendar of State Papers and Manuscripts Preserved in the Archives of Milan.

CALVIN, JEAN. Lettres, ed. Jules Bonnet. Paris, 1854.

CAPEFIGUE, J-B. Histoire de la réforme, de la Ligue, et du Henri IV. Paris, 1834–35.

CASTELNAU, MICHEL DE, SIEUR DE LA MAUVISSIÈRE. Memoirs. London, 1724.

CATHERINE DE MÉDICIS. Lettres. ed. Baguenault de Puchesse. Paris, 1901.

CENIVAL, PIERRE DE. "La Politique du Saint-Siège, et l'élection de Pologne," École française de Rome: Mélanges d'archéologiques et d'histoire, Vol. XXXVI (1916–17), pp. 108–203.

CHALAMBERT, VICTOR DE. Histoire de la Ligue. Paris, 1898.

CHAMPION, PIERRE HONORÉ. Catherine de Médicis présente à Charles IX son royaume. Paris, 1937.

_____. Charles IX. Paris, 1939.

_____. Henri III, roi de Pologne. Paris, 1943–51.

_____. La Jeunesse de Henri III. Paris, 1942.

CHARLES IX. Lettres de Charles IX à M. de Fourquevaux, ed. C. Douais. Paris, 1897.

CHÉRUEL, ADOLPHE. Histoire de l'administration monarchique en France. Paris, 1855.

_____. Marie Stuart et Catherine de Médicis. Paris, 1858.

CHEVERNY, PHILIPPE. Mémoires. Vol. XXXVI, Petitot.

CHOISNIN, JEAN DE. Mémoires. Vol. XI, Michaud et Poujoulat.

CIMBER ET DANJOU, eds. Archives curieuses de l'histoire de France. Paris, 1834–40.

COLIGNY, GASPARD DE. "Lettres," BHPF, Vol. XXI (1872), pp. 451–63.

CONDÉ, LOUIS DE BOURBON. Mémoires de Condé. London, 1740.

Cronique du roi Françoys premier de son nom, ed. G. Guiffrey. Paris, 1860.

CROZE, JOSEPH DE. Les Guises, les Valois, et Philippe II. Paris, 1866.

DARESTE DE LA CHAVANNE, RODOLPHE. "François Hotman et la conjuration d'Amboise," Bibliothèque de l'école des Chartes, ser. 3, Vol. V (1854), pp. 360–75.

_____. "Hotman d'après de nouvelles lettres," RH, Vol. XVIIC (1908), pp. 297–315.

D'AUBIGNÉ, THÈODORE AGRIPPA. Histoire universelle, ed. A. de Ruble. Paris, 1886–1909.

_____. Mémoires, ed. M. Lalanne. Paris, 1854.

DAVILA, ENRICO. *The Historie of the Civill Warres in France.* London, 1647.

DE CRUE, FRANCIS. *Anne de Montmorency.* Paris, 1885.

———. *Anne, duc de Montmorency, connétable et pair de France.* Paris, 1889

———. "La Molle et Coconat et les négociations du parti des Politiques, *RQH,* Vol. VI (1892), p. 325–94.

DEFRANCE, EUGÈNE. *Catherine de Médicis: ses astrologues et ses magicien envoûteurs.* Paris, 1911.

DELABORDE, JULES. *Gaspard de Coligny.* Paris, 1882.

DESJARDINS, ABEL, ed. *Négociations diplomatiques de la France avec la To cane.* Paris, 1859–86.

DESORMEAUX, JOSEPH. *Histoire de la maison de Montmorenci.* Paris, 1764.

DE THOU, JACQUES-AUGUSTE. *Histoire universelle.* London, 1734.

———. *Mémoires.* Amsterdam, 1713.

"Deux altercations entre le cardinal de Lorraine et le chancelier l'Hôpital, *BHPF,* Vol. XXIV (1875), pp. 409–15.

DIANNE DE POYTIERS. *Lettres inédites,* ed. G. Guiffrey. Paris, 1866.

DIGGES, SIR DUDLEY. *The Compleat Ambassador.* London, 1655.

Discours du grand et magnifique triomphe faict du mariage de François et Mar Stuart. Roxburghe Club, 1818.

"Discours merveilleux de la vie . . . de Catherine de Médicis," *Arch. Cur* ser. 1, Vol. IX, pp. 1–113.

"Documents authentiques sur la Saint-Barthélemy," *RR,* ser. 1, Vol. V, p 358–72.

"Documents originaux relatifs au rôle du duc d'Alençon," *RR,* ser. 2, Vol. \ pp. 226–92, 321–66; Vol. VI, pp. 113–44, 349–406.

"Documents originaux sur la Saint-Barthélemy," *RR,* ser. 2, Vol. III, p 193–97.

DUBELLAY, MARTIN. *Mémoires.* Vols. XVII, XVIII, XIX, Petitot.

DUPLESSIS-MORNAY, PHILIPPE. *Mémoires et correspondance.* Paris, 1824–25.

DUPRÉ-LASALE, ÉMILE. *Michel de l'Hôpital.* Paris, 1875–99.

"Élection et règne de Henri d'Anjou en Pologne," *RR,* ser. 1, Vol. IV, p 34–108.

ERLANGER, PHILIPPE. *Diane de Poitiers.* Paris, 1955.

———. *Henri III.* Paris, 1948.

———. *Le Massacre de la Saint-Barthélemy.* Paris, 1960.

ESTIENNE, HENRI, ed. *Discours merveilleux de la vie de Catherine de Médici* Paris, 1574.

FERRIÈRE, HECTOR DE LA. "Catherine de Médicis et les Politiques," *RQH,* Vo LVI (1894), pp. 404–39.

———. "Les Dernières Conspirations du règne de Charles IX," *RQH,* Vo XLVIII (1890), pp. 421–70.

_____. "L'Entrevue de Bayonne," *RQH*, Vol. XXXIV (1883), pp. 457–522.

_____. *Le XVI Siècle et les Valois*. Paris, 1877.

_____. *Les Projets de mariage de la reine Elisabeth*. Paris, 1882.

ꟾLEURANGE, ROBERT III DE LA MARCK. *Mémoires*. Vol. V, Michaud et Poujoulat.

ꟾORNERON, HENRI. *Les Ducs de Guise et leur époque*. Paris, 1877.

_____. *Histoire de Philippe II*. Paris, 1887.

ꟾOURQUEVAUX, RAYMOND DE ROUER, SIEUR DE. *Dépêches*. Paris, 1896–1904.

ꟾREER, MARTHA. *Henry III, King of France and Poland*. London, 1858.

_____. *The Life of Jeanne d'Albret, Queen of Navarre*. London, 1862.

_____. *The Life of Marguerite d'Angoulême*. London, 1854.

ꟾRÉMY, EDOUARD. *Un Ambassadeur liberal sous Charles IX et Henri III*. Paris, 1880.

_____. *Essai sur les diplomates du temps de la Ligue*. Paris, 1873.

ꟾODEFROY, THÉODORE. *Le Ceremonial français*. Paris, 1649.

ꟾOULART, SIMON. *Mémoires de l'état de France sous Charles IX*. Meidelbourg, 1578.

_____. *Mémoires de la Ligue*. Amsterdam, 1758.

ꟾRANVELLE, ANTOINE PERRENOT, CARDINAL DE. *Correspondance*, ed. C. Piot et E. Poullet. Brussels, 1877–96.

_____. *Papiers d'état*, ed. C. Weiss. Paris, 1841–52.

ꟾUILLAUME, P. "La Mort de François II," *Bulletin du société archéologique d'Orléans*, Vol. I (1960).

ꟾARRISON, G. B. *Letters of Queen Elizabeth*. New York, 1935.

ꟾATON, CLAUDE. *Mémoires*, ed. F. Bourquelot. Paris, 1857.

ꟾENRI II. *Lettres inédites*, ed. J.B. Gail. Paris, 1818.

ꟾENRI III. *Lettres de Henri III*, ed. P. Champion. Paris, 1959–65.

ꟾENRI IV. *Recueil des lettres missives*, ed. Xivrey et Gaudet. Paris, 1843–76.

ꟾÉRITIER, JEAN. *Catherine de Médicis*. Paris, 1959.

_____. "Les Premières Années de Catherine de Médicis," *Les Oeuvres libres*, Vol. 218 (1939), p. 283–319.

ꟾÜBNER, ALEXANDER VON. *Sixte-Quint*. Paris, 1870.

ꟾUME, MARTIN. *Courtships of Queen Elizabeth*. London, 1906.

ꟾEANNE D'ALBRET. *Mémoires et poésies*, ed. A. de Ruble. Paris, 1893.

ꟾENSEN, DELAMAR. *Diplomacy and Dogmatism*. Cambridge, Mass., 1964.

ꟾOURDA, PIERRE. *Marguerite d'Angoulême*. Paris, 1930.

ꟾJournal de ce qui s'est passé en France durant l'année 1562," *RR*, ser. 1, Vol. V, p. 81–116, 168–212.

ꟾERVYN DE LETTENHOVE. *Documents inédits relatifs à l'histoire du XVI siècle*. Brussels, 1883.

_____. *Les Huguenots et les Gueux*. Bruges, 1883–85.

————. *Relations politiques des Pays-Bas et d'Angleterre*. Brussels, 1882 1900.

KIERSTEAD, RAYMOND F. *Pomponne de Bellièvre*. Evanston, Illinois, 1968.

LABANOFF, ALEXANDRE. *Lettres, instructions, et mémoires de Marie Stuar* London, 1844.

LA FOSSE, J.B. *Journal d'un curé ligueur de Paris*. Paris, 1866.

LA HUGUERYE, MICHEL DE. *Mémoires inédits*, ed. A. de Ruble. Paris, 1878.

LA LANNE, LUDOVOC, ed. *Journal d'un bourgeois de Paris*. Paris, 1910.

LA MOTHE-FÉNELON, BERTRAND DE SALIGNAC, SEIGNEUR DE. *Correspondanc diplomatique*. Paris, 1838–40.

LA PLACE, PIERRE DE. *Commentaires de l'état de la religion et républiqu* Paris, 1565.

LA PLANCHE, LOUIS REGNIER DE. *Histoire de l'estaat de France . . . sous règne de François II*. Paris, 1576.

L'AUBESPINE, SÉBASTIEN DE. "Dépêches," *RHD*, Vol. XIII (1899), pp. 583 607; Vol. XIV (1900), pp. 289–302.

————. *Négociations, lettres, et pièces diverses*, ed. L. Paire. Paris, 1841.

LAUZUN, PHILIPPE. *Itinéraire de Marguerite de Valois en Gascogne*. Pari 1902.

LAYARD, SIR HENRY, ed. *Dispatches of Michele Suriano and Marc-Antoni Barbaro*. Huguenot Society of London, Vol. VI (1891).

L'ÉPINOIS, HENRI DE. *La Ligue et les papes*. Paris, 1886.

L'ESTOILE, PIERRE DE. *Mémoires-Journaux*, ed. Brunet et al. Paris, 1875–96.

L'HOPITAL, MICHEL DE. *Oeuvres complètes*, ed. P. J. Dufey. Paris, 1824–25.

LONGLÉE, P. S. *Dépêches diplomatiques*. ed. A. Mousset. Paris, 1912.

LORRAINE, FRANÇOIS. *Mémoires-Journaux*. Vol. VI, Michaud et Poujoulat.

LOUISE DE SAVOYE. *Journal*. Vol. XVI, Petitot.

LOUTCHITZKI, JEAN. "Cinquème guerre de religion," *BHPF*, Vol. XX (1873), pp. 401–13.

————. *Documents inédits pour servir à l'historie de la réforme et de la Ligu* Paris, 1875.

————. "Quatrième guerre de religion," *BHPF*, Vol. XXII (1873), p 252–68, 299–312, 352–74.

MARGUERITE D'ANGOULÊME. *Lettres*, ed. F. Genin. Paris, 1841.

————. *Nouvelles lettres*, ed. F. Genin. Paris, 1842.

MARGUERITE DE VALOIS. "Lettres inédites," ed. P. Lauzun, *Archives hi toriques de la Gascogne*, ser. 1, Vol. XI, pp. 1–46.

————. *Mémoires et lettres*, ed. M. F. Guessard. Paris, 1842.

MARIÉJOL, JEAN HIPPOLYTE. *Catherine de Médicis*. Paris, 1920.

————. *La Vie de Marguerite de Valois*, Paris, 1928.

MATTHIEU, PIERRE. *Histoire des derniers troubles de France*. Lyons, 1596.

MATTINGLY, GARRETT. *The Armada*. Boston, 1959.

———. *Renaissance Diplomacy*. Boston, 1955.

MAYER, CHARLES JOSEPH, ed. *Des États Généraux et autres assemblées nationales*. Paris, 1788–89.

MERKI, CHARLES. *La Reine Margot et la fin des Valois*. Paris, 1905.

MICHAUD, JOSEPH-FRANÇOIS, AND JEAN-JOSEPH POUJOULAT, eds. *Nouvelle collection des mémoires sur l'histoire de France*. Paris, 1836–54.

MIGNET, FRANÇOIS, "Lettres de Jean Calvin," *Journal des savants*, 1857, 1858.

MONLUC, BLAISE DE. *Commentaires et lettres*, ed. A. de Ruble. Paris, 1864.

MOTLEY, JOHN LOTHROP. *The Rise of the Dutch Republic*. New York, 1900.

MULLER, P. L., ET DIGERICK, A. *Documents concernant les relations entre le duc d'Anjou et les Pays-Bas*. Utrecht, 1889–99.

MURDIN, WILLIAM, ed. *A Collection of State Papers*. London, 1759.

NABONNE, BERNARD. *Jeanne d'Albret*. Paris, 1945.

NEALE, JOHN E. *The Age of Catherine de Medici*. New York, 1939.

NEVERS, LOUIS GONZAGUE, DUC DE. *Mémoires*. Paris, 1625.

NOAILLES, HENRI EMMANUEL DE. *Henri de Valois et de la Pologne*. Paris, 1867.

NOGUÈRES, HENRI. *La Saint-Barthélemy*. Paris, 1959.

NOLHAC, PIERRE. *Il Viaggio in Italia de Enrico III di Francia*. Rome, 1890.

PAILLARD, CHARLES. "Additions critiques à l'histoire de la conjuration d'Amboise," *RH*, Vol. XIV (1880), pp. 61–108, 311–55.

———. "La Mort de François I et les premiers temps du règne de Henri II," *RH*, Vol. V (1877), pp. 84–120.

PALM, FRANKLIN CHARLES. *Politics and Religion in the Sixteenth Century*. Boston, 1927.

"Papiers de Noailles," *Le Cabinet historique*, Vol. XIX (1873), pp. 225–304.

PASQUIER, ÉTIENNE. *Lettres*. Paris, 1629.

———. *Lettres historiques*, ed. D. Thickett. Geneva, 1966.

PASTOR, LUDWIG VON. *The History of the Popes*, ed. R. F. Kerr. St. Louis, 1923–53.

PÉRÉFIXE, HARDOUIN DE. *The History of Henri IV*. London, 1653.

PETITOT, CLAUDE-BERNARD, ed. *Collection complète des mémoires relatifs à l'histoire de France*. Paris, 1818–29.

PHILIPPE II. *Correspondance de Philippe II sur les affaires des Pays-Bas*, ed. L. Gachard. Brussels, 1848–79.

PICOT, ÉMILE. "Les Italiens en France," *Bulletin italien*, Vol. I–IV.

PITTEURS, M. A. "Un Ambassadeur d'Angleterre," *RHD*, Vol. XXIII (1909), pp. 290–305.

READ, CONYERS. *Mr. Secretary Walsingham and the Policy of Queen Elizabeth*. Cambridge, Mass., 1925.

Recueil des choses mémorables avenues en France. Paris, 1595.

Recueil de diverses pièces servant à l'histoire de Henri III. Cologne, 1599.

Recueil des fragments historiques sur les derniers Valois, ed. E. du Gord. Paris, 1869.

REUMONT, ALFRED VON. *La Jeunesse de Catherine de Médicis,* traduit, annoté et augmenté par A. Baschet. Paris, 1866.

RIBIER, GUILLAUME. *Lettres et mémoires d'Estat . . . sous les règnes de François I, Henri II, François II.* Paris, 1666.

RICHARD, P. *La Papauté et la Ligue française.* Paris, 1901.

ROBINSON, A. M. F. "Queen Elizabeth and the Valois Princes," *EHR,* Vol. II (1887), pp. 40–77.

ROBIQUET, PAUL. *Paris et la Ligue sous le règne de Henri III.* Paris, 1886.

ROCQUAIN, FÉLIX. *La France et Rome pendant les guerres de religion.* Paris, 1924.

ROELKER, NANCY LYMAN. *Queen of Navarre: Jeanne d'Albret.* Cambridge, Mass., 1968.

ROMIER, LUCIEN. *Catholiques et Huguenots à la cour de Charles IX.* Paris, 1924.

————. *La Conjuration d'Amboise.* Paris, 1923.

————. *Les Origines politiques des guerres de religion.* Paris, 1922.

————. *Le Royaume de Catherine de Médicis.* Paris, 1922.

RONSARD, PIERRE DE. *Oeuvres complètes,* ed. P. de Nolhac. Paris, 1923.

RUBLE, ALPHONSE DE. *Antoine de Bourbon et Jeanne d'Albret.* Paris, 1881–86.

————. *L'Assassinat de François de Lorraine, duc de Guise.* Paris, 1897.

————. *Le Colloque de Poissy.* Paris, 1889.

————. *Jeanne d'Albret et la guerre civile.* Paris, 1897.

————. *La Première Jeanesse de Marie Stuart.* Paris, 1891.

————. *Le Traité de Cateau-Cambrésis.* Paris, 1889.

SAULNIER, EUGÈNE. *Le Rôle politique du cardinal de Bourbon.* Paris, 1912.

SULLY. *Memoirs of the Duke of Sully.* Edinburgh, 1819.

SUTHERLAND, N. M. "Calvinism and the Conspiracy of Amboise," *History,* Vol. XLVII (1962), pp. 111–38.

————. *Catherine de Medici and the Ancien Régime.* London, 1966.

————. *French Secretaries of State in the Age of Catherine de Medici.* London, 1962.

————. *The Massacre of St. Bartholomew and the European Conflict.* New York, 1973.

TAVANNES, GASPARD DE SAULX DE. *Mémoires. Vols. XXIII, XXIV, XV,* Petitot.

TAUZIN, J. J. C. "Le Mariage de Marguerite de Valois," *RQH,* Vol. LXXX (1906), p. 447–98.

TOMMASEO, M. N., ed. *Relations des ambassadeurs vénitiens sur les affaires de France au XVI siècle.* Paris, 1838.

"Les Trespas et obsèques de Charles IX," *Arch. Cur.*, ser. 1, Vol. VIII, pp. 257–70.

TURENNE, VICOMTE DE. *Memoires*, ed. Baguenault de Puchesse. Paris, 1901.

VALOIS, CHARLES, ed. *Histoire de la Ligue*. Paris, 1914.

VAN DYKE, PAUL. *Catherine de Médicis*. New York, 1922–27.

VARCHI, BENEDETTO. *Storia Fiorentino*. Colonia, 1721.

VIEILLEVILLE, MARÉSCHAL DE. *Memoires de la vie*. Vol. IX, Michaud et Poujoulat.

VILLEROY, NICOLAS DE NEUFVILLE. *Mémoires d'état*. Vol. XLIV, Petitot.

VIVENT, JACQUES. *La Tragédie de Blois*. Paris, 1946.

WHITEHEAD, A. W. *Gaspard de Coligny*. London, 1904.

WRIGHT, THOMAS, ed. *Queen Elizabeth and Her Times*. London, 1838.

ZELLER, BERTHOLD. "Le Mouvement Guisard en 1588: Catherine de Médicis et la journée des barricades," *RH*, Vol. XLI (1889), pp. 253–76.

Index

Index

Adrian VI, Pope, 18, 19
Alamanni, Luigi, 39
Alamanni, Vincenzio, 182
Álava, Don Francisco d', 108, 119, 120, 126, 135
Alvárez de Toledo, Fernando. *See* Alba, Duke of
Alba, Fernando Alvárez de Toledo, Duke of, 47, 114, 115, 116, 117, 120, 132, 146, 169, 268–69
Alba, Duke of (son), 155
Albany, Duke of, 23
Albret, Jeanne d', Queen of Navarre, 46, 87, 89, 109, 119, 127, 128, 166, 172, 194, 294; marriage negotiations for son Henri, 142–46; death, 146
Aldobrandini, Silvestro, 21–22, 319
Alençon, Duc de (Hercule), 37, 74, 77, 152, 185, 191, 195, 200, 202, 215, 221, 239, 275, 283, 339; marriage negotiations with Elizabeth I, 172–76, 188, 252–54, 260–63, 264, 267–68; description, 173–74, 268; Huguenot sympathies, 185, 188–89, 219; and leadership of Politiques, 189–90, 219; escape attempt, 191–93; and death of Charles IX, 194, 195; enmity between Catherine and, 189, 191, 192–93, 209, 260, 264, 279; pardon, 211; collaboration with Condé, 211, 214; desire to

rule, 211–12; escape from court, 212–14; and peace of Beaulieu, 216; return to court, 219; and siege of La Charité, 229; enmity between Henri III and, 231, 236; as "defender" of Netherlands, 231 ff., 237, 251–52, 255, 256–57, 259–60, 263–67; friendship with sister Marguerite, 232–33; second escape from court, 236–37; and peace of La Fleix, 256; and relief of Cambrai, 259, 261, 278; illness and death, 277–81, 283; funeral, 280
Alexandrini, Michele Cardinal, 144
Amboise, château at, 214
Amboise, Conspiracy of, 60–65
Amboise, Edict of, 61
Amboise, Peace of, 116
Andelot. *See* Coligny, Andelot de
Anet, château of, 36
Anjou, Henri de. *See* Henri d' Anjou; Henri III
Anjou, province of, 230
Angoulême, Marguerite d'. *See* Marguerite of Navarre; Marguerite de Valois.
Antonio, Don, of Portugal, 268, 269
Antwerp, Fury of, 265–66
Aretino, Pietro, 44
Ariosto, Lodovico, 18
Armada, 311–12, 329
Army of the East, 229